D. BROUGHTON KNOX

SELECTED WORKS

VOLUME I

THE DOCTRINE OF GOD

EDITED BY

TONY PAYNE

MATTHIAS MEDIA

D. Broughton Knox, Selected Works, *Volume I: The Doctrine of God*
© Matthias Media, 2000

Published in Australia by:
Matthias Media
PO Box 225, Kingsford NSW 2032
ph +61-(0)2 9663 1478
fax +61-(0)2 9662 4289
email: info@matthiasmedia.com.au
Internet: www.matthiasmedia.com.au
(St Matthias Press Ltd ACN 067 558 365)

Distributed in the U.K. by:
The Good Book Company
Elm House,
37 Elm Road, New Malden,
Surrey KT3 3HB
ph (020) 8942 0880
email: admin@thegoodbook.co.uk

Distributed in South Africa by:
Christian Book Discounters
ph (021) 685 3663
email: peter@christianbooks.co.za

A NOTE ON BIBLE VERSIONS.
In the course of his lectures and writings, Dr Knox characteristically quoted
from either the King James Version or the Revised Version, and sometimes in
a combination of both. We have retained this feature.

ISBN 1 876326 28 x

Design and typesetting by Joy Lankshear Design Pty Ltd.

CONTENTS

$\mathcal{D}$. BROUGHTON KNOX WAS ONE OF the most important Christian thinkers of the 20th century. This may seem a startling claim on behalf of an obscure Australian theologian, largely unknown by most contemporary Australian Christians, let alone internationally.

Yet Broughton Knox was responsible, more than any other thinker, for the current vitality of Reformed evangelicalism in Sydney and beyond. His extraordinary grasp of Scripture and his talent for teaching theology shaped the minds and ministries of a generation of preachers; and these are in turn now leading a resurgent evangelical Christianity that is not only growing in Australia but is having a remarkable influence overseas.

It would be wrong, however, to suggest that Broughton Knox's importance ought to be measured purely on the grounds of how many people he has influenced, or what has been achieved 'in his name'. This would no doubt have been considered an unacceptable criterion by Dr Knox himself. He would have wished to be measured by one rule only—whether his writings conformed to, and faithfully expounded, the truth of God, which is found in Scripture. Against this yardstick, as readers of this volume will discover, Broughton Knox was indeed a giant among us. His penetrating and original mind was forever casting new light on the Scriptures, and expressing with fresh clarity its unchanging truth.

The introductory pieces that follow tell something about Broughton Knox the man, and sketch the general contours of his thought. All that remains is for me to make a few remarks about the organization of this volume and those that will follow it (God willing).

Part I of this volume contains Dr Knox's most widely known work, *The Everlasting God*. This extraordinary treatise, which had fallen out of print, is reproduced here unabridged, including an appendix on

'The implications of the doctrine of the Trinity for theology and for ordinary life' that is not included in all previous editions of the work. The only change we have made (apart from minor editorial corrections) is to add extensive scriptural footnoting to take advantage of Dr Knox's fondness for writing in sentences packed with biblical allusion. Readers can now chase through these allusions and quotations for further reflection.

Part II consists of a variety of theological writings on the doctrine of God under the general title 'The Christian Worldview'. These writings have been chosen primarily for their individual qualities, but also because they demonstrate the breadth and range of Dr Knox's thought, and the various contexts in which he taught and wrote. There are examples of sermons, theological papers, scholarly articles, book reviews, exegetical studies of particular passages or themes, and fragments from his personal papers. There are also a number of pieces that were first delivered on Dr Knox's regular radio broadcast, 'The Protestant Faith'.

This volume is one to dip into and savour, rather than to read cover to cover; a nourishing meal to be enjoyed with pleasure over time, rather than a hamburger to be devoured immediately. Here are some suggestions for making the most of this volume:

- read *Part 1: The Everlasting God* (and its appendices) continuously as one work; this will provide an overview of Dr Knox's thought; use the miscellaneous writings in Part 2 to pursue particular ideas further.
- while *The Everlasting God* is best read as a whole, the miscellaneous writings in Part 2 can be taken in any order; set yourself the goal of reading one a week (or one a month) with Bible open.
- use the index of Bible passages as a program for personal Bible study.
- use the collection of 'Knox Gems' (at the back) as a way into the contents of the volume; take an insight or subject that interests you, read the 'gem', and then read the article or chapter in which it is contained.

It is hoped that this current volume will be the first of three volumes of Dr Knox's Selected Works. Later volumes will contain material focused on the Christian life, and on church and ministry.

In some ways, I imagine that putting the doctrine of God into one volume, and Christian living and fellowship into other volumes may not have pleased Dr Knox. He was an integrative thinker, who saw the doctrine of God as being closely related to our personal and corporate lives, and vice versa. This is reflected in the material in this first volume. It is by no means dry theory. There are constant applications to how we should live, and how we should bring the gospel of Christ to a needy world.

I pray that this rich teaching would be as much food for your soul as it has been for mine.

ACKNOWLEDGEMENTS

My thanks goes to the many people who have assisted in the production of this volume:

- to Peter Jensen and the staff at Moore Theological College, for access to their extensive collection of Broughton Knox's literary works, for encouragement to pursue the project, and for helpful guidance as to the selection and arrangement of material;
- to the *Reformed Theological Review* and *New Creation Publications* for their permission to reprint certain texts;
- to Paul Whiting for his extensive (and voluntary) labours in copy editing;
- to my colleagues Kirsty Birkett, Greg Clarke and Ian Carmichael for their contribution to the painstaking work of editing, proofing and compiling indexes;
- to Mrs Ailsa Knox, Broughton's widow, for her kindness and cooperation;
- and perhaps most of all to Denis Ryan, a good friend and colleague of DBK, who was instrumental in launching the 'Knox publishing project', and who has been both a tireless aid in locating and sifting through manuscripts, and a constant encouragement during the long process of publication.

To God be the glory.

Tony Payne,
Editorial Director, Matthias Media
NOVEMBER, 2000

II. DAVID BROUGHTON KNOX[1]
By Marcus Loane

A VOLUME OF ESSAYS IN HONOUR of David Broughton Knox was published in 1986; it was entitled *God Who Is Rich In Mercy.* The first essay was an Appreciation of his life and work by Archbishop Robinson, and I can do little more than traverse the same ground with added detail to fill in a few gaps. Broughton was born on December 26th, 1916 in Adelaide, where his father was the Rector of St Luke's Whitmore Square, a parish in the heart of the city. Broughton's father had come out to New South Wales from Ulster as a child of five in 1880, and was always marked by a strong Celtic temperament and equally strong Protestant convictions. Broughton's mother had brought to the marriage the rare sweetness of a woman who lived in the sunshine of God's presence. Broughton was the first son but the third child in a home in which four boys and six girls were to be born. He was six years old when in 1922 his father left St Luke's and returned to the Diocese of Sydney as Rector of St Michael's Wollongong. Two years later there was a further move when he became Rector of St Paul's Chatswood. It was in this parish that Broughton passed from childhood to boyhood, and the home life of his parents was of paramount importance in his development. It was a home in which readings from the Bible and prayers were the rule every morning and evening; a home in which love and truth reigned supreme for all alike, "as well the small as the great, the teacher as the scholar" (1 Chr 25:8); a home that was also darkened with great sorrow. Gareth, at the age of eighteen months, died from meningitis in 1926; Margaret, who was four years old, died from the same cause as a complication from measles in 1927; and the eldest daughter Mary died from blood poisoning at the age of nineteen in 1931. That terrible

---

1. A slightly revised version of the first chapter of M. Loane, *These Happy Warriors*, (Blackwood: New Creation, 1988).

succession of family bereavements meant that love and sorrow were to unite the whole family with bonds of uncommon strength and affection.

The eight years at Chatswood were the formative years in Broughton's boyhood. He spent his teens at Knox Grammar School from 1928 onwards. He was not over fond of games, but was a lover of books, of words, of debate and argument. His great friend was Kenneth Jacobs, who in later life would become a Judge of the Supreme Court in New South Wales and then of the High Court of Australia. Broughton's father left Chatswood in 1932 to become Rector of Christ Church Gladesville, and Broughton left school at the end of 1933. He spent the next twelve months on his uncle's properties at Daylesford and Rocklynne, between Orange and Cudal. It would not be easy to tell whether he enjoyed this experience, but it was not without value. Then in 1935 he enrolled at the University of Sydney as an Arts Student in Greek and English. One of his fellow students was Gough Whitlam; they both aimed at first class honours in Greek, but were thwarted by the arrival of a new Professor at the very end of 1937. This was Enoch Powell, who had obtained the appointment at the early age of twenty-six and arrived just in time to mark the papers of the final examinations. To Broughton's great disappointment, he was only awarded second class honours in his degree. Those mid-thirties were also the years in which the fledgling Evangelical Union was winning its spurs within the University. Broughton and his friend Geoffrey Parker were interested, but stood somewhat aloof. Broughton would not join the Evangelical Union merely because that was thought to be the right thing to do. He was determined to establish his independence; he would act for himself rather than walk in the shadow of his father's reputation. This was a test of his integrity as a responsible person who had to reach maturity in his own right.

The year 1938 was spent as a Catechist with his father in the parish of Gladesville; this gave him time to test his call with a view to ordination. He was steadily growing in the conviction that this should be his goal; but where should he be trained? Although he had applied to enter Moore College, that year had brought a breach of understanding between Broughton's father and T. C. Hammond of Moore College, and that in turn led his father to think in terms of theological study overseas. As I was in England during 1938, I was asked to make inquiries concerning Wycliffe Hall in Oxford, Ridley

Hall in Cambridge, and St John's College at Highbury, which was better known as the London College of Divinity. Broughton travelled to England with his parents early in 1939 and enjoyed the summer with them before they returned to Sydney. It was finally decided that he should go to St John's where Dr T. W. Gilbert was the Principal, as it was the clearest evangelical college. He therefore enrolled at St John's in October, a month after the outbreak of war. Two years later he graduated with a First Class as an Associate of the London College of Divinity and a Second Class as a Bachelor of Divinity in the University of London, rising from a sickbed to take the latter exams. But he did not return home to Sydney. He was ordained Deacon in 1941 and Priest in 1942 by the Bishop of Ely and served as a curate in the parish of St Andrew-the-less in Cambridge. His work in the parish was light enough to allow him to become a member of Fitzwilliam College and to begin to read for the Theological Tripos under such mentors as Wilfred Knox and C. H. Dodd. But those were dark and troubled years in England. The summer of 1940 had seen the fall of France and the Battle of Britain. The month of June 1941 saw the Nazi onslaught on Russia, and December saw the destruction of the American Navy at Pearl Harbour. Broughton was bound to be caught up in the maelstrom of war; but for him there had been a short lull during his first two years in Orders.

During those years Broughton was drawn into vital contact with the Inter Varsity Fellowship. A small group of men in 1938 had formed the Biblical Research Committee with a single-minded resolve to roll away the reproach of anti-intellectualism so long levelled against Evangelicals. Broughton joined this Committee in the course of 1941 and soon became a close friend of Stuart Barton Babbage, who was to become its Honorary Secretary. They both took part in a small conference held at Kingham Hill in July that year; it was to prove pregnant for the future. Dr Douglas Johnson, General Secretary of the Inter Varsity Fellowship, liked to recall what he described as Broughton's sevenfold "No, No, No…" when he voiced his dissent. There were few that could say No so persistently and so effectively. July 1941 was almost the darkest month in the whole course of the War, but this conference drew up plans of a far-reaching character. Eventually, they led to the formation of the Tyndale Fellowship, with its Summer Schools and lectures in post-war years. Broughton was credited with the idea that led as well to the purchase of Tyndale House in Selwyn Gardens, Cambridge, and its development as a residential research library. Douglas Johnson was the mainspring in this movement, though he remained in the background. He drew very able men to his side and they began to provide an upsurge of first class Evangelical literature. One of their first ventures was the *New Bible Handbook,* though it did not appear until 1947. It included an article from Broughton: a small beginning, but a promise of things to come. But all these interests were interrupted in December 1943 when Broughton resigned from his parish to become a Chaplain in the Royal Naval Volunteer Reserve.

Broughton's service in the Navy began only six months before D-Day; it was to give him a direct share in one of the grand events in World War Two. After a brief spell at Devonport, he was posted to a Combined Operations base at Garelock in the Firth of Clyde, where men were training for the Normandy invasion. Early in the new year, Broughton had some reason to think that his name would not be listed for that operation. This led him to lodge a special application to be allowed to go, on the ground that he was a single man who had no dependents. As a result he joined the Depot ship which was to anchor off Sword Beach on D-Day plus one, June 7th, 1944. His ship was forced to move further west when things went wrong on the beach, but it remained off the coast for three months. He was then sent back to Rosyth before being appointed to serve in the first 'Monab' (Mobile Naval Air Base), which was to accompany the Squadron destined for the Pacific. It was believed that the war with Japan would go on for at least twelve months after the collapse and defeat of the German Forces, and the plan for Monab was that it should form an on-shore base in support of the Marines who were to storm island beaches. Broughton's ship the Emperor of Japan (code-named J1) reached Jervis Bay in December 1944; he was home for Christmas. But the war with Japan did not outlast VE Day in Europe by more than a few months; plans for Monab were shelved. Broughton was transferred briefly to H.M.S. Anson, and then to H.M.S. Vindex, an Aircraft Carrier ferrying supplies to the Occupation Forces in Japan. This ship sailed at last for England in 1946, via Durban and Simonstown. Broughton then chose to be discharged from the Navy in his own home country, and the voyage back to Sydney brought him home once more in time for Christmas; a civilian at last.

Archbishop Mowll had for some time been anxious to build up the staff of Moore College, and he spared no effort to arrange for Broughton to go into residence in February 1947 as a tutor and lecturer. His long absence overseas meant that he was scarcely known among his contemporaries, but a surprising episode in his early months at the College brought his name to the fore in church circles. A small group of laymen in a country parish had brought a suit against the Bishop of Bathurst on the ground that certain forms of Ritual, authorized in what was known as the Red Book, contravened the law of the Church of England. The case was heard by the Chief Judge in Equity; it turned very largely on the nature of the nexus between the Church in New South Wales and the Church of England. Sir Adrian Knox had delivered a crucial Opinion on this question in 1912. T. C. Hammond was asked in Court if he was in agreement with this Opinion, and he replied, "Yes, insofar as I understand it". Broughton, to the surprise of most people, was then called to appear before the Court as an 'expert' witness. Mr R. W. Kitto, K.C., later a Judge of the High Court of Australia, appeared for the Bishop of Bathurst, and set out at once to discredit Broughton by a rigorous cross-examination. Had he read the Opinion by Sir Adrian Knox? He had. Had he just read it in preparation for this case? No; he had read it some years before. How was that? When he was a boy of sixteen, he had taken it down from one of his father's bookshelves: he had read it then and had formed a conclusion about which he had seen no reason to change his mind. Did he consider himself an expert? Broughton was quite unfussed in his reply; "I would not describe myself in that way; but there are others who do". Kitto threw his papers down; it was said to have been the first time that he was rattled by a witness. Broughton's view as to the legal nexus based on Sir Adrian's Opinion was endorsed by Mr Justice Roper. It was a triumph for the 'expert'!

Broughton's advent to Moore College in February 1947 marked the beginning of a lifelong commitment to its affairs. The College in 1947 had begun to expand with new buildings and an influx of ex-Servicemen as students. The staff consisted of the Principal, Vice-Principal, and two resident tutors and lecturers, and the course of study prior to ordination was increased to three full years. T. C. Hammond was at the peak of his career when he left the College at the end of September that year to spend eighteen months on leave in

Britain. Broughton was his understudy in lectures on doctrine, and it became clear that his primary interest lay in Theology. He was never nervous, but was rather hesitant in his manner of speech; he had yet to acquire the easy, self-confident, fluent style of later years. He was single, restless, struggling with study, finding his balance; he was devoted to his family, but determined to establish his own independence. He pursued his studies with patience and perseverance until he gained his M.Th. degree from the University of London in 1949, having concentrated on Biblical and Historical Theology. Then in 1950, at the age of thirty-three, he married Ailsa Lane, a singularly happy marriage. Academic success and a happy marriage brought him a new maturity, and in 1951 he was granted three years leave of absence in order to pursue a Doctorate overseas. He and Ailsa settled down in Oxford, where he read in the Bodleian Library and lectured at Wycliffe Hall in New Testament. Among his students was J. I. Packer, later so well known as an author and teacher of Theology. Archbishop Mowll arranged for him to attend the Faith and Order Conference at Lund in 1952, and he was elected to the Geneva Faith and Order Commission of the World Council of Churches. Meanwhile he was attached to St. Catherine's College and in 1953 he was awarded his degree as a Doctor of Philosophy. His thesis was subsequently published as the *Doctrine of Faith in the Reign of Henry VIII*. It had involved valuable research in books printed in black letter in the early sixteenth century, and is now a standard work of reference for students in that period of history.

On his return to Sydney in early 1954, Broughton took up his work at Moore College as its Vice-Principal. T. C. Hammond's resignation at the end of 1953 had left Broughton with a clear field for his future work in Theology, to which he would devote himself for the rest of his life. His contribution to College and Church affairs during the next five years was richly varied. He drew largely on his English experience in replacing the Annual Convention with a College Mission in various parishes. He played a key role in establishing Halls of Residence for University students in two former hotels at Broadway in 1954. He had become a member of the Australian Committee of the World Council of Churches on the nomination of Archbishop Mowll, and was one of the Australian delegates to the Assembly at Evanston in 1954. This was followed by the Anglican Congress at Minneapolis, at which he was also present. Then in 1955, he took part in a Faith and

Order Conference at Christchurch, New Zealand. But this marked the end of his ecumenical involvement. His contributions in debate at meetings of the Australian Council of Churches were too strong for the more liberal emphasis which was predominant. Meanwhile he took up his father's mantle on behalf of the *Australian Church Record*, which he valued highly as an independent paper serving the Evangelical cause. He was responsible for much of the editorial work, and its columns provided a regular vehicle for the expression of his viewpoint during the next three decades. He became a member of General Synod in 1952 and its Constitution Committee in 1954. He soon began to make his voice heard in debate in the Diocesan Synod and its Standing Committee, and he became a member of the Cathedral Chapter in 1961, being elected to fill his father's canonry after his death. He had always cherished a large vision for the future of the College, and his growing prestige made it clear that he would go much further.

On the death of D. J. Davies in May 1935 and the resignation of T. C. Hammond as from the end of 1953, Archbishop Mowll had cast his net wide before settling on the appointment of a new Principal. So it was towards the end of 1958, as it turned out, Broughton's appointment was almost the Archbishop's last decisive act before his death on October 24th that year. Broughton came to his new office in February 1959 knowing that he had won the Archbishop's confidence and support, and he took up his duties in an eventful period. The Billy Graham Crusade in May that year was to trigger off an explosive expansion in College enrolments in the early sixties. The provision of Commonwealth Scholarships for University students and then of free Tertiary education brought about a steady rise in the calibre of candidates for ordination. The staff increased to match the growth in the overall enrolment; a four-year course became the norm, with the London B.D. as its goal. The principle of assessment for the College had been established by the Diocesan Synod in 1955, and the financial status of the College was further strengthened by a succession of legacies. There was extensive property development with a series of new buildings which were to transform the whole style of College life. Broughton's priorities never wavered; he set his heart on a highly qualified staff, on a wisely developed library, and on academic excellence. He was active in the affairs of the Australian College of Theology and of the Board of Studies in Divinity in the University of Sydney. He took a long view of College affairs and was single-minded in his pursuit of the ultimate objective. When it seemed to him that Archbishop Gough's policy was likely to encroach on the independent status of the College, he entrenched himself more firmly than ever against all outside pressure. He never courted popular sentiment, was sometimes misunderstood, and did not always command the goodwill of older clergy. But he was venerated by his own students and left an indelible mark on the character of the ministry.

Broughton's resignation from the Principalship took effect on February 28th, 1985. He had held office for twenty-six years, longer than any of his predecessors. It was arranged that he should continue to lecture in Theology until he reached the age of seventy-two at the end of 1988. His great contribution to the character of the ministry in the Diocese during his long term in office was due to what he was as a man and as a theologian. He had never ceased to read widely and to think deeply about the issues of Theology. He had gone on Sabbatical leave in 1968 and again in 1980 in order to pursue his reading in England. His Moore College Lectures in 1979 were published as *The Everlasting God,* and his book on *The Lord's Supper from Wycliffe to Cranmer* in 1983. Broughton was the natural successor to T. C. Hammond as a theologian, but differed from him in his fundamental approach. T. C. Hammond, himself a Gold Medallist in the school of Philosophy, always held that Philosophy was the proper handmaid of Theology. His Theology was rooted in the metaphysics of the medieval Schoolmen, much as Scottish Theology was rooted in German philosophy. Broughton on the other hand was primarily concerned to develop a Biblical Theology: his teaching was rooted in the textual study of the New Testament as practised in Cambridge. In his research for his Oxford thesis he had perceived that John Frith was the first English writer to insist that only what is taught in Scripture may be required as an essential article of faith: "Faith leaneth only on the Word of God, so that where His Word is not, there can be no good faith." [2] But Frith went still further. There are many doctrines taught in Scripture, but it is not necessary to hold them all under pain of damnation.

2. J. Frith, *The Writings of John Frith and Dr Robert Barnes,* (London: Religious Tract Society, 1930), p. 49.

This was incorporated in the language of the sixth Article of Religion: "Whatsoever is not read therein [in Scripture] nor may be proved thereby is not to be required of any man that it should be believed as an article of Faith or be thought requisite or necessary to Salvation." That was the ground on which Broughton took his stand.

Broughton's teaching was all rooted in his understanding of the integrity and authority of Holy Scripture as God's supreme written revelation of truth. He was never a blind adherent of Calvin, or Cranmer, or any other Reformation Divine; he carved out his own very independent line of approach. He admired Calvin rather than Calvin's more extreme disciples, and he followed Amyraldus rather than the latter in his view of predestination. He was not at ease with the doctrine of imputed righteousness, but followed Sanday and Headlam in treating it as a legal fiction. This led him to prefer the concept of reconciliation rather than of justification as the criterion for a standing or falling church. As for the church, Broughton and D. W. B. Robinson hammered out a much more radical assessment of the Anglican tradition in their emphasis on the church as "only and always a congregation of believers, whether on earth or in heaven". [3] Broughton's mind was very subtle, but he had a tendency to crystallize his thinking in short dogmatic statements which over-simplified the situation. On his return from England in 1953, Faith was the keyword in his teaching: he liked to say that the exercise of Faith is Worship. After 1968, the keyword was Fellowship: the main purpose of a Christian assembly is to enter into Fellowship with the Lord of the church and with its members. After 1980, it was Relationship: the ideal of Relationship in the Triune Godhead is the perfect pattern of his people. But the thinking that lay behind such keywords was acute. W. J. Lawton was to say that Broughton's ideas had shaped the mind of a whole generation of clergy in their understanding of the doctrine of the church and had had a disturbing impact on parish life in the Diocese of Sydney. [4] Its full effect for good or ill will not become self-evident until a whole generation has passed away. But it is not too much to say that no other contemporary

3. B. Webb (ed), *Church, Worship and the Local Congregation*, (Sydney: Lancer, 1987), p. 5.
4. Webb, p. 83.

Australian Churchman has had a more original mind or has shown a more penetrating insight into questions of pure Theology, and that insight was derived from his understanding of the supreme revelation of truth in the Bible.

Broughton's activities covered a wide spectrum of church life and affairs; they stretched from a body like the General Synod Commission on Canon Law to his role as the President of the New South Wales Council of Churches. He had a shrewd mind, which revealed itself in his grasp of church law and his highly intelligent approach to matters of finance. He had no nervous qualms in debate, and was never afraid of controversy. He was sometimes enigmatic, sometimes provocative; but he held on with a tenacity that could not be shaken. He was obstinate in argument, maddening in committee; but he survived where others were ignored. His dedication to Theology and the training of men for the Christian ministry led him into a new venture when he undertook to establish a new Theological College for the Church of England in South Africa as from October, 1988 He had mellowed since he retired and was always relaxed in his own home circle. The fine shape of his head with its shock of white hair gave him an amazing resemblance to his father: their portraits were almost interchangeable. He honoured his father, but worked out an independent line in thought and practice. He sat loose in a way that his father never did to clerical conventions and Anglican traditions. It was pointed out by Archbishop Robinson that he was more at ease with Grindal than with Hooker,[5] and this streak of Puritan nonconformity manifested itself in his indifference to the outward forms of clerical decorum. His was phlegmatic in some respects, but deeply emotional in others. He learnt to ski with his children and built a boat to sail with them on the harbour. He had no ear for music, but always delighted in Ailsa's singing, and drew strength and encouragement from her unfailing cheerful support. His home life, his College career, and his general ministry were all in the same mould. It would have been said of him, as of Nehemiah's colleague as they built the walls of Jerusalem: "He was a faithful man, and feared God above many".[6]

5. P. T. O'Brien & D. G. Peterson, *God Who Is Rich in Mercy*, (Sydney: Anzea, 1986), p. xii.
6. Nehemiah 7:2.

Broughton was 72 years old when he went out to South Africa to found the George Whitefield College for the Church of England in South Africa. He went to serve a small and embattled Church in a country racked by political turmoil and racial violence. He and Ailsa took up residence in Kalk Bay and opened the College for black and white. He struggled for funds, for books for the library, for housing for the students. Four years later, in December 1992, he retired, leaving the College as a steady going concern. It had been the crowning work of a distinguished ministry. As events turned out, he had little more than twelve months back in his own country, but that last year brought two great joys in his family circle: his youngest daughter was married in September, and his younger son was ordained to the priesthood in December. He died as the result of a massive cerebral haemorrhage on January 15th, 1994.

BROUGHTON KNOX ON TRAINING FOR THE MINISTRY[1]

By Peter Jensen

INTRODUCTION

*T*HE BUILDING IN WHICH WE MEET TODAY is named after David Broughton Knox, Principal of Moore College from 1959 to 1985, and one of its greatest leaders. More than any other person Dr Knox created the modern College. He had many gifts, but pre-eminent among them was his gift of teaching God's word, and it is fitting that this centre for teaching and learning bears his name.

While he was still at university, Broughton acted as a catechist in his father's parish. During that time he visited extensively in the district, following the pattern of Paul at Ephesus, "teaching (you) in public and from house to house, testifying both to Jews and to Greeks of repentance to God and of faith in our Lord Jesus Christ".[2] It seems that during this time he engaged profoundly with the Lord in prayer. Several times before his recent death he referred to the way in which he had at that earlier time asked earnestly that the Lord would make him "a man after his own heart",[3] perhaps in the pattern of King David. His prayer was that he may be used of God in fruitful service.

We may testify that this was an answered prayer. In the 1920s and 30s, Anglican evangelicalism in England and Australia had reached a low ebb, not least in the area of evangelical thought. Broughton was one of that group who helped engineer a significant renaissance. He played a part, for example, in the birth of the Tyndale Fellowship and

---

1. This introduction to Dr Knox's thought, and his philosophy of ministry training, was delivered as the first lecture in the newly opened 'Broughton Knox Teaching Centre' at Moore College on February 28, 1994.
2. Acts 20:20, 21.
3. 1 Samuel 13:14.

Tyndale House and hence the Tyndale commentaries. His greatest contribution, however, was the creation in Australia of the modern Moore College, with its excellent library, learned faculty and strongly motivated students. He was, it must be said, principal at a time when the community was raising its academic standards dramatically. But it was his genius which enabled Moore to do the same, and to do it in a way which forwarded the gospel rather than betrayed it.

When he retired in 1985, he left the College in a flourishing condition, poised to make an international contribution through the teaching and writing of its faculty, markedly influential through its graduates, beginning to gain a reputation in some circles at least for offering a distinctive vision of what theological education should be. When I had the opportunity of visiting theological colleges overseas in 1987, I was able to see clearly what Broughton had achieved and how much we owed to his wisdom. Much of it we take for granted and assume as obvious; it is only when we see that it is missing elsewhere that we begin to realise that determination and wisdom were needed. Broughton had that understanding.

What was it that Broughton Knox insisted on in theological education, and how do we benefit from his insights today? His achievements arose from his theology, and we should turn there first.

1. THE KNOX THEOLOGY

In context
It is a perennial temptation of theology to turn itself into anthropology; to talk about man rather than God. In Broughton's time, various types of man-centred theology held the attention of many in the church. There were ecclesiastical versions, in which the church and its sacramental system intruded between the person and God with the result that the Bible was supplemented. There were rationalistic versions, in which human reason became the norm for our talk about God, with the result that the Bible was diminished. There were experiential versions, in which the human spirit was thought to relate in revelation to God's Spirit, with the result that the Bible was bypassed. Broughton's lectures at various times were marked by strenuous critique of anglo-catholicism, of liberalism and of Arminianism. He offered such critiques not in a spirit

of combativeness, but because he saw in these versions of Christianity distortions of the gospel and an assault on the Godness of God. To this extent he was in sympathy with the neo-orthodoxy of the middle years of this century, but he was not a Barthian or even a Calvinist in any strict way. He was without doubt an evangelical, reformed, Anglican churchman, but his attachment to the Bible freed him from strict adherence to any particular school of thought.

In method

Since Broughton believed that God speaks uniquely and sufficiently in Holy Scripture, the exposition of the Bible occupied the central role in his method. He was not averse to natural theology, but only as natural theology was interpreted through Scripture. Because he believed this so firmly, he broke with a tradition of systematic theology in which doctrine consists of commenting on the views of others whether historical or contemporary. It is true that his first year lectures seemed to be an exposition of T. C. Hammond's *In Understanding be Men*. I personally always imagined that this was a sort of joke on Hammond, whose own method was to critically expound E. J. Bicknell on the 39 Articles! But the difference between Knox and Hammond was profound. When Hammond was Principal of the College, he worked his way through Bicknell page by page. For Knox, Hammond's book was a mere adjunct to his lectures. The real text-book was Scripture itself. Broughton was far from ignorant of historical theology; but he left no doubt that he was grappling with Scripture, not with the writings of others, no matter how sharp or how learned.

In substance

Under these circumstances, we can see where the heart of the Knox theology was. It was not in the doctrines of Scripture or the church, though he was well-known for his views in these areas. The heart of things was the Lord God himself and especially the Lord in his relationship to the world. Broughton attacked man-centred theology because he was God-centred. Do not get me wrong here; he cared deeply about humanity. But the Saviour of humanity is the Lord God, and it is by focusing on him that we learn what it is to be human.

Broughton's doctoral thesis was on justification by faith alone. This doctrine is only another way of saying God reigns, Jesus is Lord. It is a declaration of God's complete sovereignty in our salvation. I once asked Broughton to write two or three articles on 'The Christian Worldview'. I was expecting something like what Francis Schaeffer was then providing—the Christian idea of science, of philosophy, of culture. I received back articles on the sovereignty of God and the cross of Christ. This was the Christian worldview, according to Broughton. After some reflection I could see how right he was, and what made his theology perennial.

Its consequences

By focusing on God in his relationship to the world, Broughton determined the shape of theological education. There were two chief consequences of his approach, the first to do with the Bible and the second with relationships. We have already seen that this involved the task of putting the Bible at the centre of everything, since the Bible is the living and active word of God. If to you this sounds fairly obvious, be assured that making the Bible central is not on everyone's agenda in protestant theological education. The lack of such a centre is mourned, and frequent attempts are made to provide a substitute. Most lately it has been suggested that the action of God in the congregation should be the revelatory centre for theological study. Even in evangelical seminaries, the centrality of the Bible cannot be assured in practice as other worthy subjects crowd the curriculum. But Broughton never wavered in according Scripture its sovereign place.

The second consequence of the Knox focus on God was his emphasis on relationships. This arises from what he called "the foundation of the Christian religion",[4] namely the doctrine of the Trinity. For Broughton, God was no lonely monad, but the triune centre of love and fellowship, of what he frequently called 'other-person-centredness'. Trinitarian Christianity, true Christianity, had to be about fellowship, about relationships. God is not solitary, and we are not intended to be alone.

How did these emphases on Scripture and relationships shape the business of training for Christian ministry? I intend to expound each in its turn in a moment. But first let us see how Broughton envisaged the Christian ministry, what he thought of its tasks and calling. He once put it thus:

4. See p. 73, below.

The minister of the congregation is the teacher of God's Word to the congregation. This is his main task. He will have other duties and opportunities of service as a Christian, but his main task is that of teacher. He is to open up the Word of God, so that the congregation can see what the verse, or the paragraph or the chapter or the Book, or even the Bible as a whole, on which he is preaching, is actually saying. In this way the minister's word, being plainly seen to be what God is saying to the hearer, is received into the mind as God's word, and so reaches the conscience of the believer, suffuses his emotions, moves his will and issues in a godly life—friendship with God and loving actions towards others.

The minister is the teacher. This was our Lord's ministry. 'Teacher' was the title the people gave him and which he accepted. It was Paul's ministry. He told the Ephesians amongst whom he ministered for three years that he had "taught" them in their homes and publically "the whole counsel of God".[5]

And it is the teaching ministry that has been entrusted to the modern minister. As Paul told Timothy, "What you have heard from me before many witnesses entrust to faithful men who will be able to teach others also".[6] The modern minister of the congregation is the last in this line of apostolic succession in the teaching ministry, and it is his great privilege and task in his turn to teach others also the whole counsel of God.[7]

We may say the congregation was the pre-eminent scene of the ministry, and teaching its distinctive role. Lest we think, however, that this was one-sided or even novel, let me say that to my mind Broughton's picture of the minister was always shaped by the ordination of priests in the Book of Common Prayer. Furthermore, we should remember the picture of him visiting door to door in Gladesville, or on a College Mission in Newtown. It is no accident that Richard Baxter's *Reformed Pastor* was one of his recommended books for many years. I ought also

5. Acts 20:20, 27.
6. 2 Timothy 2:2.
7. "Report by David Broughton Knox to the Executive of the Synod of the Church of England in South Africa on Theological Education" (1986), p. 1.

to point out that his doctrine of the church was one that encouraged
the exercise of the gifts of the Body of Christ. Now let us turn to the
themes of Scripture and of relationships.

2. SCRIPTURE

You will have noticed, I am sure, the characteristic Knox appeal to Acts
20:27, "I did not shrink from declaring to you the whole counsel of
God". It was one of his favourite biblical references. In practical terms,
he understood the whole counsel of God to be the Scriptures, and the
task of the ministry to expound the whole of God's revealed word.
There are four consequences of this that I draw to your attention.

First, the normative role of Scripture

In the Knox theology everything had to be tested by Scripture, and the
business of systematic theology was to be biblical. Broughton used to
denounce the practice of giving the name 'Biblical Theology' to the
course taught by his esteemed colleague Donald Robinson, since he
claimed, with some justice, that his doctrine course was biblical
theology. He had no aim to introduce studies of modern theology, and
even historical theology was a mere hand-maid to the chief business.
Not for him, therefore, the division that exists almost universally
elsewhere between exegesis and theology, between biblical studies and
doctrine. All studies in the curriculum fed into the central study—the
knowledge of God and of his ways as revealed in Scripture; all served
this central focus. He insisted that, come what may, theology was the
central study of the theological college—not practical ministry or
psychology, not even Old Testament or New Testament as such. In the
service of this view he consecrated his great intellectual gifts, distilling
the wisdom given to him by God in clear, illuminating, fresh phrases
which brought life through truth. Whatever else he taught his
students, he taught them to ask, "What does the Bible say?"

I ought to add another element to this, in order to avoid
misunderstanding. It could be thought from what I have said that there
was a detached and cool appraisal of Scripture, that the objective side
left no room for the subjective, that we are dealing with a hard and
scientific approach to revelation. But there is no truth in that at all.

Knox taught that the Bible is God's personally directed speech; it is addressed to us; as we tremble at God's word, we encounter not just print on a page, but the Lord himself. Broughton's own profound personal piety, his faith in God, his prayers, demonstrate that here was a man who walked with God and who, like Abraham, was a "friend of God".[8] By putting what God has done for us first, he was able to enjoy to the full what God is doing in us, with us and through us. To take on board Broughton's great emphasis on God and to remain experientially unmoved is to miss the whole point.

Second, the whole breadth of Scripture

Over the years, theological colleges have modified their academic offerings dramatically. So many new subjects have clamoured for attention and have received admittance, and so tight have the finances become, that the study of Scripture has shrunk. The biblical languages receive less treatment, and any attempt to give a holistic account of Scripture is abandoned. The student involves himself or herself in electives, and can pass through a College with minimal attention to the Old Testament.

Broughton Knox totally opposed these trends. To him, the pastor must know "the whole counsel of God". The context of any passage was the whole of the Bible. To be ignorant of one part of Scripture was to diminish your grasp of the other parts. He insisted on time being given to study—the four year program was a minimum not a maximum in his view. He insisted on as much Scripture as possible being studied in College. He insisted above all, on the plain, continuous reading of Scripture, preferably in its original languages. For many students Scripture knowledge consists mainly of the study of the opinion of experts about Scripture. Not so for Broughton Knox. First must come Scripture; whatever else you do, there must be Scripture; the best commentary on Scripture is Scripture itself. This is the first great hermeneutical key.

The College which lives by this insight will need to be committed to the highest academic standards. This is a paradox little understood. According to liberal dogma, the so-called fundamentalists are intellectually inferior. For a few decades there was some truth in this

8. James 2:23.

charge. But you cannot be focused on knowing God in Scripture and also be content to feed your soul with pious nonsense. A true evangelicalism will demand a mind consecrated to Christ and at full-stretch for him.

Our present danger is not a lack of rigour or intellectual demand. It is, rather, that our community, faculty and students will treat the Bible as exam-fodder, as merely the way to achieve professional advancement. We may become experts in the law and lack the inner core of the matter—the heart that trembles at God's word. "How I love your law!" cries the psalmist.[9] So too must we, if we are to be educated theologically and avoid mere professionalism.

Third, the unitive nature of our study

One of the great debates in all theological institutions is the divide between the academic and the pastoral, the theoretical and the practical. At the moment, and not surprisingly given the poor understanding of so many, the so-called 'practical' is in the ascendant. Students wish to be taught the 'how-to' of their subject rather than the 'what', the Bachelor of Ministry rather than the Bachelor of Theology.

Contrary to popular opinion, Broughton encouraged the introduction of ministry subjects at about the same time as they were introduced in England and the USA. He saw that homiletics, evangelism, psychology and education were valuable in training for the ministry. The consequence is that Moore has as much or a greater amount of practical training as appears in any other college.

But Broughton refused to allow the divide which is in so many minds, or to set the subjects at odds with one another. He was very wary of electives—if a subject is needed, let all do it; if not, do not include it at all. But since the heart of his concern was God—let all subjects relate to this centre: "Anything academic which is not pastorally orientated ought not to be in the ordinand's training; anything pastoral which is not fully informed by the whole counsel of God…is unworthy and inadequate".[10]

This was a philosophy which infused the College and led to that

9. Psalm 119:97.

10. A remark recorded in the Minutes of a meeting of Principals of Anglican Theological Colleges held in 1975.

clarity of mind and strength of purpose which both friends and foes have recognised as typical of Broughton's students. It never crossed his mind that his teaching was pastorally irrelevant or merely speculative. Theology was the most practical discipline of all, for it was the truth. He never sought to give a version of the truth; he sought to expound the truth. Theology classes were practical ministry classes, and vice versa.

Fourth, the critical nature of our study

It is truly strange to see Dr Knox described as a 'fundamentalist'. I remember a fellow student making a violent attack on biblical criticism in the College chapel. In the very next lecture Broughton publicly corrected the student, pointing out the great advances that biblical criticism had brought to the study of the Bible, and castigating the blinkered obscurantism which motivated the sermon. Broughton was fully prepared to learn from all sources, and at this level alone the Library remains one of his finest achievements. Other theological colleges, even in the 1960s, kept some books under lock and key. Other libraries may not have purchased evangelical books. But the Moore College library buys books representing all points of view and students have free access to them. Broughton argued that as long as the central theological foundation, that the Bible is God's very word, is secure, all else can minister to the discerning mind.

3. RELATIONSHIPS

God graciously reveals himself to us, and we discover that our God is three in one and one in three, that relational love is at the heart of the universe. How did that shape Broughton's attitude to the study of theology?

All great men have their critics and sometimes the criticism is fierce. One of the first times I ever heard Dr Knox criticised was (I think) in the early 1960s when someone told me that he actually encouraged students not to use his title, but to call him by his Christian name! This was a characteristic Broughtonian fault. I would have described him as a somewhat diffident or shy man in personal contacts. But he knew that relationships were both the heart and the fruit of the gospel, and he valued the family of God, the brothers and sisters whom God had sent his way. I would say that few in our part of the world have done more to provide us with a proper concept of church, freeing it from unnecessary and inhibiting structures and making room for authentic, evangelical fellowship.

To Broughton, "Fellowship is a basic and delightful human experience. The acme of fellowship is Christian fellowship... The essential principle of friendship and of fellowship is unselfishness, the centring of your interests on the welfare of the other, sinking your own self-interest in the welfare of all. This generates great enjoyment." He linked it directly with God—"Ultimate reality, God, is persons in relationship. Thus there is no experience more ultimate than personal relationship, or more blissful, for this is how God's being is, and God is ultimate blissfulness."[11]

How does this relate to theological study? Clearly we may and should think of God in private; clearly you may study theology on your own. But God places us in relationship, to receive and give his blessings to one another, and fellowship is the natural and appropriate context for our life of knowing God. Normally this fellowship is found in the home or in the church but, when we have the opportunity to give ourselves to God's word in preparing for ministry, it is a wonderful blessing to experience Christian relationships at this point too.

The impact of this theology on a college is obvious. The whole idea of residence, for which Broughton fought tenaciously, flows from it. To him the College dining room was as important as the classroom and the chapel. The corporate life of prayer needs to be undergirded and sustained. Unlike the practice of American colleges, chapel at Moore remains a frequent and obligatory experience—not to teach us liturgy, but so that we may together respond to the presence of God in our midst. Unlike the practice of British colleges, we never meet without the exposition of the word of God, since it is this activity which helps define the church, and preaching is God's instrument for ruling us and making us more like Jesus. Knox was fond of quoting the apostolic description of ministry: "But we will devote ourselves to prayer and to the ministry of the word".[12] Here was a description of the essence of his College.

It is evident, I hope, that sanctification was a great concern to

11. Quoted in B. G. Webb, *Church, Worship and the Local Congregation*, Explorations 2 (Sydney, 1987), 59.
12. Acts 6:4.

Principal Knox. His own standards were high and he expected it in his faculty and students. He had a particular dislike for anything coarse or uncouth. But his study of the doctrine of justification by faith saved him from that noisy Arminian piety which draws attention to itself and claims to be the only one interested in godliness. Some of his sermons were riveting attacks on sin and exhortations to repentance; he preached with great power and great effect for godliness. A college which cared nothing for holiness would be anathema to him. He especially emphasised prayer as the chief work of faith. But the real test of holiness is neither the capacity for clapping in chapel nor the correctness of formal worship, but faith in God and love for others. You are put here in a residential college so that you can learn to exercise both to the good of all.

At the very heart of the human relationships at the College, however, was the relationship between teacher and student. Dr Knox knew full well that a college was its faculty, and that campus, and even library, took subsidiary places. In many other colleges may be found the unfortunate breed of theological academics, persons who do well in their primary degree and decide of their own volition to follow a path of scholarship. They gather their funds and take themselves off to a place of higher learning, the more prestigious the better. They then offer themselves as teachers, replying to the job advertisements of those institutions which advertise for staff. Having qualified themselves to doctoral level, they are eager to teach their dearly purchased speciality and hence contribute mightily to the splintering of the theological curriculum and the impracticality of theological education. It shall not be so among you!

Broughton was extremely careful in his choice of faculty. He was first and foremost concerned to recruit those who had a proven track record in the ministry of the gospel. Naturally, they must also be academically gifted, and no one did more than Dr Knox to raise the academic standards of the faculty of the College. He gave every support to those involved in further study or writing books and articles. I need hardly say that he chose as his colleagues those who were capable of teaching the Anglican faith in its reformed and evangelical expression, but I, for one, was never conscious of inhabiting a theological straightjacket. I differed from him in a number of areas on which he held passionate convictions—evolution being one example—but it never raised difficulties between us. Dr Knox's mind was so original, indeed so radical, that he was forever challenging us to deeper and better thought. "By what right was the Book of Esther retained in the canon of Scripture?" he wanted to know one morning. "What were we to make of the five comings of Jesus?" "How could we prove that water-baptism was intended in Matthew 28?" He was himself a great teacher, with the capacity of enthusing his students. In the end, we must not fret even if our campus is run-down and ugly—the teacher-student relationship is what really matters

Which brings us, I suppose to this new building. Among his other virtues, Dr Knox was a visionary and a shrewd businessman. He purchased the land for the campus, or most of it. He foresaw the College as it would need to be. I cannot be sure that he approved my initiative in erecting this building. I suspect he thought that there were more purchases to be made, more houses, more shops. I know that he was not content with what we have, and given the choice between fixing a house and buying a new one he never hesitated: buy first, fix second! Nonetheless, I did not hesitate for long myself. The College needed this building and I have no regrets at all in initiating its development. For myself, I believe that education best occurs in surroundings which are both comfortable and stimulating. I think that beauty matters, and you will find that this building reflects my concern for you whether as a teacher or a learner. But I want to endorse thoroughly the priorities of my revered teacher and friend: in order to serve students best—first faculty, second library, third campus.

CONCLUSION

Obviously, the half has not been told about this remarkable man. Most modern students of this College have never heard him lecture or preach. Yet believe me, they are taught by him everyday and owe him far more than they can imagine. He prayed earnestly that he be "a man after God's own heart", and I believe that his prayer was fully answered. Naturally he had his faults, personal and theological: faults of judgement, faults of character. He was fearless in his ministry of God's word, and there were those who were stung by him and disliked it. Others found him difficult, especially when he insisted on matters of principle above mere friendship. If you ask me about his limitations, I believe that they chiefly arose from his being a child of his own times; he represented a Protestant ascendancy which had a place in the church and society which is now a half-forgotten dream. We need to develop an approach to our world far more in touch with its modern realities than we can now learn directly from Broughton. And yet, he laid the foundation for this by being an original thinker. The Christian view of the world remains the sovereignty of God and the centrality of the cross.

When Dr Knox was buried recently, the gathered crowd sang two hymns. They will tell you finally of the simplicity of the man, and of what really mattered to him. For, despite his formidable and subtle intelligence, there was a pure faith in his Saviour. We sang:

What a friend we have in Jesus,
All our sins and griefs to bear
What a privilege to carry
Everything to God in prayer.

Finally, and most appropriately, we joined in the child-like song which summed up so much:

Turn your eyes upon Jesus
Look full in his wonderful face
And the things of earth will grow strangely dim
In the light of his glory and grace.

DBK would say nothing else to us. His faith was centred on Christ, and his hope was to be with Jesus. Christ was his gospel, and Christ is the foundation of this building. That is to say, Christ crucified must be the theme of all the teaching and learning which will occur here. We will never surpass Christ in wisdom, never grow richer than we already are in him. By teaching Christ, we will consecrate this building to God's service and best honour our friend and teacher, who himself pointed to Jesus both in life and in death.

PART 1

THE EVERLASTING GOD

Chapter 1
THE LIVING AND TRUE GOD[1]

*T*HE DOCTRINE OF GOD IS OF THE utmost importance, for it controls the whole of life. As a person thinks about God, that is to say, as he thinks about ultimate reality, so his standards of behaviour, values and relations with other people are determined.

Everyone has a doctrine of God, even if it is only the negative doctrine that God does not exist. On such a view, the objectives and values of life and relationships with other people will be very different from what they are when ultimate reality is conceived as a personal God who will judge the world by his standards of right conduct, which are written in the human conscience. On the other hand, if a person's doctrine of God has the Christian dimension of self-sacrificing love, then behaviour and attitudes will again be different from what they would be without a belief in the existence of God. Everyone has a doctrine of God, that is, of ultimate reality, which will influence every aspect of life—the emotions, the decisions of the will, the hopes of the future and day-to-day behaviour. If the thinker is consistent, so that his

---

1.   *The Everlasting God* was first delivered as the Moore College Lectures in 1979, and was first published in Australia by Lancer. It is Dr Knox's most well-known and widely appreciated literary work. It should be noted, however, that Dr Knox did not consider the structure or organization of *The Everlasting God* to be definitive or comprehensive. On being criticised at one point for not including more on the doctrine of the Spirit in *The Everlasting God*, Dr Knox responded: "I must emphasise that this book is a reprint of five lectures given to a lay audience. The five subjects chosen are subjects of importance, but I could not choose every subject of importance on the doctrine of God. But they were subjects which I believed needed emphasis in the context of my hearers. They were not the only subjects which needed emphasis, but a choice had to be made of five. The Spirit is God, and what is said of God is said of the Spirit."

actions correspond with his thoughts, then his doctrine of God will control his behaviour completely. But most of us are inconsistent, and this does not add to our happiness or enhance our effectiveness.

Since this doctrine is so influential, and a true doctrine consistently held and practised is a source of great benefit, it is a matter of great importance to investigate what may be known of the character and nature of God.

Deity is a concept congenial to the human mind. The existence of divine being is not an abstruse or difficult concept, like, for example, that of the infinitesimal calculus, which has to be struggled with before it can be apprehended; for even the simplest and youngest mind finds the notion of deity easy to accept and to understand. The idea of deity may be said to be innate, not in the sense that a child is born with the idea fully formed in his mind, but in the sense that the concept is readily understood and accepted by the child as soon as he is told about it. Strictly speaking, it is responsiveness to the concept of deity which is innate, though in actual fact there has been no child born into the world who has not early in his life learned from his elders of the concept of deity. For religion and belief in the divine are co-extensive with humanity. As far back into history as we can push our knowledge of the human race, religion is found, and among the nations and tribes that make up humanity at the present day, religion is a universal activity. So every child, early in his life, comes to hear of the concept of deity, and when he hears he understands it, and he has little problem in accepting it, if he learns it from one with whom he is in sympathy.

The ingredients that make up this universally held concept include personality and everlastingness, as well as knowledge, power and relatedness. The deities, as humanity conceives of them, are eternal, superhuman beings who influence our lives and who in turn may be influenced by a right approach to them. Belief in the existence of such a being or beings is found throughout humanity. There is no race known to history, or to archaeology, or to anthropology, who did not or who does not believe in deity. The concept is filled out in different ways, and apart from Christianity, Judaism and Islam, deity is always conceived of as a plurality of divine beings. Only in the sophisticated society of the ancient world or of modern times has the reality of deity been denied.

Although it obviously would be to the advantage of self-centred humanity that deity should not exist, the notion of deity is so natural to the human mind that the acceptance of its non-existence can only be maintained by constant propaganda, and even this fails and the concept returns in one form or other. It would be strange indeed if this universal and tenacious concept of deity had no correspondence with reality. The alternative to the reality of deity is that people have made up the belief because their nature needs it. But this explanation contains within it a contradiction. For if people's nature is solely the creation of their environment, as the atheist affirms, how does it come about that the real environment has created in humans a need which can only be satisfied by something which does not exist—a need so real and basic that no human race has existed without its fulfilment in religious belief? The environment has not done this for any other form of life. How are we to believe then that it should do so simply for human life? It is self-contradictory to believe that ultimate reality, in this case for the atheist, material reality, has shaped humanity so that man is only truly man, only truly human, only truly related in a human way in societies, and only prospers, if he believes and devotes himself in worship to a nonentity, to something which is not there at all. If such were the case with regard to humanity, *homo sapiens* would be a sardonic misnomer.

PERSONAL DEITY SELF-REVELATIONAL

Although sophisticated thought is able to arrive at the concept of impersonal deity, and ultimately at the concept of the non-existence of deity, the universal view of deity, as received among the nations of the world from the time that history began, is that deity is personal. Now if this is true, it follows that men can have no knowledge of deity apart from deity's own volition. The gods have always been conceived of as persons, yet persons cannot be known unless they reveal themselves. To reveal themselves or not to do so remains within the will of persons.

Similarly, if the universally held view of humanity is true, if deity not only exists but is personal, the possibility follows that deity may reveal itself to humans. This possibility is inherent in personality. We ourselves, being persons, may take the initiative and reveal ourselves to whom we will; so, too, with personal deity, it may reveal itself to whom it will. But, of course, such events are unpredictable, just as our own decision to speak to this one, but not to that one, is unpredictable. The matter rests entirely within ourselves. But once deity has acted to reveal itself, then the event passes into history. From that moment on, it is an historical event which cannot be eliminated with the passage of time. It is written in the ongoing pages of history. Now in the history that is written in the Scriptures it is affirmed that deity has addressed itself to humans in this way. For example, while Abraham was living with his relatives, idol-worshippers in Mesopotamia beyond the river Euphrates, God Almighty spoke to him, and commanded him to leave his home in Ur and his kinsmen, and to go out into a land which God would show him, and Abraham believed God and obeyed. In this way, through this word and response, Abraham, who up until then had been ignorant of God, began to know God. It is plain from the Old Testament narrative that God spoke with Abraham on many subsequent occasions. Abraham's personal relationship to God was so full that he was called the "friend of God".[2] Indeed this was God's own designation of Abraham: "Abraham my friend".[3] Friendship arises through personal conversation, personal association, one speaking to the other, the other responding, and vice versa. God took the initiative and spoke to Abraham, Abraham responded, and the friendship began which deepened over the years as Abraham came to know God more and more.

Another example from the history of the Old Testament of God's taking the initiative to make himself known was the incident of the burning bush in the desert of Sinai. Here God spoke to Moses, told Moses his name and something of his character, gave him directions how he should act and commissioned him to lead his people out of Egypt. Subsequent revelation of God to Moses was so complete and full that God himself said of Moses that he spoke to him face to face like a friend speaks to a friend.[4] A third example is at Mount Sinai where God addressed the children of Israel directly, giving them the Ten Commandments.[5]

2. James 2:23.
3. Isaiah 41:8.
4. Exodus 33 11; Numbers 12:8; Deuteronomy 34:10.
5. Exodus 19-20.

PERSONS ARE SELF-AUTHENTICATING

We could multiply such illustrations, but it is sufficient to say that, when a person addresses another person, such action carries with it its own authentication. We know this from our own experience. So, too, when God addresses anyone, the person knows that he is being addressed. All necessity for proof of the existence of God falls away when you meet God. What is true on a human level when we meet with one another is all the more true when God, the Creator on whom we depend, wills to meet and speak with us his creatures and to establish personal relationships with us. Those to whom God speaks will have a firm and clear conviction of God's existence and of the fact that he is addressing them. God's words are self-authenticating to the hearts and minds of those whom he addresses. It could not be otherwise. When God spoke to Abraham, there could not be a moment's doubt in his mind that God was speaking to him, any more than there could be in Paul's mind any doubt that the Lord Jesus was addressing him on the Damascus road. So, too, with Moses and with all those to whom God speaks.

God's word authenticates itself, and must do so, because it is a personal word addressed to a person and heard by that person, for that is the purpose of God's speaking, and his purposes do not fail. Personal words addressed to us by someone else, when received as personal words, carry within themselves their self-authenticating character; that is to say, when we hear someone addressing us, we know the reality of the existence of that other person, and if we listen to him we become, by the act of listening, personally related to him. So, too, when God addresses people, God's existence is known by those who hear, with a conviction which all theories can never attain. The universal view of humanity drawn from their contemplation of creation, namely that deity exists, is proved to be true at the moment that God addresses us, as he addressed Abraham, as he addressed Moses and as he addresses all his children.

When the superhuman Person whom we know as God addresses any one of us, in that approach by God to us, in that word which he speaks to us, and which we receive because it is addressed to us by our Creator, we know God to be the true and living God. We know that he exists, we know that he has addressed us, we know that he is the living God, the true God, for only the living and true can speak. The gods of the philosophers never come to life. We cannot relate ourselves to them because they do not address us. They are dead. They do not exist. The same is true of the gods of the idolaters, only more conspicuously so. As the psalmist says, "They have mouths but they do not speak".[6] They do not address us; they are non-gods. But the God who addresses us is known in that action not only to be, but to be the living God and the true God, and we know that we are in his presence.

GOD IS KNOWN IN HIS WORD

Humanity's universal belief in deity, that is, in a superhuman person of everlasting character, of power and in a relationship with us, is confirmed as true in the only way that it can be confirmed—namely, by the deity approaching us and establishing a relationship with us through personal intercourse—that is to say, through his word, for words are the medium of personal relationship. God has spoken and in that address to us we know him—we know him to be existent, we know him to be living and we know him to be the only true God, because his Word carries conviction and he affirms that he alone is God. We know this to be true because, knowing him, we know his character that he is true.

God has not confined himself to speaking to Abraham and to Moses, but he has continued to speak to those whom he has chosen to address, and he has made known abundantly what his character is, through this ongoing relationship of person to person. In the same way as we learn the character of a friend as years go on and as our fellowship with our friend deepens, so, too, God has spoken to his people through the centuries in different ways. The most characteristic way by which God's Word came in Old Testament times was through prophets; that is to say, through the men and women in whom God's Spirit dwelt and whose words were controlled by the Spirit of God so that they were God's words though also remaining the words of the prophet. The prophet prefaced what he had to say with the introductory phrase "Thus saith the Lord" and then went on directly to speak in the first

6.   Psalm 135:16.

person singular in God's name. So the prophet was, as it were, God's mouthpiece, and those who heard the prophet heard God, and in hearing God's words learned of God's character. Now the Spirit of God was both giving the words through the prophet and confirming the words in the hearts of those to whom they were addressed.

The phenomenon of prophecy was not an occasional occurrence among the people of Israel but was characteristic of their relationship to God. God was present in the words of his prophets and the people were related to their divine Lord through his Word. As the Hebrew text so quaintly puts it, God rose up early and sent his prophets.[7] There was a succession of prophets right through Old Testament times who through their messages made clear the character of God and his will for men, and in this way gave to the hearers the opportunity of response through faith and obedience and so brought them into a personal relationship with the God who gave the Word.

The movement of the true and living God in revelation of himself to humanity was not confined to the prophets, but reached its apex in the incarnation of the Son of God himself. In Jesus of Nazareth God was present with us. Jesus was Emmanuel and his words were the words not of a prophet, but of the divine Creator himself. No longer does the divine message need the preface of "Thus saith the Lord", but Jesus speaks directly with the divine 'I': "I say unto you".[8] Christ's words were the words of God, and were received as such by those who believed him. In the words of Jesus and in the example of his life, God spoke to us, revealing his character and his will for us, and enlarged the possibilities of our relationship with him.

The revelation of God in Jesus was completed through the apostles and New Testament prophets. Jesus himself foretold that the Spirit of God, whom the Father would send at the Son's request on his ascension, would lead the apostles into the fullness of truth about those things which he himself could not yet teach them because of their immaturity. And so it came about. The Spirit of prophecy was conspicuously present among New Testament Christians.

7.   As reflected in the KJV rendering of Jeremiah 7:13.
8.   Matthew 5:21-22, 27-28.

THE INSCRIPTURATED LIVING WORD

But there is a further point to add. God not only spoke directly to Abraham and to Moses, and to the children of Israel at Mt Sinai. He not only spoke through the prophets and once again directly in the Lord Jesus Christ, but he has spoken to us also, through the written Word of Scripture. We meet with him in his Word, which he addresses to us. The lifeless, the dead, the fictional gods of the nations do not speak. We may speak about them, theorize about them, mythologize about them. But the true and living God speaks, not only in the past but in the present also, for he has inscripturated his Word in the Bible. The Bible does not become out of date. It is the Word of God to the present-day reader, for what was spoken, for example, to Moses, was spoken by God not only to Moses, but also to us. Thus Jesus, quoting from Exodus, asked the Sadducees, "Have you not read that which was spoken to you by God?".[9] The writing may be ancient, but today's reader meets God in that Word, for God speaks to him in it and this was the divine intention from the time the Word was first spoken centuries before.

The Scripture is the true Word of God, as true a word as the word that Moses or Abraham heard or as Isaiah spoke in the name of the Lord, indeed as true a word of God as Jesus spoke (and expressed in his life) in Galilee. This is a great comfort. The words that Jesus spoke are no longer available for us to listen to with our outward ears, as the disciples did, nor can our eyes observe his character. Undoubtedly Jesus is pre-eminently the Word of God. Yet we can no longer observe his actions, and his words have ceased to echo in the Galilean hills. The words that Moses heard have similarly perished. But what we do have is the imperishable written Word, and our Lord and the apostles unite in affirming that this written Word is as prophetic a word as the word that was spoken for example by Isaiah, as true a divine word as that which was spoken by Jesus or his apostles, or uttered by God directly from heaven at Sinai or to Moses in the desert. As Paul put it, the written Word of Scripture is God-breathed, just as our words are breathed by us.[10] He called the Scriptures the oracles of God, that is, divine statements, spoken by God

9.   Matthew 22:31.
10. 2 Timothy 3:16.

himself.[11] This is in fact the uniform testimony of all the New Testament writers. In this they were following the teaching of Jesus, who taught that what was said in the Scripture was spoken by God to us and that it could not be falsified.[12] It is essential for Christians not to deviate by a hairsbreadth from what Jesus taught about God, for he is the divine Son of God, and if he is wrong in what he believed and taught about God and God's relation to his creation, his words can carry no intrinsic authority in any other sphere of his teaching. Now with regard to Scripture, Jesus taught that this feature of creation is related to God in a way which makes the words in every respect God's words. It follows that the Scripture then, as the Word of God, is infallible, and without error in all that it affirms. The character of its divine author assures the reader of its truth and reliability. The reader knows *a priori* that it is true, that is, that it is infallible.

The Bible as the Word of God has the same characteristic as any human word, that is to say, it remains fully and truly the word of the speaker and expresses his mind, whether or not it is understood or even listened to. If it takes the form of a command, the Word of God is to be obeyed even though the hearer does not acknowledge its Author, and if the form of a promise, it is to be trusted even though it is not listened to. This is because it is the Word of God addressed to all those of whom he is the gracious Creator. But (and in this respect, too, it is just like any human word) the Bible as the Word of God does not establish a personal relationship with the speaker unless there is a glad response by the hearer. When it is heard in this way it authenticates itself to the hearer as being the word of the speaker, in the same way as any human word does.

Since it is the Word of God, Scripture is self-authenticating to those who receive it. It authenticates itself to the Christian heart. We hand it on as God's Word to those who come after us, just as we ourselves received it from those who went before us,[13] having for ourselves found it to be God's Word, in which God speaks to us, and through which we have fellowship with him.

This conviction may be tested for its reasonableness and its truth by

11. Romans 3:2.
12. Matthew 19:4, 5; 22:31; John 10:35.
13. 2 Timothy 1:13-14; 2:1-2.

other considerations. For example, our contemporaries, whose spirituality we know, lend their testimony to our own experience that the same spiritual experiences as ours are theirs through reading the Scriptures. Great saints, whose religious views are of the weightiest, have affirmed God's relationship to Scripture. Such are Paul and Peter. Jesus Christ himself testified that the Scripture received by his fellow Jews was indeed the Word of God. Furthermore, the perceived character of Scripture confirms its divine origin. The loftiness of its religious and ethical teaching, its consistency with itself throughout its pages, though composed over a period of a millennium, and the rationality of its world-view—all confirm the reasonableness of the conviction that the true God has spoken and speaks to us through the Bible.

God is in his Word. He is in it not only when the Bible is read, but also when it is truly preached, or witnessed to, or reflected on in the mind; we meet him in it, and so his Word brings both knowledge and fellowship.

THE CHARACTER OF SCRIPTURE

The Word of God will have certain characteristics because of its authorship. Not only will it be infallible and inerrant in what it is saying to us, but it will be effective in its purposes, so that those to whom it is addressed will hear it and be able to understand it; that is to say, it will be perspicuous. These characteristics of God's Word spring from its Author. We are not able to say the same of our own words, which are fallible through our ignorance and sin. Moreover, our words may not be heard by those to whom we address them, and may not be understood, even when heard, because of our inability to express ourselves clearly. None of these things is true of the divine Word. It is effective; it accomplishes the purpose for which it is sent; it is heard by those to whom it is addressed. It authenticates itself as God's Word in the hearts of those who hear it. It is perspicuous and understandable and, of course, it is true, reliable, infallible, inerrant in what it is telling us.

This puts the Word of God into a classification quite distinct and different from all other words that we may hear. Peoples' words share all the defects of our sinful imperfect nature, but God's Word is altogether different. It is perfect, whether spoken by God directly, or through prophets, or by the incarnate Son of God, or by the inspired writers of Scripture. For us, the only Word of God that we have is this last, the Holy Scripture. We are not in a position to leave our job to go out to listen to Jesus speaking on the hills of Galilee. We do not hear God addressing us directly from heaven as did those assembled in the church at the rock of Horeb,[14] nor are there prophets in our midst who are able to say with truth, "Thus saith the Lord". We do, however, have Holy Scripture which Peter himself said is more sure than even his own memory of the Galilean ministry of Jesus.[15]

THE CANON

The giving by God of his Word in written form immediately brings into being the concept of the canon, because God's Word, with its perfections, is set in a category of writing quite distinct from all other writings. God's Word is normative for our life. It is authoritative over our conscience. The words of our fellow men are not so. God's Word is perfect; our writings are imperfect. The canon then is a very simple concept. It is putting into one classification or pigeon-hole those writings of which God is the Author, and putting into the other pigeon-hole all other writings which people have written—with a greater or lesser degree of truth—but which are not written by the direct inspiration of the Holy Spirit to convey God's mind and Word to the reader, and are consequently not authoritative over the conscience.

The canon is a simple concept, although the exact extent of it may sometimes be a cause for investigation and reflection. But the simple concept of the canon is confused today in theological circles, and the reason is easy to find. Theologians have denied the unique character of the scriptural writings. The Scriptures are now widely regarded as merely the record of God's Word and not as themselves being God's direct and infallible Word. If Scripture is only another form of human writing and not primarily divine, the concept of the canon evaporates.

14. Deuteronomy 18:16.
15. 2 Peter 1:19, *cf.* Greek.

There are no longer two clearly distinct varieties of books that we may read—one of which God is the author, and the other of which men and women are the authors. But now all are included in the one category; all are only human writings, and this is what many modern theologians affirm. No wonder, then, that the concept of the canon is in confusion, for the word canon means a rule or measuring rod. It is the standard by which things are judged. Naturally in religious and moral matters, indeed in everything, God's Word, if we have it, is automatically the canon, and there is no other canon or standard of measurement which can compare to the Word of God. But if there is no clear Word of God, then there is no canon to rule thought, faith and conduct.

Given the view of Scripture held by many modern writers, there can be no such thing as canonicity; but this is not always realized. So all sorts of variations of the old and simple concept of the canon are held. For example, the idea of a canon within the canon has been aired, but how this can be is hard to understand. A writing is either canonical, that is to say, God's Word, and so of normative authority over life, or it is not canonical, being man's word, and however good and inspiring and helpful and true, cannot rule the conscience in the way that God's Word must. The phrase 'a canon within the canon' is used to assess canonicity by the quality of the message of a book. This is altogether too subjective and imposes our concepts on the Holy Spirit of prophecy. We cannot restrict the Holy Spirit to certain themes, as though we knew the whole mosaic of the revelation which the Spirit intends to give us. Prophecy is the only possible criterion for canonicity.

The view of the Bible current among many New Testament scholars and theologians is that it is not prophecy—that is, it is not God's Word written, but that it is a record of God's revelation, in particular, that it is a record of his revelation in Christ, who is supremely the Word of God. This modern view of the Bible suffers from many defects which render it untenable. It is contradictory to the views of Jesus himself. He regarded the written Word of Scripture as God's Word spoken in the past to the present readers. "Have you not read", he asked the Sadducees, "that which was spoken to you by God?". Secondly, it is contrary to the Nicene Creed, which states that the Holy Spirit spoke by the prophets—a reference to the prophetic writings of Scripture; so that the existence of a canon or body of authoritative prophetic writing is an article of the Christian faith.

THE BIBLE THE WORD OF GOD

The statement of the creed is based on the testimony of Scripture itself and in particular on the testimony of Jesus Christ who regarded the Bible as God's infallible Word.[16] He had plainly studied it thoroughly before his ministry began. He quoted it in reply to the temptations of the devil and asserted that our life is to be based on every word that proceeds from the mouth of God.[17] The whole of the written Scripture was regarded by Jesus as spoken by God. For example, in Matthew 19:5 Jesus quoted a comment of the writer of Genesis and attributed this comment to God himself. The writer to the Hebrews has the same view. In Hebrews 3:7 a verse from the Old Testament is introduced by the words "as the Holy Spirit says". The writer realized that though the verse was written by the psalmist, the real Author was God. Similarly in Acts 1:16, the quotation from the Bible is introduced by the phrase "the Scripture...which the Holy Ghost foretold by the mouth of David". (There are very similar words in Acts 4:25.) This is an interesting illustration of the two-sided truth that David wrote the words of the psalm naturally and freely, drawing on his experience, yet the true Author was the Holy Spirit who was infallibly directing those faculties which he himself had given to David.

There are many other illustrations of this New Testament attitude to Holy Scripture. Consequently the creed is right in affirming that the Holy Spirit spoke by the prophets and we should not circumscribe this reference to the prophets to mean simply those writers whom we call prophets, for it extends to the whole of prophetic Scripture, to 'every prophecy of Scripture', to use the phraseology of 2 Peter 1:20. The New Testament Scriptures are also included. Romans 16:26 is evidence of a body of New Testament prophetic Scripture received by the apostolic church. Paul explicitly stated that his own letters were prophetic Scripture and fully canonical.[18] He cited Luke's Gospel as Scripture,[19] and spoke generally of the revelation of the mystery of Christ, revealed through the apostles and New Testament prophets, among which he included his own writings.[20]

16. John 10:35.
17. Matthew 4:4.
18. 1 Corinthians 14:37.
19. 1 Timothy 5:18.
20. Ephesians 3:3-5.

All of Paul's Epistles are included in Holy Scripture in 2 Peter 3:16. Consequently, we ought not to restrict 2 Timothy 3:16—"All Scripture is inspired by God"—to the Old Testament, because at the time this was written there were New Testament Scriptures acknowledged and accepted in the Christian fellowship.

The existence of a canon of prophetic writings of Old and New Testament is an article of the Christian faith, taught clearly in the New Testament and affirmed Sunday by Sunday in the creed.

A third objection to the modern view, which regards the Bible not as God's Word written but only as a record of God's Word, is that it prevents the Bible from doing its proper work in convicting the conscience and so moving the will of the reader to obedience. God's Word rules the conscience, but a human record can never attain to this normative or canonical status. When the Bible is accepted as God's Word written, the preacher's task, though not easy, is simple in concept. He is to make clear to the eager listener what the Bible is teaching, and the conscience of the hearer gladly responds in obedience and faith to that Word of God clearly seen in the Bible through the preacher's exposition.

If, however, the Bible is primarily a human record of God's revelation in the past, it cannot evoke this spontaneous response in the regenerate heart of the listener. Human words must be assessed as to whether they are true and ought to be followed. For it is always possible that the record, if only human, is erroneous. Consequently, on the modern view that the Bible is a human record, the preacher's task has radically changed. Instead of expounding clearly the Word of God and enjoining it on the conscience of God's children to be trusted and obeyed, he is simply putting before his hearers ideas which they may treat as they like, according to their own judgement and assessment. In short, the preacher's distinctive ministry has disappeared if the Bible is not the Word of God. Could the reason why many clergy are uncertain about their role, and why they do not make public and private preaching and teaching their primary ministry, be that they doubt the infallibility of the Bible and so have lost their canon?

It is essential to hold firmly to the view of Jesus and the apostles that the written Scripture is God's Word, and therefore that we must believe it with joy, submit to it and obey it with alacrity and single-mindedness, so that its glorious promises set our standard of values and suffuse our life with hope.

Chapter 2

GOD OF INFINITE POWER, WISDOM AND GOODNESS[1]

*G*OD IS OF INFINITE POWER. THE notion of power is contained in the notion of deity. Wherever people believe in God (and this belief is as universal as the human race), God (or the gods) is thought of as powerful. However, the concept of *infinite and unlimited* power is not generally attributed to the gods of paganism, yet it is clearly affirmed of the true and living God of Holy Scripture. "Nothing is too hard for the Lord" is a refrain that runs through Scripture.[2] It was the sheet-anchor of Jesus' ministry. He told his despairing disciples, as they realized the difficulty of anyone being saved, that what was impossible with people is possible with God,[3] and in that last agonizing prayer in the Garden of Gethsemane, he based his request on the completeness of God's power. "Abba, Father, all things are possible to you".[4]

Two thousand years earlier, when the divine messenger had brought Abraham and Sarah the good news that Sarah would bear a son, although humanly speaking this was a physical impossibility, the assurance was given that 'Nothing is too hard for Yahweh',[5] and so it

---

1.   This phrase is taken from the first of the 39 Articles of Religion of the Church of England, which begins: "There is but one living and true God, everlasting, without body, parts, or passions; of infinite power, wisdom and goodness; the Maker, and Preserver of all things both visible and invisible".
2.   For example, Genesis 18:14; Job 42:2.
3.   Matthew 19:26.
4.   Mark 14:36.
5.   Textual note: In the original edition of *The Everlasting God*, the author used Jehovah as the traditional English transliteration of the Hebrew name of God (the 'YHWH' that is rendered in most English Bibles as 'the LORD'). In this edition, it has been rendered as 'Yahweh'. It must be acknowledged that 'Yahweh' is not a certain translation, but it is more likely to be accurate than 'Jehovah' and less confusing to the reader than 'LORD'.

came about.[6] When Jeremiah was faced with the apparent contradiction of on the one hand God's purpose in the destruction of Jerusalem, and on the other the word that came to him to buy a block of land in Judah, he cast himself onto God with the prayer, "Ah Lord Yahweh! Behold, you have made the heavens and the earth by your great power and by your outstretched arm! *Nothing is too difficult for you...* You have said to me, O Lord Yahweh, 'Buy for yourself the field for money, and call in witnesses'—although the city is given into the hand of the Chaldeans."

Yahweh replied, "Behold I am Yahweh, the God of all flesh, *is anything too difficult for me?*...Behold, I am about to give this city into the hand of the Chaldeans...[but] behold, I will gather them out of all the lands to which I have driven them in my anger...and I will bring them back to this place and make them dwell in safety".[7] And so it came about. There is nothing too hard for Yahweh. As Job exclaimed, "I know that you can do all things, and that no purpose of yours can be thwarted".[8] The virgin Mary received the same assurance from the angel Gabriel in response to her natural enquiry as to how it could be that the promise of a son should be fulfilled to her who had no husband. "For nothing will be impossible with God".[9]

The true and living God has revealed himself as a God of infinite power. The only things impossible to him are those which contradict His character. He cannot lie, he cannot change, he cannot cease from being good.[10]

CREATION

The clearest example of God's power is the act of creation. All that we see around us is the result of God's creative power. The universe came into being through his Word, "For he commanded and they were created" as the psalmist put it.[11] The concept that God created everything

6. Genesis 18:14.
7. Jeremiah 32:15-37.
8. Job 42:2.
9. Luke 1:37.
10. E.g. Titus 1:2; Malachi 3:6.
11. Psalm 148:5; cf. Psalm 33:5-9.

out of nothing is fundamental to the Scripture and is found throughout its pages. The God of Holy Scripture, the God of revelation, is the
Creator God, the God of infinite power. Nor did his powerful acts
cease with creation, but he controls what he created. His infinite mind
controls absolutely, all the time, every detail of created things. We find
this thought a difficulty, but it ought not to be so, for we believe that
we have evidence that our own minds to a limited extent may sometimes be able to influence matter, even though it is not created by us.
God's infinite mind controls everything and he can as easily alter it at
any moment as create it in the first place. God spoke and it was done,
and God's Word continues to have the same infinite power. Whatever
he wills comes to pass, and nothing comes to pass except in accordance
with what he wills. Chance and luck are non-existent. They are simply
words to describe that which is unforeseeable by us.

The Bible puts before us a consistent world-view based on the infinite power of God. Thus Jesus said that God makes the sun to rise and
sends the rain.[12] In saying this Jesus is simply repeating the consistent
teaching of Scripture that the natural phenomena are the direct results
of God's will, whether there are rain and fruitful seasons, or whether
there is a drought. Our minds have difficulty with this. We see only the
proximate causes (the meteorological laws as we call them) or the laws
of cause and effect. But it is the mind of God which gives all these laws
their motive force. It is God who makes the sun to rise. It is God who
raises up the stormy wind.[13] It is God who makes the storm to cease.[14]
It was God who sent the flood.

After the flood God promised Noah in the covenant with creation
recorded in Genesis 9 that his dealings with the world would be on the
basis of consistency, that seed-time and harvest, cold and heat, summer
and winter, day and night would not cease so long as the world lasts.
This consistency is part of the purpose of God, for without it human
life as we know it could not be sustained. If, for example, there were no
consistency in the seasons, we could neither sow nor reap. But this
consistency of God's working must not be mistaken for an inevitable

12. Matthew 5:45.
13. Psalm 107:25.
14. Psalm 107:29.

and inexorable law of cause and effect. Ultimately, God is the only cause, and it is his mind and will which cause all things. God wills consistency, and that is why we experience consistency. Although we speak of the laws of nature governing physical events, this is a misnomer. The laws of nature are not laws in the true sense but are observed consistencies of sequences of past events. They do not govern the future. God's consistent mind governs the future as he has governed the observed past.

If in his wisdom God wills that an event in nature should differ from the unbroken sequence before or after (for example, that the sun should stand still), then it will differ.[15] We shall call it a miracle. Others who do not know God's power will deny that it happened. But there is no reason for this denial. Since God is a free Person we cannot lay down in advance how he will create the world or how he will order events within it. We know that he is loving, righteous and holy in all he does, but we cannot know the mind of the Lord for physical phenomena. Experience is our only source of this knowledge.

However, since God is a God of order and faithfulness, it is possible to develop the discipline of natural science. For science works through prediction based on precedent, that is, on the observed sequences of the past, 'the customs of the Creator'. We call these customs of the Creator natural laws. But God's will is the basis of each event. However, since God has linked events in 'causal' chains, it is possible to understand the whole series of events without reference to God. God is an unnecessary hypothesis for science, but not for the reflective scientist. For it is not a contradiction, but rather a necessary element of the whole concept, to realize that every 'cause' in the chain has the will of God as its own underlying and true cause. God holds all things together and in them he is working all things after the counsel of his own will.[16]

The doctrine of God the Creator is vivid throughout the pages of Scripture. The gods of the nations are not creator gods and, as the interesting little Aramaic insertion in Jeremiah puts it, the gods that did not create the world will perish, as indeed they have.[17] In our own times idol-

---

15. Joshua 10:12-13.
16. Ephesians 1:11; Colossians 1:17.
17. Jeremiah 10:11.

atry, which was a universal substitute for the creator God, has been replaced by the widely held theory of evolution. Both are substitutes for the concept of the creator God. Just as the ancients and the heathen today deified and worshipped the creature as the creator, modelling images of man or birds or animals or reptiles and worshipping these, so for Western secular people the modern theory of evolution deifies nature and acknowledges it as creator of all we see around us. All the beauty and intricacy and all the marvellous arrangements of the natural world are supposed to have been evolved by a thoughtless, purposeless, mechanical operation of nature, and in this way the God who made the world is as effectively shut out of the minds of those who are enjoying the blessings of his creation as he was by the false religions of idolatry. Just as the idolaters could not see the foolishness, indeed the stupidity, of worshipping gods of wood and stone, which have no life nor purpose nor mind, so modern believers in the theory of evolution cannot see the foolishness of that theory, which not only lacks evidence to support it, but also runs counter to such evidence of origins as is available. Nevertheless, this false world-view is being indoctrinated into children in the schools with the aid of public money and placarded in natural history museums as though it were the only explanation of the world around us, while those who criticize and expose the theory receive the same intense religious hostility as did those who denounced idolatry in earlier days. The Bible says that if we refuse to have the creator God in our mind, God gives us up to a reprobate mind.[18]

God's infinite power controls what he has created. We have seen that Jesus taught that the phenomena of nature are under God's control. That is why we may pray for favourable weather. To describe the weather as under God's control is not mere poetry, but a direct description of the facts. It may not be God's will to alter the consistent way by which he regulates the weather—a consistency which we call meteorological laws—yet it may be his gracious will to accede to our request. When he does this, he will do it in what we would call a natural way, but the one who prayed will know the real reason why the weather changed.

18. Romans 1:18-28.

GOD'S CONTROL OVER EVIL WILLS

God's control over his creation extends to control over the wills of people. Sinful people are within this complete control of God, otherwise sin would be a marvellous achievement, if by it we could remove ourselves from God's sovereign and absolute power. But it is not so. The brigands who slaughtered Job's servants and carried off his cattle were as much under the control of God, although they did not know it, as was the wind that destroyed the house in which Job's children were gathered.[19] Job acknowledged this by his pious and true reaction to the tragic news: "Yahweh gave, and Yahweh has taken away; blessed be the name of Yahweh".[20] Ultimately, it was Yahweh who took away Job's possessions and his children. Although the agents were men and spirits of an evil and malevolent character, yet they were not outside God's control and were operating within the sphere of his perfect will and purposes. They originated the evil, but they were not able to act contrary to what God willed should come to pass. Similarly, in Isaiah 10 the prophet recounts how the Assyrians are the rod of God's anger. Those cruel armies invading Palestine were the instruments of a well-deserved judgement. Yet the Assyrians were totally unaware that they were acting under God's control and fulfilling his purpose. They attributed their success to their military prowess, but the prophet foretold that their cruelties would in due course receive retribution, just as Israel had experienced judgement through them.

Centuries before, Joseph had reassured his brothers that his captivity in Egypt was part of God's perfect will to bless: "God sent me before you to preserve for you a remnant...and to keep you alive by a great deliverance. Now, therefore, it was not you that sent me here, but God."[21] Again, a little later, he once more reassured them with the words: "As for you, you meant evil against me; but God meant it for good in order to bring about this present result, to preserve many people alive".[22] It must have been a great source of strength to Joseph throughout the bitter years of his imprisonment to realize that God

19. Job 1:13-19.
20. Job 1:21.
21. Genesis 45:7-8.
22. Genesis 50:20.

was sovereign over every event in the experiences which he was suffering. Nothing takes place in God's creation apart from God's will because God is of infinite power.

The doctrine of God's absolute and complete providence and control over every event is a ground for banishing fear from the hearts of the people of God. Thus Jesus reminded his disciples, "Are not five sparrows sold for two cents? And yet not one of them is forgotten before God. Indeed, the very hairs of your head are all numbered. Do not fear; you are of more value than many sparrows".[23] In the Old Testament the doctrine of God's sovereignty is the comfort and strength of his people. Thus through the prophet Isaiah God says, "I, even I, am he that comforts you. Who are you that you are afraid of man who dies, and of the son of man who is made like grass; that you have forgotten Yahweh your Maker, who stretched out the heavens and laid the foundations of the earth?"[24]

The creative power of God which brought all things into being is the guarantee that he is able to sustain us in every detail of life. The doctrine of creation is basic to the Christian doctrine of God.

The infinite power and the infinite mind of God, to which the marvels of creation bear witness, mean that he is able to give full attention, care and protection to every person throughout the world with the same intensity of concern that he would give if he were related to a single individual only. The infinity of God is not overwhelmed by numbers, nor stupefied by detail. God is able to comprehend, and provide for at the same time, the needs of the whole of his creation. Our heavenly Father gives each of us his undivided attention and his full friendship as though we were his only friend.

PURPOSE AND JUDGEMENT

Creation implies purpose. In contrast, impersonal evolution is purposeless—things happening by accident without plan. But creation is a personal activity of an almighty, supreme God. Personal action implies

23. Luke 12:6, 7.
24. Isaiah 51:12-13.

purpose, and this in turn implies assessment. The doctrine of judgement is closely related to that of creation. The Scriptures are full of the
truth of the judgement of God. One of the oldest passages of the Old
Testament, the song of Deborah, proclaims how turning away from the
true God brought inevitable judgement: "New gods were chosen; then
war was in the gates".[25] The events in the historical books of the Old
Testament underscore the truth that judgement follows wrongdoing.
The main theme of the prophets is the inevitability of judgement unless
God's people return and seek God's forgiveness in repentance. A passage
from Jeremiah will illustrate this. Jeremiah is told by the Lord to write
in a book his prophecies "from the day I first spoke to you, from the
days of Josiah even to this day. Perhaps the house of Judah will hear all
the calamity which I plan to bring on them, in order that every man will
turn from his evil way; that I will forgive their iniquity and their sin".[26]
Judgement is inevitable. The purpose of God's making it known to us
is that we might repent and amend our lives in the light of the
inevitability of this future assessment, and so escape judgement.

The theme of judgement is as prominent in the New Testament as
in the Old. Jesus spoke much about the doom of outer darkness, where
there is weeping and gnashing of teeth in hopeless remorse, and also of
hell (or Gehenna), where the worm does not die and the fire is never
put out.[27] He warned his hearers not to fear people who might put to
death the body, but to fear God who could destroy both body and soul
in hell.[28] Again, speaking to the Jewish leaders, he said, "You serpents,
you brood of vipers, how shall you escape the sentence of hell?".[29]

Judgement was an integral part of Paul's message. He wrote in
Romans 2 of "the day when, according to my gospel, God will judge the
secrets of men through Jesus Christ".[30] When preaching in the market-
place at Athens, his sermon reached its climax as he proclaimed that God
has fixed the judgement day when he will judge the world in righteousness by the Man whom he has chosen and he has given proof of this by

25. Judges 5:8.
26. Jeremiah 36:2, 3.
27. Matthew 8:12; 22:13; 25:30; Mark 9:43-44.
28. Matthew 10:28.
29. Matthew 23:33.
30. Romans 2:16.

raising him from the dead.[31] A final illustration from Paul will underline this point still more clearly. When Paul was a prisoner in Caesarea and had the opportunity of preaching before Governor Felix at Felix's request, he spoke about faith in Jesus Christ, "discussing righteousness, self-control and the judgement to come".[32] This summary of perhaps Paul's most significant sermon shows how central was judgement in the Christian gospel. In his second letter to the Thessalonians, Paul described this "manifest judgement of God" in most vivid terms. He wrote,

> *For after all it is only just for God to repay with affliction those who*
> *afflict you, and to give relief to you who are afflicted and*
> *to us as well when the Lord Jesus shall be revealed from heaven with*
> *his mighty angels in flaming fire, dealing out retribution*
> *to those who do not know God and to those who do not obey the*
> *gospel of our Lord Jesus. And these will pay the penalty of eternal*
> *destruction, away from the presence of the Lord and from the glory of*
> *his power, when he comes to be glorified in his saints on that day,*
> *and to be marvelled at among all who have believed—for our*
> *testimony to you was believed.*[33]

The phrase 'that day' was well understood by New Testament Christians to stand for the judgement day. It is a common New Testament phrase because judgement is a common New Testament concept.

Judgement is a central theme of the book of Revelation and is displayed vividly in a series of pictures, so that it might have its proper influence on the conscience and the will of believers.

Judgement will be thorough and complete. Jesus said that we will give an account of every idle word.[34] Idle words are perhaps the least significant of any of our actions, yet they will not escape God's assessment. God is infinite and his judgement will take into account everything, even every idle word.

The Bible is clear that God's judgement will be righteous, that is to say, it will be absolutely just and fair. The statement that God will ren-

---

31. Acts 17:31.
32. Acts 24:24, 25.
33. 2 Thessalonians 1:6-10.
34. Matthew 12:36.

der to every person according to their works runs like a refrain through both Old and New Testaments.[35] The righteous judgement of God is a consolation to his people when they are suffering wrongfully at the hands of their enemies, for God will repay, and repay righteously.[36] They will be vindicated. On the other hand the righteous judgement of God is an awful subject for sinners to contemplate. It is a fearful thing to fall into the hand of the living God.[37]

A gospel which contains judgement as a prominent strand, as does the New Testament gospel, is relevant to men and women everywhere and in every age and culture. It does not need indigenization,[38] so popular a catchword today, but requires only clarity of language and faithfulness in proclamation. The sense of right and wrong is universal in the human race and so is the knowledge that we fall below our own standards of what is right, and that this entails death. Thus the gospel that contains judgement, and salvation from judgement, is a gospel that is always relevant to the hearer, no matter to what stage of civilization he may have attained. Such a gospel does not need to be assimilated to the culture of the people who are hearing it. A theology that proclaims the God who saves from judgement by forgiveness through faith in the Lord Jesus Christ does not need to be adapted for Australian audiences, or to be turned into a black theology for the blacks of North America. Asian Christians and Western Christians need the same gospel and the same theology which is based on it, and all are able to understand it, no matter how different the cultural backgrounds of the hearers and preachers may be, so long as the proclamation is true to the New Testament gospel of judgement and salvation from judgement.

A gospel that minimizes or omits judgement must concentrate on this life and the benefits that Christ brings for this life. Most modern preaching, whether liberal or evangelical, falls into this mistake. The liberal preacher may emphasize a social gospel, for example, one of alleviation of poverty or political oppression; the evangelical may emphasize a happy life, love, joy and forgiveness.

But the Christian gospel is concerned with the future. It proclaims

35. 1 Samuel 26:23; Proverbs 24:12; Romans 2:6; Revelation 22:12.
36. Isaiah 59:17-20; Deuteronomy 7:9-10.
37. Hebrews 10:31.
38. The more current term now would be 'contextualization'.

Jesus who rescues us from the wrath to come.[39] When hearers accept the gospel for the benefits of this life, such as peace and happiness, it is a contradiction to ask them to suffer for the gospel. The whole purpose of their accepting the gospel was for some present benefit which they had been offered by the preacher. This presentation and acceptance of the gospel of Jesus Christ for benefits it brings here and now may well be the explanation of why it is that although evangelical Christianity is growing, for example in the United States, Christian influence on society is receding. There may be more true Christians in the community, nevertheless the forces of evil—as reflected, for example, in the increase of drunkenness, gambling, permissiveness, sexual immorality and dishonesty in business— continue to grow, in spite of the preaching of the gospel and the conversion of men and women to Christ. What is required, if we are to maintain a true spiritual witness against social evils, is the willingness to suffer for the sake of the truth. Such willingness to suffer will only be created by a gospel that proclaims a future judgement and a salvation from that judgement through forgiveness and justification in Christ, so that our thoughts are fixed on that future rather than on some present blessing for which we may have embraced the gospel and which is threatened by suffering. Christians today are like salt that has lost its savour, through loss of heavenly-mindedness.[40]

The modern gospel does not draw tears from the preacher as he preaches. Yet it is a characteristic of the New Testament gospel that the preacher was moved to tears. For example, our Lord wept over Jerusalem.[41] The tears were drawn out, not because Jerusalem was missing out on some present blessing, but rather because it was neglecting its opportunity of repentance and so of salvation from the inevitable future judgement when its enemies would come upon it and not leave one stone upon another, a judgement too awful to contemplate, a tribulation such as had never occurred in the history of the world before. Paul, too, wept over the impenitent. In Romans 9 he testified that he had constant pain in his heart through the unbelief of

39. 1 Thessalonians 1:10.
40. Matthew 5:13; Colossians 3:1-4.
41. Matthew 23:37-24:2f.; Luke 19:41-44.

62 THE EVERLASTING GOD

his kinsmen. In Acts 20, Paul, giving a summary of his three years' ministry at Ephesus, mentioned twice over that his preaching was accompanied by tears. Tears in the preacher are evoked by deeply felt sympathy with the predicament of those who are listening, a predicament which the preacher shares but from which he has been rescued by the gospel which he is bringing. When that gospel is rejected, tears are drawn from the preacher as he earnestly seeks the good of those to whom he has been sent. Our modern gospel does not evoke tears in the preacher because the dimension of judgement has almost completely been eliminated. A gospel without tears, because without judgement, is not the gospel of the New Testament.

Judgement is prominent in the biblical message. But the Bible has to be believed without wavering if judgement is to be prominent in preaching which at the same time is compassionate preaching. It is easy for a preacher, lacking sympathy with the human race, to throw brickbats of judgement at the heads of his hearers. On the other hand, since the world does not believe in judgement nor like to hear of it, a considerate preacher will avoid the subject unless, unshaken by private doubts, he remains firm in his belief in the reliability and truth of God's Word, which is so full of judgement.

Creation and judgement are the focal points around which human life moves. These two truths, closely related because they both spring from a supreme purposeful Creator, should not be far from the thoughts of any. They are central in the Christian gospel, but neither purposeful creation nor future assessment finds any place in the alternative explanation of reality which the modern world embraces and which goes by the name of evolution.

EVERLASTING, WITHOUT BODY, PARTS OR PASSIONS

God is everlasting, without body, parts or passions. These phrases from the first of the Thirty-Nine Articles simply draw out the thought that is contained within the concept of deity. Everlastingness, infinity in time, is inherent in the notion of deity. Humanity is conscious that its life is temporary, but the gods have always been thought of as immortal. Consequently, the epithet 'everlasting' simply draws out what is contained in the word 'God' and what is thoroughly endorsed by the

Bible, which terms God "the everlasting God".[42]

At first sight, in view of numerous passages of Scripture, it might seem strange to deny God a body, but a body is a form of limitation. God is not limited by externals; he is infinite. He is not limited as we are by location. He is omnipresent, present equally everywhere; but ubiquity is contradictory to the concept of a body. The scriptural descriptions of God in bodily terms, such as the eyes of the Lord, or the right hand, are metaphors.

'Without parts' is inherent in the concept of spirit. God is spirit and spirit is not composite, made up of parts as material objects are. Spirit is not divisible. Jesus taught that God is spirit.[43] Our knowledge of spirit comes from our knowledge of ourselves. We know we are an indivisible unity.

'Without passions' does not mean that God is without feeling, but it means that God is not subject to control from outside himself. He is not passive, he is not the recipient, willy-nilly, of the action of others, but he is the One on whom all activity depends. For he is sovereign; he is of infinite power.

OF INFINITE GOODNESS

God is of infinite goodness. Goodness may be defined as concern for other people's welfare, that is, interest in others and the desire and activity of promoting their welfare. The Scriptures constantly affirm that God is good.[44] Creation exhibits the goodness of God in a very clear manner. As the Scripture says, God saw the creation that it was very good.[45] He created the world to be inhabited,[46] and its inhabitants enjoy living within the created world. The world is beautiful and we enjoy its beauty. The tourist industry witnesses to the pleasures of beauty that are built into the creation. The whole of life in its created

42. Genesis 21:33; Isaiah 40:28.
43. John 4:24.
44. Psalm 100:5; Mark 10:18.
45. Genesis 1:31.
46. Isaiah 45:18.

nature is pleasant to live. For example, it is pleasant to eat and without eating we would not survive! The world brings pleasure to the creature.

This ought to evoke thanksgiving to the Creator. Thanksgiving is a duty, and like all natural duties, it too is pleasant, for it increases the experience of the pleasure, by minimizing self-centredness and sharing the joy, for shared joys are deepened. But as Paul says in Romans 1, this basic primary response of thanksgiving is where humanity fails and, failing at this point, the whole relationship with God is brought into jeopardy.

GOODNESS IN RELATIONSHIP INVOLVES RESPONSIBILITY

The act of creation brings the Creator into a relationship of responsibility for the welfare of his creation. For otherwise God would not be good. From the moment of creation the good God is in a relationship of care and concern for that which he has brought into being, and his care and concern are infinite and never vary or fail. In a word we may say that God is in a covenant relationship with his creation from the inception of its existence. In the true world, where goodness is basic, creation involves covenant. God has always been and will always be in covenant relationship with his creation and, since God is good, the covenant is always a covenant of grace. Its character and content will vary with humanity's situation and need.

The covenant, implicit in creation, becomes explicit in Genesis 6 and 9. In these passages, God promises that he will maintain his covenant. "I will maintain my covenant with you and with your seed after you and with every living creature that is with you."[47] The word 'maintain' indicates that the covenant was already in existence, confirming that the fact of covenant is involved in the act of creation by the good Creator. The terms of this covenant are that God will maintain the stability of the earth in order that humanity's life might prosper. There will be no more cataclysms; there will be no irregularity in the seasons but while the earth remains, seed-time and harvest, cold and heat, summer and winter, day and night shall not cease. This is God's promise and this is God's fulfilment. The consistency of the

---

47. Genesis 9:9-10 (RV).

natural phenomena is the basis of human life. We can rely upon the future and so take action in the present with a view to that future. This is part of the goodness of God. As Paul put it, he fills our hearts with food and gladness through sending us fruitful seasons.[48]

God's covenant relationship with creation, when expressed in personal terms, means that he is faithful; he fulfils that which he promises. He is the faithful God and we are to reflect his faithfulness in our relationships, not only with God, but with one another. The virtue of faithfulness must not be degraded into loyalty. Although this word has begun to appear in modern English versions of the Bible, loyalty is not a biblical notion, and is often the cause of grave injustice. But faithfulness is always a virtue and a duty. In Scripture, God is described as the faithful God.[49] The faithfulness of God is the most important aspect of his goodness. Without this divine attribute of faithfulness it would not be possible to practise the Christian religion, because the Christian religion is a relationship with God, a relationship with a God who can be trusted, a relationship which calls for the response of obedience and hope. Now obedience and hope are based on the knowledge of God's faithfulness. It is because God, who has promised, is faithful that we gladly obey him in the way that he has directed in order to attain his sure promises. The goodness of God and his covenant relationship with all that he has created are expressed in Psalm 104. The wildlife of the jungle and of the open countryside look to God for the provision of their daily food. As Jesus said, the sparrows are fed by him; how much more men and women, whom he created in his own image for fellowship with himself?[50]

RESPONSIBILITY INVOLVES AUTHORITY

Because God is responsible for our welfare, he has authority over us. Authority and responsibility go hand in hand. Those who receive benefit from the exercise of responsibility have the obligation to respond by obedience to the authority within the area of its responsibility. This

48. Acts 14:17.
49. Deuteronomy 7:9; 32:4.
50. Matthew 6:26; 10:29-31.

is true, not only in relation to God, but in all areas of human life. Thus the state has responsibility for the welfare of the citizens in the areas of justice and virtue, and therefore has authority over the citizens within those areas. It is the duty of the citizens to respond with obedience, thanksgiving and honour. Similarly, in the family it is the duty of the parents, and particularly of the father, to advance the welfare of all the members of the family while they are still dependent. He must take thought and action for their benefit. Consequently, he has authority within the area of that responsibility. If he acts beyond his responsibility, then his authority ceases at that point. But within the area of his responsibility he has authority, and consequently there is an obligation on those who benefit from his care and concern to obey him, within the area of his authority and also to be thankful for the thoughtfulness and for the action taken on their behalf and for their benefit.

Obligation to obey ceases when commands are given beyond the area of responsibility. An illustration is Peter's refusal to obey the Jewish authorities. They were giving commands which were contrary to the commands of God.[51] But since the authority of rulers is a delegated authority as the ministers of God,[52] when they give commands which contradict God's commands, they have exceeded their responsibility of being God's ministers. Yet a command that appears to be unjust to oneself may not necessarily be outside the area of responsibility and consequently is to be obeyed, as Peter reminded those unfortunate slaves who had unjust masters.[53]

Closely related to obedience and thanksgiving is honour. We are to give honour to those in authority—give recognition, that is, to their authoritative position, an authority which derives from their relationship with us of responsibility for our welfare. The obligation to honour continues even when the responsibility has been fulfilled and the authority has ceased.

God's relationship to us is one of complete responsibility for all aspects of our life and therefore his authority is complete. We on our part must recognize the authority which accompanies this responsibility by giving complete and absolute obedience to God. There is no area of

51. Acts 5:29.
52. Romans 13:4.
53. 1 Peter 2:18.

our life which is outside his responsibility, and since he is a good God he is active in discharging that responsibility for our welfare. Therefore we are to obey him in everything, to be thankful to him in everything, to honour him in everything.

God is of infinite power, but power in itself does not confer authority. God's power has brought us into being through creation, but his power alone is not the ground of our obligation to obey him. The ground of that obligation is his goodness coupled with his power, for his goodness means that he is concerned for the welfare of his creation and his power enables him to give effect to this concern. As the infinitely good Creator, he accepts responsibility for the welfare of his creation; that is, he is in covenant relationship with it. He is actively promoting its welfare, and this relationship of real responsibility confers authority and calls for the response of obedience from those who benefit, for this is their acknowledgement of the relationship.

First, there is the relationship, then there is the responsibility of that relationship. From this flows the authority which God has over all, and which leads in turn to the obligation on all of obedience, thanksgiving and honour. In short, goodness in relationship plus ability to discharge the responsibilities of that relationship are the ground for authority, not only in the affairs of humans but also in the ultimate relationship of God and his creation.

We may apply this concept to the life of the congregation and ask, 'Who has authority within the congregation?'. We answer, 'Only those who rightly have responsibility for the spiritual welfare of the congregation, and only to the extent of their responsibility'. Those who benefit from the exercise of the responsibility, with its care, concern and thoughtfulness for the benefit of the recipients, are obliged not only to honour the authority, but also to obey it within the area of its responsibility, but not beyond. If authority is exercised beyond that area of responsibility it becomes usurped authority and carries no obligation for obedience. We all have responsibility for the welfare of fellow members of the congregation and to this extent we are all to submit to one another, as Paul commanded the Ephesians.[54] But some members because of their recognized gifts have greater responsibility and so

54. Ephesians 5:21.

greater authority, which other members have the duty to acknowledge and to obey.[55]

God's infinite power coupled with his infinite goodness mean that he is not niggardly in conferring benefits on his creation. He is not, for example, like the gods of the ancient civilizations, who were thought to be envious of the prosperity of humans; but God loves his creation, cares for it and bestows blessings on it with a generous hand. As the Scripture says, "No good thing does he withhold from those that walk uprightly";[56] and again, "In your right hand there are pleasures forever".[57] As Paul said, God "richly supplies us with all things to enjoy".[58] God's goodness means that he is other-person-centred. He has created us in his image to be other-person-centred. In Jesus we have been given the example and pattern of how we should use the good things he gives us by sharing them with others. Our Lord himself has told us that it is more blessed to give than to receive.[59] The character of the blessed One is that of giving. To give and to share mean to enlarge the benefit as well as to increase the joy of relationship.

THE WISDOM OF GOD

God is of infinite wisdom. Wisdom may be defined as knowledge applied in purposeful activity to achieve good ends. Knowledge applied purposefully but not towards the good of others is not called wisdom but cunning. Wisdom must always be good. Wickedness is incompatible with wisdom.[60] God is of infinite power, infinite goodness and infinite knowledge. God's knowledge differs from ours in that it is prior to the existence of the things known. They exist because he knows them. Human knowledge is derived from observation and arises from experience. God does not have to wait on the event to know it as we do; he knows it before it happens and it only happens because he

55. 1 Corinthians 16:15, 16.
56. Psalm 84:11.
57. Psalm 16:11.
58. 1 Timothy 6:17.
59. Acts 20:35.
60. Proverbs 8:7, 8.

knows it and wills it.

It may be asked, 'How can knowledge be infinite, if knowledge has an object, for objects are limited?'. It is because God knows possibilities as well as actualities. Thus God's knowledge is co-extensive with reality—not only actual reality, but all possible reality, which is infinite, so that he is of infinite knowledge. He knows all the actuality of reality as well as the infinity of its possibilities. This means that he knows how human wills will react to the circumstances in which they find themselves and which he himself controls. Therefore nothing takes God by surprise. He knows the end from the beginning.[61] His infinite knowledge coupled with his infinite power and infinite goodness mean that he has infinite wisdom. Consequently, he infallibly achieves his purposes and those purposes are beneficent. He is active in forwarding the true interests of his whole creation.

God's wisdom is marvelously displayed in the created world. As the psalmist exclaims, "O Yahweh, how many are your works! In wisdom you have made them all".[62] The world has been created to accomplish ends of blessing, of joy and of fellowship with God. It marvellously achieves these ends. Take for example our body, that aspect of creation about which we know most. It has plainly been created in order that we might enjoy life. Our five senses all are vehicles of pleasure, as we see the beauty of the world, as we hear the sounds of music, as we taste the food which we need to sustain our life, as we enjoy the fragrance of a flower, as our bodies feel the sensation of the surf or of the wind. All these things are aspects of God's wisdom in conferring on us joys. Looked at from another point of view, the body is marvellously contrived to accomplish its ends of relationship, with all the pleasure, physical, mental, emotional, spiritual that relationship brings. The eye, the face, the language structure of our brain, are designed to express our inner being to one another. Our sexual natures, both psychological and physical, are marvellously designed to relate us in joyous fellowship.

God's wisdom is manifest in creation but is even more marvellously displayed in redemption and the restoration of fellowship with God. God has indeed bestowed upon us every spiritual blessing. These blessings are in Jesus Christ. He is the wisdom of God. He is so described by

61. Isaiah 46:9-10.
62. Psalm 104:24.

Paul in 1 Corinthians 1:24. God's beneficence comes to fruition in Christ and in his cross. Paul expresses this in Colossians 2:3—"Christ, in whom are all the treasures of wisdom...hidden".

Jesus described himself as the wisdom of God. In Luke 11:49 we read, "The wisdom of God [said], 'I will send to them prophets and apostles'". Comparison of this passage with its parallel in Matthew 23:34 shows that Jesus was speaking of himself.

A further example of our Lord's self-identification as the wisdom of God is in Matthew 11:19 and its parallel in Luke 7:35. In these passages, Jesus described the attitude of his generation who were rejecting the counsel of God. He compared them to children in the market-place. John the Baptist had called to them and they had taken no notice. Now Jesus called to them and they again took no notice. In Proverbs, wisdom calls in the market-place to the passers-by, but her call is disregarded. "I have called and you refused. I have stretched out my hand and no man regarded; you have set at nought my counsel".[63] Luke 7:30 states explicitly, "The Pharisees and the lawyers rejected for themselves the counsel of God", and Jesus commented, "Wisdom is justified of all her children". In Matthew the same sentiment is put in different words: "Wisdom is justified by its works".[64] Jesus, the Wisdom of God, saw that his ministry was rejected by the Jews, but nevertheless it is justified by what it accomplishes in those who are the children of wisdom.

Our Lord's knowledge that he was the wisdom of God spoken of in the Old Testament may be behind the somewhat unusual activity of public proclamation by Jesus when on the last great day of the feast he stood and cried, "If any man thirst, let him come to me, and drink". "This spoke he of the Spirit", says the evangelist.[65] Proverbs 1:21-23 reads, "[Wisdom] cries in the concourse... 'I will pour out my spirit upon you'", and in Proverbs 9:5 wisdom invites the passer-by, "Come, eat of my bread, and drink of my wine", a phrase that may have been in our Lord's mind also when he chose bread and wine to be symbols of his death, for the cross of Christ is pre-eminently the wisdom of God.[66]

Through the death of Jesus on the cross, God's wisdom is working

---

63. Proverbs 1:20ff; 8:1; 9:3.
64. Matthew 11:9.
65. John 7:37-39.
66. See 1 Corinthians 1:18-2:6.

out God's purposes—wisdom not guessed at for a moment by the rulers of this world, otherwise they would not have crucified the Lord of glory.[67] God's object, which he achieved through the death of Christ, was to overthrow evil, the great marring alien element in his creation, and to release those who are bound and blinded by Satan. This Christ accomplished by his death. So the cross is the wisdom of God. God accomplishes his ends through it. To the Jews it was a scandal, to the Greeks foolishness, but to those who were called, both Jews and Greeks, Christ the power of God and the wisdom of God.[68]

Christ as the wisdom of God is displayed not only in the cross, where most unexpectedly the very success of the evil powers in bringing Christ to destruction involved them in their own defeat, through the perfection with which Jesus bore all that evil which they brought upon him,[69] but is also seen in the way that the salvation of Christ is administered.

The whole work of our salvation is the wisdom of God. In 1 Corinthians 1, Paul pointed out that the way people are chosen is all part of God's wisdom. At first sight it would not appear the way of wisdom, for God chose the foolish in the world, God chose the weak, God chose the base things of the world and the things that are despised, in order that he might display his power and his grace in overthrowing and bringing to shame those who are boasting in their own strength apart from God.[70]

In Romans 11, Paul returned to the theme of God's wisdom as displayed in his predestinating purposes in carrying out the scheme of salvation and bringing the benefit of Christ's death to the world. In Romans 9, Paul reviewed the surprising turn of events where the people of God reject the provision of God for their salvation. In chapter 11, he drew out the consequences—that through this unexpected rejection by God's people of God's Word, the Gentiles have been brought into that blessing which in due course will embrace the Jews themselves, as a result of the very rejection of the gospel which had opened up the way for the conversion of the Gentiles. The apostle exclaimed, "Oh, the

67. 1 Corinthians 2:7, 8.
68. 1 Corinthians 1:23, 24.
69. 1 Corinthians 2:6-9.
70. 1 Corinthians 1:26-31.

depths of the riches both of the wisdom and knowledge of God! How unsearchable are his judgements and unfathomable his ways!"[71] And again, "God has shut up all unto disobedience that he might have mercy upon all".[72] The infinite wisdom of God is completing his purposes of blessing and salvation.

71. Romans 11:33.
72. Romans 11:32.

Chapter 3
GOD IN TRINITY

$\mathcal{T}$HE DOCTRINE OF THE TRINITY IS the foundation of the Christian religion. Unless this doctrine is held firmly and truly, it is not possible to be a Christian. For the Christian is one who acknowledges Jesus as Lord, yet adheres to the religion of the Bible which emphasises so strongly that there is only one God.

The Christian message is "Believe in the Lord Jesus, and you shall be saved, you and your household".[1] Yet Jesus of Nazareth was a man who himself prayed to the Lord. Jesus was a man, yet his disciple Thomas acknowledged him as his Lord and his God, without thereby abandoning any tenet of his ancestral faith.[2] A knowledge of the doctrine of the Trinity resolves this conundrum and enables the Christian to believe in the Lord Jesus and in the God of the Bible.

The classical statement of the doctrine of the Trinity is the Athanasian Creed. Although it is fashionable today to denigrate the strong asseverations of the Athanasian Creed, and indeed this creed has been dropped by certain parts of Christendom, the statements of the creed remain true, in particular its opening statement: "Whosoever will be saved, before all things it is necessary that he holds the catholic faith. Which faith except everyone do keep whole and undefiled, without doubt he shall perish everlastingly. And the catholic faith is this that we worship one God in Trinity and Trinity in unity, neither confounding the Persons nor dividing the Substance". The Athanasian Creed may be old fashioned in its language, but it is succinct and correct. Its strong words, that it is not possible to be saved without believing in the Trinity or in the reality of the incarnation, only spell out the gospel message that salvation is found only in Jesus the Lord. For Jesus cannot be called Lord apart from the doctrine of the Trinity.

1. Acts 16:31.
2. John 20:27-29.

A DOCTRINE OF REVELATION

The doctrine of the Trinity is derived entirely from the pages of the Bible. Its basis is the doctrine of the unity of God. God in his Word has revealed that he is God alone. There is but one living and true God. There is no other God. Monotheism is a doctrine of revelation. It is not a truth arrived at by human reflection. Ethnic religions are polytheistic. The three monotheistic religions, Judaism, Islam and Christianity, derive their faith in the unity of God from the Bible. The knowledge that there is but one God comes to us from God himself. He who speaks to us declares that he is the only divine being. All others are phantoms. This is the starting point. God reveals that he alone is God. God is one.[3] It is a truth which once known satisfies human thought. The human mind is monistic, and seeks to find a unity in experience. The doctrine of the unity of God, though not arrived at by human thought, confirms this human aspiration.

The doctrine of the Trinity waited for its full revelation with the unfolding of the experience of salvation in Jesus Christ, and it depends on the authenticity of the revelation in Scripture. The Trinity is not a concept that the human mind can arrive at from its own resources. It is a historical fact that this doctrine has never occurred to anyone in any of the religions of the world outside the Christian revelation. Nor is it a doctrine that commends itself to the secular mind. At best it appears to be incomprehensible; more frequently it is scoffed at as absurd. Nevertheless, the doctrine is the glory of the Christian religion. Through it we understand not only God's nature and his relationship to us, but our own nature and our relationships to one another.

The doctrine of the Trinity is entirely drawn from the revelation of Holy Scripture and depends on the authority of Scripture. If the Christian view of the infallibility of Scripture, as taught by our Lord and his apostles and held uniformly throughout the Christian church up until a century or so ago, is abandoned, then the doctrine of the Trinity cannot stand. A great deal of modern theological writing is a tragic illustration of this fact. Once belief in the full inspiration, infallibility, reliability and trustworthiness of the whole of Scripture as the written Word of God is modified, then the doctrine of the Trinity is quickly

3.   Deuteronomy 6:4.

lost. Knowledge of the trinitarian nature of God is only attained and understood if every word of Scripture is accepted as given by God's Spirit so that every word is given its full place in revelation. Scripture must be interpreted in accordance with Scripture, for the Spirit of God is uniform in his revelation. All Scripture is God-breathed and profitable for doctrine.[4] Apart from Scripture there is no ground for believing that God is Trinity and then in turn it becomes impossible to believe in the lordship of Christ without falling into polytheism.

THE TRINITY REVEALS THAT REALITY INVOLVES RELATIONSHIP

The doctrine of the Trinity is the glory of the Christian religion. It tells us that ultimate reality is personal relationship. God is ultimate reality, and is the ground of all other reality, and yet God is not a single monad or an impersonal absolute, but God is relationship. God is Trinity. He is not the unconscious, unmoved mover of Aristotle; nor is he the ground of our being, the one who lets be, of modern theology; but he is Father, Son and Holy Spirit. That God is a living God becomes plain when he addresses us. That he is a God of infinite goodness becomes plain not only from the content of his Word to us, but also from our confirmation of that goodness through our reflection of our own experience in the world.

Through the revelation of the Trinity we learn that the living God, the good and true God, is a God who has relationship within himself, and that the values of relationships ultimately belong to reality in its most absolute form. In the light of this doctrine, personal relationships are seen to be ultimate, arc seen to be the most real things that are. The characteristic of true relationship is other-person-centredness. God is good, God is personal, God has relationship within himself, and because God is good these relationships within the Trinity have the characteristic of other- person-centredness. Thus the Scriptures reveal that the Father loves the Son, and gives all things to the Son,[5] and that he shows him all that he does.[6] The Son in response does always that which pleases the

4.   2 Timothy 3:16.
5.   John 3:35.
6.   John 5:20.

Father.[7] His obedience springs from his love: "I love the Father, and as
the Father gave me commandment, even so I do".[8] There is complete
other-person-centredness in this relationship of the Father to the Son
and of the Son to the Father. The Son does nothing of himself, but as the
Father taught him.[9] The same is true of the relationship of the Spirit to
the Father and the Son. The Spirit is self-effacing. He does not speak
from himself, but he takes the things of the Son and shows them to
believers; he glorifies Christ.[10] Ultimate reality is good, personal, relational. And these relationships are other-person-centred, as all good true
relationships must be. This is the character of God and this is how creation has been made. We have been created in God's image for relationship, and this relationship must be other-person-centred.

The doctrine of the Trinity contradicts modern philosophical and
social concepts. The idea of self-expression as the primary objective of
life is very popular nowadays. Even in Christian circles we are being
told that the first thing is to love ourselves. But these modern ideas are
in contradiction to reality, to God in Trinity.

Similarly, the humanist ideal of the balanced complete life as the
object of living is again contrary to what is actual, for humanism is self-
centred in ultimate analysis. God is Trinity; Trinity is relational. The
relationships are good and personal and other-person-centred. The
famous slogan of the French Revolution, which was the fruit of the
Enlightenment, namely, 'Liberty, Equality, Fraternity', is in fact a denial
of genuine relationship. Bestsellers today reflect the modern ideal of
expressing yourself, of loving yourself, of liberating yourself from your
relationships with other people, which constrict the development of
your own personality. Through the revelation of the Trinity believers
can see that this popular philosophical concept and social objective is
contrary to reality and therefore will not bring the hoped-for benefits of
happiness or peace. A renewal of understanding of the Trinity and its
implications for the way human life should be based will lead to the
recognition that personal relationships which are other-person-centred
are ultimate in value for living, even though it should turn out that in

7. John 8:29.
8. John 14:31.
9. John 8:28.
10. John 16:13,14.

serving these relationships it becomes impossible to pursue the chimera of gracious living, the balanced life and so-called authentic existence. Even life itself may be lost, but eternity will vindicate the reality of the basis of such actions. The modern philosophy of life known as existentialism concentrates on self-expression, 'living an authentic life', and this is translated into everyday language by the phrases 'doing your own thing', or 'doing what you like'. This is a very popular way of understanding true living today. People feel that they must express themselves, that they cannot be trammelled by their relationships with other people, whether with husband or wife or with children. They must be independent and pursue their own goals. This is not the way in which the Trinity relates. Eastern religions popular in the Western world today have the same concept of reality. Their followers are invited to 'meditate on yourself, worship yourself, repeat the mantra going on within you; God dwells within you as you'.

The doctrine of the Trinity contradicts and corrects these modern thoughts and attitudes. It teaches that reality seeks the welfare of the other person. Reality is good, it does not serve itself but serves others. And since this is ultimate reality, any philosophy of life or any social theory which contradicts this reality will certainly be running into the shallows.

UNDIVIDED BUT DISTINCT

The relationship within the Trinity is very close. Jesus said, "I am in the Father and the Father in me",[11] and on another occasion, "The Father is in me and I am in the Father".[12] It is impossible to find a form of words which expresses a closer relationship. The words, "I am in the Father and the Father in me", maintain the distinction of the Persons, yet unite them so closely with one another that they are, as it were, identified with one another in their distinctness. The Father dwells in the Son and does the works that the Son does, and at the same time the Son dwells in the bosom of the Father and does everything that the Father shows him. The Father is in the Son, the Son is in the Father— a close intimate relationship. The same is true of the relationship of the

11. John 14:10.
12. John 10:38.

Spirit to the Father and the Son.

This close unity of relationship within the Trinity is expressed in the theological dictum that in all God's works in the world, the Trinity is not divided. This truth reflects the language of Scripture. Thus in the supreme work of God in the world, the redemption of his people, scriptural language makes clear that the Trinity is not divided. Jesus bore our sins in his own body on the tree,[13] yet God was in Christ on the cross reconciling the world to himself,[14] and on the cross Jesus offered to the Father, through the eternal Spirit, the perfect sacrifice.[15] Though there is specific order in God's work in the world, yet this does not exclude the truth that the works of God in the world may be ascribed to any of the Persons of the Trinity. This is exemplified by our Lord's language when he promised his disciples divine assistance when they are brought to trial for their Christian faith. In Matthew 10:20 Jesus said, "It is not you who speak, but it is the Spirit of your Father who speaks in you". In Mark 13:11 he said, "It is not you who speak, but it is the Holy Spirit", and in Luke 21:15, "I will give you utterance".[16] Thus Father, Son and Spirit each receive the emphasis with regard to the same work of grace in the Christian. Similarly, in the works of Jesus' ministry, it was Jesus who was casting out devils. Yet he cast out devils by the Spirit of God, as he himself told his interrogators.[17] And yet it was the Father who was doing the works. Jesus was doing nothing of himself, but only what the Father taught him.[18] The Father who dwelt in him did the works: "The words which I say to you I do not speak on my own initiative, but the Father abiding in me does his works".[19] Father, Son and Spirit are one God. God is not divided in the works that he does in the world.

The unity of God is the basic concept underlying the revelation of the Trinity. The Persons of the Trinity are very closely related, yet they remain distinct but not separable. This close relationship is expressed

13. 1 Peter 2:24.
14. 2 Corinthians 5:19.
15. Hebrews 9:14.
16. Literally, "I will give you a mouth".
17. Matthew 12:28.
18. John 8:28.
19. John 14:10.

by Jesus in the words "I am in the Father and the Father in me".[20] Jesus' relationship with the Spirit, and the Father's relationship with the Spirit, are expressed by the Spirit being named the Spirit of Jesus[21] and in another place the Spirit of the Father.[22] That is why the addition to the creed of the words "and from the Son", with regard to the relationship of the Spirit to the Father, is true and, although it was a late addition, it ought not to be removed simply to satisfy antiquarian interests or from a false ecumenism.

The first Christians were Jews who had come to acknowledge that Jesus of Nazareth was the Messiah promised by God to the Jewish people. In becoming Christians they did not change their religion. They continued to regard the Bible, that is, the Old Testament, as the oracles of God, believing, as Jesus taught them, that God spoke to them as they read. One of the most fundamental truths constantly reiterated and underlined in the Old Testament is that God is one. How did it come about that those who held the truth of the unity of God so firmly also came to believe in the doctrine of the Trinity? It was the result of their experience of the facts. They could never give up the truth that God is one. That is so clearly taught in God's Word and written into the experience of the Jewish people. Yet they realized that Jesus was God. They applied Old Testament passages which speak of Yahweh directly to Jesus. There are many examples of this. One is the passage which begins with Paul's description of how "the Lord Jesus shall be revealed from heaven with his mighty angels in flaming fire, dealing out retribution to those who know not God".[23] Almost the whole of this passage is composed of quotations from Old Testament prophecies of which Yahweh is the subject.

From the beginning, Christians prayed to Jesus. Christians are described by Paul as those who "call upon the name of our Lord Jesus Christ" (that is, pray to Jesus).[24] Stephen is an example from the early chapters of Acts. He prayed as he died, "Lord Jesus, receive my spirit".[25]

---

20. John 14:10.
21. Acts 16:7; Philippians 1:19.
22. John 15:26; Romans 8:9-11.
23. 2 Thessalonians 1:7ff.
24. 1 Corinthians 1:2.
25. Acts 7:59.

Christians recognized Jesus as their God. As Thomas put it when he first met the risen Christ, "My Lord and my God".[26]

It would have been easy for those brought up in the Greek culture to acknowledge many gods and many lords, but this was impossible for those brought up within the context of the revelation of God given to his people. To them, as Paul emphasised, there is only one God, and only one Lord.[27] But Jesus was God, and yet Jesus was not the Father; he himself prayed to his Father and described the Father as his God.[28] So the facts were simple, although perhaps difficult to comprehend. The Father was God and Jesus was God, and Jesus was not the Father and yet God was one. Fortunately in the Greek language there is a synonym for God, namely, Lord. This term had been used in the Greek translation of the Old Testament to translate the divine name 'YHWH', Lord of hosts. Paul makes use of this synonym in saying that for Christians there is one God the Father and one Lord Jesus Christ. God and Lord are synonyms, and yet the Father and Jesus are distinct. We have here the basis of the doctrine of the Trinity, which arose from the Christian experience of God in Jesus Christ and which was taught indeed by Christ himself. The revelation of the doctrine of the Trinity waited on the unfolding of the events of redemption, namely the incarnation of the Son and the pouring out of the Spirit.

NEW TESTAMENT DOCTRINE

The character of God is other-person-centred, and thus Jesus in his earthly ministry was not given to drawing attention to himself. He did not bear witness of himself, and therefore his affirmation of his deity was not direct so much as indirect. It was very clear, nevertheless, and his followers came to a firm and clear conviction, based on our Lord's actions and teaching, that Jesus was divine, their Lord and their God. The miracles of Jesus testified not only to his messiahship, as when he reminded John the Baptist how Isaiah's prophecy of the Messiah was being fulfilled—the blind were seeing and the poor had the gospel

26. John 20:28.
27. 1 Corinthians 8:5, 6.
28. John 20:17.

preached to them[29]—but his miracles also pointed to his deity. In Psalm 107, it is God Almighty who makes the storm to cease, the waves to be still, and brings the mariners to the haven where they wish to be. This our Lord did for his disciples on two occasions. He calmed the storm, the winds ceased, the waves subsided and they found themselves at the land where they were going. Again in the psalms, the people of Israel are depicted as complaining on their journey from Egypt to the promised land that they were left by God to starve in the desert, and they asked the question, "Can God prepare a table in the wilderness?".[30] God did so, sending them quails and manna. In the New Testament, the disciples of Jesus asked, "Where would we get so many loaves in a desert place to satisfy such a great multitude?",[31] but Jesus fed them, breaking and distributing the bread and the fishes. He provided a table in the desert.

It is, however, in John's Gospel, in the discourse in the upper room at the end of his ministry, that Jesus made quite clear to his disciples his equality with the Father and the intimate relationship between Father and Son. He told them that in as much as they had seen him, they had seen the Father. "He who has seen me has seen the Father" and "I am in the Father and the Father is in me".[32] John 17 is perhaps the most trinitarian chapter in the Bible. Absolute equality between the Father and the Son in the divine attributes is clearly enunciated. Although the Spirit is not mentioned specifically in this chapter, the Spirit is implied in the glory which Christ had given to his disciples, and which he himself had received from the Father. He is also the One who unites the disciples into one, and through whom Jesus indwells the disciples and the Father. So, too, in the last verse of the chapter, the Spirit is implied in the love with which the Father loved the Son, and which is in the disciples and which is equivalent to Jesus being in them. The Spirit is also implied in the unity arising from the mutuality of indwelling of the Father and Son and of believers with the Father and the Son.[33]

Everything that Jesus had, he had because it was given to him by

29. Matthew 11:1-6.
30. Psalm 78:19.
31. Matthew 15:33.
32. John 14:7, 9, 10.
33. John 17:21.

the Father; this extends to his divine glory as well as to his human mission—note the constant repetition of "you gave me" in John 17, and also the statement "All yours are mine".

The Father is related to the Son, and the Son to the Father, through the Holy Spirit, as we are related to God through the Spirit: "As you, Father, are in me, and I in you, that they also may be in us".[34] The Spirit is love. "You loved me before the foundation of the world"[35] refers to an eternal relationship within the Trinity—before the foundation of the world. The Spirit is the glory, that is, the manifestation of the character of God. Christ prays for his return to the previous relationship of glory which he had with the Father from eternity

"Glorify me together with yourself, Father, with the glory which I had with you before the world was".[36] Christ has given us this same relationship of glory through the gift of the Spirit. It is a relationship one with another, similar to the relationship of the Father and the Son. The glory is the bond of unity between ourselves, one with another, as well as between ourselves and God. "The glory which you have given me I have given to them; that they may be one, just as we are one, I in them and you in me…".[37] The Spirit is the glory, for the Spirit is the bond. Christ's prayer for unity of his followers with one another and with God was fulfilled at Pentecost with the gift of the Spirit. The Spirit is the oneness. The Spirit is the glory. The Spirit is love. The Spirit is the bond between Father and Son and between God and the believer, for the Spirit is the glory and the love. The Spirit's presence is the presence of Christ and the presence of love. Christ prayed, "The love wherewith you loved me may be in them, and I in them".[38] It is a grave theological mistake to think that our Lord's prayer for the unity of Christians is still to be fulfilled. It was answered at Pentecost.

The clearest teaching of the doctrine of the Trinity is given by our Lord in his final words to his disciples as recorded in Matthew 28:19. He sent them to baptise the nations into the knowledge of God and he puts it this way: "Baptising them in the name of the Father and the Son

34. John 17:21.
35. John 17:24.
36. John 17:5.
37. John 17:22, 23a.
38. John 17:26.

and the Holy Spirit, teaching them to observe all that I commanded you". "The name of the LORD" was a frequent Old Testament phrase, which the disciples would be familiar with from their earliest youth.[39] Jesus took this phrase and expanded it. No longer is it the name of the Lord, that is, the name of Yahweh or Jehovah, but the name of the Father, Son and Holy Spirit. The unity of God is preserved by the singleness of the name, and the Trinity of the Persons by the expansion of the term "the LORD" into Father, Son and Holy Spirit. God is three Persons, equal yet distinct. This verse has been rejected without grounds by some as a composition of the evangelist, but it is actually inconceivable that the Christian church did not have the doctrine of the Trinity from its earliest days, because from its foundation it regarded Jesus as God and prayed to Jesus as God, and yet maintained the distinction between Jesus and the Father, and the unity of the Father and the Son in the unity of God. At the same time it believed in the deity of the Spirit, whom Peter, for example, identified with God in his rebuke of Ananias.[40] The Spirit is the Spirit of God, yet is personal, for his actions are personal. He guides,[41] he grieves,[42] he intercedes.[43] He is a divine Person along with the Father and the Son. Even if Matthew had not recorded that Jesus had clearly taught his disciples the doctrine of the Trinity before his ascension, we should be compelled to conjecture that he had done so, in order to explain the worship of the first Christians.

It is a mistake to think that the New Testament church grew in its doctrine of the Trinity. The Christian church certainly grew in its ability to articulate the doctrine and to preserve the doctrine from the errors of heresy, but it held the doctrine from its earliest days, because of its experience of redemption in Christ and of the presence of Christ and the Father through the Spirit. These things were factual experiences of the early church and they were put into their theological perspective by our Lord's teaching of the doctrine of the Trinity in the

39. Genesis 4:26; 12:8; Exodus 33:19; Psalm 102:15, 21; and some 80 other references.
40. Acts 5:3, 4.
41. Romans 8:14.
42. Ephesians 4:30.
43. Romans 8:26.

words of the great commission. Through these words the unity of God, so clearly taught in Scripture, is maintained; and the distinction, personality and equality of the persons within the Godhead are understood so that the three Persons in the one God may each be honoured and worshipped.

The New Testament is trinitarian to the core. God is praised in the Persons of the Trinity—Father, Son and Holy Spirit. Perhaps the most outstanding example of this is the opening chapter of Paul's letter to the Ephesians, which is trinitarian in structure. God the Father, God the Son and God the Holy Spirit are each in turn related to our redemption, to the praise of the glory of God's grace: "Blessed be the God and Father who... fore-ordained us... to the praise of the glory of his grace... the Beloved, in whom we have our redemption through his blood... to the praise of [God's] glory;... you were sealed with the Holy Spirit... to the praise of his glory".[44]

OLD TESTAMENT DOCTRINE

The doctrine of the Trinity is a doctrine of the New Testament. It is not revealed in the Old Testament, and cannot be gathered from the Old Testament alone. Yet it is present there, and this is not surprising, because the God of the Old Testament is the God of Trinity, and his Word in the Old Testament from time to time reflects this truth. Thus in the opening words of the Bible, "In the beginning, God created", the word for God is in the plural, literally "Gods", but the verb "created", governed by this plural subject, is in the singular. Thus in the first verse of Scripture we have an indication of plurality, yet unity in the Godhead. In the same chapter we read, "And God said, 'Let us make man in our image'".[45] Whom is God addressing when he uses the plural "us"? Why is the plural "Let us make man in our image" followed immediately in the next verse by the singular, "God made man in *his* own image"? The phraseology is easily understood when it is remembered that the one true God here speaking is triune, three Persons in the relationship of unity. It is especially appropriate that this

44. Ephesians 1:3-14 (RV).
45. Genesis 1:26.

plurality of Persons in the Godhead should come to the surface in the Word of God at this point. For God is making man in his own image. Man is a relational person just as God himself is relational and the verse very neatly draws attention to this fact. It runs, *"In the image of God created he *him:* male and female created he *them"*.[46]

There are other interesting variations of language in the Old Testament which are intimations of the Trinity. In Genesis 32:24, it is said that Jacob wrestled with a man, yet Jacob commented, "I have seen God face to face".[47] Hosea said that Jacob had power with God and in the next verse that he had power over the angel.[48] In Exodus 23:20, the Lord said, "I will send an angel before you" and in the next verse "My name is in him". The one sent by Yahweh is Yahweh himself. In Malachi 3:1, we read, "The Lord whom you seek shall come suddenly to his temple, even the messenger of the covenant whom you delight in, behold he comes, says Yahweh of hosts".[49] The temple, of course, is God's temple, so that the messenger of the covenant, the hoped-for Messiah who is distinguished from Yahweh of hosts, is himself divine—a prophecy fulfilled by the coming of Christ. In Isaiah 48:16, a threefold distinction within the Godhead is reflected in the words of God: "From the time that it took place, I was there. And now the Lord Yahweh has sent me, and his Spirit". In this verse, there is a threefold distinction. The sent One is God, and yet he is sent by the Lord Yahweh with the Spirit of God.

But the clearest indication in the Old Testament that there is plurality in the Godhead is in the prediction that the Messiah whom God sends will be divine, as in the famous verse Isaiah 9:6: "For a child will be born to us, a son will be given to us; and the government will rest on his shoulders; and his name will be called Wonderful Counsellor, Mighty God, Eternal Father, Prince of Peace". This is an unambiguous prophecy that the Messiah will be divine. He will be both man and God: "a child will be born to us, a son will be given to us", yet this young child is also given the name "Mighty God, Everlasting Father", a prophecy which was fulfilled in Jesus, both God and man. The prophet adds, "The zeal of Yahweh of hosts shall perform this". Yahweh of hosts

46. Genesis 1:28.
47. Genesis 32:30.
48. Hosea 12:3, 4 (RV).
49. Following the RV.

is the Sender. But the sent One, the child to be born, is also divine—Mighty God, Everlasting Father.

We see, then, that the doctrine of the Trinity is simply the fuller statement of the truth that God is one, and a consequence of the revelation of himself in Jesus Christ and of the gift of the Spirit in the redemptive process. It waited on the completion of that process for its full revelation. This doctrine comes to the Christian, not as a burden on the mind, as the non-Christian assumes, but as a help in understanding the facts of redemption and the Christian experience of God. The Christian knows God as Father, he knows God as Son, he knows God as Spirit; yet it is not three Gods whom he knows, but one. The doctrine of the Trinity is an aid to his understanding of his experience of salvation.

PERSONS

The doctrine of the Trinity also fits our experience of personality. God is the highest being that we can conceive, and personality is the highest mode of being known to, or conceivable by, us. We believe that God is personal, but personality cannot exist in a monad, that is, in complete singularity of being. Personality requires relationship. The attributes of God are personal attributes. Justice is a mode of relationship. It is impossible to be just and righteous and fair in absolute isolation. So, too, wisdom has no meaning or content if there is no relationship. And this is particularly true of love. Only persons love; only persons are able to be loved. Indeed we may define a person as one capable of loving and of being loved.

Since we do not believe that God began to be righteous, wise and loving at creation, but is eternally so, we must either posit an eternal creation, as does the pantheist (but which is denied by the Scriptures and by common observation), or we must affirm the doctrine of the Trinity—that God is eternally relational, that there are eternal Persons within the unity of God, who are related righteously and lovingly. Indeed the doctrine is required to give a basis to our understanding of values. Love, self-sacrifice, goodness, fairness, faithfulness, are pre-eminent in our scale of values. They are personal and relational values, but if they do not exist in ultimate reality they cannot themselves be ultimate. But we believe them to be such, which we may dare to say approaches a proof of the doctrine of the Trinity, that is, that ultimate reality is relational, personal and good.

God is Trinity. This is clear from revelation. We may not know the fullness of God's being, but it would be foolish to say that the concept of Trinity is incomprehensible. For nothing that God has revealed is incomprehensible to those to whom he reveals it.

The doctrine of the Trinity throws light on the age-old philosophical problem promulgated by Plato of the one and the many. How can both universals and particulars be real? From the Trinity we realize that the relationship of one and many, in which the reality of the unity and the distinctiveness and reality of the particular are both preserved, is part of ultimate reality itself.

The doctrine also sheds light on our understanding of human life. From it we realize that personal relationship is of the essence of reality, and we also learn something of the quality of that relationship. It is a relationship of other-person-centredness. The Father loves the Son and gives him everything.[50] The Son always does that which pleases the Father.[51] The Spirit takes of the things of the Son and shows them to us. He does not glorify himself.[52] We learn from the Trinity that relationship is of the essence of reality and therefore of the essence of our own existence, and we also learn that the way this relationship should be expressed is by concern for others. When Jesus lived among us he summed up his own life by the phrase: "I am among you as the one who serves".[53] The Trinity in its relationship was manifested in human relationships where the man Christ Jesus served others as God serves us, and as within the Trinity itself there is concern by the Persons of the Trinity one for another.

THE WORD AND THE SPIRIT

From the doctrine of the Trinity we also see the appropriateness of the Son's becoming incarnate. He always does that which pleases the

50. John 3:35.
51. John 8:29.
52. John 16:13-15.
53. Luke 22:27.

Father. He does nothing of himself, but only as he is taught of the Father.[54] He is in this way the expression of God, and therefore when God expresses himself in human life by becoming man yet remaining God, it is the Son whom the Father sends. It is the Son who becomes incarnate. The Father has given the Son everything.[55] It is the Son who serves mankind by giving his life.[56] The Son, or the Word of God, is the expression of God within the Trinity and therefore the expression of God towards us in the incarnation. It is the eternal Word that becomes flesh.[57] The Son is the One sent and he expresses among us the words and actions of the Father who is in him, and he in the Father.

The names of the Persons of the Trinity, as revealed in Holy Scripture, reflect the eternal relations of the Trinity as well as the work of the Trinity in the world. The Son is the Word of the Father. Our words are us. They are the expression of our minds, and our words are conveyed to others by our breath. Now the Spirit is the breath of God— 'spirit' and 'breath' are identical both in Hebrew and Greek. It is by God's Spirit or breath that we are related to God through his Word. Breath is movement from God to us; we know God through his Word by means of his breath, by means of his Spirit. But breath in itself is nothing; it must carry words to be the means of relationship; so the Spirit of God does not testify of himself but takes of the things of Jesus, who is the Word and expression of God, and shows them to us.[58]

Secondly, breath is the sign of life. At the beginning of the world, in the gloom and chaos, the breath of God was present brooding over the waters.[59] The breath was the agent in bringing the world and its life into being, for God spoke, "Let there be light". He spoke his word through his breath, and the world, pulsating with life, came to be.

At the creation of man God breathed into man and he became a living soul,[60] and at the recreation of the sinner into the child of God, it is the breath or Spirit of God who brings life through the Word of God.

54. John 8:28-29.
55. John 3:34-35.
56. Mark 10:45.
57. John 1:1-14.
58. John 16:13-15.
59. Genesis 1:2.
60. Genesis 2:7.

God, the Word of God, the breath or Spirit of God are divine and eternal and, as we learn from the New Testament, all are personal and distinct, yet one God.

MAN, THE IMAGE OF GOD

The doctrine of the Trinity also enables us to understand what is meant when it is said that God created man in his own image. God has created us for relationship, for he is relational. We know that our nature is relational, for we do not like being isolated. Loneliness is horrid. The way the human race is structured shows clearly that we are created for relationships. Genesis 1:27 runs, "God created man in his own image. In the image of God created he him; male and female created he them." Men and women together make up the human race. Men and women complement each other and together make up humanity.

Theologians have puzzled over whether the Fall has meant the loss of the image of God or simply its marring. Both are true. Fallen man is still in the image of God according to Genesis 9, and yet he is very far from the image of God. That image has been restored in Christ, who is the image of God.[61] So from one point of view the image has been lost completely, but from another it is an inalienable part of human nature. It is not difficult to reconcile these two apparently irreconcilable concepts when we realise that the image of God means relationship. The Trinity is relationship, and humanity is relationship. So that when God created us in his own image, this has a double aspect. Firstly, he gave to us the basic faculties and characteristics on which relationships are based, and then on these he built the perfect flowering of that relationship in the first human pair. Adam and Eve were perfectly related to one another and perfectly related to God. The possibility of relationships is based on personal attributes, that is to say, on such things as reflective self-consciousness, and mind which is able to remember the past and plan for the future; on will, which is able to direct actions towards purpose; on a moral sense and consciousness, which assess actions in accordance with relationship; on a religious sense, from which we learn that we are dependent on a superior being; and on the faculty of language,

61. Colossians 1:15.

through which one mind is able to relate to another. These characteristics, which enable humanity to be persons, have never been lost and that is why in Genesis 9 we are told we are not to raise our hand against our fellow man because he has been created in the image of God. Our fellow man is in relationship with God and with us as a person. That is why Genesis 9 forbids us to kill him though the same chapter gives permission for the killing of animals for food.

Yet personal relationships, although they are based on personal characteristics and gifts, do not flower into true relationships unless they are crowned with moral actions and attitudes such as love, kindness, faithfulness, service and consideration. It is these moral virtues that have been lost through the Fall, so completely that instead of the relationship being one of serving one another, as is the case within the Trinity, and as God serves us and as he intended that we should serve one another, this relationship has been completely marred. The moral gifts by which the relationship is perfected and expressed have been lost. Self-centredness has taken the place of service and devilish character has begun to supplant the character and image of God. However, in Christ that image has been restored in its entire and moral perfection. He was a human person relating to his fellow men through all the personal structures of our nature, but he also built on those structures the perfection of personal relationships in a way we never achieve. He was always in a personal relationship of perfect love, trust and obedience with his heavenly Father, and in a perfect personal relationship with his fellow men, loving them, forgiving them, having compassion on them and serving them. Jesus is the perfect image of God, being perfect Man, and as we come to him and dwell in his company we are transformed by his Spirit into the same image, reflecting more and more the glory, that is, the character and Spirit of God.[62]

The doctrine of the Trinity helps solve another problem which troubles modern theologians. How is it possible that human language drawn from human experience can be an adequate vehicle for describing the ineffable God? Must all language be merely analogical when it is used to describe the realities of religion? That is a very popular view. Religious language is thought to be analogical and not direct description, but if this were true it would mean we have no sure knowledge of God, for we

---

62. 2 Corinthians 3:18.

cannot be sure how an analogy fits unless we already know the object which the analogy describes—that is, unless we already know God, we cannot know whether analogical language fits the God of whom we are speaking. In other words, this line of thought means that we have no sure knowledge of God and this is a conclusion of much modern theology.

However, the doctrine of the Trinity reminds us that human life has been created in the image of God. Human relationships reflect the image of the Trinity. It follows that human language reflecting these human relationships is a suitable vehicle to describe God's relationships within himself and with humanity, for we have been created in his image and our relationships correspond to his relationships, for they are an image of them. It follows that when God chooses human language to describe his relationships, not only within himself but especially his relationships to us, he is not using analogical language but a direct description of reality, for the language being used is language drawn from the image of that reality. It is God who is using the language (for he is inspiring the prophet), and the vehicle that he is using (human language) is adequate, indeed exact, to describe what would otherwise be beyond our powers of knowing. Because we have been created in the image of God, the revelation of God to us becomes a possibility. We may know him truly through our own human language. Had this not been so, it would not be possible to have the Christian religion, which is a religion of faith, trust, obedience and love. For it is not possible to relate personally to one who is only known by analogy, to one about whom you are not sure and of whom you only have vague and general concepts. But God reveals himself to us personally in a direct and literal and not merely analogical way, and so we are able to respond in a real and true way and enter into real personal relationships with God. All this follows from the fact that God is Trinity and has created us in his image, that is to say, to be relational, so that the language which describes our relationships is an adequate vehicle when used by God himself to describe the real relationships that he has within himself and with us. In other words, religious language is not analogical but direct and univocal. We may rely on it. When God uses it to describe the relationship between himself and us it has the same meaning as when used to describe our relationships with one another, because human life has been created in the image of God who himself is relational.

ORDER

There is order in the Trinity: Father, Son, Spirit. This order does not imply inferiority but is an order among equals; yet it is not reversible, for irreversibility is of the essence of order. The very terms 'Father' and 'Son' indicate order, and it is of the essence of order that it cannot be disturbed or reversed without creating disorder and disharmony. From the doctrine of the Trinity, we learn that there is order in ultimate reality. God is a God of order. This suggests that there is also order in created life. If the order of relationships in created life is confused, the relationships will be jarred. Paul saw this very clearly in church life at Corinth. He said God was a God of order and therefore things should be done in proper order;[63] and he commended the Colossians for their order.[64] Order does not imply subservience or inequality. Father/Son indicates an order which is not reversible, but which is equal. The Father is greater than the Son, but not as we evaluate greatness; for according to the real values of God, the servant is the greatest; subordination is not an indication of inequality but of order. There cannot be subservience where there is complete love, complete other-person-centredness. In the Trinity, although there is order there is no dominance on the one hand or subservience on the other, but only a relationship of love.

The doctrine of the Trinity shows us that order is of the essence of reality, so it is to be expected that God has created the world with order. This is in fact plain if we look at the created world around us where we see the different species all ordered. Genesis 1 describes how God created order from chaos in six ordered stages. So, too, in the creation of humanity God has created order. Though men and women are equal they stand in an order of relationship. There is an order of headship and of response, an order which reflects the character of God as constituted in the Trinity. The world in general, and humanity in particular, have been created by God and all that fills the earth is a reflection of his character. Christian congregations and Christian homes should reflect this order, which is a reflection of the character of God himself. The outsider should be able to see God's character

63. 1 Corinthians 14:31-40.
64. Colossians 2:5.

reflected in the way the congregation orders itself and Christian families should learn from the order of the congregation how their own homes should be conducted. The conduct of the congregation should not contradict the order that God has structured in the world and in human society, and in particular in married life, which has specially been created in the image of God, as Paul pointed out in Ephesians 5.

Paul made clear what this order in created humanity is when he said that the head of every man is Christ, the head of woman is the man and the head of Christ is God.[65] Some modern translations have obscured Paul's meaning by limiting his statement to married women. But the Greek shows that it is not so. And this modern translation is objectionable, for it implies that on entering the divinely ordered state of matrimony a woman exchanges freedom for subservience. The problem in Paul's statement must not be resolved by restricting headship to marriage, but by understanding the true meaning of headship as exemplified by God's headship of Christ and Christ's headship of humanity. Headship implies order and the order of the congregation should acknowledge God's created order in humanity, and not turn it topsy-turvy or reverse it. This means that men (whether a group or individuals) must not dominate in the congregation, for the head of *every* man is Christ. The congregation will have leaders, to whom all should submit within their area of leadership, but the leadership must not be that of dominance or autocracy, for the head of every man is Christ, and Christ alone. This order must also be reflected in the relationships between men and women in the congregation. Headship implies responsibility and initiative in welfare, and if this is to be discharged properly all must acknowledge that God has created order in relationship in humanity, and it will be a help to see that this reflects the order eternally subsisting in the Trinity. If we destroy order in the congregation, we will destroy order in the Christian home and that will bring great sadness. We will also set an example which will destroy order in society. Our homes and our society, as well as our congregations, should reflect the order which is part of their constituent created nature and is an image of the order in the Trinity. The Son does not strive to be the Father or feel inferior because he is not the Father.

65. 1 Corinthians 11:3.

From the relationship of the Trinity we understand what headship means. There is no hint of dominance in it, simply initiative in service. This and this only is the headship that God has conferred on men in respect to women. So, too, from the relationship within the Trinity we learn what the response of obedience is. There is no hint of subservience in it, only the glad and grateful response to the initiatory service and care of the head. Sin has debased headship into dominance and obedience into servility. This is the way the Gentiles behave.[66] But it is not to be so among Christians, for God has given the grace of his Spirit to enable them to live and to relate to one another in the way he intended when he created men and women in his image.

There is equality yet order among the Persons of the Trinity. This is the key for human relationships in the congregation, in the home and in society. Yet equality in the Trinity is not sameness, nor does it mean the disregard of what is implicit in order. Jesus said, "I and the Father are one"[67] and "All that is mine is yours and yours mine".[68] But he also said, "The Father is greater than I".[69] It is possible so to stress equality, for example, within the congregation, that disorder and lack of relationship emerge; or on the other hand, so to stress order that dominance emerges and destroys relationship. It is especially important that the congregation, which is the outward and visible sign of Christ's church and of the heavenly life, should reflect the principle of equality and order, which is basic to reality itself, so that the rest of society may learn from the way it sees Christians ordering their lives.

66. Mark 10:42-45.
67. John 10:30.
68. John 17:10.
69. John 14:28.

Chapter 4
ONE LORD, JESUS CHRIST

*T*HE FRIENDS OF JESUS BELIEVED THAT he was God. They were all devout Jews and if there was any truth that they believed from the bottom of their heart it was that there is only one God. Every morning they would say those words from Deuteronomy "Hear O Israel! Yahweh is your God, Yahweh is one".[1] Yet they believed that Jesus was God and worshipped him as God.

It is not a view that they came to suddenly, but it grew over the months and years that they knew him, so that at the end they were able to affirm with complete conviction and sincerity that Jesus was God. Thomas is recorded as ascribing deity to Jesus with the apostrophe, "My Lord and my God".[2] John begins his Gospel with the statement that the Word, that is, Jesus of Nazareth, was God. In Hebrews 1, the writer applied the Old Testament psalm to Jesus "Thy throne, O God, is for ever and ever".[3] Paul described Jesus as "God over all".[4] Though it is true that some modern English translations separate this ascription of deity from Christ, in doing this the translators are not following the text but their own theological presuppositions. Every grammatical and stylistic consideration makes clear that Jesus was the One to whom Paul was referring when he spoke of "God over all, blessed for ever". In Titus 2:13, Paul very clearly spoke of Jesus as "our great God and Saviour" whose appearing we are all awaiting expectantly.

Jesus' friends did not hesitate to apply to Jesus passages from the Old Testament which refer to Yahweh. Thus Mark began his Gospel by saying that John the Baptist was the one who fulfilled the prophecy of Isaiah: "The voice of one crying in the wilderness, make ready the way

1.   Deuteronomy 6:4.
2.   John 20:28.
3.   Hebrews 1:8.
4.   Romans 9:5.

of Yahweh, make his paths straight".[5] That prophecy is referred to John the Baptist's preparation for the ministry of Jesus. Jesus was Yahweh, whose way John the Baptist was making ready.

Not only the New Testament but also contemporary secular literature endorses the fact that the first Christians believed that Jesus was God. About 80 years after the crucifixion, Pliny, the Governor of Bithynia on the shores of the Black Sea, wrote a letter to the Roman emperor in which he described Christian worship and said that Christians in his area would come together early in the morning to sing hymns to Jesus as God. From the beginning of the Christian church, Christians prayed to Jesus. This is the way that Christians are defined by Paul in 1 Corinthians 1:2. They are people who call upon the name of the Lord. For a Jew or a believer in the Old Testament to pray to Jesus meant that he regarded Jesus as the one and only God.

The Old Testament prophets foretold that the Messiah, that is the Christ, would be God Almighty, their Lord, Yahweh. The most famous passage is Isaiah 9, "For a child will be born to us, a son will be given to us...and his name will be called...Mighty God, Everlasting Father".[6] The Messiah is Emmanuel—God with us.[7] Isaiah's contemporary, Micah, predicted that the ruler in Israel who should come from Bethlehem should be one whose "goings forth are from long ago, from the days of eternity".[8] Ezekiel, in his prophecy of the good shepherd, brought into one the Lord Yahweh and the coming Messiah: "Thus says the Lord Yahweh, "Behold, I myself will search for my sheep and seek them out... I will deliver them... I will bring them out from the peoples and gather them... I will feed them in a good pasture... I will feed my flock and I will lead them to rest", declares the Lord Yahweh. "I will seek the lost, and bring back the scattered, bind up the broken and strengthen the sick".[9] And in verse 23, God speaks, "My servant David...will feed them; he will feed them himself and be their shepherd". Thus Yahweh is the Good Shepherd and Yahweh's servant David

5. Mark 1:3; Isaiah 40:3.
6. Isaiah 9:6.
7. Isaiah 7:14; Matthew 1:23.
8. Micah 5:2.
9. Ezekiel 34:11-16.

is the Good Shepherd. Both are the one shepherd who feeds God's sheep. This prophecy of Ezekiel was applied by Jesus to himself.[10] He is the Good Shepherd who sought for his sheep, who brought the sheep out from the nations and gathered them into one fold, who protected them and provided for them, leading them out into good pasture and who in the end laid down his life for the sheep. He delivers them and none is able to pluck them out of his hand, and yet it is not he alone, but the Father in him, and none is able to pluck them out of the Father's hand.[11]

Jesus' self-testimony

Jesus knew himself to be God. This became plain at the end of his ministry. He knew that he came forth from God and that he was going to God.[12] Jesus' knowledge of his deity is reflected in his question to the Pharisees about David's son and David's Lord.[13] It was an indirect affirmation, asking the Pharisees to reflect on what they had already received from the Old Testament. This indirectness is in keeping with the character of God. Jesus did not bear witness to himself, did not take the initiative in announcing his own person with clear and bold affirmations, but the truth of his person was reflected in his actions, in his miracles—for example, when he met the needs of his hearers by providing them with loaves and fishes through a miraculous divine creation.[14] Jesus' identification of himself with the wisdom of God is an affirmation of deity, for wisdom is inalienable from God. God's wisdom cannot be divorced from God himself. Moreover, it is the prerogative of God alone to send prophets to speak in the name of God. In the Old Testament God is characterized as one who sends prophets to his people.[15] Yet Jesus says, "I will send prophets",[16] and again "The

10. John 10:1-18.
11. John 10:28-29.
12. John 13:3.
13. Matthew 22:42-46.
14. Mark 6:33-44.
15. 2 Chronicles 36:15; Jeremiah 7:25.
16. Matthew 23:34.

wisdom of God says, 'I will send prophets'".[17] Christ is the wisdom of
God and Christ is divine.

An interesting affirmation by Jesus of his deity, so indirect that it is
hardly noticed, is the message that he told his disciples to give to the owners of the colt on which he was to ride into Jerusalem.[18] When the owners asked the disciples what they were doing loosing the colt, they replied
as Jesus had instructed them, "Its owner needs it".[19] The contrast between
the human owners and Jesus is clear in the Greek. Thus at the end of his
ministry, our Lord made it clear that he is the divine Owner of all things.
He is the sovereign God the Creator. He is Lord of all.

From the beginning of his ministry, Jesus recognized his divine
authority. His words were as true and as authoritative as were the Ten
Commandments which had been spoken directly by God from heaven.
"You have heard that the ancients were told, 'You shall not commit
murder'...But I say to you...".[20] Jesus placed his words, spoken to the
disciples from the mountain in Galilee, on the same level as the words
spoken by God from Mount Sinai. For Jesus was the Lord Yahweh.
Jesus was conscious that in himself God was present with his people.
The Father was in him and he was in the Father.[21] He is the One whose
name is "I am".[22]

Thus the whole of Scripture, Old Testament and New, Jesus himself,
his apostles and the early Christians combine in testimony to the marvellous miracle that God dwelt with men in Jesus Christ. Not that there
was any change in the Godhead, for God is unchangeable, but there was
a change in God's relationship to creation. The Creator had come into a
new relationship with his creation by taking the nature of men, whom
he had created to have dominion and to be in his image. For although
Jesus was fully God and there is no doubt as to the Bible testimony to

17. Luke 11:49.
18. Luke 19:28-35.
19. This is not reflected in most English versions. The Greek of Luke 19:33
reads, translated literally, "And as they were untying the colt, its masters (*kurioi*)
said to them, 'Why are you untying the colt?' And they said, 'Because its master
(*kurios*) has need'".
20. Matthew 5:21, 22.
21. John 14:10-11.
22. John 8:58.

this truth, he was at the same time truly and fully man. None of his contemporaries doubted that. His physical life was human. From time to time he was tired[23] and hungry,[24] and his life terminated in pain on the cross. He died and was buried. His emotional life was human. He had friends;[25] he wept.[26] His religious life was human. He prayed and trusted God.[27] His knowledge was human. It grew and increased from babyhood onwards.[28] There were times when he was surprised at the way events turned out. There were things which he did not know. In taking our nature and becoming man, Jesus accepted all the limitations of perfect human nature. Thus he accepted the limitation of knowledge which goes with human life. For example, he did not know what was, humanly speaking, contingent either on other people's wills or on the events of nature. For example, he did not know who touched him in the crowd. This is plain from the way Luke described the incident.[29] Nor did he know that there were no figs on the fig tree when he made a detour to it in order to satisfy his hunger.[30] He did not know the moment of his arrest, as a careful reading of the synoptic accounts makes clear. And Jesus himself told his disciples that he did not know the day or the hour of the inauguration of God's final kingdom.[31]

It is plain from the narrative that our Lord in his earthly life did not have the omniscience of God, and yet his knowledge was well beyond ours—not only his knowledge of the Father, but his knowledge of man. We read that he knew what was in man and did not need anyone to bear testimony to it.[32] He knew who it was who should betray him. Our Lord's knowledge was human knowledge, yet it was knowledge drawn from his close association and unity with the Father. That relationship was perfect and so his knowledge was perfect, though not

---

23. Mark 4:38.
24. Matthew 21:18.
25. John 15:14-15.
26. John 11:35.
27. Matt 26:39.
28. Luke 2:52.
29. Luke 8:43-48.
30. Mark 11:12-13.
31. Mark 13:32.
32. John 2:24-25.

complete. It was perfect because it was according to the will of God. Just as his words and works were not from himself, but he taught and did what the Father showed him, so, too, we may say that his knowledge was drawn from his relationship with the Father. There were some things which the Father retained in his own hands. These things our Saviour did not know in his incarnate life. What he knew he learnt from the Father, doubtless through what we would call natural means, though no doubt sometimes through direct revelation.

We do not know the process by which our Lord learnt, though some part of it at least would be the same as that by which we learn, that is, studying the Old Testament, observing how things happen, meditating and reflecting on all this and asking questions of those who knew more than he did. But in addition there would be that very close relationship with the Father which brings a deepening understanding and knowledge, which humanity, cut off from God through rebellion, does not have, but which Christians, through their renewed relationship to God through the Spirit, begin to appreciate and understand. Had it not been for the Fall, our relationship with God would have continued perfect, growing daily in depth so that our knowledge would have been perfect, for we would have been taught of God, and have grown daily, and in this way humanity would have avoided all those natural evils and disasters which cause some to stumble in their faith in the God of infinite power and love.

Although our Lord's knowledge was limited, as all human knowledge is, yet his sinlessness, or in other words his perfect relationship with God, prevented him from saying anything which he knew to be beyond his knowledge. Therefore all his words are utterly reliable and none will pass away, as he himself affirmed.[33] Limitation in knowledge in no way implies error in knowledge.

JESUS, OUR COMPLETE EXAMPLE

Our Lord was truly human and perfectly human. Because of his perfect humanity and the divinity of his person, Jesus is the complete example of how human life should be lived, the values on which it should be

33. Matthew 24:35.

based and the attitudes which should characterize it. For in Jesus, the Designer himself was living his product. God the Creator was living the life he intended to be lived. Though much could be said under this heading, one or two points will suffice, suitable for the present times.

The first is that Jesus set the example of a life free from materialism. He chose to live a simple life. He was brought up in the country village of Nazareth. During much of his ministry, he had no permanent dwelling-house,[34] and he inculcated, not only by example, but by direct teaching, the need for men and women to be freed from material-mindedness. He gave the command: "Do not be anxious for your life, as to what you shall eat, or what you shall drink; nor for your body, as to what you shall put on".[35] This command is perhaps the one which is most consistently and flagrantly disobeyed by Christians in our society. It is regarded simply as a piece of idealistic advice, but our Lord couched it in the form of a command. We are to seek God's kingdom, knowing that God will look after and provide for our needs.[36] Put more colloquially, if we look after the affairs of God, he will look after our affairs. But most of us put our own affairs on an equality with those of God. We seek to look after both together. It cannot be done, but if we wish to look after our own affairs God allows us to do this, yet we are in actual disobedience and therefore cannot expect to grow in spiritual depth. For it is a failure of faith. It shows that we do not believe the clear teaching of Jesus that God, who provides for the birds their daily food, will much more provide for us if we give our attention, our time and our activity to seeking and advancing his kingdom and his righteousness. Materialism may be disguised by our telling ourselves that we are really seeking the advantages of our family when we seek for higher pay or better housing or more ample superannuation. But this is simply to deceive ourselves and to make the end justify the means.

Another example that our Lord has given is the example of service. Jesus summed up his life in the phrase, "I am among you as the one who serves".[37] In this, he was reflecting the character of God, whose tender mercies are over all his works[38] and who provides for our needs, for men

34. Matthew 8:20.
35. Matthew 6:25.
36. Matthew 6:31-34.
37. Luke 22:27.
38. Psalm 145:9.

and women as well as for the rest of creation.[39] The Christian's aim should be to serve those with whom he is brought into contact by the flux of events. God controls the events that enter our lives, and they are for the purpose of our exhibiting the character of Christ.[40]

In the managing of our money the same principle holds. We should serve those with whom we are brought into contact by our money. For example, property owners should serve their tenants. Christ in his human life set us the example that we are to serve, even though that service is costly as it was in his case. He told his disciples he came not to be served, but to serve to the extent of giving his life as a ransom for others.[41]

PERFECT FAITH

The chief example that our Saviour has left us is the example of faith. He lived his life in perfect faith in God. Faith is a human activity. It is the response that we should make to the faithfulness of God. God is faithful and he expresses his faithfulness in promises. We exercise faith towards that faithfulness of God by believing those promises and living our life in the light of them. This is how Jesus lived and so he has become the exemplar of faith. In Hebrews 11, there is a catalogue of the heroes of faith. Beginning with Abel, the list includes Enoch, Noah, Abraham, Jacob, Joseph, Moses, right through to David, Samuel and the prophets. But the chief of all is Jesus. He is the One to whom we are to look, for he is the Captain and Perfecter of faith, who for the joy that was set before him endured the cross.[42]

Faith is a human activity; it looks to the unseen;[43] it cannot be exercised in the sphere of omniscience. Faith is impossible if knowledge is complete. But human knowledge is limited, and this limitation of knowledge is the occasion for our exercising faith in the Word of God, who knows the future in a way that we do not.

39. Psalm 104; see especially vv. 27-28.
40. Ephesians 2:10.
41. Mark 10:45.
42. Hebrews 12:2.
43. Hebrews 11:1; cf. Romans 8:24-25.

The events leading up to the crucifixion are an example of how Jesus lived by faith. To go up to Jerusalem for the Passover was a religious obligation on every Jewish man. It was commanded in the law of God. But it was plain that for Jesus to go up to Jerusalem for the Passover was a very hazardous undertaking. Especially since the raising of Lazarus, the Jewish authorities had been seeking to arrest Jesus, and he had been staying away in the desert the other side of Jordan.[44] To go to Jerusalem was full of risk. His disciples warned him against it. They knew real danger to life, not only for Jesus, but for themselves was impending at Jerusalem. Jesus did not shrink from his duty, yet he took every precaution. During the day, from early morning, he was teaching in the temple surrounded and so protected by the crowds. The upper room where he ate the Passover was only known to himself, and the two disciples who prepared it were directed there by what was apparently a prearranged sign between Jesus and the householder. Afterwards he retired to a secret place known only to his disciples. It was here that Judas, one of those who knew, turned traitor and revealed to the chief priests how they could arrest Jesus away from the crowds.

Jesus knew how things were turning out. In the Garden of Gethsemane he took the opportunity of the silent night to beseech his Father in prayer that events might be reversed, that the cup which was looming might pass away from him.[45] He set three of his disciples to watch while he prayed. He said to them, "My soul is deeply grieved to the point of death; remain here and keep watch".[46] Though he felt the need of prayer as never before, yet he took precautions. This was his duty, for it is never right to take unnecessary risks. The three disciples failed him and the Jewish and Roman soldiery, led by the disciple Judas, approached undetected. At the end of his time of prayer, he told his disciples that they might go on sleeping and take their rest, presumably because he would take over the duty of watchfulness.[47] Jesus, however, became aware that Judas' band was close at hand. He reversed his concession to allow them to go on sleeping. "Stop", he said, "the crisis has arrived; I am betrayed; get up; let us go".[48] But it was too late.

44. John 11:54 (cf. 7:1; 10:40).
45. Mark 14:36.
46. Mark 14:34.
47. Mark 14:41 following the RV.
48. Paraphrasing Mark 14:41-42.

While he was still speaking, Judas burst through the darkness, came up to him and kissed him. It is interesting that all three synoptic Gospels emphasize the fact that while Jesus was still speaking, the denouement came. And both Matthew and Mark say that our Lord's last words were "Let us go", but it was too late.[49] The events showed Jesus that his prayer had been answered in a way that he had hoped it might not be. He saw the events that were overtaking him as the cup which his Father was giving him, and so he willingly drank it. He gave himself up in order that his disciples might escape.

CALVARY

Jesus' faith never failed, even when it was tested to the limit on the cross. There, during those three hours of darkness, the Lord laid on him the iniquity of us all.[50] He was made sin.[51] He was cursed by God with the curse that every sinner deserves to experience. He became a curse for us, as Paul put it.[52] Yet through it all there was never a moment of recrimination; never a fist shaken, as it were, in the face of God; never a thought of self-pity. His thoughts and words were only for others: a word to secure the safety of his disciples at his arrest;[53] a look to secure the recovery of Peter after his denial;[54] a prayer for the forgiveness of those who were crucifying him;[55] a word of comfort and promise of heavenly bliss to a fellow sufferer now repentant;[56] a word of provision for the dear one left desolate.[57] Towards his heavenly Father there was full faith. His love and trust of God never wavered, even when he was deserted by God (and deserted justly, for he was the sinbearer) and was experiencing the depths of what sin does for

49. Mark 14:42; Matthew 26:46.
50. Isaiah 53:6.
51. 2 Corinthians 5:21.
52. Galatians 3:13.
53. John 18:8.
54. Luke 22:61.
55. Luke 23:34.
56. Luke 23:39-43.
57. John 19:26-27.

humanity. He was forsaken by God.[58] God gave the sinner up, as Paul put it in Romans 1.[59] Christ was identified with our sin. He who knew no sin was made sin for us.[60] He bore our sins in his own body on the tree.[61] He went down into the very depths of hell, symbolized by the darkness[62] and the cursed tree, but experienced in reality and expressed by the cry from the cross, yet in the extremity of this experience his love and faith in God never wavered. God was still his God, the one to whom he could pray and address his petition: "My God, my God, why have you forsaken me?".[63] He came out of that experience justified, and he died committing his soul into the hands of his heavenly Father: "Father, into your hands I commit my spirit".[64]

OBEDIENCE

Faith leads to obedience and faith expresses itself through obedience. The two are inseparable. Jesus' faith was perfect, and so his obedience was complete.[65] His faith was tested in a way that ours never will be. God asked of him a form of obedience which he never will ask of us. God asked that he, the perfect man, should identify himself so completely with sinful man that he became sin for us and experienced all that sin involves. His faith and obedience are an example to us that we also should trust and obey. In this sense, our faith and obedience are similar to our Lord's. They have the same formal character. We are to be perfectly obedient to God.[66] Nevertheless, the material content of how we are to obey is very different. For our part, we are to keep the law of God and follow the example of Christ of loving God with all our hearts, and loving and serving one another. Jesus also fulfilled all

58. Mark 15:34.
59. Romans 1:24, 26, 28.
60. 2 Corinthians 5:21.
61. 1 Peter 2:24.
62. Matthew 27:45.
63. Mark 15:34.
64. Luke 23:46.
65. Hebrews 5:8, 9.
66. Matthew 5:48.

this and was fully obedient and perfect in all these human duties. His faith was tested throughout his life.

We are given a glimpse of this testing in the narration of the temptations at the beginning of our Lord's ministry.[67] There was no corner of human experience which was not explored by Satan to bring our Lord to disobedience. Finally, on the cross with all its cruelty and indignities, and in the depths of hell, Christ triumphed over Satan. On the cross, Jesus was asked by his heavenly Father to undergo an experience through which mankind has been saved; namely, to undergo the experience of bearing our sins, bearing them perfectly and obediently without any failure of faith or of love. In this way Jesus achieved what humanity had never yet achieved—perfect obedience to God tested to the fullest extent imaginable. In him, the Father was always well pleased.[68] And because he has borne the pangs of hell obediently and lovingly, he has triumphed over all that Satan and evil are able to effect.[69] He was the Victor, and God vindicated him by raising him from the dead and exalting him to the throne, crowned with glory and honour.[70]

It is Jesus' obedience to the will of his Father that is the ground of our salvation. It was a full and complete obedience, tested in every way that obedience can be tested. It was to be obedient that Christ became man. Paul indicated this when he summed up Jesus' ministry by saying that he humbled himself, becoming obedient even unto death, yes, the death of the cross.[71] Paul went on immediately to say that because of this obedience Christ has been glorified. His obedience was the victory which has been rewarded with glory and with that name which is above every name, that at the name of Jesus every knee should bow and every tongue confess that Jesus Christ is Lord to the glory of God the Father.[72]

The Epistle to the Hebrews states that it was to be obedient to the will of God that Christ became incarnate and that through the doing of this will he has brought salvation to his people. "'Behold, I have come to do thy will'… By this will we have been sanctified through the

67. Matthew 4:1-11.
68. Matthew 3:17.
69. Colossians 2:15.
70. Hebrews 2:5-15.
71. Philippians 2:8.
72. Philippians 2:8-11.

offering of the body of Jesus Christ once for all".[73] Christ's obedience to God is the ground of our salvation and its result is the defeat and binding of Satan, and the release of those held captive by him. Forgiveness is the ground of their release. Sin, Satan and the law have no more claim on them.

The New Testament has more than one way of referring to Christ's obedience. One example is the cross of Christ, where the place of his obedience stands for that obedience. Similarly, the death of Christ refers to the manner of his obedience. The blood of Christ is a phrase drawn from Old Testament sacrificial terminology, as is also the description of his death as a sacrifice. Both are metaphors drawn from the worship of the Old Testament to describe what Jesus did on the cross, which is called in Hebrews 13 our altar.[74] In Leviticus 17:11, the blood poured out at the altar covered sin. All sacrifices atoned for sin. Christ is our sacrifice, the cross is our altar, his blood metaphorically poured out in God's presence covers our sins. All these phrases are metaphorical ways of saying that Christ's perfect obedience to the will of God, tested to the full on the cross, makes atonement for sin in his bearing our penalty, fulfilling our obligations and defeating our enemy.

Man's fundamental sin in the Garden of Eden was disobedience and it remains disobedience today. Christ reversed that disobedience, being the first man ever perfectly to obey the will of our heavenly Father and to obey it in every conceivable manner of testing, even that of having our sins laid upon him, of being made sin and bearing the curse of separation from God—all of which he bore with perfect obedience and with perfect love towards God, receiving it as the cup which his Father had given him. The contrast between Adam's disobedience and Christ's obedience is very clear in Romans 5, where Paul stated that it is Christ's obedience which is the ground of our justification. "For as through the one man's disobedience the many were made sinners, even so through the *obedience* of the one the many will be made righteous".[75]

All men everywhere should obey God in the daily circumstances of

73. Hebrews 10:9, 10.
74. Hebrews 13:10.
75. Romans 5:19.

life. None of us is exempt from this ongoing obligation and duty, a pleasurable duty for those who know God as their Father, a duty nevertheless for all those who have been created by God and given life through his goodness Jesus fulfilled this obedience in his daily living, as we also should. In this sense, he is the exact pattern for us to follow.[76] His obedience and ours are of the same character. Nevertheless, as we have already seen, his obedience went further than we will ever be called upon to obey. The Father asked the Son to obey in bearing the sins of his people. This was the cup which the Father gave him. The content of his obedience was unique, and our Lord accepted it in complete filial obedience, in love and faith. It was a unique obedience—the character the same as our obligation, the content unique. It is the content of his obedience which saves.

It is important to recognize and maintain the distinction between formal obedience to God–a duty which we share equally with Christ–and the material obedience of Christ, which was unique to him. A failure to observe this distinction misled the Lambeth Conference Committee into enunciating a doctrine of the Lord's Supper in which the Christian's willing obedience in daily life is the same as the obedience of Christ on the cross which the Lord's Supper commemorates.[77] This confusion leads to an erroneous doctrine of the Lord's Supper, where the supper is thought of as an extension of our Lord's sacrifice instead of a remembrance of it.

Our suffering as Christians may be described as a partaking of the sufferings of Christ.[78] Formally, they are identical, but the content of the suffering is different. Christ suffered by bearing the consequences of justice which a righteous judge awards sinners; we suffer (as Christ also did) by bearing the consequences of injustices which sinners inflict on the righteous. But both are suffering in the cause of righteousness and both, by bearing the suffering in the right way, defeat Satan and roll back his kingdom. In this way we fill up what was lacking in the sufferings of Christ.[79]

---

76. 1 Peter 2:21-23; 4:1-2.
77. *The Lambeth Conference 1958* (SPCK), 2.84: discussed further on pp. 253ff. below.
78. 1 Peter 4:13.
79. Colossians 1:24.

THE SAVIOUR

Our Lord's obedience was unique and its effect was coextensive with humanity. There is no limitation in the work of our Lord on the cross. What he fulfilled at Calvary he fulfilled for every man. Thus he fulfilled every man's obligation to be completely obedient to the will of God. Whatever God wills for us, that is what we must obey. Our Lord obeyed in everything that the Father willed that he should do. Every man is obligated to obey the will of God. Jesus obeyed in everything; his obedience was complete. He could not have obeyed more completely, more perfectly, whether he was bearing the sin of one man only or of an immense multitude. Thus Christ fulfilled every man's obligation to walk in all the things written in the book of the law to do them.[80]

Secondly, Jesus bore every man's penalty. Every man deserves, and all outside of Christ will receive, the penalty of separation from God, of being cast out into outer darkness, of partaking of the everlasting punishment prepared for the devil and his angels.[81] That is what each one of us in ourselves deserves, and that is what our Lord endured. God laid on him the sin of us all. There are no depths of penalty that could be added to what our Lord underwent. His obedience was tested to the full; his sinbearing was complete. He drank the cup of God's wrath against sin to the dregs,[82] and he drank it without any breach of faith or trust or love in the God who was giving it to him to drink, who was laying on him the iniquity of us all. Thus our Lord bore every man's penalty, the punishment that every man deserves. It is impossible to conceive of the limitation of our Lord's work on the cross, as though he would have borne more suffering, more punishment had his merits been applied in the mind and purpose of God to more sinners. The atonement is not quantitative, as though God added up the sins of the elect and placed the penalty for these and these only on Jesus; but the atonement is qualitative. Our Lord experienced fully the penalty for sin.

Thirdly, on the cross our Lord overcame every man's enemy. He brought to nought the devil who keeps every man in subjection

---

80. Galatians 3:10.
81. 2 Thessalonians 1:9; Matthew 25:41.
82. Psalm 75:8.

through fear of death.[83] Viewed from this angle, once again it is seen that our Lord's death on Calvary and what he accomplished there are coextensive with humanity. All are enslaved to Satan, who is the strong man who through the fear of death keeps us all in bondage. He is the strong man whom Jesus, the stronger, has bound and whose goods he is now spoiling at his own discretion.[84]

Thus Jesus discharged every man's obligation to keep the law. He bore every man's penalty of separation from God. He overcame and bound every man's enemy, the devil. The redemption our Lord achieved on Calvary was unlimited with regard to humanity—he took every man's nature; he underwent every man's curse; he fulfilled every man's obligation; he overcame every man's enemy. There is no limit in the provision of forgiveness which Jesus achieved at Calvary. All the children of Adam may share it if they call upon the name of the Lord.

Christ commanded his disciples to proclaim forgiveness of sins in his name throughout the world.[85] There is provision of salvation for every hearer of the gospel. For if there were no provision for some, there could be no offer of salvation to these; and if there is no genuine offer, there is no responsibility or blame in rejecting the offer, indeed, only commendation for not being taken in by a spurious invitation to come to Christ for salvation, which in fact is not available. But there is provision of salvation for everyone who hears the gospel. It was made by Christ on Calvary, when he gave his flesh for the life of the world,[86] and so became the Saviour of the world.[87]

JESUS' FAITHFULNESS IS OUR SALVATION

We have seen that the New Testament ascribes our Lord's achievement of our salvation to his obedience: "Through the obedience of the one shall the many be made righteous".[88] Now obedience is the overt

83. Hebrews 2:14.
84. Mark 3:27.
85. Luke 24:47.
86. John 6:51.
87. 1 John 4:14.
88. Romans 5:19.

expression of faith. Faith and obedience are closely linked. They are in fact one concept. Faithfulness to God is only another way of saying obedience to God. To put faith in God is expressed outwardly by obeying God, that is why James said in his letter, "I will show you my faith by my works".[89] A person who says that he believes, yet does not obey, is deceiving himself. We may therefore put the matter of our salvation in more than one way. We may say that we are saved by our Lord's death, as is so frequently said in the New Testament, or that we are saved by our Lord's obedience, as in Romans 5, Philippians 2 and Hebrews 10. Or again we may say that we are saved by our Lord's faith expressed in faithfulness to God.

Now Jesus' faith is frequently mentioned in the New Testament as the ground of our salvation, but this has not been noticed in the English translations. The phrase "the faith of our Lord Jesus Christ" is normally interpreted in the English versions of the Bible as our faith *in* Jesus Christ. The Greek can mean this. But the contexts show that it ought to be understood and translated in a more straightforward way as the *faith* or the *faithfulness* of Jesus Christ, that is to say, the obedience of Jesus Christ. An example is Galatians 3:22. This reads in the Revised Version, "That the promise by faith in Jesus Christ might be given to them that believe". It makes better sense and removes the double reference to believing if the Greek is translated more exactly: "That the promise based on the faithfulness of Jesus Christ might be given to them that believe". In Philippians 3:9, there is again a double reference to faith which is tautological in the normal English translations but which becomes full of significance when we realize that the first reference to faith is to the faith or faithfulness of Jesus, while the second reference is to our faith in him. Thus it should be translated: "The righteousness which is through the faithfulness of Christ, that is, the righteousness which comes from God upon our faith".

Similarly in Romans 3:22, the text in the Revised Version reads: "The righteousness of God through faith in Jesus Christ unto all them that believe". Once again, it makes better sense of the Greek, as well as theologically, if it is translated: "The righteousness of God through the faithfulness of Jesus Christ unto all them that believe". The phrase "the righteousness of God" expresses the truth that God gives believers in

89. James 2:18.

Jesus the status of being righteous, and this gift of God is based on the faithfulness, that is, the obedience of Jesus Christ in life and death, and it is given to all who believe in Jesus as Lord. That is the meaning of the sentence, and is in conformity with the rest of the teaching of the New Testament. However, this meaning is lost when it is translated in the customary way.

A similar consideration applies to the translation of that famous verse Romans 1:17, where Paul sums up the gospel. It is normally translated, "The righteousness of God from faith to faith", a phrase to which it is difficult to give any real sense—a fact witnessed by the various paraphrastic translations attempted in the modern English versions. However, the meaning becomes crystal clear when it is seen that the first reference to faith is to Jesus' faith and the second reference is to the faith which we in response exercise towards him. In this sentence the apostle states that the gospel is the news of a righteousness which comes from God by way of gift, based on the faithfulness of Jesus, and is given to those who have faith in Jesus as Lord. Interpreted thus, the verse makes very good sense both grammatically and theologically.

It may be that the reason why what is plain in the Greek has never been expressed in the translations is that a very long tradition in theology has upheld that it is impossible for the incarnate Son of God to exercise faith because, being God, he is omniscient. But, as we have already seen, the Scripture makes clear that Jesus did not share the omniscience of God in his human life, but that his knowledge was based on his relationship to the Father and on the Father's will. Therefore there was room for faith. Indeed, Scripture reveals that Jesus lived the life of faith and describes him as "the prince and perfecter of faith".[90] It also makes clear that it is our Lord's faith which is the ground of our salvation. God's gift of righteousness, without which we cannot stand in his presence, is based on Christ's work which may be summed up either as his obedience or as his faithfulness. The words 'faith' and 'faithfulness' are, of course, the same word in the Greek because the concepts are identical.

Our faith in Jesus, by which we are saved, is closely linked to his faith in God, which is the ground of our salvation. It is wonderful to think

90. Hebrews 12:2 (RV).

that by exercising faith in Christ we are walking in the footsteps of our Saviour, working the same work of God, which won from his Father the encomium: "In you I am well pleased".[91] We fill up, as it were, in our own body that which is lacking in the sufferings of Christ, as we live our daily life in faith in the same way as the Saviour walked the path of faith before us. He is our example of faith, as Hebrews 12:2 puts it.

COMING ON THE CLOUDS TO THE THRONE[92]

On account of his victory on the cross, Jesus is exalted to God's right hand, which is the symbol of rule and government. He has received the kingdom which Daniel 7 foretold was to be given to the Son of Man who, coming in the clouds of heaven to the Ancient of days, would receive the kingdom on behalf of the people of God, a kingdom which would be without end. The passage in Daniel reads,

I kept looking in the night visions,
And behold, with the clouds of heaven
One like a Son of Man was coming
And he came up to the Ancient of Days
and was presented before him.
And to him was given dominion,
Glory and a kingdom,
that all the peoples, nations and men of every language
Might serve him.
His dominion is an everlasting dominion
Which will not pass away;
And his kingdom is one
Which will not be destroyed.[93]

The vision is interpreted at the end of the chapter thus: "The kingdom, the dominion, and the greatness of all the kingdoms under the whole

91. Matthew 3:17; 12:18; 17:5.
92. For an exposition of the different 'comings' of Jesus and their meaning, see 'The Five Comings of Jesus' below, pp. 213-227.
93. Daniel 7:13-14.

heaven will be given to the people of the saints of the Highest One; his kingdom will be an everlasting kingdom, and all dominions will serve and obey him".[94] This prophecy was repeated at the annunciation[95] and was fulfilled at the ascension.[96] Jesus had referred to its fulfilment several times during his ministry. In his Olivet discourse, he predicted (with great emphasis on the reliability of his prediction) that the generation who heard him would not pass away until they had seen the Son of Man coming in the clouds with great power and glory.[97] To the Sanhedrin, a day or so later, he predicted that from that time onwards they would see the Son of Man seated at the right hand of God and coming with the clouds.[98] "To come with the clouds" is a reference to the prophecy of Daniel, that the Son of Man would come with the clouds to the throne of God and receive the kingdom, a prophecy fulfilled through the cross and symbolized in its fulfilment by the ascension, when our Lord ascended in the clouds to heaven and to his throne.

This "coming with the clouds" to the Father's right hand to receive the kingdom at the ascension is to be distinguished from the coming of the Son of Man at the end of the world when he will come in the glory of his Father with the holy angels to sit on his throne of judgement.[99] The coming in the clouds was fulfilled, as Jesus predicted, within that generation. But the time of the coming of the Son of Man in judgement at the end of the world, on 'that day' as the New Testament phrase has it, has not been made known. The Father has kept that time within his own power,[100] so naturally our Lord made no prediction as to when it would be. The confusion between the coming with the clouds to the Father's throne, predicted in Daniel and fulfilled at the ascension, and the coming to his judgement throne in flaming fire at the end of the world, has led to a great deal of misunderstanding of what is otherwise the plain text of Scripture. Both comings are foretold in Daniel 7, for Jesus is the Son of Man, coming in the clouds

94. Daniel 7:27.
95. Luke 1:32-33.
96. Matthew 28:16-20.
97. Mark 13:26, 30.
98. Mark 14:62.
99. Mark 8:38; cf. Matthew 25:31.
100. Acts 1:7.

to the throne, and he is also the Ancient of Days, coming in fire with his holy angels for judgement.[101]

COMING IN JUDGEMENT

The judgement on the final day will be judgement by the Son of Man. Jesus described how, in that day, the Son of Man will come in his glory and all the angels with him, and he will sit on the throne of his glory with the nations gathered before him for judgement.[102] Judgement is from eternity associated with the Son. Jesus told the Jews, "For not even the Father judges anyone, but he has given all judgement to the Son",[103] and again, "he gave him authority to execute judgement, because he is the Son of Man".[104]

The judgements of God are not restricted to the last day but have been experienced throughout history. Just as the final judgement will be that of the Son of Man in his day, so these earlier judgements which humanity has experienced are "days of the Son of Man".[105] Judgement means the vindication of the right, and the righteous rejoice when they see the judgement of God. As Psalm 98 puts it, "Sing joyfully to Yahweh, all the earth… let the mountains sing together for joy before Yahweh, for he is coming to judge the earth; he will judge the world with righteousness and the peoples with equity".[106]

Jesus foretold that the days would come when the disciples would long for vindication of righteousness through judgement, but they would not experience it, for it was not then God's time. He said, "The days shall come when you will long to see one of the days of the Son of Man, and you will not see it".[107] 'Day' is a New Testament term for judgement, as the Greek of 1 Corinthians 4:3 makes clear.[108] Abraham

---

101. Daniel 7:9-10, 21-22.
102. Matthew 25:31.
103. John 5:22.
104. John 5:27.
105. Luke 17:22.
106. Psalm 98:4, 8-9.
107. Luke 17:22.
108. 1 Corinthans 4:3 reads, literally: "But with me it is a very small thing that I should be judged by you, or by any human *day*".

had seen one of those days of the Son of Man when, rising early in the morning and standing on the place where he had met the Lord the day before, "he looked down toward Sodom and Gomorrah, and toward all the land of the valley, and he saw, and behold, the smoke of the land ascended like the smoke of a furnace".[109] God's judgement on Sodom was the coming, the *parousia*, the regal presence of the Son of Man.[110] It was "one of the days of the Son of Man" for the Father has given all judgement to the Son.

The destruction of Jerusalem was an even more signal day of the Son of Man, when the blood of the innocent, from the blood of righteous Abel to that of righteous Zechariah, was required by God at the hands of the inhabitants of Jerusalem in a tribulation which has never been exceeded.[111] It was a day when God was present in judgement, a day of the *parousia* of the Son of Man. Like all the comings of the Son of Man, it was as sudden and as clear as a lightning flash,[112] or as when eagles swoop upon a carcass.[113]

The judgements of the Son of Man are never expected by the recipients. People go on their way eating and drinking, marrying and giving in marriage until the flood of judgement comes and destroys them all.[114] So, too, the final denouement in the day when the Son of Man is revealed will be unexpected by all except those who are waiting for it.

KINGDOM AND DOMINION

At the creation, God purposed that the dominion should be given to mankind. The New Testament sees this purpose of God as fulfilled in Jesus, in the dominion that he received through the cross at his ascension. 1 Corinthians 15, Ephesians 1 and Hebrews 2 make it clear that the Genesis narrative, taken up in Psalm 8, is fulfilled in Jesus of

---

109. Genesis 19:27, 28.
110. Cf. John 8:56—"Your father Abraham rejoiced to see my day; and he saw it, and was glad."
111. Matthew 23:35.
112. Luke 17:24.
113. Luke 17:37.
114. Matthew 24:38.

Nazareth. He is the One to whom all things have been subjected. God's purposes for mankind have been fulfilled in him and in those who are in him. He is not only the image of God, as we have already seen, but he is the One to whom dominion has been given and so the words of Genesis are fulfilled: "Let us make man in our image after our likeness and let them have dominion".[115] On two occasions Jesus taught his disciples that the dominion had been given to him. He began his prayer on the eve of his crucifixion with the words: "Father…[you] gave [the Son] *authority over all mankind,* that to all whom you have given him, he may give eternal life".[116] And on the eve of his ascension he assured his disciples, *"All authority has been given to me in heaven and earth.* Go therefore and make disciples of all the nations".[117]

Salvation comes to sinners by their acknowledgement of this dominion of Jesus. To acknowledge Jesus as Lord is the touchstone of being a Christian.[118] When in the New Testament it is said that salvation comes through faith in Jesus, it means faith in Jesus as Lord. That lordship was accomplished on the cross so that his Lordship and his saviourhood are identical concepts. He saves by victory over sin through bearing sin perfectly, and all sinners who call upon him as the victorious Lord will be saved. Our acknowledgement of the dominion of Christ does not only look back to Calvary, though that is its basis, but it takes in its scope the present and the future also. His dominion is exercised at the present moment. He is reigning and must reign, says Paul, until every enemy is put under his feet.[119]

The dominion of God is a very different sort of dominion from what we understand by the word in ordinary human relationships. As Jesus pointed out, the nations of the world exercise dominion over one another by force.[120] Had Jesus' dominion been of that sort, were his kingdom of this world, his disciples would doubtless have used force to protect and extend his kingdom or rule. But the dominion of God is a dominion which flows from righteousness and love. This is how God

115. Genesis 1:26.
116. John 17:2.
117. Matthew 28:18-19.
118. Romans 10:9; cf 1 Corinthians 12:3.
119. 1 Corinthians 15:25.
120. Matthew 20:25.

exercises his dominion in heaven and therefore also on earth. In heaven, the will of God is done because those who are there love God and love the rightness of God's will. God exercises his dominion through the glad obedience of perfect hearts. Christ in his earthly life followed and expressed this kingdom or dominion of God. In heaven, it is unalloyed joy to express the kingdom of God. In this sinful world, the joy is mingled with suffering—suffering at the hands of sinners—but it is also the occasion for victory over sin, and so the extension of the dominion or kingdom of God. Christians share the dominion of Christ. "They reign upon the earth" as the best manuscript of the book of the Revelation puts it.[121] The Christian's reign upon the earth is a present reality. And like their master, their exercise of the dominion of God, their expression of God's kingdom will involve them in victory. Satan the prince of this world will be repulsed, and the kingdom or dominion of God, God's rule, will be extended. Their faith (which is expressed in their obedience) is the victory which overcomes the world.[122]

The lordship of Christ is manifested not only in the past at Calvary, and in the present through the victory that his servants win by suffering righteously in this world of sin, but it will also be manifested at the Last Day. Consequently the acknowledgement of Jesus as Lord comprises not only the past and present, but also looks forward to the future. That future look was very characteristic of Christians of the New Testament. They were awaiting their Lord from heaven.[123] They lived by hope, as we should, too. Their expectation was put very vividly by Paul in his second letter to the Thessalonians when he spoke of

your perseverance and faith in the midst of all your persecutions and afflictions which you endure. This is a plain indication of God's righteous judgement so that you may be considered worthy of the kingdom of God, for which indeed you are suffering. For after all it is only just for God to repay with affliction those who afflict you, and to give relief to you who are afflicted and to us as well when the Lord Jesus shall be revealed from heaven with his mighty angels in flaming fire, dealing out retribution to those who do not know God and to

121. Revelation 5:10.
122. 1 John 5:4.
123. 1 Thessalonians 1:10.

those who do not obey the gospel of our Lord Jesus. And these will pay the penalty of eternal destruction, away from the presence of the Lord and from the glory of his power, when he comes to be glorified in his saints on that day, and to be marvelled at among all who have believed.[124]

All this is included in the belief that saves. For Jesus is Lord, Lord of the future, as well as Lord of the present and the past. The apostles told the Philippian gaoler, "Believe in the *Lord,* Jesus, and you shall be saved, you and your household".[125]

124. 2 Thessalonians 1:4-10.
125. Acts 16:31.

Chapter 5

'The everlasting purpose of God to deliver those whom he has chosen in Christ'[1]

$\mathcal{T}$HE SUBJECT OF PREDESTINATION IS one that often puzzles Christians. The question of how to think about predestination is an important one; it affects our whole attitude to life and salvation and to our trust and joy in God. The doctrine of predestination is simple to state. It is that from eternity God has chosen some for salvation in Christ, but has left others to their own choice of rebellion against him. On some he has mercy, drawing them to Christ; others he has hardened by allowing them to harden themselves, or rather to be hardened and blinded by Satan, whose slaves they have willingly become.

We do not by nature like the doctrine of predestination, for it appears to make us puppets on the one hand, and it appears unfair on the other. Yet it is a doctrine that is amply taught in Holy Scripture. It is based on the nature of God, who is sovereign and merciful; it is based on the nature of men, rebellious and dead in sin; and it is based on the character of salvation, which is a free gift.

The basic concept of the Christian faith is that God is gracious. This is clearly revealed in the Old Testament when God declared his character to the children of Israel in the early days of the desert wanderings: "Yahweh, the God Yahweh, compassionate and gracious, slow to anger, and abounding in lovingkindness and truth; who keeps lovingkindness

---

1.   This opening quotation is from the Anglican 39 Articles, article 17, 'Of Predestination and Election'.

for thousands, who forgives iniquity, transgression and sin".[2] God's tender mercies are over all his works.[3] The love of God is the motive for salvation: "God so loved the world, that he gave his only begotten Son".[4]

But an equally important truth to remember (and one that we are much more ready to forget) is that God is Creator of everything, and sovereign Lord over all that he has created. His sovereign lordship is not only over the impersonal happenings of nature but also over the lives of men and women, who are a part of his creation. His sovereignty in our lives is not exercised in an impersonal way, but through our natures that he himself has made. To think that God has withdrawn from any area and given over his sovereignty would be an unbearable thought. To think that God is unable to remain sovereign, having created men and women with true human natures and human wills, is, of course, absurd. The Bible teaches clearly, and common sense confirms, that God is sovereign over every aspect of his creation, over the great and over the minute, over men and women, their actions, thoughts and wills, and even over evil men and their wills.[5] He is sovereign over death—he can bring the dead to life by his word as easily as he brought creation into existence out of nothingness in the first place. His sovereignty is not diminished because of man's rebellion against him.

Alongside the goodness of God and the lordship of God, the Bible places the rectitude of God. He is upright in his thoughts and actions and he has implanted the same sense of rectitude in our minds and consciences. We approve righteousness and justice, and the Bible is very clear that God approves righteousness and justice. He is the vindicator of the right, and the awarder of rewards and punishments in accordance with desert. How frequently we read in the Bible that God will judge every man according to his works![6]

It is here that the human problem becomes acute. Our own sense of rectitude and our own conscience tell us that we do things which deserve not reward but punishment. Our future is a fearful expectation of judgement whenever we remember that God is righteous and sover-

2. Exodus 34:6, 7.
3. Psalm 145:9.
4. John 3:16.
5. See chapter 2.
6. E.g. Romans 2:6; 2 Timothy 4:14.

eign, and that he will judge the whole creation in righteousness and truth. God's rectitude will ensure that justice and right are vindicated. Our problem is that in a world where justice will be vindicated we are unjust. The Bible is clear that there is none of us righteous, no not one; we have all turned aside,[7] we are all under God's condemnation and without power of self recovery. None of us can be saved unless God saves us. As Jesus said, "No man can come to me, unless the the Father who sent me draws him".[8] As Jeremiah put it, "Can the Ethiopian change his skin, or the leopard his spots? Then you also can do good who are accustomed to do evil".[9] Or, in Paul's words, "The mind of the flesh is hostile towards God; for it does not subject itself to the law of God, for it is not even able to do so; and those who are in the flesh cannot please God".[10] Because we choose to do what we know to be wrong, God gives us up to our choice. That is fair, but it means hell for all of us; it means eternal separation from God; it means the outer darkness where there is weeping and gnashing of teeth. There is no difference; all have sinned.[11] By disobedience, we all cut ourselves off from God, the source of life. We have involved ourselves in death—in physical death—but more importantly in spiritual and eternal death. We are dead, says Paul, in our trespasses and sins.[12] We are by nature children of wrath, under God's eternal condemnation of death. Dead people cannot save themselves. We need new life, a completely new start, a new creation, as it were, a spiritual resurrection, a new birth, as Jesus told Nicodemus.[13] And it is God, the Creator, the sovereign Lord, who alone can bring about this radical change and this new start, this new creation, this spiritual resurrection. We must be born by the power of God's Spirit.[14] The doctrine of predestination is simply the consequence of man's nature (dead in trespasses and sins), and of God's nature (goodness and mercy), and of his sovereignty and power,

7. Romans 3:10-12.
8. John 6:44.
9. Jeremiah 13:23.
10. Romans 8:7, 8.
11. Romans 3:22-23.
12. Ephesians 2:1-3.
13. John 3:3.
14. John 3:5-8.

through which he recreates those who are dead in their sins, to be his
sons and daughters, choosing according to his own wise and loving and
righteous will.

THE BIBLICAL FOUNDATION

Passages of Scripture which teach the doctrine of election and predestination are very many. One or two illustrations will suffice. Paul wrote,

> *He [God] chose us in him [Christ] before the foundation of the*
> *world, that we should be holy and blameless before him. In love he*
> *predestined us to adoption as sons through Jesus Christ to himself,*
> *according to the kind intention of his will, to the praise of his grace,*
> *which he freely bestowed on us in the beloved... In him also we have*
> *obtained an inheritance, having been predestined according to his*
> *purpose who works all things after the counsel of his will, to the end*
> *that we who were the first to hope in Christ should be to the praise*
> *of his glory.*[15]

In 2 Thessalonians 2:13 the apostle wrote, "God has chosen you from
the beginning for salvation through sanctification by the Spirit and
faith in the truth. And it was for this he called you through our gospel,
that you may gain the glory of our Lord Jesus Christ." Peter wrote his
letter to those whom he described as having been "chosen according to
the foreknowledge of God the Father".[16] Luke described the result of
the preaching of Paul and Barnabas with the words: "As many as had
been appointed to eternal life believed".[17] Likewise Paul wrote, "God
causes all things to work together for good to those who love God, to
those who are called according to his purpose. For whom he foreknew,
he also predestined to become conformed to the image of his son."[18]
But it is in the next chapter, Romans 9, that Paul wrote most fully on
the doctrine of predestination. First, he stated that God chose Jacob
rather than Esau simply because of God's own decision. There was

---

15. Ephesians 1:4-12.
16. 1 Peter 1:1-2.
17. Acts 13:48.
18. Romans 8:28, 29.

nothing in the children which evoked that choice. The apostle concluded, "He has mercy on whom he desires, and he hardens whom he desires".[19] Then in the rest of the chapter the apostle made clear by the way he answered objections that God's choice is not conditioned by anything in those who are predestined.

The intellectual problem

The doctrine of predestination provides an intellectual as well as an ethical problem. The intellectual problem is that of the relationship of our wills, which we know to be real wills, with the sovereign will of God who chooses for salvation. The ethical problem is the question of the fairness of God's choice: why one and not the other?

First let us look at the problem of the intellect—the relationship of the will of God and our wills. This problem of the relationship of the supreme will of Almighty God and the subordinate but real wills of men and women is a difficult one, because there is no parallel in our experience to help us understand it. Our imagination finds difficulty in comprehending how our wills, which we know to be real, can remain true wills within the sovereign will of our Creator, in whom we live and move and have our being[20] and who, so we are clearly taught by revelation, works all things after the counsel of his will.[21] Philosophical theology stumbles over the problem, but there is no problem within the experience of the converted, regenerate Christian. For example, the Christian who is in personal fellowship with his heavenly Father prays with complete confidence to God for guidance through the intricacies of life. In this, he is following numerous spiritual injunctions to commit his way to the Lord who will direct his paths. As the Christian looks back over life, he can see clearly that God has fulfilled and is fulfilling his promise to answer this prayer for guidance, yet the guidance experienced comes through entirely natural means. At no point is the Christian conscious that his own natural God-given faculties are suspended in order that the guidance might be piped to him, as it were. Every step of the road is his step, every decision is his, made, if he has these particular gifts, by intellectual reflection and decision, otherwise

19. Romans 9:18.
20. Acts 17:28.
21. Ephesians 1:11.

perhaps through the influence of friends and their intellectual wisdom. Thus the Christian is conscious both of the over-ruling guidance of God and of the true and full working of his own nature and of circumstance in the receiving of this guidance. Reason may find difficulty in reconciling these two but experience finds none.

Or take another illustration from the field of human relations. The Christian does not hesitate to pray for divine protection from external dangers, whether through natural forces or from malevolent people. He is conscious that God is able to restrain human wrath; indeed if God did not do this, who would survive? Thus the Christian prays with confidence that God will protect him, for it never enters his mind to think that the answer to his prayer might be that God has limited his authority because he has given humanity free will, and that therefore the supplication should be directed to the malevolent person rather than to Almighty God.

In these two areas of Christian experience we have examples of the relationship between the free will of man and the sovereign will of God. God is sovereign, yet the reality of our nature and our free will is not infringed. The Scripture abounds with examples. Thus Joseph answered his brothers, "It is not you who sent me here, but God";[22] and "You meant evil against me, but God meant it for good".[23] Every action which led to Joseph's position in Egypt was God's action. God sent him to Egypt, yet at the same time it remained truly human action, freely decided on, so that those who perpetrated the wrong remained responsible.

Job's reply to his misfortunes has always been recognized not only as very pious, but also as very true: "Yahweh gave, and Yahweh has taken away".[24] The ultimate truth was that the Lord Yahweh took away Job's possessions, for the Lord was in complete control of the Chaldeans and the other brigands who, inflamed by greed and lust for loot, destroyed Job's servants and drove off his livestock.[25] The Lord was not only in complete control of the brigands and all their actions, which they freely undertook and which sprang from their evil natures,

22. Genesis 45:8.
23. Genesis 50:20.
24. Job 1:21.
25. Job 1:13-17.

but he also controlled the maliciousness of their demonic master, set-ting strict limits to his actions,[26] which his wicked nature originated.

On the day of Pentecost Peter told the Jerusalem crowd, "you nailed [him] to a cross by the hands of godless men and put him to death".[27] These men acted freely according to their own lawless natures. But everything that happened was, as Peter put it, according to the "predetermined plan and foreknowledge of God".[28] Similarly, the first Christians acknowledged in their prayer that Herod and Pontius Pilate with the Gentiles and the people of Israel were gathered together to do "whatever your hand and your purpose predestined to occur".[29] From the point of view of history, the crucifixion was just an ordinary event indistinguishable from any other. It was the result of the ordinary interaction of men and women. But the Bible sees every detail as pre-ordained by God's predetermined plan. What is true of Calvary is true of every event everywhere throughout human history.

FREE WILL

The problem of the relationship of God's will to the created will is not to be solved by denying God's sovereignty, as though through the creation of human wills and demonic wills he had delimited an area within his creation over which he had given up control. Not only is this contrary to the whole of revelation, but it would be unbearable and terrifying were it true, and prayer and trust would become impossible. God has not limited himself in any way at all. The Bible knows nothing of such an idea.

Nor is the problem of the relationship of God's will and ours to be solved by denying the reality of the human will, as though it were not what we experience it to be, namely a true will. The word 'free' adds nothing to the meaning of the word 'will', and the denial of the word 'free' is meaningless, so long as we are talking about what we experience as will, which is the only will of which we have direct knowledge.

26. Job 1:12.
27. Acts 2:23.
28. Acts 2:23.
29. Acts 4:27, 28.

Although our wills are free wills, it is incorrect to say that they are independent wills over against God's will. The possibility of this concept was the false suggestion of the devil to Adam, grasped at by man but certainly not achieved by him, though man thinks he has attained to it and that he is in fact free from God's sovereignty. Adam's mistake was that of thinking that by rebelling against God he would become sovereign. But no creature can ever become sovereign over against its almighty Creator, and no will can be free if by this is meant independent of its Creator.

The regenerate man does not wish to have a will operative outside the sphere of God's sovereignty. The concept is repulsive. The unregenerate man may desire this, but he certainly does not possess it. The poet may inveigh,

> *It matters not how strait the gate,*
> *How charged with punishments the scroll,*
> *I am the master of my fate,*
> *I am the captain of my soul.*[30]

But his sentiments are baseless. This attitude of independence of man over against God is what the natural man would like. It is what Adam grasped at, but it is a chimera. Sin does not remove us from God's sovereignty, otherwise sin would be a tremendous success. God remains sovereign; we remain true men and women, enslaved now to the devil against our nature, instead of to our true Master, but nevertheless still within the sovereignty of God who is Lord over heaven and hell. It sounds good to boast against heaven, "I am the master of my fate, I am the captain of my soul", but it is false. God controls his creation; he does not originate moral evil or sin, for this originates from the created will (or rather, person), yet he remains in control of its effects. He is also able to re-create the will and free it from sin, in accordance with his own decision and choice.

The freedom, that is to say, the reality of our will, is not infringed by God's sovereignty, because he exercises his sovereignty only in accordance with the natures of his creation. Thus in working in us he works through our natures, which he has created, and which he foresaw in determining his plan, indeed which he created for the

---

30. From "Invictus", by William Ernest Henley (1875).

purpose of fulfilling his decrees. Thus God's working out his sovereign will appears to us entirely natural, that is to say, in accordance with the nature of things, as in the case of God's guidance and protection. The problem of reconciling God's sovereignty and the reality of our will remains with the intellect, but it is not a problem of experience or of revelation, which is clear and unwavering on the subject.

PERSEVERANCE

Although converted Christians do not differ among themselves on the reality of God's guidance and protection, there has been strong controversy about the sovereignty of God in the transformation of the rebellious sinner into a son of God, into a new creation in Christ, and his perseverance to the end. Yet it must be said that there does not seem to be any real room for denying that the testimony of Scripture is overwhelmingly in support of the sovereignty of God in all aspects of salvation as in every other sphere of human affairs.

It is sometimes argued that the exhortations and especially the admonitions and warnings of Scripture are a proof that there is a real possibility that God's elect will fall away and fail to persevere to the end. This is to misunderstand the purpose of these exhortations and warnings. God works through our natures so that in bringing his children to glory he will work with them through their response to his Word. Their regenerate wills will gladly follow his exhortations and take heed to the warnings. It always remains true that if a person continues in sin he will not inherit the kingdom of God. Paul reiterated warnings that fornicators and drunkards and idolators and money-makers will not inherit the kingdom of God.[31] This remains true. All of us know that we can at any time choose to give ourselves to these things and so fall away and be lost eternally. Indeed, left to ourselves, it is certain that we will fall into one or the other of these sinful ways of life. Nevertheless, by the grace of God we do not, for the warnings are the means by which God saves us from these fatal falls, just as the warning erected in front of a precipice is effective to prevent anybody falling over. The warning notice does not mean that someone must

---

31. 1 Corinthians 6:9; Galatians 5:21.

have fallen down the precipice before it was erected, or that someone will fall over in the future, but it simply indicates that if you ignore the warning you will be killed; however, no-one need ignore it. Indeed, no-one will who reads it. So too in Holy Scripture the warnings are to ensure our perseverance and they achieve this.

Salvation is through faith, which is expressed in obedience. Now faith and obedience are the work of our own personality, but are also the work of God in the heart of the believer. God works through our natures, and in his working he does not destroy or suspend these natures, nor do the natures get in the way of his working. It must always be remembered that God works out his purposes through the nature of his creatures. He does not find the nature which he has created an obstruction to his will. Thus he has created men and women with responsible natures and true wills. In calling his elect and bringing them to glory God does not need to suspend our nature or overrule our will, but he accomplishes his purposes, determined on before the creation of the world, through our free will.

So faith and obedience are both the work of God and at the same time our own work. Since faith is the work of man we must preach the gospel and exhort people to believe, and must ourselves believe and persevere in our obedience; yet since it is a work of God we must look to God, trust him that he will give faith according to his will, and give him thanks when we see evidence of that creative will; for ourselves, we must rely on his faithfulness to keep us to the end, according to his promises. In the case of the unregenerate hearer of the gospel the warnings and promises are not indications of an ability to respond, for they are disbelieved and ignored through sin. Yet they remain indications of reality. The warning is true and the promise is true. When God creates once again our natures, then we both believe the promises and act on the warnings, and they are the instruments by which God brings his children, whom he has chosen, to his eternal home. Warnings are quite compatible with confident assurance of ultimate salvation. Indeed, these warnings and the careful attention to duty that ensues, are the means of obtaining that salvation.

Take two simple illustrations from current life. The driver of a motor vehicle has confidence that he will attain his destination, but at the same time he remains fully vigilant and he is aware that if, for example, he goes to sleep at the wheel he will be killed. His care and wakefulness in no sense diminish his confidence but are the grounds for it. The warnings alert him so that he avoids the dangers which they indicate. Or, again, in space travel an awareness of the frightful dangers and the inevitable death that would follow even one careless slip does not diminish the confidence of the astronauts in the successful completion of their mission. Vigilance against known dangers, and warnings which make these dangers known, are simply the means of ensuring the successful completion of the mission. They do not reflect any lack of confidence of success, neither is there any need for an accident to take place to make the warnings real and true. So, too, with the warnings of Scripture. There do not need to be any apostates, any of God's true children failing to attain, for the warnings in the Scripture against apostasy to be real and true.

ASSURANCE

The Christian's perseverance rests on the character of God, and the Christian's assurance of his salvation rests on that character being known to him through God's promises of faithfulness. The Christian is confident that he will not come to grief, and that no-one will pluck him out of his Father's hand.[32] His confidence is well based and will be justified, for God is faithful and almighty.[33] Yet the Christian knows full well that were he to turn away from God, or were he to fail to do what is necessary, for example, in the buffeting of his body, he would be lost.[34] So we can expect to discover in the New Testament the fullest confidence in the sureness of salvation, along with the clearest warnings against the dangers of drifting away. For these warnings are the instrument by which God makes real and actual that sure salvation. The Christian's assurance of perseverance flows from his realization of the faithfulness of God, who will continue the work which he has begun. Yet every Christian at the same time knows that no fornicator or unclean person will inherit the kingdom of God, so he buffets his body

32. John 10:29.
33. 1 Corinthians 1:9; 1 Thessalonians 5:23-24.
34. 1 Corinthians 9:27.

lest he become such and so be a castaway. The two concepts of faith in God's faithfulness to keep souls which we have committed to him, and of diligence to make our election sure,[35] fit together like a hand in a glove. They are not in contrast or apparent contradiction, but complement each other, for it is God who works in us as we work.[36]

It is a fatal misunderstanding to think that full assurance of final perseverance is incompatible with warnings and exhortations against falling away, and to take the occurrence of such warnings and exhortations in Scripture as proof that the writers of Scripture did not believe in predestination and final perseverance, even when they explicitly said that this was their belief. Equally it is a mistake to believe that the will is free against its own Creator. That is the attitude of rebellious man, but it is not true in reality. We cannot be free against our Creator, nor should we wish it. It is sufficient for us if we are free against the influence of all that is not God. As sinners we are very far from free in this respect; we are always slaves to our passions and led captive by the devil. But restored in Christ, we become free in the only way a creature can be free—that is, free to follow its God-given nature; not free against the Giver, but only truly free when it is responding to the overwhelming grace of God, as our natures were created to do.

THE ETHICAL PROBLEM

The ethical problem in the doctrine of predestination arises from our God-given sense of fairness. Fairness, righteousness and justice are the basis of all our relationships with one another. But we are on dangerous ground if we set up our sense of fairness, that is to say, what we believe to be due to us and to others, as the criterion for judging God's dealings with his rebellious creation. A rebel *deserves* nothing but condemnation and condign punishment. Since salvation, however, is in the realm of mercy, not punishment, it is difficult to see how the concept of fairness plays any part in it. If God is to be fair and just to rebels we all deserve and will receive punishment. But mercy supervenes, and

35. 2 Peter 1:10.
36. Philippians 2:12-13.

mercy is apart from the realm of justice. In fact, the two concepts are mutually exclusive. That which is deserved is not mercy but reward. Mercy is that which is held out and given to those who have absolutely no claim on it. Consequently the rebellious sinner who is the recipient of God's mercy can hardly discuss and make demands about this mercy on the basis of his sense of fairness.

Mercy is a completely different category from justice. The Lord's parable of the labourers in the vineyard warns us against the fatal error of impugning God's goodness in seeking to judge his acts of mercy and overflowing benevolence by our judgement of what is fair.[37] The Judge of all the earth will do right[38]—of that we may be sure—but he will not be judged by us. It is a very dangerous activity for us to set up as a criterion our sense of what it is fair for him to do to rebels in his distribution of his unmerited mercy, especially when the results of this judgement of ours fly in the face of the overwhelming testimony of revelation.

The Bible constantly testifies that salvation and eternal life are God's gifts.[39] Now a gift is in the complete disposal of the giver; he may give it, or he need not. The same is true of mercy. It is completely at the disposal of the merciful. He may show mercy, or he need not. Salvation is a gift. The Giver may give it, or he need not. If salvation is deserved, it ceases to be a gift. It then becomes reward for merit, wages which have been earned. But salvation is entirely a gift from beginning to end. It therefore means that it must be given according to God's will and choice. The character of salvation as a gift, the merciful provision of salvation, is bound up with the doctrine of God's complete freedom in election and predestination.

IN CHRIST

To understand the doctrine of predestination correctly we should view it from the standpoint of a Christian who is experiencing and enjoying fellowship with his heavenly Father in the Holy Spirit through the forgiveness in our Lord Jesus Christ. The Bible regularly treats the subject from

37. Matthew 20:1-16.
38. Genesis 18:25.
39. E.g. John 10:28; Romans 6:23.

this point of view. As a Christian reflects on the grace of God which he is experiencing in his own life, he cannot but attribute it all to God's goodness. In himself he knows he deserves nothing. Paul said, "Nothing good dwells in me, that is in my flesh".[40] There is nothing in us of ourselves which deserves God's favour, but only God's condemnation,[41] and yet how wonderfully Christians experience this favour, for the Christian life is one of peace with God through forgiveness, joy in his presence and love towards him and others by his Spirit, faith in daily life and sure hope for the future, a daily fellowship with God through prayer and his Word. This relationship to God is God's gift, and it springs entirely from God's initiative. Jesus said to his disciples, "You did not choose me, but I chose you".[42] Our present Christian experience and our future hope are attributed in the Bible to God's decision, a decision which was made from the beginning of creation with regard to us personally: "God has chosen you from the beginning for salvation through sanctification by the Spirit and faith in the truth";[43] and "God has not destined us for wrath, but for obtaining salvation through our Lord Jesus Christ".[44] Speaking of Christians, Paul said that they are "vessels of mercy, which he prepared beforehand for glory".[45] As we experience our Christian status as adopted sons of God, all the glory and the thankfulness of this state of things must be given to God. It is not shared partly with ourselves, as though we had contributed the vital link which made the difference between death and life.

GOD'S SOVEREIGNTY IN SALVATION

The clearest illustration of God's sovereignty in salvation is the life of the apostle Paul. He was a man totally immersed in his prejudices. On his own initiative, he had asked for authority to journey to Damascus to arrest and imprison believers.[46] He certainly did not seem a bright

40. Romans 7:18.
41. Romans 5:18.
42. John 15:16.
43. 2 Thessalonians 2:13.
44. 1 Thessalonians 5:9.
45. Romans 9:23.
46. Acts 9:1-2.

prospect for conversion, nor was he. His conversion resulted from an extraordinary intervention by God on his behalf. He was converted because as the risen Lord himself put it, he was "a chosen instrument".[47] A light shone around him and he heard the voice of Jesus addressing him. Indeed the heavens were opened and he had a vision of our Lord so bright that he was blinded. It is not surprising that after such an experience he should recognize Jesus as Lord and give his life to his service. It is plain that his conversion is to be attributed entirely to God. It took extraordinary means to bring this 'chosen instrument' into the kingdom. The same is true of the conversion of everyone, though normally it is not so spectacular. The initiative lies entirely with God. It must be so because in ourselves we are blind and cannot see the truth.[48] The mind of the flesh is at enmity against God and is not subject to God's will, nor indeed can it be.[49] God must intervene. He alone can open the eyes of the spiritually blind,[50] take away the stony heart,[51] and re-create the personal relationship with himself. For when a man is in Christ, said Paul, "he is a new creation",[52] and it is God the Creator to whom alone this new creation is to be attributed.

The doctrine of predestination is another way of saying that God is sovereign in salvation; it is he who chooses those whom he adopts as sons.[53] It is he who re-creates them from dead sinners to living saints. Even our response of faith is God's gift, given according to his purpose. Thus Paul told the Philippians that it was God's gift to them that they believed on Jesus.[54] Frequently in the Bible, repentance is said to be the gift of God,[55] and this is natural because we have not the power of self-recovery within ourselves to turn back from a self-centred life to a God-centred life. If anyone repents in this radical way, it is God's gift to him. Christians know this to be the case. As they reflect on their

47. Acts 9:15.
48. 2 Corinthians 4:4.
49. Romans 8:7.
50. 2 Corinthians 4:4-6.
51. Ezekiel 36:26.
52. 2 Corinthians 5:17.
53. Ephesians 1:5.
54. Philippians 1:29; cf. Ephesians 2:8-9.
55. Acts 5:31; 11:18; 2 Timothy 2:25.

own experience, they recognize that were it not for the grace of God they would still be living the old life of self-centredness and sin.

PREDESTINATION IS FULL OF COMFORT

Belief in the doctrine of predestination does not come naturally; it is only because it is so clearly taught in Scripture that anyone holds it, and yet when it is firmly grasped it has a tremendous effect in releasing our spirits from anxiety and stress. The evangelist who knows that God is sovereign in salvation does not feel driven to all sorts of expedients to get people converted. He rests in confidence in God. He will rely primarily on prayer and on preaching the clear truth of the gospel in the context of love and relationship, because he knows that the word of the cross is the power of God to salvation.[56] He will not be driven to obtain decisions by methods and expedients which may be unworthy of that gospel with which he has been entrusted, for he knows that it is God who gives repentance and faith in fulfilling his purposes of grace and salvation. Not that belief in God's sovereignty in salvation will excuse lethargy in prayer or slackness in preparation on the part of the minister or individual Christian, or sitting back with the pretext that God will save those whom he has predestined, for God works his purposes of grace through us and through our natures and our gifts, and we must be obedient in the use of our gifts and opportunities, for we are responsible and will have to give an account before the judgement seat of God.[57]

There is a two-sidedness which cannot be escaped. God is sovereign in salvation; we are responsible in our obedience. The writer of Acts found no contradiction here. In Acts 13:48, he described the results of the preaching of Paul and Barnabas in terms of God's sovereignty: "As many as had been appointed to eternal life believed". A few verses later in 14:1 he put the other side, attributing the result to the fervency of the preachers: "[The apostles] spoke in such a manner that a great multitude believed". Both are true at the same time; God is sovereign–we are

56. 1 Corinthians 1:18.
57. 1 Corinthians 4:1-5.

responsible. Those who believe and receive salvation, reconciliation, adoption and the Spirit's presence, and are made inheritors of God's kingdom are to understand that their decision for Christ was God's gift in accordance with his purpose, determined on before creation began. Paul said we are "vessels of mercy, which he prepared beforehand for glory".[58] The destinations of the lost and the saved are separated more widely than any gulf imaginable.[59] It would be intolerable if our being on the blessed side of this awful distinction were to be attributed to some virtue in ourselves, some cleverness, some response initiating within ourselves. It would be monstrous if we were to attribute to ourselves the fact that we have received the unspeakable blessings of being the inheritors of God's kingdom,[60] of having his name on our foreheads, of seeing his face and dwelling in his presence for ever.[61] And yet this would be the case if our salvation depended in any way at all upon our own decision apart from God's prior decision. Only the doctrine of predestination prevents us from being engulfed in such an impious doctrine as to attribute the difference between ourselves in heaven and those lost in hell to some response or decision that we ourselves contributed. Of ourselves, we are all the same, lost through our own deserts. The difference between those who are lost and those who are being saved rests in God's decision made before the world was. God is righteous, God is wise and God is loving, and he has mercy on whom he will.[62]

UNBELIEF

As the preacher contemplates the great number of people who reject the message of God's grace which he has delivered in God's name, he cannot help but weep over them as Christ wept over Jerusalem. Yet it is interesting to note that the ultimate explanation that the Scriptures offer for this unbelief is the predestination of God. Thus Peter said that "they stumble because they are disobedient to the word, and to this

58. Romans 9:23.
59. Luke 16:26.
60. Matthew 25:34.
61. Revelation 22:3-5.
62. Romans 9:18.

doom they were also appointed".[63] As John contemplated the ineffec-
tiveness of Jesus' ministry in drawing the Jewish people to himself, he
rested in the predestinating purposes of God, made known long before
through the prophet Isaiah: "Who has believed our message? And to
whom has the arm of Yahweh been revealed?".[64] "For this cause", John
went on to say, "they could not believe, for Isaiah said again, 'He has
blinded their eyes, and he hardened their heart; lest they see with their
eyes, and perceive with their heart, and be converted, and I heal them'.
These things Isaiah said, because he saw his glory, and he spoke of
him".[65] In this John was following and echoing the thoughts of his
Master. For when Jesus was reflecting on the rejection of the gospel by
Capernaum and Bethsaida and Chorazin, he prayed, "I praise you, O
Father, Lord of heaven and earth, that you hid these things from the
wise and intelligent... Yes, Father, for thus it was well-pleasing in your
sight".[66] Again when Jesus was confronted with the impenitent unbelief of his Jewish hearers he found the explanation of this extraordinary
phenomenon, that the people of God should reject the Word of God
delivered by the Son of God, in the predestination of God. "You do not
believe", he told his hearers, "because you are not of my sheep. My
sheep hear my voice";[67] and again, "For this reason you do not hear
them, because you are not of God".[68] He also said, "No one can come
to me, unless the Father who sent me draws him";[69] and "No one can
come unto me, unless it has been granted him from the Father";[70] and
"All that the Father gives me shall come to me".[71] When John reviewed
the ministry of Jesus, he attributed to the predestination of God its failure to evoke faith. When Paul faced the same extraordinary fact that
the people of God rejected the Messiah of God, he too found the
explanation in the predestination of God

63. 1 Peter 2:8.
64. Isaiah 53:1, quoted at John 12:38.
65. John 12:38-41, quoting Isaiah 6:10.
66. Matthew 11:25, 26.
67. John 10:26, 27.
68. John 8:47.
69. John 6:44.
70. John 6:65.
71. John 6:37.

It is not as though the word of God has failed. For they are not all Israel who are descended from Israel...for though the twins were not yet born, and had not done anything good or bad, in order that God's purpose according to his choice might stand, not because of works, but because of him who calls, it was said to her "The older will serve the younger". Just as it is written, "Jacob I loved, but Esau I hated".

What shall we say then? There is no injustice with God, is there? May it never be! For he says to Moses, "I will have mercy on whom I have mercy, and I will have compassion on whom I have compassion". So then it depends not on the man who wills or the man who runs, but on God who has mercy.[72]

The unbelief of his hearers should fill the preacher's eyes with tears and his heart with yearning, as it did for Jesus and Paul, but the preacher knows that the unbelief of the hearer of the gospel is not outside God's predestinating purposes. In this way it will not discourage him nor make him relax his efforts to fulfil the commission to preach the gospel to the whole creation; but the knowledge of God's predestination will relieve him of tension; it will help him to escape unworthy methods and to avoid psychologically damaging introspection. He will know himself to be the Lord's servant and messenger gathering the Lord's people, that is, Christ's elect, according to God's eternal purposes[73]—purposes which the Scriptures reveal to be of infinite and overwhelming blessing to the world.

THE GOLDEN CHAIN OF BLESSING

Because the Bible so clearly teaches the doctrine of predestination, Christians ought to embrace it without hesitation, for it is certainly true and we should adjust our attitudes in conformity with it. There is a wonderful passage in Romans 8:28-30:

And we know that God causes all things to work together for good to those who love God, to those who are called according to his purpose.

72. Romans 9:6-16.
73. Acts 18:10; Matthew 24:31.

For whom he foreknew, he also predestined to become conformed to the image of his son, that he might be the first-born among many brethren; and whom he predestined, these he also called; and whom he called, these he also justified; and whom he justified, these he also glorified.

Notice the emphasis on God's purpose, which he is fulfilling in our lives that we might be conformed to Christ's likeness. Notice the golden chain "whom he predestined, these he also called; and whom he called, these he also justified; and whom he justified, these he also glorified". None is missing; no link is broken; all attain glory. Those whom he had predestined in due course he called, justified and finally glorified by conforming them to the image of Jesus. It is the work of God. Thanks be to God!

The doctrine reminds us that it is God's purpose to confer blessing. The Scriptures tell us that God chose Abraham in order that he might bless him,[74] and Paul began his letter to the Ephesians with: "Blessed be the God… who has blessed us with every spiritual blessing… he chose us in [Christ] before the foundation of the world… He predestined us to adoption as sons". The realization of this goodness of God, totally undeserved by us, should make us humble and cause us to appreciate our blessings.

PREDESTINATION NOT BASED ON PRE-VISION

In considering the doctrine of predestination we must exclude from our thoughts any concept that God's predestination is based on his foresight of our response, or of our virtues or our faith. God's choice was based entirely on his own character. Moses made clear that God's choice of the Israelites was not based on anything within themselves: "Yahweh did not set his love on you, nor choose you because you were more in number than any of the peoples, for you were the fewest of all peoples, but because Yahweh loved you".[75] Our salvation is the result of God's mercy, and mercy is always unmerited.

74. Genesis 12:1-3.
75. Deuteronomy 7:7.

In Romans 9, Paul unravelled the problem that although Jesus the Messiah had come to God's people, the majority of the Israelites had rejected him. It was a very depressing problem for Paul. He wrote, "I have great sorrow and unceasing grief in my heart. For I could wish that I myself were accursed, separated from Christ for the sake of my brethren, my kinsmen according to the flesh, who are Israelites."[76] In spite of all their privileges, the majority of the Jews were rejecting the Messiah. How was it to be explained? Paul attributed it simply to the choice of God. God was having mercy on whom he was having mercy.[77] It has always been so, and at that time also there was a remnant according to election and "the rest were hardened, just as it is written, 'God gave them a spirit of stupor, eyes to see not and ears to hear not'".[78]

We must remember that we have no claims on God. In the first place we were created by him. Can the pot dictate to the potter?[79] There is no unrighteousness in God; all his ways are perfect.[80] We cannot probe the purposes of God beyond what he has revealed to us in Scripture. We know his character of love and graciousness, of wisdom and righteousness. He is dealing with a sinful and rebellious race, creatures who reject their Creator, yet he has mercy; and his actions of salvation spring from within his character of wisdom and love and righteousness. God chooses. Of Abraham's children it was Isaac whom God chose, and of Isaac's two children, who were twins and so absolutely equal, Jacob was chosen, not Esau the elder.

Paul is aware of the intellectual problem posed by God's sovereign discrimination, but he does not answer it in any simple manner. He imagines an objector saying that God's choice of one rather than another is unjust, but Paul will not allow any thought that God could be unjust. God, who is the source of our sense of justice, will not contradict what is just by any of his actions. But God is free in choosing on whom he will have mercy. Mercy springs entirely from within the one who is merciful. No rebellious sinner (as we all are) can *demand*

76. Romans 9:3.
77. Romans 9:18.
78. Romans 11:8.
79. Isaiah 29:16; cf Romans 9:20-21.
80. Deuteronomy 32:4.

that God should be merciful on him or on anyone else. But God has mercy on whom he will, and whom he will he hardens.

Once again the apostle imagines an objector saying that this is unfair. The apostle replies:

> On the contrary, who are you, O man, who answers back to
> God...What if God, although willing to demonstrate his wrath and
> to make his power known, endured with much patience vessels of
> wrath prepared for destruction? And he did so in order that he might
> make known the riches of his glory upon vessels of mercy, which he
> prepared beforehand for glory, even us, whom he also called...[81]

Paul recognized the problems of the doctrine of predestination, but he did not take the easy way out, and say that God's decisions are based on his foresight of our response, for this is not true. On the contrary, our response, our reaction, is based on God's foreordination, and his decisions are based only on himself, on his goodness and mercy, on his wisdom and his will. We must not allow ourselves to adopt a solution of which Paul knows nothing as he grapples with this problem of pre-destination. Yet God's hardening of the sinner is not apart from the sinner's hardening of his own heart. "He hardens whom he desires", said Paul,[82] but on the other hand the Scripture addresses a word to us: "Do not harden your hearts".[83] Of Pharaoh, the Bible says both that God hardened his heart and that Pharaoh hardened his heart, for both are true at the same time.[84] Pharaoh's will is within the sovereign will of God. Pharaoh wanted to harden his heart, he willed to harden his heart, and God willed that Pharaoh should harden his heart, so that from this sin of Pharaoh God should bring salvation to the world.

We sinners have no right to be angry with God because of the way things happen. We all deserve God's judgement, and if we are not experiencing that judgement to the full immediately, that is due to God's long-suffering. Sinners have no claims on God, no right to be angry with God, for we all deserve a great deal more than anything that might be happening to us at present. If we receive any blessings, and

---

81. Romans 9:20-24.
82. Romans 9:18b.
83. Psalm 95:8.
84. Exodus 7:3, 22; 8:15.

especially if we receive restoration of fellowship through salvation in Christ, it is because of God's mercy.

Immediately after our Lord had reflected on the mystery of God's predestination with regard to the blindness of the townspeople of Capernaum with the words "I praise you, Father... for thus it was well-pleasing in your sight", he repeated the gracious invitation of the gospel: "Come to me, all who are weary and heavy laden, and I will give you rest".[85] There are always these two sides of the truth to be kept in mind at the same time. On the one hand, there is God's sovereignty, having mercy on those who could not possibly be saved apart from his mercy; and on the other, our responsibility to respond and to believe the gospel. Paul kept both sides of the truth before his readers in Romans 9-11. In chapter 9, he emphasised God's sovereignty in pre-destination and election, but he completed his discussion of this sub-ject in chapter 11 by reminding his readers that those who are lost are lost through their own unbelief, while if his readers hope to be saved it can only be by their continuing in faith. Otherwise, they too will be lost like the rest.

Yet we must not jump to the conclusion that this faith originates in ourselves. It is our faith, it is true, but it is God's gift to us. And because it is God's gift to us we may look to the future with confidence that he will continue to give us the grace to believe. As Hebrews puts it, Christ will save to the very end those who come to God by him.[86] If we are Christ's sheep, none can pluck us out of his hand.[87] Our con-fidence for the future (and we should all have this confidence) rests in God, not in ourselves, for God has promised to be faithful and to com-plete that which he has begun in us.[88]

Assurance of future salvation is sometimes said to be presumption. It is anathematized by the Council of Trent for this reason.[89] But it is a question of the ground on which this assurance rests. If it rests on our good works, it would indeed be presumptuous of us to assume that these are good enough to merit salvation or that we will have the strength to

85. Matthew 11:25-28.
86. Hebrews 7:25.
87. John 10:27-28.
88. 1 Thessalonians 5:23-24; Philippians 1:6.
89. *Session 6, chapter 9* and *Canon 16.*

persevere. But if our assurance rests on a knowledge of God's promises and his faithfulness, it is not presumption but an act of true faith. Such assurance should be possessed by every believer. So long as the child of God is looking into the face of God, assurance is God-honouring. But to look away from God and to base assurance on something in ourselves, and not solely on God's grace and promises, is indeed irreligious presumption. Yet it is God's will that every child of his should have assurance of his perseverance and future salvation. One of the objects of John's First Epistle is that his readers might possess this full assurance, for without it Christian joy is diminished and fellowship with God defective.[90]

It is a very important aspect of the doctrine of predestination that God will be faithful and that we may rest in this faithfulness. He will keep his promise, for he is faithful and will do it.[91] If our salvation were to depend on ourselves it would be presumptuous for us to be sure that our future will be in heaven. But since salvation is entirely God's gift from beginning to end, we may rest in thankfulness on his faithfulness, that he will complete the salvation of those whom he chose before the foundation of the world. And we may accept with equanimity, indeed with joy, the events which his goodness allows to enter our lives, knowing that all things work together for good to those that love God, to them who are called according to his purpose. For those whom he called, them also he predestined to be conformed to the image of his Son. We may work in his service without the tension of thinking that everything depends on ourselves, and we may trust him for the future, knowing that those whom he foreknew he also called, and those whom he called he also justified and those whom he justified he also glorified. For God has not appointed us to wrath but to the attaining of salvation through our Lord Jesus Christ.[92] We should put an inestimable value on our inheritance.[93]

Paul completed his discussion of the doctrine of predestination in Romans 9, 10 and 11 by reminding his readers of the wisdom of God manifested in the extraordinary and unexpected event that, through the

90. 1 John 1:3, 4; 2:26-27; 3:18-20; 5:13.
91. 1 Thessalonians 5:23, 24; 1 Corinthians 1:8, 9.
92. 1 Thessalonians 5:9.
93. 1 Peter 1:3-5.

rejection of the Messiah by the people of God, the Gentiles are blessed, and in turn through God's work among the Gentiles, the Jews themselves will be converted. He apostrophizes the wisdom and knowledge of God, who has shut up all unto disobedience, that he might have mercy on all. God's wisdom is not fully revealed to us. We do not understand all that lies behind God's purposes in predestination, but we may rest in his wonderful wisdom and believe that the future will be more full of blessing for the whole world than even the present is.

For those who have been chosen by God to be his sons and daughters, not only should there be profound thankfulness to God for his mercy, but a very deep sense of responsibility. We have been chosen that we might become like Jesus in character. This is God's purpose for us and we should make this the chief object of our life, to conform ourselves to the image of his Son. What a glorious purpose God has for us! We have been chosen to set forth God's praise, that we might be to the praise of the glory of his grace.[94] Our lives should be such that God's glory is seen and praised.[95] We have been chosen to be blessed and to be a blessing, that through our lives and our words we might bless others with the knowledge of Christ. The privilege is great and the responsibility real.

94. Ephesians 1:6.
95. Matthew 5:16.

Appendix A

THE RELIGIONS OF THE WORLD
AS A SOURCE
OF KNOWLEDGE OF GOD

*S*INCE HUMANITY UNIVERSALLY BELIEVES that deity is personal and since persons and, *a fortiori,* a personal God are only known in as far as they reveal themselves, the question arises where (if indeed anywhere) deity has revealed itself to mankind. We have seen in chapter 1 that the Bible states that God has revealed himself through the centuries by personally addressing men and women whom he has chosen to receive these communications and his fellowship. This revelation culminated in the presence of Jesus of Nazareth in Palestine in the first century. The Bible further states that this revelation has been inscripturated by God so that the revelation and fellowship are also fully available to us. But has the self-revelation of God been confined to the Christian religion? To extend the concept of revelation to all the religions of the world is a natural answer and it has been given classic expression in *The Constitution of the Church, Lumen Gentium,* one of the official pronouncements of the Second Vatican Council of the Roman Catholic Church. In paragraph 16, the Second Vatican Council affirmed, "The plan of salvation also includes those who acknowledge the Creator. In the first place among these are the Moslems who, professing to hold the faith of Abraham along with us, adore the one and merciful God who in the last day will judge mankind. Nor is God far distant from those who in shadows and images seek the unknown God, for it is he who gives all men life and breath and all things and, as Saviour, wills that all men be saved". The view expressed in this document is very widespread. It was given expression at the Anglican Congress in Toronto in 1963 when the secretary of an important missionary society challenged his hearers to flex "the muscles of our imagination far enough to recognize God's presence in the cave outside Mecca, under the Bo tree and at other points in man's religious pilgrimage".[1]

NO REVELATION IN THE ETHNIC RELIGIONS

However, the knowledge of deity that may be gained by examining the religious notions of humanity, whether Muslims or idolaters, does not extend beyond the knowledge of the existence of a superhuman, powerful, knowledgeable, personal, everlasting being to whom we are related. The religions of the nations do not give a knowledge of the character of God, for the notions of deity in those religions are so diverse that they cancel one another out. We may conclude that although mankind believes in the existence of personal deity it has no personal relationship with deity because it has no consistent or universally held view of the character of deity, which would not be the case if men were in fact related to the same deity through the multiplicity of human religions.

This conclusion is also the view of the Bible. The worshippers of the religions of the world are regarded by the Bible as being ignorant of the true God. When Paul was walking through the market-place at Athens he noticed that it was full of altars to the various deities of the Athenian pantheon. The one that he chose as closest to reality was the altar inscribed "to the unknown God", and taking this inscription as his starting-point, he told the Athenians, "What you worship in ignorance, this I set forth to you".[2]

For Paul, the nations are "without God".[3] They are ignorant of God. "The Gentiles walk", he said, "in the vanity [that is, emptiness] of their mind, being darkened in their understanding, alienated from the life of God because of the ignorance that is in them, because of the hardening of their heart".[4]

This last phrase "the hardening of their heart" points to the reason why the ethnic religions are not in touch with the true God. The religion of the nations is the consequence of the hardening of their heart.

1. *Report of Anglican Congress 1963* (S.P.C.K.) p. 21.
2. Acts 17:23.
3. Ephesians 2:12.
4. Ephesians 4:18.

Ethnic religions are the result of turning away from God; they are not a feeling after him in order to find him. Such feeling after God to find him is always open to mankind, for he is not far from any of us.[5] But it is a possibility that is not taken. This is plain from Paul's argument in Romans 1. There the apostle makes clear that the religions of the world are the result of rebellion against the true knowledge of God given to man in creation. For through the things that have been made, it is possible to perceive God's everlasting power and divinity, but instead of responding to that knowledge in the way that our consciences tell us we should, namely by glorifying God and giving him thanks for all the benefits that creation has brought us and in this way coming to know God, mankind has refused to have a knowledge of God and has become vain in its reasoning and its ignorant heart has become darkened. Mankind has refused to respond to God known in creation, it has refused to give him the glory due to him and the thanks for benefits received through his benefaction. Men have turned their back on God, hardened their heart against him and have developed false religions to be a substitute for the true God whom we have refused to acknowledge in the way that we know God should be acknowledged, that is, by thankfulness and praise. The religion of rebels does not yield a knowledge of the true God.

THE RELIGIONS OF REBELS CONTAIN NO KNOWLEDGE OF GOD OR RELATIONSHIP WITH HIM

The religions of the world are the creation of rebellious men as a substitute for worshipping the true God. Universally mankind has made and worshipped idols as a substitute for acknowledging the true God—a substitute which on analysis is absurd, namely, idols of mortal men, of birds, of animals and of reptiles, as though these were ultimate reality. Truly "their senseless heart has been darkened".[6] There is therefore no knowledge of the true God to be found in the worshipping that goes on in connection with the religions of the nations. It is not there that we can seek for knowledge of God. The Bible is quite clear on this.

5. Acts 17:27.
6. Romans 1:21.

The Old Testament constantly describes the religions of the nations around Israel as emptiness, vanity. The idols, their gods, are nonentities. It is not to be expected therefore that knowledge of the true God is to be found by examining the religion and worship of nonentities.

There is a further and perhaps more compulsive reason still for rejecting the study of religion as a way which leads to the truth about divine things, for the idols of the nations, in themselves nonentities and the result of God giving men up to their disobedience, become the opportunity by which the evil spirits of the demonic world obtain a control over the minds, hearts and lives of those who worship idols. Paul says in 1 Corinthians 10:20, "The things which the Gentiles sacrifice, they sacrifice to devils, and not to God", and this is fully in keeping with the repeated testimony of the Old Testament with regard to the idolatry which the children of Israel fell into from time to time. For example, in the song of Moses, "They sacrificed unto demons which were no God, to gods whom they knew not, to new gods that came up of late, whom your fathers dreaded not",[7] or again in Psalm 106:37, "They sacrificed their sons and their daughters unto demons". In Revelation 9:20 the worship of the religions of the world is said to be the worship of devils.

The conclusion is clear that in the ethnic religions, both of the ancient world as well as of our modern times, there is no knowledge of God to be found. The worshippers of those religions are not in fellowship with God; they are not related to God through their religious worship. They open themselves up to the influence of demons and are in fact worshipping evil spirits under the veil of their idols, so that we may conclude that their notions of deity are devil-inspired. This biblical teaching is very different from that of modern theological thought, reflected for example in the trend in universities to substitute the study of religions for the study of Christian theology.

The New Testament constantly warns Christians to have nothing at all to do with idolatry. John concluded his letter with the words: "My little children, guard yourselves from idols" and Paul in several places warned his converts that idolaters will not inherit the kingdom of God, but on the contrary the wrath of God will overtake those who

7.   Deuteronomy 32:17.

follow this form of religion.[8] In New Testament times there was no other form of religion among the nations except idolatry, so in condemning idolatry the New Testament condemns all the religions of the nations and the terms of its condemnation are the severest possible. If the New Testament is to be normative for our thinking about God and where he may be found, we must not yield to the temptation of seeking him in the thought structures created by the ethnic religions which even today are essentially idolatrous. This exclusivism is very unpleasant to the modern mind but it expresses the New Testament emphasis which is fully in keeping with that of the Old. Israel was to have nothing whatever to do with the religions of the nations for there was no truth to be found in them.

ETHNIC RELIGIONS ARE NOT SEEKING GOD

There is nothing in the world or in God's relation to it which prevents us from finding God in the world. Nor has God left himself without witness, in that he did good, giving us rain and fruitful seasons, filling our hearts with food and gladness. The fault is in ourselves if we do not perceive this witness. For the god of this world blinds the eyes of the unbelieving. Even those whom the apostle was addressing as he reminded them of this witness were at that very moment engaged in idolatry.[9] They were ignoring the witness. God has promised that those who seek him will find him. He will respond to those who with a true heart seek him, because he is not far from any of us. But the Bible teaches that "there are none who seek after God. They have all turned aside".[10] Instead of seeking God we turn our backs on him; instead of making the right response we refuse that response. We refuse to have knowledge of the truth and make a false god in its place. The consequence is that our relationship with God is cut. There is no knowledge of God in our lives and the religions of the world which we create in the place of the true God are not a means for knowing him or a way by which we may relate ourselves to him. It is true that there remains

8.   1 Corinthians 6:9; Ephesians 5:5.
9.   Acts 14:18.
10.   Romans 3:11, 12.

much that is noble in human nature and in human relationships, through the grace and long-suffering of God, but this genuineness in human relationships, man with man, should not be mistaken for knowledge of God. Knowledge of God and relationship with him has perished through sin.

To sum up, the Bible states that human religion is the result of rebellion against God, and no knowledge of God is in it. Because they would not have God in their mind, the nations created for themselves idols which on a moment's reflection should have been seen to be the most ridiculous form of god. Secondly, the Bible says that the idols and gods of the nations are empty, vanity, nonentities. Nothing corresponds to them in reality, therefore it is plain that no knowledge of God can be found from the philosophy and the reasoning that surrounds these religions. Thirdly, the Bible says that the religions of the world are directed towards the demon world. It is as though the vacuum caused through turning away from the true God is filled by evil spirits from the spiritual world that is in rebellion against him. Fourthly the Bible is clear that there is absolute ignorance of God in the religions of the world. For these reasons it is plain that a knowledge of God, that is to say, a relationship with the true personal God, is not to be arrived at through these religions. Religious studies will help the student understand human nature and human culture but will not contribute to his understanding of God. Anthropology is important, but it is not theology.

Appendix B

THE IMPLICATIONS OF THE
·········· DOCTRINE OF THE TRINITY ··········
FOR THEOLOGY
AND FOR ORDINARY LIFE

THE TRINITY AND THEOLOGY

*T*HE TRINITY, GOD HIMSELF, IS AN awesome subject. God is the high and lofty one who inhabits eternity, whose name is holy. He dwells in the high and holy place, but also with those of a contrite and humble spirit, to revive the spirit of the humble and to revive the heart of the contrite ones.[1]

Because of the humility of God in dwelling with us and speaking to us, we may speak to him and speak of him to one another.

The doctrine of the Trinity is the glory of the Christian faith. It is drawn entirely from revelation. It depends on the absolute truth of the sentences through which the Scriptures teach us about God and his nature, his character, his purposes, his actions and promises. The doctrine depends, for example, on the infallibility and inerrancy of the teaching in St John's Gospel, or the Epistle to the Ephesians or the last paragraph of St Matthew's Gospel, because the doctrine of the Trinity is not enunciated fully in any one passage but is gathered from many statements of the Scriptures. If we cannot rely on the verbal inspiration of Scripture, the doctrine of the Trinity has no basis.

The teaching of Scripture about the trinitarian nature of God is succinctly summarised in articles one, two and five of the Thirty-Nine Articles of the Church of England. But its classical statement is in the Athanasian Creed. This creed is regarded with disfavour by some people at present, especially its opening and closing statements that the Christian faith is "we worship one God in Trinity and Trinity in unity;

---

1. Isaiah 57:15.

neither confounding the persons nor dividing the substance", and that unless a person holds this faith he cannot be saved. However, the truth of the creed is confirmed by Peter's words that Jesus is "the head of the corner and in none other is there salvation"[2] and that "whoever calls upon the name of the Lord shall be saved".[3]

For it is not possible to hold the unity of God and to call on Jesus as Lord unless you believe the doctrine of the Trinity.

The doctrine of the Trinity was believed by the Christian church from the beginning, for from the beginning believers acknowledged Jesus as their Lord and their God and prayed to him, though he had prayed to the Father. Yet they remained orthodox Jews, saying in their devotions twice a day, "Hear, O Israel, the Lord is our God, the Lord is one Lord".[4]

Josephus ascribes the command to say the shema twice daily to Moses.[5] The Mishnah takes the saying of the shema twice daily for granted.[6]

In fact, if it had not been recorded in Matthew 28:19 that Jesus taught the disciples the doctrine of the Trinity, we would have to postulate that he had done so. These words of Jesus in Matthew 28:19 encapsulate the doctrine of the Trinity. The name of the Lord remains one name, yet now God is to be known as Father, Son and Holy Spirit—distinct, personal and equal.

The fact that God is Trinity shows that personal relationship is basic reality, that is, that:

(i) There is nothing more ultimate than personal relationship. Being, considered in itself, is an abstraction. Ultimate, true and real being is and always has been being-in-personal-relationship.

(ii) It follows that metaphysics of the Absolute or a theology of an impersonal God, such as Aristotle's, and any theology of Being which is not thought of as being-in-relationship has an error at its centre.

(iii) It follows that the subject matter of theology is not God, but God in his relationship, for the essence of God is in eternal relationship. Relationship with God and with one another is the subject matter

2.   Acts 4:11-12.
3.   Acts 2:21, cf. Paul in Acts 16:31; Rom 10:13.
4.   Deuteronomy 6:4.
5.   *Antiquities* 4:7.
6.   *Beracot* 1:1-2.

of Scripture. It teaches the infallible truth inerrantly on these matters. God is Trinity eternally. The first words of the Bible are "In the beginning God created the heaven and the earth", that is, revelation begins with a statement of God in relationship with our environment and ourselves.

THE TRINITY AND PERSONAL RELATIONSHIPS

1. Other-person-centredness

Personal relationship is ultimate reality. The basic requirement for the establishment and maintenance of true personal relationship is *other-person-centredness*, that is, genuine interest in the other person and his welfare and the forwarding of that welfare by every appropriate means at one's disposal. This means that absolute other-person-centredness is the most real thing in being a person.

There can be no trace of self-centredness in true personal relationship. The smallest degree of self-centredness diminishes the relationship. Complete self-centredness is the negation of any personal relationship. The complete absence of relationship between persons is hell.

Since God is *actus purus* (i.e., there is no mere potentiality in him), his other-person-centredness is complete, and active in conferring benefits on the other person all the time.

Thus we read that in the Trinity the Father always gives the Son everything:

> *...as the Father has life in himself, even so he gave to the Son to have life in himself.*[7]
>
> *The Father loves the Son and has given all things into his hand.*[8]
>
> *The Father loves the Son and shows him all things that he does.*[9]

Similarly of the Son we read of his true personal response to the initiatives of the Father:

7. John 5:26.
8. John 3:35.
9. John 5:20.

I seek not my own will, but the will of him that sent me.[10]

The Son's response springs from his other-person-centredness:

I love the Father and as the Father gave me commandment, even so I do.[11]

The Son does nothing of himself but as the Father taught him.[12]

The Spirit, too, is other-person-centred within the Trinity:

He shall not speak from himself; but whatsoever things he shall hear, these shall he speak.[13]

He does not glorify himself but glorifies the Son, just as the Son does not seek his own glory but the Father's. In the Trinity there is complete mutual other-person-centredness, as:

All things that are mine are thine and thine are mine... All things whatsoever the Father has are mine.[14]

This complete other-person-centredness and mutual self-giving one to the other makes personal knowledge of each other possible. Thus:

The Father knows me and I know the Father.[15]

No-one knows the Son except the Father and no-one knows the Father except the Son and he to whom the Son wills to reveal him.[16]

You shall know that I am in my Father, and you in me and I in you.[17]

Other-person-centredness is activity; it is not merely benevolence but beneficence.

It is more usually described by the Hebrew word *chesed,* the Greek *agape,* the Latin *caritas,* and the English *love,* all of which are terms for other-person-centredness in attitude and action.

10. John 5:30.
11. John 14:31.
12. John 8:28.
13. John 16:13.
14. John 17:10; 16:15.
15. John 10:15.
16. Matt 11:27.
17. John 14:20.

God's centre of his activity is in the welfare of the other. It is not confined to the relations between the persons of the Trinity, but being basic to his nature of relationship extends to his creation. Thus:

The Lord is good to all and his tender mercies are over all that he has made.[18]

He makes his sun to rise on the evil and the good and sends rain on the just and the unjust.[19]

He is kind to the unthankful and evil.[20]

This absolute other-person-centredness, which is the inalienable element in perfect, personal relationship, as in the Trinity, is the ground of our salvation.

God commended his own love toward us, in that while we were yet sinners, Christ died for us.[21]

God so loved the world that he gave his only Son.[22]

It is a great assurance to know that God is infinitely concerned with our welfare and with advancing it. His whole infinite being is absolutely and always centred on each of us, and he is always engaged in advancing our benefit.

The most ultimate thing that can be said of God is that he is Trinity. He always has been, always will be. Three persons in one God, one God in personal relationship within himself.

He has created man in his own image and likeness. This means that man is fundamentally a being in personal relationship, in relationship with God and with his fellows.

Therefore, humanity's nature is created to facilitate personal relationship to God and to one another.

The establishment, maintenance and deepening of personal relationship is the true object for human activity, relationship with God and with fellow men.

18. Psalm 145:9.
19. Matthew 5:45.
20. Luke 6:35.
21. Romans 5:8.
22. John 3:16.

Human beings are spirits, created for fellowship with God. Deepening of friendship with God is the object of our spiritual life. Biblical spirituality is friendship with God, that is, growing in knowing God. Jesus calls those who follow him his friends. He shares with them what he has received from the Father.[23] There is a mutual dwelling of us in the Father and the Son, as the Father and the Son indwell us by the Spirit.[24]

Contrast this biblical faith and spirituality with what goes under the name of religion and spirituality.

Religion arises out of ignorance of God as the result of rebellion. Those who refuse to have God in their knowledge, God gives up to religion.[25]

But the Christian faith is friendship with God, knowing God or, rather, being known by him, indwelling him and he indwelling us, through the Spirit. The Christian faith and the Christian life are firmly trinitarian.

Holiness is knowing God and obeying him as a result of personal relationship with him, through knowing and meditating on his word and consequently being consciously in his presence. This is biblical spirituality.

Humanity was created in the image of God to have fellowship also one with the other. Thus the establishment and deepening of personal relationship between one another is also the true object of human activity.

Since God is in personal relationship within himself it follows that true personal relationship is blissful and is the basis of happiness. This truth is confirmed in human experience. We find that enjoyment is deepened when it is shared.

Men and women are to imitate God in being absolutely other-person-centred, without any trace of self-centredness. That is, they are to be benevolent and beneficent to everybody, in attitude and action, to forward the welfare of others, as their own circumstances and responsibilities allow.

23. John 15:15.
24. John 14:23; 17:21, 23, 26.
25. Romans 1:18-32.

The virtues which are peculiarly Christian virtues spring from this absolute-other-person-centredness. Such virtues are, for example: forgiveness, humility, meekness and long suffering.

In the non-Christian world these characteristics are not regarded as virtues but are seen as weaknesses (cf. Sulla's self composed epitaph).[26] But they are strongly and consistently inculcated in Scripture and are exemplified in the lives of the biblical saints, and pre-eminently in Jesus.

The concept of other-person-centredness controls the content of these virtues. For example, humility is not servility, but a forgetfulness of self in the presence of the other person. Meekness is not weakness and timidity, but the absence of self-assertiveness, the absence of self-centredness. Moses was by no means a weak man, yet he is described as the meekest man in all the earth.[27]

Humility is an essential virtue if other-person-centredness is to be perfect and complete. Humility is the taking of one's thoughts off oneself in order to be mindful of the welfare of the other. In true relationship between persons, neither should be thinking of themselves at the expense of the other.

God is humble. He does not direct attention to himself for his own sake. He is not concerned with status, but he is concerned that others should recognize their relationship to him, for this is their welfare, for this is truth. The ignoring of the truth, or its denial, is always to the disadvantage of those who do this.

God does not blow his own trumpet! He does not bear witness to himself, except when knowledge about the truth, about himself, is to the advantage of the hearer. Thus Jesus does not proclaim his deity, except indirectly, in order that the listener might arrive at this conclusion himself; or in answer to a direct question.

God commands, "Let another man praise you and not your own mouth, a stranger and not your own lips".[28] Paul follows this injunction. He did not commend himself unless it was for the benefit of his readers.[29]

The clearest expression in Scripture of God's humility is in Isaiah

26. The Roman general and dictator, whose epitaph read: "No friend ever out-stripped me in doing good, no enemy in doing harm."
27. Numbers 12:3.
28. Proverbs 27:2.
29. 2 Corinthians 12:19.

57:15: "For thus says the high and lofty One who inhabits eternity, whose name is Holy: I dwell in the high and holy place, with him also that is of a contrite and humble spirit, to revive the spirit of the humble and to revive the heart of the contrite ones".

Humility characterized the life of Jesus.[30] He invited the burdened in spirit to learn from him in this respect: "I am meek and lowly in heart". "I am among you as he who serves."[31] This self-testimony was for the purpose of our following him for our good.

Other-person-centredness is only another way of saying love; that is, love in its biblical meaning.

2. Communication

The second essential requirement for personal relationship is personal *communication*. There must be mutual indwelling of person with person through mutual communication of person to person. Thus in the creation narrative we read of God conferring within the Trinity. God said, "Let us make man in our image, after our likeness..."[32] It is entirely appropriate that there should be an intimation of the trinitarian nature of God at this point, for the narrative had reached the stage of the creation of man "in the image of God", that is to say, a being-in-personal-relationship. This verse is not a proof of the doctrine of the Trinity, but since God is eternally Trinity, as is established from elsewhere in Scripture, and since all Scripture is spoken to us by God,[33] it is perverse not to acknowledge that his trinitarian nature is reflected in the language of revelation at this most appropriate juncture. "God created man in his own image, in the image of God created he him; male and female created he them." No sooner had he created them thus, as personal-beings-in-relationship, as he is personal-being-in-relationship, than he spoke to them communicating his mind and will to them, telling them that he was giving them his own dominion over his creation and that he was providing plenteously for their needs.

Communication is essential for personal relationship. Communication is a mutual activity. One party must speak and the other hear

30. Matthew 11:28, 29.
31. Luke 22:27.
32. Genesis 1:26.
33. 2 Timothy 3:16.

and respond by speaking, which in turn must be heard and responded to. Failure in communication results in the atrophy and death of the relationship.

In our relations with one another we must give ourselves to one another, we must communicate our minds and our feelings by our words to one another, whether through voice, or gesture, or expression, or action. We dare not indulge in the sinful luxury of huffiness. Refusal to communicate weakens and kills personal relationship in which happiness is alone to be found. If we are to have personal relationship with God, God must speak to us, communicating himself to us. We must hear his word and respond by faith, believing that word, trusting it and obeying it, for to us God is his word. We, in turn, must respond by communing with God, speaking to him in praise and thanks and prayer.

God has created men and women as persons, to be in personal relationship with him and with one another, and to speak to one another, expressing their thoughts, feelings and personality to him and to one another.

The image of God, which is persons in relationship, is built on the attributes of conscious thought, will, feeling, sense of right and wrong and of justice and of judgement, the concept of God and a sense of his existence, the gift of language with similar attributes. On these are built the relationship of friendship and fellowship, and the sharing of a common life through mutual self-giving.

When man broke his fellowship with God through self-will and disobedience, his personal relationship with God and with his fellow man was marred and progressively destroyed. Thus he lost the image of God which is perfect personal relationship, which expresses itself in active other-person-centredness and for which he had been created. In this sense, he irretrievably lost the image of God. He became irreversibly self-centred towards God and towards his fellows. But in another sense he retained it, for he remained a person, created for personal relationship. Thus, after the Fall, man is still said to be in the image of God, and this is the ground why murder is forbidden[34] for murder is the nadir of personal relationship; no action less other-person-centred can be imagined, nor more out of keeping with the image of God in which we were created.

34. Genesis 9:6.

It is in Jesus Christ that God's image in man has been restored. He was perfectly other-person-centred, actively supplying our needs, fully trusting and obeying his Father. Through the Spirit of Jesus, those who are in Christ are being transformed into that same image[35] and so the purpose of God in creation is being fulfilled.[36]

In the Garden of Eden, God began personal communion with man but man broke off that relationship by disobedience. Had God accepted the breach there would have been no further need for God to speak to us. But it was his will and purpose to restore the fellowship, and this meant that he continued and continues to speak to mankind. He has done this in a variety of ways but for us today he speaks through Scripture, his written word.

Since humanity's relationships reflect God's relationships, being the image of God, human language, which describes them, is a true vehicle for God to use to communicate his relationship to us. Thus our God-talk is univocal and not analogical. We may know God truly though still dimly, in this life. He has spoken to us, and speaks to us, in the words of Scripture.

God had each of us in mind when he breathed out the words of Scripture. Our mind boggles at the idea that God had each of us in mind when he inspired the written, and therefore unchangeable, words. But God is infinite in knowledge and power. It presents no problem to him. As Paul says, "What was written before time was written for our instruction",[37] and "All Scripture has been breathed out by God (i.e., spoken by God) that God's man (i.e., person) might be thoroughly equipped for every good work" (i.e., the Bible is sufficient to guide us in all our relationships).[38]

In this connection Jesus' words to the Sadducees are most interesting. He asked them, "Have you never read what was spoken to you by God".[39] Notice it is the Scripture that Jesus said was spoken by God. Something we have in our hand, something permanent, and which we can read. But note especially that these words are spoken by God to the

35. 2 Corinthians 3:18.
36. Romans 8:29.
37. Romans 15:4.
38. 2 Timothy 3:16f.
39. Matthew 22:31.

present day reader. In Scripture God speaks to us. He communicates with us. Of course it is through the Holy Spirit who indwells us that we hear those words, just as it was through the Holy Spirit that the words were addressed to us in the first place, so many centuries ago.

If the words of Scripture are God's words to us which he is addressing to us in order to communicate himself to us (and this is the clear view of Jesus and the apostles),[40] it follows that what God is saying, what he is communicating to us, is infallible and inerrant. This is axiomatic for the God of Truth. If anything we regard as Scripture is wrong in what it is saying to us about God and ourselves and his will for our relations with him and with one another, that is, about "every good work", or if the Scripture is deceiving us about its own character, then *ipso facto* it is not Scripture, not breathed out by God. It has got into the canon by mistake.

The testimony of our Lord and the apostles is to the Scripture, that is, to what we have in our hand, not to the thoughts of the writers, or to their background, but to the propositions they have written and which we may read. It is this word that God is speaking to us. The way to understand what we read is by the historico-grammatical method, not the historico-critical. The study of sources, dates, authorship, is interesting and may be useful for apologetics, but unless it makes clearer the meaning of the written words, unless, that is, it makes clearer what God is saying to us, it is ultimately irrelevant knowledge. But, for the most part, the meaning of Scripture is on the surface, especially if the reader knows the text of the whole of Scripture and in particular the Old Testament as well as the writer did, for Scripture illuminates Scripture, having ultimately only one author, God.

It is important to maintain the view of Scripture which Jesus held and which the apostles held and which the whole Christian church held till recently. Otherwise it is not possible to continue to be a Christian, that is, to have fellowship with God through knowing him, to submit to the lordship of Christ and so be saved, to live the life of faith, and to have a sure and steadfast hope, for it is only through God communicating with us that we can know him personally. Communication is essential for personal relationship.

40. Matthew 19:4, 5; 22:31; Acts 4:25.

3. Fairness

A third equally essential element of true personal relationship is *fairness* or righteousness or justice. This consists of treating people according to what they deserve.

Thus constantly we read in Scripture that: God renders to every man according to their works,[41] and that God is no respecter of persons.[42] Justice is essential for personal relations. Any trace of injustice breaks down the relationship. Thus we read not only "God is love"[43] but first we read "God is light and in him is no darkness at all".[44] God is a righteous God.

In the Trinity, the relationships between the person are eternally unchanging, but in human life relationships admit of degrees, and the degree of relationship modifies what is deserved.

Thus a rich man who has no relatives would be acting righteously if he left in his will all his estate to be distributed equally to the inhabitants of his village, say $100 to each of the 1,000 inhabitants; but he would not be acting righteously if he were to include wife and children equally with the other inhabitants.

Thus, though on the one hand God's tender mercies are over all his works,[45] yet he works all things together for good to those who love him, to those who are called according to his purpose.[46] His righteousness, i.e., his giving to those what they deserve, expresses itself in the salvation of his people. The God-given victories of the people of God over their enemies are "the righteous acts of the Lord".[47] God's righteousness and his salvation of his people are the same.[48]

4. Faithfulness

A fourth essential for personal relationship is *faithfulness* (i.e., steadfastness to the relationship).

41. Proverbs 24:12; Romans 2:6.
42. Acts 10:34.
43. 1 John 4:8.
44. 1 John 1:5.
45. Psalm 145:9.
46. Romans 8:28.
47. 1 Samuel 12:7.
48. Isaiah 51:5; 56:1.

Faithfulness is not the same as loyalty, in spite of the fact that it is translated by loyalty in some modern English versions of the Bible. Faithfulness is based on truth. Where loyalty does not coincide with faithfulness, it is a vice, and not a virtue.

God is a faithful God. Thus is his description in both Old and New Testaments.[49] He remains true to the relationship he has entered into.

5. Order
Order is the fifth necessity for personal relationship.

Order arises out of differences. There are differences within the Trinity. The Father, the Son, and the Spirit share one essence but are distinct. There are differences among the members of the human race.

The most obvious difference is the difference in sex. Men and women share an identical nature but there are observable differences physically, emotionally and mentally. The differences are not differences in equality, but make men and women distinct. The same is true of individuals. Each is distinct. They are not mere clones.

The distinctions of creation are purposeful, since they are the result of a wise sovereign creator. They are for the purpose of experiencing and strengthening relationships, of advancing the image of God within us. That is to say, they are for the purpose of serving one another, for this is the image of God.

Were mankind to be identical clones there would be no need or opportunity of serving one another, for all would have identical resources within themselves. That is to say there would be no possibility of personal relationship through mutual self-giving.

The distinctions within mankind are opportunities for service, that is, for reflecting the character of God who is among us as one who serves.[50]

Order is the structure in which service functions smoothly.

We see order exemplified in the Trinity. The personal relationship within the Trinity is an ordered relationship—Father, Son, Spirit. The essence of order in relationship is that it cannot be reversed without affecting the relationship. Father-Son cannot become Son-Father without changing the relationship.

Relationship implies responsibility, and if this is to be discharged,

49. Deuteronomy 7:9; 1 Peter 4:19.
50. Luke 22:27.

a priority of responsibility must be recognised in each relationship. That is to say, true personal relationships have a recognised and gladly accepted order within them.

Priority in order implies responsibility for initiating thought and action in line with the principle of other-person-centredness. This priority in responsibility is described in the Bible as headship. Too often we interpret scriptural headship in conformity with headship as exercised in sinful humanity, where it is the equivalent of dominance and the imposition of one's own will on others.

But there is no trace of this in God or in the world as God created it. There is headship in the Trinity, accompanied by the response of glad submission and recognition of authority. Divine headship consists of responsibility for initiating benefits evoking the corresponding response of thanks and obedience.

Thus the Father loves the Son and shows him everything he does and the Son acknowledges the Father is greater than the Son.[51] The Father sends the Son.[52] The Father gives him everything.[53] As the Father has life in himself, so he has given the Son to have life in himself.[54]

These relationships between the Father and the Son are eternal relationships. They do not have a beginning. The relationship of Father and Son described as "the Son being in the bosom of the Father"[55] is an eternal relationship. This terminology indicates order in the relationship.

So, too, in the relationship of the Spirit to the Father and the Son, there is order. The Spirit proceeds from the Father[56] and is poured forth on believers by the Son.[57] He is sent by the Father.[58] He is sent by the Son.[59]

This order in the Trinity does not imply inequality, as though, in the modern sense of the words, one is superior and the other inferior,

51. John 14:28.
52. John 4:34.
53. John 13:3.
54. John 5:26.
55. John 1:18.
56. John 15:26.
57. Acts 2:33.
58. John 14:26.
59. John 16:7.

but the order does indicate different functions and responses within the personally related Trinity.

God has created the world in accordance with his nature and has created humanity in his image, after his likeness. There is order in the creation and there is order within the personal relationship of humanity. This order within humanity does not imply inequality between the persons but it does indicate that there are different functions and responses to the persons in relationship.

In Scripture God is revealed as head of Christ and Christ as head of the church.[60]

The Father takes the initiative with regard to the Son, showing him everything he does, giving him everything, sharing with him his life-in-himselfness (John 5:19-27).

The Son responds by always doing that which pleases the Father, by always doing and only doing what the Father shows him, by doing always that which the Father commands.

Similarly, in humanity, God has created order. In the same Scripture passage, which teaches that God is the head of Christ and Christ the head of the church, God has revealed that man is the head of woman.[61] This passage controls the meaning of the word "head". Man's headship in relation to woman is of the same character as the headship of God to Christ and of Christ to man, and of Christ to the church. The divine headship which God has conferred on man in the man-woman relationship contains no element in it which is not found in the Father's headship in the Trinity, or Christ's headship in humanity. That is, it is entirely other-person-centred, without so much as a trace of self-centredness. Our Lord affirmed, as we all experience, that in the world headship has been twisted into something quite different. "The kings of the nations have lordship over them… but you shall not be so… I am in the midst of you as he that serves".[62] Headship after the divine pattern is responsibility for taking thought and initiative in forwarding the welfare of those of whom one is head. It consists of nothing else. The responsibility is to further the welfare to the best of one's abilities and circumstances of the other party in the relationship.

60. 1 Corinthians 11:3, Ephesians 5:23.
61. 1 Corinthians 11:3.
62. Luke 22:25-26; cf. Mark 10:42-45.

We all have this responsibility towards others, but in each relationship there is a priority which circumstances or created nature indicates. Authority accompanies the discharging of true responsibility. The response should contain the recognition of this, thanks for the benefit and abiding honour of the one who is giving or has given himself in furtherance of one's welfare.

All men and women have responsibility for one another's welfare according to the changing circumstances of their relationship. It is the relationship which creates the responsibility. In the flux of the circumstances of life, men and women come into many and often changing relationships which carry with them the responsibility of advancing the other's welfare. This responsibility arising from the circumstances of the relationship, carries with it authority for beneficent action. The recipient of the benefit should acknowledge the authority and receive and give thanks for the benefit, and honour the giver.

There are, however, some personal relationships which are not the result of changing circumstances in life but are permanent, such as those which result from birth. Our relationship with God and the relationship between men and women partake of this permanent character. The Scriptures make clear that man is the head of woman. Men and women together make up humanity. Men and women are almost 100 per cent the same in physical, emotional and mental make up. Yet there are differences between them, not only physically, which is obvious, but also emotionally and mentally, as careful observation will confirm. These differences do not make one sex better than the other or superior to another, but they further the different responsibilities which belong to the order of their relationship. The differences between masculinity and femininity is part of creation and is consequently purposeful, to enable the responsibilities of the relationship to be perfectly fulfilled.

Sin, which is essentially self-centred, has not only destroyed the personal relationship which man has to God, namely the response of honour, faith, thanks and submission, but has also greatly marred the relationship of men and women. Men have turned headship into self-centred lordship and dominance. They have used their natures, physical, mental and emotional, not to serve but to dominate. Women, too, may use their gifts of nature to dominate.

The re-creation of men and women in Christ does not destroy the order in their relationship but restores it to its divine character in being motivated and directed by love, that is, biblical, divine love of other-person-centredness in attitude and action.

Relationships may change—e.g., the parent-child relationship begins at the point of conception, grows to the birth, remains stable through childhood but changes again with growing maturity, and may reverse itself in old age. Each stage in the relationship means a change in the responsibility and thus of the authority inherent in it. But the obligation of honour does not evaporate when the responsibility ceases.

So, too, in the *ad hoc* relationship of daily living and secular life. Circumstances may create a relationship and hence the responsibility for caring for the other's welfare, and changing circumstances may reverse the relationship and hence the responsibility and its consequent authority.

Relationship within the Trinity is unchanging and immutable, and so the order of Father, Son, Spirit remains stable.

But many relationships in modern society are flexible and so responsibility for the other person's welfare is flexible and is determined by the flux of circumstances.

However, there are some human relations that are more stable than this, being based on human nature as God has created it.

These include the relationship of men and women as such. But even in this, it is possible to imagine unusual situations where the normal order of responsibility is affected by the circumstances.

But only those involved in such circumstances can determine what those circumstances require. Thus in the congregation, only the congregation can determine who should lead it in the circumstances they find themselves in.

Absolute ordinations are condemned by the sixth canon of Chalcedon.[63] Yet these days all ordinations are absolute. If this were

---

63. "No man is to be ordained without a charge, neither presbyter, nor deacon, nor anyone who is in the ecclesiastical order; but whoever is ordained must be appointed particularly to some charge in a church of a city, or in the country, or in a martyr or monastery. But as regards those who are ordained without any charge, the holy synod has determined, that such an ordination is to be held void, and cannot have any effect anywhere, to the reproach of the ordainer." Canon 6 of the Council of Chalcedon, 451.

remedied, so that only those are ordained who are recognized as minis-
tering to a congregation as their ministers, and they remained ordained
only so long as they minister acceptably in that congregation unless they
are called and recognised by another congregation, then it would be
possible for women to be ordained, at least in theory, for in practice it
would not be often (perhaps never) that a spiritual, Bible-instructed
congregation concluded that the circumstances it found itself in meant
that it should recognise a woman as its teacher and chief minister.

The sin in the Garden of Eden involved a reversal of the created
order of relationship. Instead of God, man, woman, animal, the
priority became animal (the serpent), woman, man and God, and his
word was excluded altogether.

After the Fall, God re-established the order, but now, because of
sin, it would be accompanied by pain.

God is ultimate reality. The revelation that his nature is Trinitarian
brings us the knowledge that personal relationships are ultimate reality,
and are blissful. The revelation of his character brings us the knowledge
how we may go about establishing our relationship with God and with
one another more perfectly, by loving God with all our heart and
loving our neighbour as ourselves, by giving ourselves in personal
communication to one another, by absolute fairness and faithfulness in
our dealings with each other, and by being mindful of the order and
priority which God has created, so that our relationships may flower
with the bliss that God intends for us in our friendship with him and
with one another.

PART 2

THE
CHRISTIAN
WORLDVIEW:

MISCELLANEOUS
WRITINGS

The following selection of theological writings represents the breadth of Broughton Knox's thought on the doctrine of God. After a short introductory piece on the importance of clear thought and doctrine ('As a man thinks, so he is'), the remaining works cluster around three major subjects:

1. *God as the Sovereign Creator and Judge of all (chapters 2-6)*
2. *The centrality of Christ: his person, his work, his continued presence with us through the Spirit (chapters 7-14)*
3. *The nature and authority of the Scriptures as God's revelation (chapters 15-23)*

Chapters 24 and 25 are exegetical papers, serving as examples of Dr Knox's approach to the Bible.

Chapter 1

AS A MAN THINKS, SO HE IS[1]

*T*HE BIBLE ENUNCIATES AN IMPORTANT principle of human behaviour in a verse in Proverbs 23:7 which reads: "As [a man] thinketh in his heart so he is".[2]

Modern Western life (of which Australia is a part) has very little thought for anything else except having a good time and seeking its own pleasure. The emptiness of modern Western life and thought means that we have neither principles nor determination by which to resist the inroads of error, whether in the form of immorality or Communism. We modern Christians are involved in the Western predicament of unbelief. Our neighbours don't believe, the group in which we mix don't believe and as a consequence we are tempted to water down our own faith. As a whole it is true to say that we modern Christians have relaxed our trust in God as Sovereign Lord, the Creator and Controller of all. We have relaxed our belief in God's holiness, and thus in his judgement, in spite of the fact that the Bible clearly says that God's judgement is so complete that every idle word will come up for examination. We have relaxed our conviction on the centrality of Jesus Christ in history, Jesus who came from God to be our Saviour, who is the one through whom God has come into a relationship with mankind for the purpose of blessing and salvation. "As a man thinks, so he is." Our modern Christianity has become weak in faith and as a result is flabby in witness. It has no real message to the God-forgetting society around us. As individuals we engage in little personal evangelism, and as congregations we have a very weak witness. I do not say that we don't invite people to church, but do we testify to Jesus Christ as the only Mediator between God and man? Because our beliefs are weak we turn aside from evangelism whether personal or

1.   Protestant Faith Broadcast, 12 September 1976.
2.   KJV.

corporate and instead engage our attention in building up our institutions and church organisations. These church institutions and organizations appear to be more tangible to those weak in faith because they are things of this world.

If we modern Christians are to be saved in the judgement which is inevitable, we must deepen our faith in God as Sovereign Lord, in the Holy God who judges, who is yet the loving God who saves. We need to renew our faith in the purposes of God which find expression in Jesus Christ crucified, risen and coming again. For God's purposes did not cease 2,000 years ago at the resurrection but are still being completed and will be completed. We need to renew our faith in Christ as Lord and in his coming kingdom. If we believe these things we will have something to say to our God-forgetting community, but we cannot generate a renewed faith out of our own resources. First we need to pray for one another's faith, for faith is the gift of God; and secondly we need to have fellowship with one another on the basis of our common faith; for fire kindles fire, and fellowship strengthens faith.

"As a man thinks, so he is." This principle implies that if we are to be Christians we need to keep in the forefront of our minds the facts of revelation. We should think constantly on the great truths that God is Creator and Judge and Saviour; that we have a great future inheritance; that Jesus Christ is the one in whom God has a relationship with us, and through whom we become the sons of God and inheritors of God's purposes. Jesus Christ is Lord!

Chapter 2

*"Then I saw another angel flying in midheaven, with
an eternal gospel to proclaim to those who dwell on
earth, to every nation and tribe and tongue and people;
and he said with a loud voice, "Fear God and give him
glory, for the hour of his judgement has come; and
worship him who made heaven and earth, the sea and
the fountains of water. Another angel, a second, followed
saying, "Fallen, fallen is Babylon the great, she who
made all nations drink the wine of her impure passion."
(Revelation 14:6-8)*

ARTICLE 1 OF THE 39 ARTICLES OF
the Anglican Church states that God is of infinite power, wisdom and
goodness, the creator of everything. We have been considering the
power of God in the gospel, but now I want for a moment to consider
an antecedent manifestation of the power of God; God's power
manifest in creation. The Christian doctrine of creation is very clearly
based in the Bible, it is a very simple and lucid doctrine. It is that mind
controls matter and that God's mind controls everything that we see
around us because he brought it into existence simply by his will and
word. In Genesis 1, "God spoke", or as the opening verse summarises
it "in the beginning God created the heaven and the earth", full stop.
God is the source of your life; of all that you possess, of your whole
environment and of everything in the universe. Or as Psalm 148 puts

---

1. Moore College Chapel sermon, 30 March 1979.

it, "He commanded and they stood fast" or as Revelation 4:11 puts it, "you are worthy to receive honour and glory and power because you have created all things and by your will they were created". So the doctrine of the creation of all of our world, ourselves included, by the will and word of God is a basic doctrine of Scripture. It is the first thing we are taught, and as we have seen, it runs right through into the Book of Revelation and is here in our text. It is a universal truth for everyone: "worship him who made the heaven and the earth, the sea and the fountains of water".[2]

It is a gospel that has to be proclaimed to every nation, tribe, tongue and people. We find it for example very close to the piety of the first Christians in their prayer in Acts 4. They began by addressing God as the creator of the heaven and the earth and of the sea and everything in it. So too it is very prominent in the sermons of the apostles; for example when St Paul is preaching in Athens, he begins by saying he is preaching to them about the God who made the heaven and the earth and the sea. So it is right in the forefront of the Christian news, because creation reflects the power of God and we need to get our world view clear on that point. The almighty, personal God has brought all the world into being through his will expressed in his word, and we, as part of that world, need to adore our creator, to honour him and to praise him and especially to give him thanks. The adoration and praise and thanksgiving should be basic as we worship God, as we come into his presence.

Especially we should thank him, because creation not only reflects the power of God, but also reflects the character of God, his goodness, since creation is very beautiful and good. In Genesis 1 we read, "when God completed his creation he saw it was very good," and that is affirmed by our own judgement. Life is good, relationships and friends are good, the world is beautiful, our bodily functions, appetites, feelings, all bring us pleasure. All of this is built into our nature in order that we might enjoy God's created world and enjoy our friendship with one another. Or as St Paul puts it when he is speaking to the pagans of Asia Minor, "God did good, satisfying your hearts with food and gladness through the fruitful seasons, through the created world".[3] Now it is true that only those who have had their eyes opened by the Saviour

2 .   Revelation 14:7.
3.   Acts 14:16-17.

are able to see the goodness of God in creation. Other people take it for granted, and we are often too inclined to take it for granted ourselves. Nevertheless we should pause and give God thanks daily for his goodness to us in creation. God as a creator-God (creation reflects and expresses his character of goodness) means that he is one who will care for that which he brings into being, having brought it into being through his word. He doesn't just leave it like that because he is good. He is in relationship with his creation through being its creator, and being a good God he will be responsible and will care for his creation. This is hymned and sung about in the Psalms. His tender mercies are over all his works, over the whole of his creation which he cares for. He makes the sun to rise on the just and the unjust because he cares for all. He is responsible for all, having brought them into being, and that responsibility expresses itself in concern for their true welfare. Now responsibility involves authority: if you are responsible for someone then you have authority for that person's welfare in the area of your responsibility. God is responsible for every aspect of our life, he cares for every aspect of our life, and therefore he has authority in every aspect of our life. Now that authority should evoke in us a response of willing and glad obedience and of trust in his care. That is the only response appropriate to authority. If you recognise someone's authority in an area of your life then you obey in that area, you trust in that area. So too God, having tender mercies for us all, has authority over us, and that authority is complete because (as our creator) he has complete responsibility. Therefore we should acknowledge that authority gladly and not rebel against it and seek to be our own authority as though we could be responsible for ourselves. Many people seem to think this way, but it is an absurd notion. They want to go their own way; they take responsibility for themselves in areas where God is responsible, in areas where we should be obeying him. We who belong to him need to be aware of this temptation and turn from it, gladly giving him our obedience and our will. We must acknowledge God's authority by glad obedience and complete and full trust, responding to him as he draws near to us in his goodness.

God's power in creation, of course, doesn't stop with creation. It is complete and absolute. There is a phrase that runs through the Old and New Testament, "nothing is too hard for the Lord". We seem to think that things which are too hard for us may be too hard for God.

That is not so. It cannot be so, of course, and we have got to absorb that truth. Even the evil wills of men are within his complete control. For example, in Isaiah 10:5-19 God speaks of the Assyrians, that blood-thirsty and cruel nation that had developed modern methods of warfare and were sweeping away the old fashioned variety of folk armies. God says that, in their cruelty and in their success, they are in reality the axe in God's hand to bring about his purposes of judgement, the rod in God's hand to bring about his purposes of chastisement; but they are quite unaware of it. They think it is their own cleverness that has achieved their results, they haven't glorified God, nor do they in any way submit to him. Yet in spite of their sinfulness, they are completely within the power of God; he has them in his hand and they cannot possibly shake him though he shakes the Assyrians as a rod to chastise the armies of the nations. There is nothing in the world outside God's sovereignty and our Lord reminds us that this should comfort us. "Do not fear", he says, "even the hairs on your head are numbered, the sparrows that fly through the sky, none of them is outside God's control; how much more you".[4] And so God's sovereignty is a ground for our comfort and strength in his service.

Creation implies purpose. It is the act of a will, and will is purposeful. Purpose will imply an objective and it will of course include an assessment as to when the objective is attained. It will include judgement—and so this is the second great truth of the gospel. The first is that God is sovereign, the second that God will be judge. Both are contained in our verse: "I saw another angel flying in midheaven with an eternal gospel to proclaim to those who dwell on earth, to every nation and tribe and tongue and people; and he said with a loud voice, 'Fear God and give him glory, for the hour of his judgement has come; and worship him who made heaven and earth, the sea and the fountains of water.'" Judgement is the most important truth for us to realise. Running parallel with the concept of God as creator is the fact of God as judge. Now neither of these truths is limited by culture. We all understand our dependence on God and therefore we will all understand that he is our creator, once it is brought to us clearly and with authority from Scripture. And we all

4.   Matthew 10:29-31.

have a guilty conscience, therefore we all understand the rightfulness of judgement, and so it is a message that belongs to every nation, tribe, tongue and people. You don't have to turn it into your own culture, you don't have to have an 'Australian theology' on these truths or on any other to tell you what is true, because the doctrine that God is your creator and sovereign Lord of the world overleaps every culture, the most primitive or the most sophisticated. All can apprehend it and it meets a truth in their own experience of the world. That God is going to be their judge also overleaps every cultural barrier and meets the truth of the experience of their own hearts.

Now people don't like judgement; you don't like judgement and I don't like judgement. It upsets the present most abominably, but it is a truth. It must be true if God is God, but people find other methods of avoiding this concept of God. The ancient world had idols, and idols are an impoverished sort of God, with no creative power, no real interest in people's rightful behaviour and no capacity for judgement. Today idols of that kind are out, but we have a way of avoiding the truth of God as creator, and therefore as judge, by appealing to evolution, to explain the world around us by a lot of mechanical accidents. It is a theory which has no evidence to support it, a theory contradictory to the evidence such as there is, and of course, a theory which runs counter to all our understanding of the way the physical world works when you actually observe it running down rather than running up. Nevertheless it is extraordinarily widespread, and doubtless it lodges in your mind as a truth because you have been told it is so. But nevertheless it is a foolish theory without any foundation, and it takes the place of believing that by the will of the Creator, things are what they are. He may have used whatever process he liked or he need not have had any process. You can have whatever views you like on that, so long as you know that it is the word of God that brought everything into being exactly as it is now. The word of God and nothing else is the source of the power which has created this world in the form we have it, and we are therefore in the world very close to God. He is its creator and he is a purposeful creator, and therefore he will be an assessor and a judge, and that judgement will be complete. We will have to give an account of every idle word and if of every idle word, then everything else will certainly be brought within the net of God's judgement. This truth will include us; we will stand before the judgement seat of Christ to give an account of things done in the body.

Therefore as we bring before those to whom we minister the truth of God's judgement, it won't be, as it were, standing back dispassionately, but it will be with tears. If you aren't able to preach the judgement of God with tears, you haven't apprehended either the awfulness of the judgement or the reality of your own or your hearer's situation. That is why when St Paul in Acts 20 gives us a thumbnail sketch of his ministry, and tells us how he did it, he mentions more than once that it was "with tears". Now those were not tears because of what he was suffering, but they were tears because of his sympathy with the predicament of his hearers in urging them to turn to God and save themselves from this wicked generation. So if we don't preach with tears we will not be preaching truly and we certainly won't be preaching effectively. We must, in other words, preach with deep sympathy. You may not be an Eastern Mediterranean type who weeps, nevertheless you must have the same attitude of deep sympathy with those to whom you bring the gospel. Otherwise your words will not be of any use, for they won't be the words of Christ, who wept over Jerusalem as he saw the judgement that was coming.

When St Paul preached before Felix, you may remember, he preached righteousness, self-control and judgement to come. Now Felix was married to a Jewess of sorts, and so presumably he would know the doctrine of creation very well. For him, Paul didn't need to begin with the Creator as he did at Athens, with their pantheon of gods who hadn't created the world and who weren't going to judge the world. There, he began with creation, and finished with judgement. Now when he preached to Felix, he preached about righteousness, self-control and the consequence of all that, namely, judgement to come, and he preached with such effect that Felix trembled, so we read in Acts (24:25).

Now unless you understand your predicament, you won't understand the gospel, because the gospel is a gospel of salvation from an awful predicament, a real predicament—which the world is in, which Jerusalem was in and for which its people suffered severely. Every individual is in this predicament and will suffer the consequences when after death comes the judgement, as Hebrew 9:27 puts it. But it is Christ who rescues us from the judgement to come, because God in his care and love for his creation has provided a way of escape, has provided a salvation in Christ. Christ then is the power of

God to exercise God's sovereignty in rescuing us from the predicament we have involved ourselves in by refusing to thank him or to obey him or to trust him, although he cares for us and has given us all things. And so the gospel will certainly centre on Christ and him crucified. But it doesn't make much sense unless you understand why Christ was crucified. It is so that he might rescue us from the wrath to come. And God's judgement also reminds us that in it all, as we preach the gospel, he will vindicate us and we are able therefore to commit our cause to him. We may be suffering wrongfully in this world as we preach the gospel. St Paul certainly experienced that, and so did St Peter. But Peter reminds us that those who suffer righteously for God's sake should commit their cause to God, the faithful creator and the one who judges righteously, and we will be vindicated as we serve him and bring this eternal gospel to every tribe, nation, tongue and people.

Chapter 3

They did not know that I gave them the corn and multiplied the silver and gold which they used for Baal. Therefore will I take back my corn in the time thereof and will pluck away my wool and my flax.
(Hosea 2:8-9)

I WILL TAKE THESE TWO VERSES OR parts of them as an introduction to a theme that runs through the Bible. These verses refer to a period of ancient Israel when they were suffering from drought. We ourselves are in one of our most severe droughts and our sympathies and our prayers go out to those who are bearing the brunt of the drought, who are seeing their livelihood diminishing, perhaps vanishing, and yet are not able to do anything about it; their life's work disappearing before their eyes. Our sympathy should go out to them and our prayers should go out to those who are suffering like that.

Droughts are natural disasters like earthquakes and floods. But their evil consequences are the result of sin. Had we not fallen into sin we would have been given, by our relationship with God, the knowledge to eliminate the evil from natural events. For example, Agabus in Acts was given a word from God about a famine, by which word the Christians were able to avoid very largely, the evil in that natural event. We also know, many centuries before, that Joseph was given a word from God warning the people of Egypt that there would be seven years of drought. That warning came from the power of God through his Spirit and they

1. An address delivered at St Paul's Anglican Church, Chatswood, Sydney on 6 September, 1982, and also given as a sermon in the Moore College Chapel.

were able to take measures to alleviate the evil of the event.

I believe that had we continued in true fellowship with God, the evil of these natural disasters would have vanished. You may remember what Jesus said in John 5:20, "the Father shows me everything that he does". Jesus' relationship with the Father was so complete and perfect that there was a common exchange of knowledge in this matter, and I am quite sure that had we remained in the fellowship with God which he intended for us in this world, the evil of these natural events would have been eliminated through our fellowship with the Father. And so we can say that the evil of the natural events is a result of humanity's sin. It is not, of course, necessarily the sin of the people who are suffering most; we know that very clearly from holy Scripture.

Natural catastrophes, though they fall on us, (and we can't say we don't deserve them), don't necessarily fall on those who especially deserve them. For example, Jesus said of the man who was born blind that neither he nor his parents had sinned; nevertheless that blindness was doubtless the result of humanity's sin.[2] Again, he said of those on whom the tower of Siloam fell, "don't think that they are especially sinners above everybody else; that is not so. They were sinners but you also are sinners. Unless you repent you will receive the same judgement".[3] In the events of life, whatever they might be, whether sickness like the man born blind, or a natural event like the fall of the tower of Siloam, or a political event like Pilate mingling the blood of the Galileans with their sacrifices and putting them to death,[4] if we turn to God he will be in it with us. The Lord Jesus shared the consequences of man's sin in the life he lived on earth. God allows these things to happen to us in this sinful world for good purposes, if we are his children. We know that from the story of Job.

It was to the glory of God and for his growth in the knowledge of God that those terrible disasters overtook Job. They didn't overtake him especially for his sinfulness, because we are told that that wasn't the case. And so as we get involved in sadnesses and events that are disastrous from one point of view, let us never take our eyes off our Heavenly Father who controls every event and has promised that

2.   John 9:1-3.
3.   Luke 13:1-5.
4.   Luke 13:1-2.

nothing will take place in our lives which is not for our good. He works in all things for good for those who love him. And so an event like a drought is an opportunity for us to turn back to him. We need to thank him for the forgiveness that wipes out the sin and thank him for the promise of hope for the future and especially that promise of eternity. So this is a time for turning back to God in prayer; as Peter says in chapter 5 of his first letter, "humble yourselves under the mighty hand of God and he will exalt you in due time". Or as James says in chapter 5 of his letter, "is anybody in trouble? Let him pray".

Sometimes God allows a natural disaster to overtake a country for the purpose of bringing that country back to repentance. We wonder in awe that they are a chastisement for some gross breach of the will of God of which the inhabitants are guilty. Take, for example, the story of Saul and the Gibeonites.[5] The Gibeonites, as you know, were people of Hittite origin who lived in the land before the Israelites arrived there, but through stratagem managed to get Joshua to promise them by God that they would be allowed to go on living where they were. Now that must have been a notorious fact: everyone must have known it. These Gibeonites were not Israelites, but were living amongst the Israelites. Why? Well, of course, the children would be told "Joshua had promised them that they might continue there". However, King Saul sought to eliminate them. That was a clear breach of the covenant and God visited the whole land with drought as a punishment. The purpose of this punishment was to bring the Israelites to recognise that they couldn't flout God's will, which they know well, and avoid the wrath of their creator, the God with whom they were in covenant relationship.

Now the verse that I quoted at the beginning came many years after the time of King Saul, and there was another drought. This time the prophet makes clear that God was sending the drought because the people of God were completely oblivious to him, attributing all the fertility of the soil not to the God of heaven and earth, but to their little local fertility gods, their Baals. They were oblivious to God, "they did not know that I gave them the corn therefore I will take back my corn and my wool".

Now surely this is exactly what Australia's situation is at the present

5.   2 Samuel 21:1, 2.

moment. If there is any country that is oblivious to God, it is Australia. Take for example, what is taught in schools. Is there ever a word taught that the beautiful world which we are enjoying and all its blessings, with its wheat and its wool, is God's gift to us through creation? Not a word of it, we are all told the whole thing is accidental, from protoplasm, the result of successive mutations. Nature has created itself: that is what we are taught to believe. And there is no acknowledgment that God is Lord of heaven and earth (to quote Jesus' description of him), no recognition that his providence controls every detail, that not a sparrow flies through the air without God, no ant crawls on the ground in the Amazon forests apart from the God who created it. We are oblivious to God, we haven't acknowledged that God has given us the wheat and the wool, and we are completely self-centred too. The strike is an illustration; it is an illustration of what we are all like. People going on strike for a few extra dollars and putting everybody to inconvenience is entirely selfish, but it is not true only of those people; we are all exactly the same. Or think of the greed that is going on in the continual increase in gambling, with Lotto and casinos and so on. It is just greed, wanting money, wanting more without any effort or giving anything in exchange for it. And we have had plenty of revelations in the paper about the corruption that is going on in our community in the business and perhaps in the political world.

Now I want to remind you that God is a God of judgement and that he doesn't allow us to get away with it. To do so would be a denial of reality. You may remember that in the church of Corinth, Christians who should have known better were ignoring one another in the Lord's Supper, each taking their own supper (1 Cor 11). St. Paul said that some of those Christians had been judged by God. In fact the whole group had been judged by some of them being sick and others even dying. God doesn't change. He doesn't deal with the Corinthians, that tiny little group way back there two thousand years ago, but let Australia off or let each of us off. We have got to judge ourselves, if we don't want the judgement of God to fall on us. And so the drought should be an occasion, because that is what is intended. God has allowed it to happen in order that it might call us back to him so that we might cease to be forgetful of him, cease to be unthankful. He wants us to change so that we thank him for the benefits we are receiving, thank him for the fruitful seasons that fill our hearts with food and gladness. And it should be a reminder to us of the final judgement. Joel 2 reminds us of that.

There was a drought in the days of Joel. Joel has three things to say about it: first, it is an occasion to remind people of the final judgement of God. This is only, as it were, a foretaste, because there will be a judgement when God will assess how we have used our opportunities of responding to him and, whether sickness or drought or whatever sort of suffering it may be, has caused us to turn back to God. We recognise that we deserve it but in his grace he is merciful. That is the first thing, to remember that we are under his judgement.

Secondly, Joel says, it should be a call to repentance. And as we repent we turn in faith to Christ and remember the graciousness of God who has in his love sent the Saviour so that we do not need to perish. He has sent Jesus who rescues us from the wrath to come. We thank him not only for forgiveness and peace of conscience, but also for all the other benefits that we continue to enjoy.

Thirdly, says Joel, it is an occasion for a call to prayer. Now what I believe we should pray for is not just simply rain, for what is the use of rain if we haven't learnt the lesson that God wishes to teach in withholding the rain? St Paul says that when God chastens us it is in order that we might not be condemned finally; we have got to repent. I believe what we need to pray for is that we might be given spiritual repentance and that our community might be given spiritual repentance, that it might become God-centred and not God-forgetful, that it might recognise that it is God who has given the corn and the wheat and the wool and the flax and acknowledge God as the source of these things. I would like to see all of us witnessing to this; I would like to see our leaders, our Christian leaders, inviting our political leaders to call us back to repentance. Anybody can pray and it is right to pray, and what we need is the prayer of repentance, the prayer that recognises that we have sinned in failing to acknowledge God as the creator and the giver of all good things, failing to be thankful to him for what we have received in the past and, of course, turning back to him to receive the forgiveness of our sins.

As we pray for rain and for those who are afflicted, let us pray firstly for repentance for all of us, that God might be the centre of our mind and heart and life and society. In fact, of course, he *is* the centre and if we keep ignoring him we can't expect anything else but his chastisement and judgement. Well then we should pray: pray to him that he might be gracious to us and as Joel puts it, that the Lord might return and bless us as a result of our prayers.

In conclusion then, what can we do? Well, we can repent ourselves and make God central in our own thoughts. Secondly, we can witness to the sovereignty of God. It is God who sends the rain, as Jesus said, it is God who makes the sun to rise, it is God the creator who holds the whole world in his hand. How else will the world know? How will Australia know unless we witness to God as creator and God as sovereign? And we must witness too to his righteousness, that he does not treat lightly the continual ignoring of him that leads to sin, selfishness, crime and corruption of every sort. God is a righteous God and that means that he is a God of judgement. So we repent ourselves, bear witness to God in his character of sovereign righteousness and judgement, and above all pray because God is gracious. That is his essential character; he is a God who forgives all who turn back to him. He has provided the way of forgiveness in the Lord Jesus Christ so let us take the opportunity, whether it is drought or any other event which gives us the opportunity of turning to him in fervent prayer for ourselves and for our fellow citizens.

Chapter 4
"WE PREACH JUDGEMENT"[1]

My text is Acts 10:42-43.

He ordered us to preach to the people, and solemnly to testify that this is the one who has been appointed by God as judge of the living and the dead. Of him all the prophets bear witness that through his name every one who believes in him has received forgiveness of sins.

*W*HAT WAS THE MESSAGE THAT CHRIST sent his apostles to minister? A comparison of sermons in the book of Acts reveals that when the apostles were preaching to the Gentiles they began at a point different from when they preached to the Jews. When preaching to the Gentiles, they began with God as Creator. This was necessary because the word "god", which everyone uses, has different meanings in different cultures. In the Graeco-Roman world, no one believed that God was Creator, and yet that is the essential truth from which the preacher starts, for God as Creator is the basic doctrine of the Bible. That is where the Apostles began. The sermons in Acts 14 and Acts 17 illustrate this.

In today's world, too, God as Creator has slipped out of mind. Nevertheless, God the Creator is the God whom the Christian preacher is speaking about—the One who brought the world into being by his word, who controls the world by his word, who has no

---

1.   A sermon preached at the Church of England in South Africa (CESA) Clergy Conference, Natal, 1991 Synod. Subheadings did not appear in the original manuscript.

problem with any miracle which is in line with his character because he brought everything into being by a word and can change it by a word if that is his will.

When the apostles preached to Jews, they started at a different point because the Jews firmly believed in God as Creator. They started with the news that Jesus was God's anointed one, the Messiah, who was crucified. Paul said that he would know nothing in Corinth except the Messiah crucified. Crucifixion was death by being "hanged on a tree" and the apostles drew attention to that by using that old-fashioned phrase. It would have reminded the Jewish hearers of the statement in Deuteronomy 21:23 that whoever is hanged on a tree is cursed by God. No wonder that the Jewish contemporaries of the apostles found the gospel an enormous stumbling block. How could Jesus be God's Messiah if he was cursed by God? The Messiah cursed? And yet that is what crucifixion was a sign of: that Jesus was under God's curse. But the apostles were preaching that Jesus was the Messiah. Paul was determined to know nothing at Corinth except this truth: that God's Messiah was cursed by God.

Jesus is our message: Jesus the Messiah, Jesus crucified, Jesus cursed by God, Jesus glorified! When the New Testament writers or preachers mentioned that Christ had been crucified, or more specifically that he had been hanged on a tree, in the very next clause they said that God raised him. Here is a paradox, cursed by God, raised by God, that is, vindicated by God. The reason is that Christ's work on the cross was totally successful. He fulfilled God's law, God's will, perfectly, which we were all obligated but unable to do. He bore our curse because he is our substitute. He overcame our enemy when he overcame death. God raised him and crowned him King, so when Peter was preaching to Cornelius, on this occasion, he said that God had commanded the apostles to preach that Jesus is the Judge and then, secondly, that whoever calls on his name receives forgiveness of sin.

Jesus is the Judge because he is our King. Jesus is our Saviour because he is our substitute. Each of these comes from his victory on the cross. This is our message: Judgement, and salvation from judgement. The requirement is righteousness and therefore people need to repent. The need is to call upon the Saviour in order that we might be found 'in him', having his righteousness, a righteousness from God and not from our own efforts.[2]

So, Peter told Cornelius that God had commanded the apostles to preach that Jesus is the Judge.[3] Nothing more than that! Jesus is the Judge because he is the King. The administration of justice is the task of the king and Peter added that there is forgiveness in Jesus. Judgement is fundamental to the message. These days we describe the message as good news. The word 'gospel' means primarily 'news'. The notion of good is not basic to the meaning of the word *euangelion*.[4] In actual fact it is primarily very bad news for those who hear it, because it is news of the imminence of God's judgement day when he will judge mankind. Those who are rejected will be burnt up with unquenchable fire, while those who are accepted will be gathered into his heaven. Our basic message is the imminence of the Judgement Day.[5] That is what Paul's sermon on the Areopagus climaxed with: "God has fixed the Judgement Day. He has given proof of this by the resurrection of the judge from death".[6] This is what he told the leading citizens of Athens when he was given the opportunity of explaining his message to them.

But the most startling example of the centrality of the message of the imminent coming judgement in the New Testament preaching is Paul's sermon to Felix, the governor of Palestine. What a wonderful opportunity the apostle had been given! Paul was a prisoner, but the governor of the Holy Land—God's own land—invited him to address his court when he himself and his lady were present. And we read in Acts 24:24 that the invitation by the Governor was to speak to him "concerning faith in Christ Jesus". It was to this that Paul had been giving his whole life, namely, seeking opportunity to speak publicly "concerning faith in Christ Jesus".

Luke sums up the sermon in a sentence, but we may be sure that Paul went on for longer than that! What is interesting, however, is how Luke summed up that sermon. He wrote: "Paul reasoned of righteousness, self-control and judgement to come".[7] That is how he summed

2. Philippians 3:9.
3. Acts 10:42.
4. Cf. the LXX (Greek) version 2 Samuel 18:26-27.
5. Matthew 3:2, 7, 12; 4:17.
6. Acts 17:31.
7. Acts 24:25.

up the whole powerful sermon "concerning faith in Jesus Christ". Does that sum up our message to our congregations and to the community?

PAUL'S THREE-PART SERMON

Let us consider the elements of Paul's summary. The first is *righteousness*: God's requirement of us to be perfect.

How do you and your congregation think they are going to get to heaven? How does the community think that they are going to get to heaven? There is only one way: righteousness. But you have got to be perfect. You will not enter God's presence in heaven just because you are a little better than somebody else. To reach God's presence and to be approved by him requires a one hundred per cent pass. "He is of purer eyes than to behold iniquity".[8] Adam only sinned once and out of the garden he went. That is common sense. It is the ordinary rule of justice. One offence makes a person a criminal. But there is perfect righteousness in the Lord Jesus Christ and it is certain that Paul stressed that. We have to be righteous to escape the judgement. But how can we be righteous, since we are sinners? Only through the forgiveness that is in Jesus Christ; only by being found in Christ the righteous one.

Paul's second point was *self-control*. Here he came pretty close to the bone because Paul knew something about the private life of Felix, who was not given to temperance. His life was notorious. Paul was speaking directly to his audience, in their situation, about God's requirements for our life.

Thirdly, he spoke about *judgement to come*. Our Creator and our Redeemer is not going to leave the whole situation up in the air. As John the Baptist foretold, he is going to assess us, he is going to judge us, he is going to gather the wheat into his barn and burn up the chaff with unquenchable fire. Judgement will come. No wonder Felix trembled. It was the teaching about judgement that got through to him. He postponed the matter, saying "I'll listen to you again another time". He never did, of course.

The Christian minister is to preach the judgement of God. After establishing the fact that the God of whom he speaks is Almighty, the

8.   Habakkuk 1:13.

Creator of everything, we are to make clear that he will judge us all in righteousness. Moreover, this judgement is near, as near as death, as near as the coming of Christ.

So our message is, believe this and change your way of life, change your attitude to God and ask for forgiveness from the Lord Jesus Christ, King, Judge and Saviour.

THE BIBLE ON JUDGEMENT

It was Jesus, loving Shepherd of his sheep, who preached the judgement, that is, the kingdom, and who taught the reality and the awfulness of the eternity of hell. The consequences of the judgement for those of us who remain unrepentant, unbelieving, self-centred, God-ignoring, disobedient to our conscience will be awful beyond imagining.

Most of the awful imagery in which the sufferings of the lost are described is found in the discourses of our Saviour Jesus Christ.

> *Jesus could never have warned so frequently and earnestly against the fire that never shall be quenched, or the worm that does not die, had he known that there was no future peril corresponding to them.*[9]

Here are some of Jesus' words:

> *Depart from me, you cursed, into the everlasting fire prepared for the devil and his angels…into everlasting punishment.*[10]
>
> *If your hand causes you to stumble, cut it off; it is better for you to enter into life maimed rather than having your two hands to enter hell, into the unquenchable fire… and if your eye causes you to stumble, gouge it out; it is better for you to enter into the Kingdom of God with one eye, rather than having two eyes to be cast into hell where the worm does not die and the fire is not quenched.*[11]
>
> *The rich man died and was buried and in Hades.*[12]

9.   W. G. T. Shedd, *The Doctrine of Endless Punishment*, (Scribner, New York, 1886).
10. Matthew 25:41, 46.
11. Mark 9:43-48.
12. Luke 16:22-23.

...being in torments...[13]

At the end of the world the Son of Man shall send out his angels and they shall gather out of his kingdom all things that cause stumbling and those who do wrong and shall cast them into the furnace of fire. There shall be the weeping and the gnashing of teeth.[14]

There are many other passages in the Gospels where Jesus solemnly warned his hearers of the awfulness of God's judgement on sinners.[15] He also spoke of the two ways of living, one road which led to life, the other to destruction on which most people were walking.[16]

John the Baptist and the apostles had the same message. For example:

The Messiah will separate the wheat from the chaff and will burn up the chaff with unquenchable fire.[17]

The smoke of the torment of the lost ascends forever and ever.[18]

And [all whose names are not written in the book of life] will be tormented day and night forever and ever.[19]

Those who do not know God... shall suffer punishment, eternal destruction from the face of the Lord and from the glory of his might.[20]

There are two things to note:

1. The awful reality of the consequences for a creature flouting the Creator and of the endlessness of these consequences. Jesus described Gehenna as where the worm does not die and the fire is not quenched.

2. We would all like to think that the consequences of sin are not as awful as Christ clearly taught they were. But any step to lessen the awfulness is a step away from the truth. That is why there is no hint in holy Scripture to lessen the fearfulness of condemnation at the judgement.

13. Matthew 13:41-42.
14. Matthew 19:49-50.
15. E.g., Luke 9:25, 12:5, 12:10, 12:46; John 5:28-29.
16. Matthew 7:13.
17. Matthew 3:12.
18. Revelation 14:11; 19:3.
19. Revelation 20:10.
20. 2 Thessalonians 1:9.

ANNIHILATIONISM

Some evangelical Christians today have adopted a theory of annihilationism, which is that sinners are annihilated by God and cease to exist. The older form of the theory of annihilationism was that sinners are annihilated at death. But this is so plainly contrary to Scripture, (e.g. the rich man in the Luke 16 parable is fully conscious in the torments of hell) that these conservative evangelicals state that God annihilates sinners after a period of punishment in hell.

A reply may be briefly made.

1. Scriptural terminology and imagery teach that hell is eternal. Sentences like "the worm does not die", "the fire is not quenched", "the smoke goes up forever and ever", indicate that there is no termination in view to the punishment sinners received as retribution for their contempt and disobedience to their Creator, if grace does not intervene. And the Scripture indicates that there is no grace after death. Today is the day of salvation and after death, the judgement.[21]

2. The meaning of the Greek words used in these verses correspond to the English word 'everlasting'. Thus Liddell and Scott's Greek Lexicon defines *aiōnios* as "everlasting" in one of its meanings, and gives quotations from Greek literature to establish this. The other Greek word used is *aidios* which has one meaning only, namely 'everlasting'. It is in parallel with *aiōnios* as it is a synonym in Jude 6 and 7. *Aiōnios* is the usual word used to indicate eternity in the New Testament. It means belonging to an age, or aeon, either a past age, or this age or the next age; but it also means 'everlasting' or 'eternal'. The imagery which surrounds it in our Lord's language and in the rest of the New Testament, as well as its association with *aidios* in Jude, makes it clear that its New Testament meaning is eternal, everlasting, unending.

> *In the vernacular, as in classical Greek, aionios never loses the sense of 'perpetuus'... In general, the word depicts that of which the horizon is not in view.*[22]
>
> *Aidios is a synonym for aiōnios.*[23]

21. 2 Corinthians 6:2; Hebrews 9:27.
22. J. H. Moulton and G. Milligan, *The Vocabulary of the New Testament*, (London: Hodder and Stoughton, 1930) p. 16.
23. G. A. Deissmann, *Bible Studies* (Edinburgh: Clark, 1901), p. 363.

"Eternal punishment" is Jesus' own phrase. Jesus used the same word in the same sentence to describe the eternity of punishment of the cursed as he did to describe the eternity of the bliss of heaven to which those blessed of the Father go after the judgement.[24]

In Mark 9:48 Jesus speaks of sinners being thrown into hell where the fire never goes out. There are many other statements of Jesus to the same effect, as well as those of John the Baptist and the apostles.

3. Annihilation at death, though unsupported by Scripture, is a notion that has some attraction if the righteousness of God is ignored, and the solemn and repeated warnings of Jesus are disregarded, and the rest of the Bible testimony discounted. But annihilation after a period of punishment, which evangelical annihilationists hold, seems cruel and illogical.

Retributive punishment does not lead to repentance and turning to God. The sinner continues to sin in hell, blaspheming God, without any repentance[25] and so continues to deserve the retribution of hell for his sins there, just as he deserved it for his sins on earth. If the Almighty annihilates the sinner some time during the ongoing experience of the punishment of hell and the ongoing blaspheming of his Creator, it seems there is no reason why the impenitent sinner should not have been annihilated at the beginning, that is, at death, the close of the day of grace. To delay awhile the annihilation of an impenitent sinner who continues to deserve punishment for his continuing rebellion, and then to annihilate him while still deserving punishment seems cruel in postponing annihilation in the first place.

4. Annihilation after a period of punishment involves quantifying punishment.

5. Hell is an awful truth, and it is not surprising that the Bible-believing Christian is tempted to lessen its awfulness. The theories of annihilation and also of universal salvation are attempts to lessen its awfulness. But the consequences of rebellion against God are unimaginably awful, and any attempt to lessen that awfulness is a step away from the truth.

The anguish of contemplating the lostness of the lost tore at Paul's heart. But he doesn't lessen the pain by a theory of annihilation.

24. Matthew 25:41, 46.
25. Revelation 16:10-11.

He wrote with great emotion,

I will tell you the truth in Christ. I do not lie, my conscience bears
me witness in the Holy Spirit, that for me there is enormous grief
and unceasing pain in my heart. For I could pray (were it possible)
that I myself should be accursed from Christ on behalf of my
brothers, my human kinsmen....[26]

Jesus felt the same. He wept as he said "O Jerusalem, Jerusalem! How
often would I have gathered you as a hen gathers its chicks, but you
would not..."[27]

The awful truth of the judgement of God on impenitent mankind
was a spur to Paul to preach the news of judgement and forgiveness
through Christ. He wrote: "We must all appear before the judgement
seat of Christ in order that each might receive what he has done in this
life whether good or bad and so knowing the fear of the Lord we are
persuading people... we beg you on behalf of Christ, be reconciled to
God".[28] Paul preached the gospel with tears.[29]

Annihilationism weakens the urgency to preach the gospel. It rests
on feelings. Thus John Stott, in explaining why he has come to hold
annihilation wrote, "Emotionally I find the concept of eternal suffering
of the impenitent intolerable".[30] But our feelings must arise from and
reflect the truth of God's Word. It is a fearful thing for us rebels to fall
unrepentant into the hands of the living God[31] and to go on throughout eternity unrepentant. We must not palliate this awfulness for it is
true, taught clearly in Scripture. The lostness of the lost is awful.

How do we deal with our emotions? I suggest we should do as
Abraham did when he felt so emotionally concerned over the judgement of Sodom, "Shall not the judge of all the earth do right?"[32] We
rest in God's character, leaving it with him. Or, as our Lord did, after

26. Romans 9:1-3.
27. Matthew 23:37.
28. 2 Corinthians 5:10, 11, 20.
29. Acts 20:19, 31.
30. D. L. Edwards & J. R. W. Stott, *Essentials: a liberal-evangelical dialogue,*
(London: Hodder & Stoughton, 1988), p. 314.
31. Hebrews 10:31.
32. Genesis 18:25.

denouncing woes over the unrepentant cities he had preached in, saying that they would go down into Hades and that it would be more
tolerable for Sodom in the day of judgement than for them, he continued: "I thank you Father, Lord of heaven and earth that you hid
these things from the wise and understanding and revealed them to
babes; yes, Father, for so it was well pleasing in your sight".[33] But it
spurred him to continue with the evangelistic invitation "Come to me
all you who are weary and heavy-laden I will give you rest".[34]

FEAR THE LORD

The most neglected command of Jesus is in Luke 12:4-5:

> *I say to you my friends, do not fear those who kill the body and after
> that have no more that they can do, but I warn you whom you shall
> fear. Fear him who, after he has killed has authority to cast into hell,
> yes, I say to you, fear him.*

Firstly, note that these solemn words were spoken by Jesus, the One
who knew God and loved God and knew men and loved mankind.
Secondly, note that they were spoken to his disciples, to those who
were earnestly seeking God's face, following Jesus the Messiah. "I say
to you, my friends…". He sat in a group of devoted followers to whom
he was giving this warning, "I say, yes, fear God."

Thirdly, it is genuine fear that Jesus is talking about, not what people call reverential fear, whatever that means. We all know what ordinary
fear means. That Jesus was using the word in this simple straightforward
meaning is clear from the passage. He began "I say to you, my friends,
do not be afraid of those who kill the body". Now we all know that sort
of fear, a very deep and understandable fear. He continued: "…but…fear
him who can not only kill the body but cast the soul into hell. Yes,
believe me, fear him." The word 'fear' has the same meaning in the same
sentence. It is genuine fear that Jesus is speaking about.

Note next that it is a command of our Lord: "Fear him": a twice
repeated command. It is a command that is not isolated but runs right

33. Matthew 11:25.
34. Matthew 11:28-30.

through the Old Testament and the New Testament. Just one example is in Paul's letter to the Romans, chapter 11. He tells the Roman Christians, "Be not high-minded but fear" (v. 20). Once again it is plain from the sentence that the word is used in its ordinary straight-forward meaning as it is through the Bible.

This is the command of God most neglected by Christians. Modern Christians seldom or never take the slightest notice of it let alone anyone who is not a Christian. How often is genuine fear of God preached about? Christians neglect it and society scoffs at it.

God has commanded us to preach the judgement and this is a fearful message. It is the preliminary to preaching forgiveness. The preacher must remember he is under judgement as much as his hearers. We must plead with sinners, and as foremost among them, ourselves. "Be reconciled with God. He who knew no sin became sin for us that we might become the righteous of God in him".[35]

God is not mocked, the Scriptures say.[36] What we sow we reap. And yet we refuse to face that. Christians too! But how much more those who do not listen to the Word of God? If we neglect Jesus' warning, we neglect it at our peril, because life as God created it has judgement and retribution built into it. God is our Creator and he will also assess the lives he has given us because he has given everyone a conscience to know how we ought to live, and this implies that we will be assessed and judged. This is also plain in Scripture and, if we have eyes to see it, it is plain in the life around us. But the final judgement is still to come. This warning of Jesus applies not only to deviant sex but to every activity—to dishonesty, to lying, to envy, to anger that has no real basis, to bitterness, to all disregarding of God and his character and his commandments. Jesus spoke clearly "unless you repent", he said, "you will all perish".[37]

To fear God is where true life begins. The opening sentence of the book of Proverbs states, "The fear of the LORD is the beginning of wisdom", that is, the beginning of living the right sort of life. It is the fear of the LORD, the fear of God as he has revealed himself. We do not fear an arbitrary God, a God whom we cannot be sure about, but God who

35. 2 Corinthians 5:21.
36. Galatians 6:7.
37. Luke 13:3.

has revealed himself in Christ, a consistent God, a righteous God, a holy God, a God who has generously given us life and all the world around us, and who so loves us that he gave his Son to save us.

The fear of God will save us from the fear of men and the fear of circumstances. If we fear God and obey him he will protect us in his wisdom. Jesus said "Fear him who is able to destroy body and soul in hell" and then two verses later, "the very hairs of your head are all numbered. Do not fear, therefore, you are more valuable than sparrows".[38] If we fear God we do not have to fear persons or circumstances, for God is in control of circumstances and persons, even despots.[39]

The purpose of this command of Jesus is for our blessing. It is so that we should turn away from sin, because sin brings, inevitably, the judgement of God. That is a principle built into reality. Sin brings destruction.

The warning of Jesus is for our good. It is just as foolish to ignore this warning of Scripture as it is to ignore a warning of high voltage transmission wires. If we ignore it the result is inevitable. The warning of high voltage wires is not intended to frighten us, but to keep us alive. So, too, are God's warnings in Scripture. They are like fences to turn the pilgrim back to the true path. God gives them for our good. It is vital to know the facts. It is also for the good of others. "He who turns a sinner from the error of his ways shall save a soul from death".[40]

FEAR AND LOVE: EVANGELISM

The fear of God is a stimulus to evangelism. "Knowing the fear of the Lord, we persuade people", said the greatest of all evangelists.[41]

God longs for us to fear him in order that we might keep his commandments, so that he might bless us. Mount Sinai was a very fearsome sight for the Children of Israel, and they were rightly frightened and fearful of the great awesome God who was revealing himself there. They said that they did not want to have any more close relationship

38. Luke 12:7.
39. Proverbs 21:1.
40. James 5:20.
41. 2 Corinthians 5:11.

with God, they feared him. They said to Moses, "We shall die if we hear the voice of the LORD speaking to us any longer... go near and listen to see what the LORD our God says. Then tell us... we will listen and obey".[42] Now God makes a very interesting comment to Moses. God commends the Israelites' fear. He said to Moses, "O that there was such a heart in them that they would fear me always and keep all my commandments that it might be well with them and with their children forever".[43] Notice once again that it is ordinary fear, deep fear for one's life. "We will die if we hear the voice of the Lord any longer," said the Israelites. It was of this fear that God said, "O that they would fear me always".

The fear of the Lord is the beginning of wisdom. It is not the end. The end is to know God, but we cannot know God unless we are walking in his way, unless we are walking in righteousness, unless we are in the area of reality, "keeping all his commandments". Because God is a true God, if we think ourselves in charge of our own lives and do this and do that and do the other thing as though there were no God, no judgement, no eternal punishment, that is unreal. We cannot have a relationship with God on the basis of unreality. Acknowledging God, walking in his commandments, is the pre-requisite to our knowing him and being blessed by him.

If we know him, we will know his love, we will perceive his goodness towards us, and love on our part will flow out towards him. And love overwhelms fear. "The fear of the LORD is the beginning of wisdom." We go on to know the Lord, we go on to love him, and all the terror is taken away. But if we turn away from him there is God's warning to turn us back again. The fear of God and our love for God have the same goal, the goal of keeping us walking in his way and in fellowship with him.

Jesus said that if we love him we will keep his commandments, and that he and the Father will make their home with us.[44] In Deuteronomy we read that if we fear him we will keep his commandments and He will be able to bless us. Love becomes the motive for obedience. Fear is the fence turning us back when we stray from obe-

42. Deuteronomy 5:25-7.
43. Deuteronomy 5:28.
44. John 14:23.

dience. We have to walk the narrow way if we are to get to heaven. We have to walk the narrow way if we are to have fellowship with God. That narrow way is guarded by the warning fence that keeps us from disobeying God this way or that way. As we walk along the narrow way, we do not have to notice the fence, we do not have to have fear, but if we turn aside then fear is there to turn us back again. When we are walking in love with God along the narrow way, love casts out fear. Fear provides the parameter and love provides the motive for keeping God's commandments.[45]

The early Christians are described as "walking in the fear of the Lord and in the comfort of the Holy Spirit".[46] That should describe our lives also. As we walk in the fear of God and in the presence of God (because that is who the Holy Spirit is, God's presence with us), he gives us his comfort and strength. Walking in the fear of the Lord leads to the presence of God with us as we walk.

"O that they had a heart to fear me always, that it might be well with them and with their children forever".[47] That should be our wish, for it was God's great wish at the beginning of his people's history. And that is still his wish for us, that we might fear him in order that we might remain in his love and, therefore, remain in his presence and fellowship, and in the sphere of his blessing, now and forever, and respond to his blessing with love. "We love because he first loved us".[48] "This is the love of God that we keep his commandments",[49] so our fear of God and our love of God both lead to the keeping of his commandments, so ensuring the greatest of all blessings, his presence with us.[50] "Perfect love casts out fear".[51]

Peter told Cornelius: "God has commanded us to preach to the people that Jesus is he who has been ordained by God to be the judge of the living and the dead. To him all the prophets witness that through

45. 1 John 5:3.
46. Acts 9:31.
47. Deuteronomy 5:29.
48. 1 John 4:9.
49. 1 John 5:3.
50. John 14:23.
51. 1 John 4:18.

his name everyone who believes in him will receive the forgiveness of their sins".[52]

"'Twas grace that taught my heart to fear and grace my fears relieved."[53]

52. Acts 10:42, 43.
53. From 'Amazing Grace' by John Newton.

Chapter 5

GOD IS SPIRIT, LIGHT, LOVE[1]

WHAT WE BELIEVE ABOUT GOD IS OF immense importance to the way we live and to our happiness. From God's Word in Scripture we learn that we are under God's condemnation for our wrongdoings, but we also learn that Jesus conquered sin through his death on the cross. The result is that all who accept him as their Lord and God may be forgiven and restored to the relationship of being the children of God, with the prospect of eternal fellowship and happiness in his presence, not only now but after death and throughout eternity.

The apostle John was one of the closest of Jesus' disciples and in his writings in the New Testament he makes three great statements about God's nature.

The first is in John 4:24, "God is spirit". This means that God is a person like us in that He has personal relationships. He is not merely an impersonal force or influence, but a person with interests, with purpose, with will. Jesus said "God is Spirit and they that worship him [that is to say those who are in relationship with him] must worship him in spirit and in truth". As we draw near to God in prayer we must do so from the centre of our personality. There must be nothing artificial or indirect as we speak to God. It is like friendship. You cannot be the friend of someone if you always address him or her in an artificial way or indirectly through somebody else. God is spirit and those who worship him must worship him in spirit. We should see to it that our relationship to God is genuine, sincere, from the bottom of our heart: let us ask for his full forgiveness and accept him as our true Lord and God.

Jesus added—they that worship him must worship him in spirit *and* in truth. Once again you cannot be related to a friend in the area of falsehood; if you pretend to be other than you are, that friendship has no

---

1. Protestant Faith Broadcast, 16 October 1977.

future. Our friendship and fellowship with God must be based on truth. We must acknowledge ourselves as sinners and ask for his forgiveness.

The second great statement that John makes about God is in 1 John 1: "God is light and in him is no darkness at all".[2] All our relationships with persons, if they are to be true, must be on the basis of what is right and just and fair. Justice, fairness and righteousness are the basic ingredients of all relationships with other people and this is the prerequisite of our relationship with God. God is light and we must walk in light if we are to be related to him, otherwise we simply evoke and receive his eternal wrath. That is why we need to repent of our untruthful, Godless, self-centred way of life, ask for forgiveness and be restored to his friendship, for God is light and we dare not trifle with this truth. We must walk in light, being just and fair to others as well as being true to God.

The other great statement of St John about God's nature is in the fourth chapter of his letter in which he says, "God is love".[3] This is perhaps the best known of the three and it conveys the wonderful fact that God, just and upright person that he is, is utterly unselfish. He finds his interests in us; he loves us so much that he gave himself for us in order to rescue us from the rule of darkness to bring us into his presence as forgiven children. God is love, Jesus died for us, and his love extends to every little detail of daily life. His infinite mind knows everything about us and cares for every need; we should respond by love and trust in him, and imitate his character by finding our interests in other people, in extending true love to those whom we meet and who are in our sphere of life. We must never treat people with indifference; God never does this, for God is love. God cares for us.

Thus there are three great affirmations. God is Spirit—he is a true person and we must be related to him in a true personal way. God is light—never will he overlook the slightest deviation from what is upright. And he is love—he gave himself for our sins so that we might be completely forgiven if we turn to him. And he will give us his Spirit, that is, his own presence so we ourselves may walk uprightly, doing things that are fair and just by his help and walking in love not only to God who has such a wonderful future for us, but in love for one another.

2. 1 John 1:5.
3. 1 John 4:8.

For as St John says, how can we say we love God whom we have not seen as yet, if we do not love our fellow man whom we have seen?[4]

4.   1 John 4:20.

Chapter 6
THE HOLINESS OF GOD[1]

*T*HE CONCEPT THAT GOD IS HOLY IS basic to the Bible, but it is not an idea that we think of much today. A great many of our troubles in church and society are due to this neglect. We need to bring our thinking back to the Scriptural picture of the world and God's relationship to us expressed in the concept of the *holy* God.

The essential meaning of the word 'holy' is that God is high and exalted, and separate from all that he has created; he is the everlasting king supreme over all.

The sixth chapter of Isaiah gives a picture of the Holy God. The prophet Isaiah experienced a vision in the temple and he saw the Lord as King, high and lifted up. Around him were the cherubim who called one to the other, "Holy, holy, holy is the Lord God of hosts; that which fills the earth is his glory".[2] Here we see a glimpse of the reality of God's deity.

The modern Christian needs to recover the concept of the holiness of God, the One who inhabits eternity, who dwells in the high and lofty places, who is King supreme over all, even at this present moment. He is separate not only as Creator, but as One who is pure, separate from all that is immoral and unjust.

The function of a king in earliest times was to judge. He applied the law and judged righteously between those in dispute with each other and he judged the wrong doers, punishing them for their crimes. God as King is the God of judgement, the King over all, judging the whole earth. The fact that you may not believe it makes no difference. The Bible is very largely a message of judgement, though this is almost entirely forgotten today by those who think they are following the religion of the Bible. An examination of the contents of the Bible will

---

1.   Protestant Faith Broadcast, 11 April 1976.
2.   Isaiah 6:3.

confirm what I say, that its message is primarily a message of the certainty of judgement. The Bible asserts the judgement of God because God is the holy God, the ultimate in supremacy and loftiness and therefore the ultimate in seriousness. That he is a holy God means that life is serious. It will be assessed. God judges according to what is right. And his judgement is complete and all-embracing, including even the idle word, as Jesus said.[3] Isaiah's vision of the holy God, the King, in chapter 6 confirms what I am saying. The message that was given by God to Isaiah in that vision was a message of judgement, severe and complete.

That God is a holy God, an everlasting King and the judge of all the earth makes life serious and we need to take it into account. What we do today may be forgotten by us, but we will in due course have to stand by it and give an account for it. Our actions and attitudes, and reactions to what is done to us will be scrutinised. We may shrug them off now, but we must stand by them and receive what is due for them at the judgement seat of God, whether they are good or whether they are bad. Judgement is in the very centre of the Christian gospel.

The cross itself is judgement, for Christ condemned sin at Calvary and when Paul, the great apostle of the gospel, was preaching in Athens it was judgement that he said was the message of the resurrection. God had appointed a day when he would judge the world by the man he had appointed and "he has given evidence of this by raising him from the dead".[4] The audience broke off the sermon at that point because we sinners do not believe in judgement.

God is the Holy One, supreme over all his creatures and the Judge of the whole earth, separate from sinners and from all impurity. Yet not separate from those who are his people, for in the Biblical phrase, he is the Holy One in the midst of them. A strange contrast, holy and near, yet it is true in experience. God is the holy One who inhabits the high and lofty places yet dwells with him who is of a contrite and humble spirit. This aspect of God's holiness is expressed most clearly in Jesus Christ who is Emmanuel—God with us. If we wish to know the Holy God we look to Jesus. Jesus is a King supreme over all, he is a judge to whom all judgement has been given; he is the Saviour and indeed it is his glory that Isaiah saw. As St John declares, Jesus is the Lord of Hosts,

3.   Matthew 12:36.
4.   Acts 17:31.

high and lifted up, God with us, the Son whose name is "the Everlasting Father".[5]

Live by this worldview in which the holy God rules over all. Supreme in the highest place, at this present moment he judges every action of his creation and condemns and punishes all sin and rebellion and stubborness of heart and yet he is gracious to all who call upon him and forgives all who change their mind. The Holy God will bring everything into judgement because he treats us all seriously. He is in the midst of us in Jesus Christ the Lord, the Holy One of God, who has been exalted to the highest heaven to reign and to come again as judge, before whom we all must stand. Yet He is above all a gracious Saviour through his Spirit indwelling in the hearts of all who will receive him. Jesus Christ is Lord. This is the Christian worldview. We must make it thoroughly our own and proclaim it without flinching in a world which ignores the holiness of God.

5.   John 12:39-41; Isaiah 9:6.

Chapter 7

THE FIVE COMINGS OF JESUS
(MATTHEW 24 AND 25)[1]

"*T*HE COMING ONE" IS THE ROLE TITLE that John the Baptist gave to Jesus. Jesus by implication approved.[2] The title goes back to the Septuagint. In Daniel 7:13 *ho erchomenos*, the coming one, is seen with the clouds of heaven and is introduced into the presence of the Ancient of Days who is seated on his throne surrounded by a myriad of his holy ones, his saints. Then "the coming one", who is described as like "a son of man", receives from the Ancient of Days "dominion and glory and a kingdom, that all peoples, nations, and languages should serve him." It is an everlasting, indestructible kingdom and dominion over every race of the world.

Five different ways of applying the concept of the coming one to Jesus may be distinguished in the New Testament. Jesus' birth at Bethlehem and his entry into the world is the **first coming**. The angels in Luke's nativity account predicted the everlasting kingdom which he would receive.[3] John, in the prologue to his Gospel, spoke of Jesus as having "come to his own",[4] and throughout that Gospel Jesus himself used the concept of "having come" with reference to his ministry. He had come because God had sent him;[5] he had come as a light;[6] he came to save the world.[7] In St Matthew's Gospel, Jesus declared that "I am come to fulfil the law",[8] "I am come to call sinners to repentance",[9] and in

1. Originally published in *Reformed Theological Review*, vol. xxxiv, May/Aug 1975, pp. 44-54.
2. Matthew 11:3ff.
3. Luke 1:33.
4. John 1:11.
5. John 7:28.
6. John 12:46.
7. John 12:47.
8. Matthew 5:17.
9. Matthew 9:13.

Matthew 20:28 our Lord declared "the son of man came... to minister, and to give his life a ransom for many".

Examples could be multiplied from the Gospels to indicate that the concept of coming is applied extensively to Jesus with regard to his earthly ministry. There are, however, four other applications of the concept of coming applied to Jesus which may be distinguished in the New Testament. Matthew's great eschatological discourse in Matthew 24 and 25 will serve as a basis for explicating these. The discourse arises quite naturally, almost, from very human circumstances. On leaving the temple precinct one of the disciples drew Jesus' attention to the magnificent architecture and engineering of the building expressed in the size of the stones that Herod had used. Some of the stones, which Herod used in constructing the temple platform, are still standing, and are huge. The tenor of Jesus' reply to the question must have been unexpected, for it impressed itself on the minds of the hearers and is reproduced word for word in each of the three synoptic Gospels. "Not a stone will be left on a stone here, which will not be thrown down."[10] A little later as they sat on the Mount of Olives overlooking the temple, a small group of his closest friends asked him privately when this would happen, and what would be the sign that it was about to take place. Matthew expands the second half of the question into "what shall be the sign of your coming and of the consummation of the age?", in this way giving the meaning of what was in the mind of the disciples as they asked their question. Jesus' reply as recorded by Matthew may be divided into five sections:

(a) Predictions of troubles (24:1-14)
(b) Predictions of the circumstances surrounding the destruction of Jerusalem (24:15-28)
(c) Predictions about the preaching of the gospel (24:29—31)
(d) Advice on how to live in view of the impossibility of knowing when the hour will come (24:32-25:30)
(e) The final denouement (25:31-46).

Verses 1-14 describe in a general way the sort of events that the disciples may expect before the consummation of the age takes place. There will

10. Matthew 24:2; Mark 13:2; Luke 21:6.

be various religious claimants who will have considerable measure of success; there will be wars of aggression; there will be natural disasters such as famine and earthquake. These are not the sign of the end ("the end is not yet")—they are merely the beginning of trouble. Christians will suffer persecution and martyrdom, and many will fall away. There is only one principle for attainment, and that is, patience to the end—"he that endures to the end, the same shall be saved."[11] However, Jesus did give one sign which when fulfilled would usher in the end, and that is the preaching of the news of the kingdom throughout the world as a witness.

Presumably, when this has been accomplished, the time of the judgement will be ripe, for men will then not only have the knowledge of the law written in their hearts by nature, but will have seen the power of the message of the kingdom in their own environment, by which to be judged.

Mark[12] and Luke[13] fill out the discourse at this point with similar predictions of persecution to be experienced by Jesus' followers, which Matthew records in chapter 10 in the discourse with which Jesus briefed the Twelve before sending them out on their missionary journeys. That was the first time that the followers of Jesus went out into the world with the gospel, and so it was appropriate there should be predictions of persecution at this point, for it is a universal experience of Christians, foretold by Christ himself, that in the world they will have persecution. This flows from the nature of the message on the one hand and the nature of those who hear it on the other. The presence or absence of persecution in the experience of the witness is a test of his fidelity to the message.

The predictions of the destruction of Jerusalem (which took place in AD 70) is introduced by the statement "when you see the abomination of desolation spoken of by Daniel the prophet standing in the holy place, let him who reads understand."[14] Luke makes the innuendo explicit: "when you see Jerusalem surrounded by armies then know that its desolation is at hand".[15] It was to be a time of tremendous suffering, confirmed in actuality by Josephus's description of the siege and

11. Matthew 24:13.
12. Mark 13.
13. Luke 21.
14. Matthew 24:15.
15. Luke 21:20.

capture of the city. What is interesting in Matthew's account is the terming of the event "the coming (that is, the *parousia*) of the Son of Man" (verse 27). This **[second] coming** will be conspicuous and unmistakable, as clear for all to see *parousia* as the lightning is in heaven, or as the carcass on the ground which attracts the vultures from every point of the compass. The destruction of Jerusalem had already been described (perhaps earlier on the same day) by Jesus in terms of God's vengeance.

> *Upon you shall come all the righteous blood shed on the earth from the blood of Abel the righteous until the blood of Zechariah the son of Berechiah whom you murdered between the sanctuary and the altar. Verily I say unto you all these things shall come upon this generation. O Jerusalem, Jerusalem...your house is left unto you desolate.*[16]

Luke incorporates the same idea into the discourse itself. "These are days of vengeance".[17]

The destruction of Jerusalem was the most conspicuous example of God's judgement, that is to say, the most conspicuous example of the *parousia* or presence (translated 'coming' in our English version) of the Son of Man. Judgement is one of the offices of the Son of Man. This is explicitly stated in John 5:27 and in Matthew 25:31, and is based on Daniel 7 where the final judgement follows the reception of the Son of Man by the Ancient of Days. Every *parousia* of the Son of Man for judgement will be sudden and unexpected. When men are saying "peace" then suddenly destruction will come upon them. It will be as in the days of Noah when life ran on normally until the day that Noah entered into the ark and the flood carried them all away, or as in the days of Lot when life ran on normally until the day when Lot left Sodom and then it rained fire and brimstone from heaven and destroyed them all. So will it be in the *parousia* of the Son of Man. When men observe it coming there will be no time even to go back to get a coat. "Escape for your life" is the advice that Christ offers when that time arrives. The language he uses is reminiscent of Lot's wife who looked back as she fled.

The coming of the Son of Man in judgement will not only be sud-

16. Matthew 23:35-38.
17. Luke 21:22.

den but will also be absolutely unpredictable as to the day on which it falls. "Of that hour knows no man neither the angels or the Son."[18] This truth refers equally to the destruction of Jerusalem as to the final denouement or to any other of the comings ('presence') of the Son of Man in judgement. However for those who are awake, the general tendency of the event may easily be seen. Indeed our Lord was able to foretell that Jerusalem would experience judgement within that generation.[19] He underlined with the greatest emphasis the certainty of this prediction (24:35). Of the nature of this coming three things are said. It will overtake the man in the street with unexpected catastrophe. It will be conspicuous and for all to see as the lightning is seen everywhere or as vultures converge on a carcass. Thirdly, the exact day and hour (though known to God who governs all things after the counsel of his own will) remains uncertain in human knowledge.

Because the time of the *parousia* is unpredictable in created knowledge, Jesus told four stories to draw out the implications which flow from the certainty yet unpredictability of the Son of Man's coming. In each story the concept of coming is dominant.[20] Watchfulness, faithfulness, preparedness, diligence, are the four lessons. Mark has a saying that the coming may well be in any of the four watches of the night, that is, may be soon or long delayed. Matthew omits this saying, but in his story of the talents it is "after a long time" that the lord comes.[21]

There is a reference to the *parousia* of judgement of the Son of Man in Luke 17, where, speaking to his disciples, Jesus said that the days would come when they would desire to see one of the days of the Son

18. Matthew 24:36.
19. Matthew 23:36, 39 and 24:34.
20. Matthew 24:43, 50; 25:10,19.
21. Matthew 25:19 [Following footnote is DBK's]. There are several references to the coming in judgement of the Son of Man in the Letters to the Churches in Revelation 2 and 3. The Church is threatened, "Repent...if not, I will come to you and will remove your lampstand" (Revelation 2:5). "Repent! If not I come quickly...", (Revelation 2:16). In Revelation 3:3 the future tense is used, in association with the imagery of the thief, imagery reminiscent of Matthew 34:43: "...repent, if you do not keep awake, I will come as a thief, and you won't know the hour when I will come upon you". In Revelation 2:25 the future tense is used of the final coming at the end of the world. "Hold fast till I come", while the present tense is used of the final coming in Revelation 3:11 "I will come quickly".

of Man but they would not see it. The juxtaposition of the singular and plural, "one of the days", is interesting. The day of the Son of Man is one of a class. This phrase "a day of the Son of Man" describes the same event which Matthew refers to as the *parousia* of the Son of Man,[22] for in Luke 17:24ff, Jesus described "the Son of Man in his Day" in the identical imagery of Noah, Sodom, the man on the house top, the woman grinding at the mill and the eagles at the carcass, which he used in Matthew 24 to describe the *parousia* of the Son of Man. Thus the Son of Man in his day, or one of the days of the Son of Man, is a reference to the cataclysmic judgements which overtake mankind in vengeance for sustained wrong-doing and in vindication of the right, which in Matthew is called the *parousia* or presence or coming of the Son of Man. The Lord predicted that the time would come when his disciples would long to see one of these days of the Son of Man, that is, would long to see injustice and oppression overthrown; but they would not see it. How often is this the Christian's painful experience when with the saints under the altar he cries out "how long, O Lord!", but Jesus' words are that he must endure to the end. The time of vengeance of God is coming, but not yet. However, there will be occasions when the Son of Man is present in judgement, as in Jerusalem in AD 70. The destruction of Sodom and Gomorrah was also one of those occasions, and it may be to this day of the Son of Man that Jesus referred when he said, "Abraham rejoiced to see my day and he saw it and was glad".[23] If Lot vexed his righteous soul with the goings on at Sodom,[24] how much more would have Abraham, the friend of God, encamped as he was in close proximity in the hills above the cities. Genesis relates how Abraham saw the smoke of Sodom going up. He saw the judgement of God. It was one of the days of the Son of Man who had been active before Abraham, and will be till the consummation of all things. "Abraham rejoiced to see my day and he saw it and was glad... before Abraham was I am".[25]

The **third coming** of the Son of Man distinguished in the New

22. Matthew 24:27, 37, 39.
23. John 8:56.
24. 2 Peter 2:7-8.
25. John 8:58.

Testament is his coming on the clouds of heaven. It is a coming which takes place within the lifetime of Jesus' hearers and will be recognized by them as having taken place. Thus Jesus told the members of the Sanhedrin, "Henceforth you shall see the Son of Man sitting on the right hand of Power and coming on the clouds of heaven".[26] Earlier in his ministry he had predicted, "Verily I say unto you, there shall be some of them that stand here that shall not taste death until they see the Son of Man coming in his Kingdom",[27] and in the eschatological discourse in Matthew 24 which we have been considering, Jesus predicted "They shall see the Son of Man coming on the clouds of heaven with power and great glory... Verily I say unto you this generation shall not pass away until all these things are accomplished. Heaven and earth shall pass away but my words shall not pass away".[28] It is plain from these passages that Jesus expected with absolute certainty that the Son of Man would come on the clouds during the lifetime of his hearers. The imagery of the Son of Man coming on the clouds is drawn directly from Daniel 7:13 where the Son of Man comes with the clouds into the presence of the Ancient of Days and receives the Kingdom. This coming of the Son of Man is neither a coming into the world at Bethlehem nor the coming or *parousia* in judgement at Sodom or Jerusalem or any other of "the days of the Son of Man" but is a coming to the Father. As Jesus said in his prayer before his death, "I come to Thee".[29] He comes to the Father to receive the everlasting kingdom, to be crowned with glory and honour through his death, to sit on God's right hand asking, reigning and waiting for every enemy to be subject to him. The "coming on the clouds" is a synonym of "sitting at the right hand of God", and both stand for receiving and the exercising of dominion and sovereignty. In recording the words of the Saviour, Matthew uses both images: "henceforth you shall see the Son of Man sitting on the right hand of power and coming on the clouds of heaven".[30] Strictly speaking the images are incompatible, but they both stand for the same truth, that through his death Christ has been raised to the Father's right hand where he now reigns. The authority

26. Matthew 26:64.
27. Matthew 16:28.
28. Matthew 24:30, 34.
29. John 17:11 cf. John 14:12, 28, etc.
30. Matthew 26:64.

and kingdom is given to the Son of Man. It is this which is indicated by the phrase "the Son of Man coming in his kingdom" or "the Son of Man coming with the clouds". It is symbolic language to describe Jesus' receiving authority to subdue the Kingdom of Satan through the preaching of the gospel and the converting of sinners. The receiving of this authority is referred to in Psalm 110: "Sit at my right hand", and its exercise is referred to in Psalm 2 under the concept of the victorious Messiah imprecating for his kingdom, asking to be given the nations for his inheritance and the uttermost parts of the earth for his possession. Jesus told his disciples that as a consequence of his receiving all authority in heaven and earth he sent them out to convert the nations.[31] It is through conversion by the gospel that Jesus receives his promised inheritance of the uttermost parts of the earth for his possession. In his prayer in John 17:2 Jesus spoke in similar language, that all authority had been given to him for the purpose of saving the elect.

There is reference to this coming of the Son of Man in the clouds, that is to say, his coming to the Father and his entering into his kingship for the purpose of saving his people, in Matthew 24:39-41. In these verses the world mission follows immediately after the destruction of Jerusalem. Full weight must be given to the copulative temporal phrase "immediately after the tribulation of these days",[32] because the destruction of Jerusalem, the bringing to an end of the old order of the Old Testament dispensation, was the necessary prelude to the world mission in its full strength. Jesus had already predicted in parable that "the Lord of the vineyard shall come and will miserably destroy these miserable men", the wicked husbandmen who had ignored the prophets and killed the Son. Jesus spoke plainly, "the Kingdom of God shall be taken away from you and given to a nation which shall bring forth its fruits".[33] This took place in A.D. 70 and in the years that followed.

When Jesus first sent out his disciples with the gospel message in Matthew 10, he had confined them to the cities of Israel, for the times of the Gentiles had not yet begun. However, he predicted these times would not be long in coming, indeed the disciples would not be able

31. Matthew 28:29, 30.
32. Matthew 24:29.
33. Matthew 21:40-43.

to evangelize Jewry before the Son of Man came; before, that is, Jerusalem was destroyed and the Gentile world mission was launched in its fullness. "You shall not go through the cities of Israel until the Son of Man comes."[34] The world mission of the gospel would undermine and change established human institutions. It would, in a word, turn the world upside down. This our Lord predicted in stock imagery, used in the Old Testament to describe the break up of social and national groupings. "Immediately after the tribulation of those days, the sun shall be darkened and the moon shall not give its light and the stars shall fall from heaven and the powers of heaven shall be shaken."[35] In the Old Testament, the capture of Babylon[36] and the destruction of Egypt[37] are predicted in similar imagery. Joel uses the same imagery for the prediction of the coming of the Holy Spirit.[38]

"Then shall they see the sign of the Son of Man in heaven".[39] We have in these words probably a reference to the **fourth coming** of the Son of Man of which the New Testament speaks. This coming is the coming of the Holy Spirit. "I will not leave you orphans, I come to you" said Jesus in the context of the gift of the Spirit.[40] A verse or two earlier he had said, "I will come again and will receive you unto myself, that where I am you may be also". This verse is also probably a reference to fellowship of the Spirit of Christ in our hearts. Its language is based on Exodus 19:4 where God comes down on Mt Sinai and brings the nation of Israel to himself. So Christ through his Spirit comes to his disciples and indwells them so that they have fellowship with him, spirit with spirit. The coming of the Spirit into the heart of the believer is the coming of Jesus for fellowship. "I will come in to him and have a meal with him and he with me".[41] "My Father and I will come to him and stay with him".[42] Jesus comes to his disciples and takes them to himself, that where he is there they may be

34. Matthew 10:23.
35. Matthew 24:29.
36. Isaiah 13:10.
37. Ezekiel 32:7.
38. Joel 2:28-32; Acts 2:16-21.
39. Matthew 24:30.
40. John 14:18.
41. Revelation 3:20.
42. John 14:23.

also,[43] even seated with him at the right hand of God in the heavenlies.[44] So they may be said to have already come to the heavenly Jerusalem and to Jesus.[45] They have been introduced by Jesus into the presence of God, as the Son of Man was so introduced in Daniel 7. This is through the gift of the Holy Spirit. It is the first fruit of their full inheritance. As Jesus is described as *ho erchomenos*, "the coming one", so his faithful are described as *hoi erchomenoi*, "the coming ones", in Revelation 7:14. They are the ones destined to come into the presence of the Father and receive the kingdom.

The phrase "the sign of the Son of Man in heaven" is difficult, but the genitive should be taken as meaning the sign consisting of the Son of Man in heaven. In Isaiah 5 the prophet foretold that after God had judged his people he would lift up a sign to the nations from one end of the earth the other and would draw them to this standard. In chapter 11 the prophet is more explicit. It is the Messiah, the root of Jesse, who will be the sign which God will raise on high, for the peoples and for the nations, so that through this sign he will draw the Gentiles and at the same time gather his people from the four corners of the earth.[46] Jesus is this sign; he is the Son of Man in heaven, the focus of salvation for the whole earth. The Holy Spirit poured out by Christ is the visibility of his presence in heaven so that the phrase "then shall appear the sign of the Son of Man in heaven" may be exegeted as a prediction of the promised Holy Spirit. Jesus is in heaven, but the sign of the Son of Man in heaven will be visible to "all the tribes" on earth, and will have the effect of making them mourn and repent. Now the reason that we know that the Son of Man is in heaven, the reason, that is, that we know that he is reigning, is that we see the Holy Spirit poured out. "He has been exalted to the right hand of God and has received the promised Holy Spirit and has poured out this which you see and hear".[47] It is through the coming of the Spirit that the kingship of Christ is exercised and is seen to be exercised by the converting of

---

43. John 14:3.
44. Ephesians 2:6.
45. Hebrews 12:22-24.
46. Isaiah 11:10-12.
47. Acts 2:33.

the world, for "when he (the Comforter) is come, he will convict the world of sin, of righteousness, and of judgement".[48] It is a conviction related to the lordship of Christ, "because they believe not on me...because I go to the Father...because the prince of this world is judged".[49] It is the Spirit's presence which gives power to the gospel and accompanies it with signs, so that it is seen to be not merely words, but the power of God. In this way the Spirit makes visible the lordship of Christ, that he is indeed in heaven at God's right hand.

The consequence of this exercise of Christ's kingship through the work of the Spirit by the instrumentality of Christ's children ("when he is come to you") is the conversion of the elect, scattered as they are in every tribe and nation. This conversion is referred to by an image drawn from Zechariah: "then shall all the tribes of the earth mourn, and they shall see the Son of Man coming in the clouds of heaven with power and great glory".[50] The mourning of the tribes of the earth is drawn from Zechariah 12:10, where the mourning is the mourning of repentance and conversion. It is not the terror, which will accompany the last day when men will call on the rocks to cover them. It is the repentance that follows the recognition of the lordship of Christ. "Then shall appear the sign of the Son of Man in heaven, and then shall the tribes of the earth mourn." There is a reference to the same event in Revelation 1:7: "Behold he comes with the clouds and every eye shall see and they that pierced him and all the tribes of the earth shall mourn over him. Even so. Amen". The verse at the beginning of the Book of Revelation celebrates the lordship of Christ, and anticipates, according to prophecy, the triumph of the gospel in the conversion of the world, the conversion even of the Jews, who through the Gentiles accepting the faith, come to acknowledge Jesus as Lord, "who by the mercy shown to the Gentiles obtain mercy themselves".[51]

In Matthew 24, Jesus goes on to speak about his work of sending out labourers into the harvest: "[the Son of Man] shall send forth his angels with a great sound of a trumpet and they shall gather together

48. John 16:8.
49. John 16:9-11.
50. Matthew 24:30.
51. Romans 11:31.

his elect from the four winds of the earth".[52] In Revelation 14:14 there is a short paragraph which speaks of the same subject, viz., the vision of the Son of Man sitting on a white cloud crowned with a golden crown and having a sharp sickle in his hand. He receives the word to reap the harvest of the earth. This is the imagery of conversion which is the work of the crowned Son of Man, and is quite distinct from the image that follows where another angel with another sickle gathers the grapes of the vine of the earth into the wine press of the wrath of God.

The present is the hour of salvation and the Son of Man sends forth his angels or his messengers (for this is the normal translation of the Greek word *angelos*). Sending forth his messengers is accompanied by the sound of a trumpet, another Old Testament image,[53] and the purpose of sending forth these messengers is to gather Christ's elect from under the whole of heaven. We recall our Lord's prayer to the Father in John 17:2, "You have given him authority over all flesh that he should give eternal life to those you have given him". We are in this day of Christ now and we should recognize that the work of the Christian disciple, and pre-eminently the Christian minister, is to be a faithful witness so that through him the Son of Man may gather his elect to himself. Jesus referred to this same subject when he said "other sheep I have which are not of this fold; them also I must bring and they shall hear my voice and they shall become one flock, with one shepherd."[54] The sheep which the Father has given to the Son hear the voice of the Good Shepherd through the angels or messengers he sends out in his name. Paul was encouraged to persevere by the consolation that his task was to save the elect: "I have much people in this city".[55] The test of the Christian is primarily faithfulness, and patient enduring of the tribulation which faithfulness will inevitably engender. But it is a triumphant ministry; the tribes of the earth shall mourn when they see the Son of Man as Lord of all. "Even so. Amen".[56]

Jesus made clear that all these things were about to take place. When

52. Matthew 24:31.
53. Exodus 19:16; Isaiah 27:13.
54. John 10:16.
55. Acts 18:10 cf. 2 Timothy 2:10.
56. Revelation 1:7.

the fig tree puts forth its leaves, summer is approaching, so there are indications of the imminence of these great events for the discerning to see and Jesus reiterated that they would all be fulfilled within the lifetime of his hearers. He could not be more emphatic: "Verily I say unto you, this generation shall not pass away until all these things be accomplished. Heaven and earth shall pass away, but my words will not pass away".[57] No stronger language could be used to indicate the certainty of fulfilment in the lifetime of that generation. There ought, therefore, to be no doubt that not only verse 15 and 22 but also verses 27 to 31 have all been fulfilled. We do not know much of the great Gentile mission that must have followed on from the destruction of Jerusalem, for with the close of the New Testament, Christian history is silent for almost a hundred years. But when later in the second century we are able to observe how things stand with the Christian mission, we see that it has indeed spread to every corner of the known world.

One coming yet remains. After the general description of how Christians should live between the fourth and the final coming of the Son of Man which occupies Matthew 24:36—25:30, Jesus refers to the final *parousia* and coming of the Son of Man. This coming is distinguished from the coming on the clouds (or with the clouds) to receive the kingdom. It is the coming with the angels for the final judgement. The angels surround the throne of the Ancient of Days in Daniel 7:10. The Son of Man having received his kingdom comes with the angels to the throne of judgement. The imagery is probably based on the Septuagint of Deuteronomy 33:2 where the Lord comes "with the 10,000's of saints on his right and his angels were with him". Another Old Testament reference to the coming of God with his saints for judgement is Zechariah 14:5. Jesus had already referred to this coming "with his angels" in Matthew 16:27. Here too it is a coming for judgement: "then shall he repay every man". St Paul has a reference to this coming in his letters to the Thessalonians.[58]

The coming of the Son of Man in his kingdom is a reference in Daniel's imagery to Christ coming to the Father to be crowned. The coming with his angels in the glory of his Father is a coming from the Father, as it were, to the throne of judgement. It is a day of vengeance,

---

57. Matthew 24:35.
58. 1 Thessalonians 5:23, 2 Thessalonians 1:7, 8.

the reaping of the vine and the treading out of the grapes in the wine-press of the wrath of God. Its most vivid description is in 2 Thessalonians 1:6-10 where the angels and the saints are both mentioned. This final *parousia* is a *parousia* of final judgement and destruction:

> *It is a righteous thing that God deems it just to repay with affliction those who afflict you and to grant rest with us to you who are afflicted, when the Lord Jesus is revealed from heaven with his mighty angels in flaming fire, inflicting vengeance upon those who do not know God and upon those who do not obey the gospel of our Lord Jesus. They shall suffer the punishment of eternal destruction and exclusion from the presence of the Lord and from the glory of his might, when he comes on that day to be glorified in his saints, and to be marvelled at in all who have believed, because our testimony to you was believed.*

This final and fifth coming of Jesus is very prominent in the New Testament. When our Lord ascended in the clouds to the Father in Acts 1, the angelic messengers assured the disciples that this same Jesus would come in like manner as they had seen him go into heaven.

According to the New Testament, the Christian life should be characterised by the expectation of the righteous judgement of God.

It is worth noting that in Daniel 7 there are two comings. There is the coming of the Son of Man with the clouds to receive an eternal kingdom and dominion (7:13) and there is the coming of the Ancient of Days (7:22) which is followed by the judgement and the consummation of the kingdom. In the New Testament, Jesus, the Son of Man, is the subject of both comings. He is the Ancient of Days,[59] the Son whose name is Everlasting Father.[60] This identification of Jesus with Jehovah is one of the numerous biblical examples of testimony to the full deity of the Messiah.

The message of Jesus' lordship will be "the witness" on that day separating those who have been "ashamed of Christ", "those who have not obeyed the gospel of our Lord Jesus", from those who have ministered to his little ones, his brethren. A man's attitude to God, as

59. Revelation 1:14.
60. Isaiah 9:6.

expressed in his attitude to Christians, Christ's brethren, as to whether he has empathized and identified with them in their persecutions, and rejection by the world, will be the criterion of the judgement. The work of God[61] is to believe in God, that is, to believe in the one who is sent by the Father and is his express image. And this belief in Jesus is manifested in a man's attitude to his people, even to one of the least of the brethren of the King.

Each coming of Christ is celebrated with the sound of the trumpet, but this final coming will be accompanied by the last trumpet. The heavens will be rolled up like a scroll. Destruction and the punishment of consignment to the bottomless pit will overtake all sinners, human and demonic. Christ's people will be united with him forever in the new heaven and the new earth in which dwells righteousness.

61. John 6:29.

Chapter 8

OUR LORD'S LIFE OF FAITH[1]

*J*ESUS LIVED THE LIFE OF FAITH WHICH should characterise the lives of men and women. His enemies taunted him with "He trusts in God".[2] There was never a truer statement made, for on the Cross our Lord's faith was tested to the fullest imaginable extent and triumphed over all the temptations that arose from his circumstances and from the devil's suggestions.

Our Lord prayed earnestly in Gethsemane that he might not have to undergo what he saw in the future. Throughout his ministry he had sought to avoid arrest, for this was his duty to do so. He continued to do this during the last week in Jerusalem, which he had visited because of the obligation to the Passover, and he continued to seek to avoid arrest right up to the moment of Judas' appearance in the Garden of Gethsemane. He asked three of his disciples to watch while he gave himself to prayer, that he might not be arrested. When he realised that Judas was in the vicinity, he told his disciples to cancel his last suggestion that they might go on sleeping (now that his time of prayer was completed). His next comment to his disciples, "Arise, let us be going",[3] was interrupted by Judas and his posse while he was actually giving it. When our Lord saw how events were indicating the will of his Father, he told Peter, "The cup which my Father has given me shall I not drink it?"[4] Here was faith expressing itself in complete obedience.

Faith and obedience are really one. The loving obedience which the Christian should offer to his heavenly Father springs from the consciousness of his Father's presence, his Father's power, wisdom,

1. An unpublished essay. The only date referred to is in a note saying: "retyped 10th August 1993".
2. Matthew 27:43.
3. Recorded in Matthew 26:46; Mark 14:42.
4. John 18:11.

righteousness and love. Not a sparrow falls to the ground apart from him. No event overtakes us apart from him. How we should react, that is, what our duty is, comes from a knowledge of God, and the consciousness of his loving presence leads to the obedience of faith.

The faith expressed in our Lord's words—"The cup which my Father has given me shall I not drink it?"—continued throughout his trial and crucifixion and reached its acme in those three hours of darkness. God was asking Jesus to obey in a way that none of us is ever asked to obey. He was laying on the Lord our iniquity and our penalty for our rebellion against him. What this meant is symbolised in the hours of darkness when, as Luther put it: "Christ suffered everything which a condemned sinner has deserved and should suffer eternally".[5]

Or as Calvin put it, "He bore in his soul the pangs of the lost".[6]

It comes to the surface in the cry of desolation. But our Lord's continuance in faith is expressed in the fact that the question on the Cross is addressed to God, "My God, my God, why have you forsaken me?" There is no breach of relationship, no break in faith. It was the most bitter test when he became a curse for us.

Adam disobeyed because he failed to believe the truth of God's Word and the goodness of God in giving him that command. The tempter suggested that the threat of death would not be true and that the reason for the command not to eat of the fruit of the tree of the knowledge of good and evil was that God wished to withhold the blessing from Adam, namely of being equal with God. Mankind accepted these statements of Satan that God's Word was not true and that God's motives for giving them were self-centred. This failure of faith in God, in his veracity and goodness, led to disobedience. Jesus reversed mankind's sin. He did not believe that equality with God was something to be hung onto but became man, and his faith and obedience were tested to the uttermost even to the death on the Cross, that is, to the death of the curse of God on sin.[7]

The New Testament makes clear that Jesus' obedience is the ground of forgiveness. "By the disobedience of the one, many were

5.   WA. 45. 240f.
6.   *Institutes* II.15.10.
7.   Philippians 2:6-8.

constituted sinners; so through obedience of the one, many were constituted righteous".[8]

Jesus' life was the life of obedience because it was the life of faith. That faith and obedience were tested by the things that happened to him. "He learned obedience by the things that he suffered".[9] This faith and obedience was finally tested in the Garden of Gethsemane and by arrest and the events that followed, culminating on the Cross and the experience of sin-bearing, reflected in the three hours of darkness and the questioning cry of desolation. Such experiences are beyond our understanding—"we may not know, we cannot tell, what pains he had to bear". But his faith triumphed. Satan was defeated. Jesus rose victorious and so became the pattern for our faith. He is the Captain and Perfecter of faith, who for the joy that was set before him overcame the temptations involved in his bearing our sin in his own body on the tree, and so he was crowned with glory and honour through the resurrection and ascension to the throne.[10]

Our disobedience in the Garden of Eden and throughout each individual's life has involved us in death. Physical death is part of this penalty and is the expression of spiritual death with the ultimate penalty which disobedience to God brings as its consequence. Our Lord underwent both physical death and spiritual death in bearing our penalty. Our Lord's physical death was very painful yet not as painful as it might have been, for he died sooner than others who were crucified; but his spiritual death is beyond imagination and, if we are in Christ, beyond what we will ever experience.

Our Lord lived the life of faith which expressed itself in perfect obedience which we should live. Our Lord was asked to obey in matters which none of those in Christ will ever be asked to obey in, namely in the bearing of the penalty of sin. He obeyed without any breach of perfect faith towards God and with perfect love towards God and others, which is the fruit of faith.

The New Testament makes clear that our Lord's obedience is the ground of our righteousness. Faith and obedience are one, so that the

8. Romans 5:19; cf. Philippians 2:8; Hebrews 10:9-10.
9. Hebrews 5:18.
10. Hebrews 12:2.

New Testament is equally clear that it is our Lord's faith which is the ground of our righteousness. But this is obscured in modern translations because it has not been thought that Christ exercised faith, for he is the second person of the Trinity. Yet it is our Lord's faith which is said to be the ground of our salvation in Romans 3:22 and Philippians 3:9. In these passages the Greek, translated in the most straightforward way, states that it is the faith of Jesus Christ. If it is translated "faith in Jesus Christ", which is a possible translation, the phrase is redundant both in Romans 3 and Philippians 3. It becomes unintelligible in Romans 1:17. But when it is recognised that our salvation is through *the faith of* Jesus Christ for all who believe, then the Greek becomes transparently clear in all three passages. (In Romans 3:25 the definite article should be translated his: "through his faith" and *autou* should be aspirated *hautou.)* For his faith is tested to the uttermost, leading to complete obedience in every possible circumstance. That is the ground of the righteousness of those who are in Christ.

Chapter 9
JESUS' KNOWLEDGE[1]

*F*ROM THE BEGINNING OF CREATION, God the Creator was in relationship with his creation. His tender mercies cared for all. When the Son of God became man, God was entering into a new dimension of relationship, a closer relationship with his creation. Mankind had been created in his image after his likeness. All things had been brought into being through the Son and when for our sakes and our salvation the Son became man, it was perfect man that the Son became. In perfect human nature, created in God's image, there is nothing which is not a reflection of God, so that when the Son took our nature in the womb of the blessed virgin, he did not take anything foreign to his own nature. Nor did the fact that his divine person was the subject of our human nature distort our nature because it was the image of his. He was truly human as well as truly divine. He remained perfect in his divinity without any change or distortion or limitation, and he was perfect in his humanity without any alien, non-human element.

His humanity is as God created humanity, and as God intended and purposes humanity to be. God's purposes never fail.

It was not God's will that Adam should partake of the tree of the knowledge of good and evil. That was a sin. It follows that Jesus' humanity was free from this.

The Genesis narrative suggests that the Tree of the Knowledge of Good and Evil represented 'independence in knowledge' just as God possesses independent knowledge. "And the Lord God said, 'Behold the man is become as one of us, to know good and evil'".[2] This suggests that man was meant to be dependent on God for his knowledge,

1.   Unpublished essay.
2.   Genesis 3:22.

as he is in every other aspect of his life, and consequently knowledge of
evil was not to be part of man's experience. This would be a blessed
state, for innocence is much better than knowledge of evil, though this
notion is derided by the world. Yet, because of the evil present in our
world, complete innocence is no longer practical or wise.

Man's created dependence on his relationship with God for his
knowledge reflects the relationship within the Trinity, in whose image
man was made. For within the Trinity the Father shows the Son
everything he does. The Son is eternally the only begotten God, just as
the Father is the source of life within the Trinity (the Father gives the
Son to have life in himself), so he is the source of knowledge. Only
God could become man without any change in what he is eternally, for
man is made in God's image. This means that God can take man's
nature to himself without change in himself, though, of course, with
change in his relationship with mankind, his creation.

No created being can become another created being without
ceasing to be what he was before; or if he remains what he was, his
assumption of humanity is merely docetive, merely appearance. But
when the Son of God became man there was no change in his
Godhead nor any mere appearance in his humanity.

Jesus of Nazareth was the eternal God, the "I Am" of eternity. The
New Testament witness to this is clear and abundant. He was God the
Son in the triune God of Father, Son and Holy Spirit, into whose name
all the nations of the world are to be converted.

God the Son expresses the Godhead. He is the word, he is the efful-
gence of his Being.[3] Thus when God manifested himself to man, it was
the Son, the only begotten God, who manifested God.[4]

Before the incarnation of the Son of God, God had already manifested himself in creating man in his image, after his likeness.[5] Thus,
the Son of God taking our nature and becoming man while remaining
himself without change in any way, presents no problem to our intellect. For there is nothing in man as God created him that is foreign to
the nature of God, not even man's body. For in a world of material

3.   Hebrews 1:3.
4.   John 1:18.
5.   Genesis 1:26.

beings, spiritual beings manifest themselves in material bodies which are real bodies and not mere phantoms. Thus Gabriel at Nazareth and the angels at the tomb had real bodies and real clothing. So too did Jesus after his resurrection. He ate and drank with his disciples.[6] So too, did the Lord, and the two angels who visited Abraham and had a meal with him. Similarly when the two angels took the hands of Lot and his family, it was real muscles which gripped those hands and pulled. This is doubtless the explanation of Genesis 6:1ff. Man's created limitations are not sinful but pin-point man's relation to God his creator, which is one of entire dependence, just as within the Godhead the Son is begotten by the Father, a relationship which is eternal and not merely preliminary to a new situation.

Within the Trinity, the Son is eternally begotten of the Father. This is the eternal relationship of the Persons and man, created after God's likeness, created to be dependent *in all respects* on God.

Knowledge is the most characteristic of human attributes. When man is compared to the rest of creation only man of all God's creation has been given knowledge, knowledge of God, knowledge of right and wrong, knowledge of the world and its workings (fallen man only values the last!). Within the Godhead however, there is a source. In the Godhead the Son receives knowledge from the Father. The Father shows him all things that he does. As he was created, man was dependent on God for all things, including knowledge. Partaking of the fruit of the Tree of the Knowledge of Good and Evil was forbidden him. He was not to be independent in his knowledge as God was,[7] but to be dependent on God. In his rebellion, man opted for independence in knowledge, as well as in other things. Of course, he did not succeed in being independent, but he did succeed in cutting himself off from the source of knowledge, God, in whom all wisdom and knowledge dwells.

Humanity is now characterized by ignorance, and very gross ignorance. Mankind suffers a great number of ills as a consequence of this ignorance. For example, all the natural evils, the loss of life and of property, which result from earthquake, flood and similar such like calamities of natural forces would easily have been avoided if mankind had remained in fellowship with God, the source of all knowledge and who, as James

6. Acts 1:1-5.
7. Genesis 3:22.

reminds us, gives freely of his knowledge to all who look to him.[8]

When the Son of God became man, it was man's nature in its pristine goodness that he took, not the defective self-centred, rebellious nature that we inherit as the entail of Adam's sin. He did not partake of the sin of independence from God, or of independent knowledge, which was forbidden man at his creation.

What he knew was the knowledge that the Father gave him through his natural human faculties for acquiring knowledge and through his unbroken filial fellowship with his Father. There was no change in his relationship with his Father as the result of his incarnation. But now that he was in a new context, having taken our nature and become man, the knowledge that the Father willed him to have, that is, the things that the Father showed him, would be fully and truly human. Thus he grew in knowledge in the way that God created men and women to grow, through the experiences of life, through the structures of their mind, through the teaching of their elders and especially through their perfect unbroken fellowship with their heavenly Father. This is how Jesus grew in knowledge and how he attained to the perfection of knowledge. The Gospels show that in some things Jesus had profound knowledge, in others complete ignorance. It is worthwhile to review the evidence.

Consider Jesus' out-of-the-ordinary knowledge. Jesus knew men's thoughts (especially their evil thoughts):

- "Jesus, knowing their thoughts, said, 'Why do you think evil in your hearts?'".[9] An alternative reading is "Jesus, seeing their thoughts", that is, visible in their faces and their mutterings. A parallel passage is, "Jesus perceiving in his Spirit that they so reasoned".[10]
- "Jesus knew their thoughts".[11]
- "Jesus, knowing their thoughts, said to them 'Every kingdom divided against itself...'".[12]
- "When Jesus saw the reasoning of their heart, he took a little child..."[13]

8.   James 1:5.
9.   Matthew 9:4.
10. Mark 2:8.
11. Luke 6:8.
12. Matthew 12:25.
13. Luke 9:47.

➤ "Jesus did not trust himself to them, for he knew all men and did not need that any should bear witness concerning man; for he himself knew what was in man."[14]
➤ "I know you that you have not the love of God in yourselves."[15]
➤ "Jesus, knowing in himself that his disciples murmured at this..."[16]
➤ "'There are some of you that believe not.' For Jesus knew from the beginning who they were that believed not and who it was that should betray him."[17]
➤ "Did I not choose you the twelve and one of you is a devil."[18]
➤ "He knew him that should betray him."[19]
➤ "Now we know that you know all things and do not need that any man should ask you. By this we believe that you came forth from God."[20]
➤ "Peter said, 'Lord, you know all things, you know that I love you'."[21]

These verses indicate that Jesus knew the heart of man. Jesus declared people's sins were forgiven because he knew their heart, that is, their repentance and faith, and he knew the mind of God, that he freely forgives the penitent.

All Christians (i.e., all those included in the Son of Man) may do the same for they have the mind of Christ, that is, the word of God and the Spirit of God and so may know a person's relationship to God, and if repentant believing sinners, may declare their sins forgiven: "whose soever sins you forgive, they are forgiven".[22] "The Son of Man has authority on earth to forgive sins".[23]

Note that what the New Testament calls the forgiveness of sins, is a declaration of an existing state. The Greek is always "Your sins have

14. John 2:24, 25.
15. John 5:42.
16. John 6:61.
17. John 6:64.
18. John 6:70.
19. John 13:11.
20. John 16:30.
21. John 21:17.
22. John 20:23.
23. Luke 5:24.

been forgiven".

The preaching of the gospel and the declaration of the forgiveness of sins are identical concepts. Thus in Luke 24, Jesus told his disciples to preach forgiveness of sins in his name. On the same occasion John puts it thus: "Jesus said 'Receive the Holy Spirit. Whose soever sins you forgive they are forgiven and whose soever sins you retain, they are retained'".[24]

All Christians have authority to declare sins forgiven. In the congregation, the public declaration of the forgiveness of sins is normally restricted to those who have authority to preach the gospel and expound God's word publicly in the congregation.

All prophecy is given for the purpose of being proved false (cf. Jonah). Prophecy does not control the future nor should prophecy control our actions in the present.

On two occasions Jesus exercised a knowledge not unlike clairvoyance. In John 1:48, "Jesus told Nathanael 'Before Philip called you, when you were under the fig tree, I saw you'". And again, in Matthew 17:27, Jesus told Peter "Go to the sea and cast a hook and take up the fish that first comes up and when you have opened his mouth you shall find a shekel." (Is it possible that this word should be taken figuratively, like praying that a mountain should be cast into the sea?)

On several occasions Jesus predicted his crucifixion and his resurrection on the third day. He also predicted the destruction of Jerusalem and the worldwide preaching of the gospel and the conversion of Jew and Gentile within the lifetime of his hearers.[25] Yet it is interesting to note that our Lord took steps right up to the last moment—"Come let us be going"—to avoid his arrest and consequent crucifixion. Jesus was a prophet, and all prophecy is contingent. Thus Jonah prophesied that within forty days Nineveh would be destroyed. His words were God's words. His prophecy was not fulfilled. Nineveh was not destroyed. Jonah had surmised that this would be the outcome of his prophecy. Prophecy is a human activity, though not absolute but contingent.

Thus Jesus' prediction of his death was God-given prophecy, as Jonah's was, but unlike Jonah, he did everything he could—including intense prayer—to ensure that it did not come true. This he should have

24. John 20:22-23.
25. Matthew 24:34.

done, as Jonah ought also to have done (and which, indirectly, he did!).

The Gospel records of Jesus' life show that he grew in knowledge from infancy onward. To grow in wisdom, as Luke testifies Jesus did[26] implies that the gaining of fuller knowledge diminishes earlier ignorance. Jesus himself said that he was ignorant of the day of judgement.[27]

There are many indications in the Gospels that Jesus' knowledge was limited in the ordinary way that human knowledge is limited. When the woman who had an issue of blood touched him in faith to be healed of her sickness, he did not know who touched him, though he was conscious by the inward sensation of his body that power had gone from him. His ignorance is shown by his turning around to see who it was and, when he failed to see, because the woman had hidden herself in the crowd, he asked "Who touched my clothes?", but received no reply. His disciples, and Peter in particular, expostulated: "The crowd is thronging you, why then ask 'who touched me?'", Jesus gave them the reason for his question. "Someone touched me, for I felt (literally 'knew') power had gone out from me." Mark adds, "he continued looking around to see who had done this thing".[28] It is plain from this narrative that Jesus did not know who touched him. The only way to avoid this conclusion is to say that Jesus' reply to Peter's genuine surprise and his continuing to look around to see who had done it after he had replied to Peter, was to deceive Peter and the other disciples as to the nature of his question; namely that, although his question was not to elicit knowledge, he wished his disciples to think that it was. And this would mean that his words and his actions were for the purpose of giving this false impression and that the evangelists Mark and Luke, were either taken in themselves in giving their account, or else cooperating in giving a false impression of the import of our Lord's question.

The straightforward interpretation of the narrative is that Jesus asked a simple question to find out what he didn't know before. This is the normal reason for asking questions. Jesus' humanity was true humanity. He grew in knowledge in the normal way. His elders instructed him. It is clear from his later ministry that he knew the Scriptures thoroughly.

26. Luke 2:40.
27. Mark 13:32-37.
28. Mark 5:30-32; Luke 8:44-46.

He was brought up in a pious home and we may assume that, like Timothy, from a child he was instructed in Scriptures by parents and grandparents.[29] We catch a glimpse of this learning process of his childhood when, at the age of twelve, Jesus visited the temple at Jerusalem and sat at the feet of the official teachers of the law "listening to them and asking them questions".[30] On his return from Jerusalem to Nazareth Luke adds, "Jesus continued to increase in wisdom."[31]

To increase in wisdom means to move from lesser knowledge to greater knowledge. The precondition of growth is previous limitation and this is an essential element of human life. Limitation in knowledge is quite different from error in knowledge. Error is failure to recognise limitation and is a consequence of sin.

There are many other indications in the Gospels that Jesus showed the ordinary human limitations in knowledge. He asked questions of others on matters he was anxious to learn.[32] Events sometimes fell out in a way he had not anticipated.[33] He expressed surprise at the turn of events.[34] He approached the fig tree with hopes which were not fulfilled.[35] From Mark's explanation it might even be gathered that Jesus did not know the agricultural seasons in the Judaean mountains, having lived all his life in Galilee, which is below sea level. His ministry did not achieve all that he aimed for.[36]

All these incidents are the natural and completely innocent expressions of our human life in which our knowledge is the consequence of our experience of events. Our knowledge is not *a priori* but follows after our experience unless we have been taught beforehand from someone else's experience.

In Mark 6:31-34 our Lord changed his intentions as the result of unforeseen events. On another occasion he changed his intentions as the result of further reflection. Jesus told his brothers "I am not going

29. 2 Timothy 1:5; 3:14-15.
30. Luke 2:46.
31. Luke 2:52.
32. John 11:34; Mark 6:38, 9:21; Luke 8:30, 45, 46.
33. Mark 6:31.
34. Luke 2:49; Mark 4:40, 7:18, 8:21, 14:37.
35. Mark 11:13.
36. Luke 13:34.

up to this feast… but when his brothers had gone up to the feast, then he also went up, not openly, but as it were secretly".[37] To change your intentions, even your expressed intentions, is an entirely blameless human action. To forbid the expression of an intention because it may later be changed would be absurd, for this would impose silence about intentions, as every intention upon matters of indifference is potentially open to change. (However it should be noted that the reading in the Greek text is not absolutely certain. Many manuscripts state that Jesus told his brothers "I am not *yet* going up to this feast").

It is plain that Jesus' knowledge was truly human knowledge, gathered in the way our knowledge may be gathered and limited as ours is, not only in heavenly things ("of that day knows no man, neither the angels nor the Son, but the Father only") but also of earthly experiences. On the other hand it is plain that Jesus had a much truer and deeper knowledge of human nature than we have and also a clearer vision of the future. The testimony to this is very clear in the Gospels. For example, Jesus declared with full assurance on several occasions that people's sins had been forgiven. Only those who know the state of a person's soul and the mind of God can do this, though Jesus did promise his disciples that they also would have this authority.[38]

On another occasion, as we have noted already, Jesus displayed knowledge akin to clairvoyance when he saw Nathanael under the fig tree.[39]

Although Jesus spent the night in prayer before he chose his disciples,[40] amongst whom he chose Judas Iscariot, John tells how Jesus knew from the beginning who it was who should betray him. Jesus' words "Did I not choose you twelve and one of you is a devil" express surprise that one whom Jesus had chosen as a disciple should have turned out the way he had.

Jesus had a true and profound insight into people. "Jesus did not commit himself to them because", as John said, "Jesus himself knew everyone and had no need that any should testify about anybody for he himself knew what was in each person".[41] At the Last Supper, the

37. John 7:8-10.
38. Peter alone: Matthew 16:19; disciples: Matthew 18:18; John 20:23.
39. John 1:48.
40. Luke 6:14-16.
41. John 2:24-25.

disciples testified of Jesus "we know that you know all things"[42] and after Jesus' resurrection Peter echoed the same truth "Lord, you know everything…".[43]

A prophet knows the future through the Spirit of God. Prophecy declares the mind of God as to what he is going to do. But all prophecy is contingent. Jonah knew this. He was apprehensive that the clear prophecy that God had given him to proclaim, and of which he fully approved (for he was a patriot) might not come true, as indeed it turned out. No prophecy of judgement need come true, if there is repentance, nor any prophecy of blessing, if there is a continuance of unrepented sin.

Jesus was a prophet. He foretold early in his ministry that the days would come when the bridegroom would be taken away. Yet he took every precaution to prevent this happening. He held a low profile. He retired to the desert when animosity grew strong.[44] This was true human behaviour. It is our duty to minimize unnecessary risks, though it is also our duty to be fully obedient to God's law. It was this later consideration that brought our Lord to Jerusalem on his final visit, though he knew the dangers and his disciples were most reluctant to accompany him.[45]

In the last weeks of his ministry Jesus became more specific in his prophecy about his imminent crucifixion,[46] especially on the last evening of his life.[47] But he was still active in seeking to avoid it to the very last moment.

It would seem that the place for the Passover supper was kept secret from the authorities,[48] who sought an opportunity of arresting him without the crowds around to protect him. The place where he slept at night was also secret and had to be betrayed to the authorities by a disciple. When, in the Garden of Gethsemane, Jesus prepared by fervent prayer for what he anticipated but which he was determined, if possible, to

42. John 16:30.
43. John 21:17.
44. John 11:54.
45. John 11:7, 8, 16.
46. Mark 8:31, 32; 9:12.
47. Matthew 26:28, 42.
48. Matthew 26:17, 18.

avoid, he asked three of his disciples to keep a look out while he prayed.[49] They also needed to avoid the test, so they should give themselves to prayer even as they watched.[50] But apparently they were quite unaware of the crisis and went to sleep, even twice. On completion of his prayer, Jesus told them they could now sleep without interruption, presumably because he would take over the watching. But he had no sooner given them this permission than he said, "Hold it".[51] He had seen Judas and his gang approaching. He explained "He who betrays me is close" and added, "Come, let us get out of here". But it was too late. He hadn't completed his sentence when Judas burst through the darkness. All three Gospels note that while Jesus was still saying "Come, let us get out of here", the posse was upon them, so making Jesus' intended escape impossible.

It was right and truly human that Jesus, though he foresaw his death prophetically, should take every step to avoid it and to hope and pray that it would not happen. These things are our duty to do. Our actions are limited only by our knowledge of God's character, that is, our knowledge of what is right. But when events show what God's will is, then those who are in true relationship with God will accept the cup which their Father is giving them, as Jesus did,[52] making every effort to avoid it if they can, as Jesus did, but not transgressing righteousness in an effort to achieve this.[53]

The basic feature of man's nature is that he is contingent, that is, that he is dependent on something other than himself, dependent on his parents, dependent on his fellows, dependent on the resources of the earth, and above all, dependent on God. Because of his sinfulness, man is fiercely resistant to and resentful of the idea that he is dependent. "I am the captain of my fate, I am the master of my soul." But a detached, disinterested examination of our human situation makes it abundantly clear that we are contingent, dependent beings.

Our knowledge is also contingent. We acquire it from observation of events and from the instruction of others who have observed events before us. God's knowledge, however, is absolute and independent of

---

49. Matthew 26:37.
50. Matthew 26:41.
51. Matthew 26:45.
52. Matthew 26:39.
53. John 18:11, Matthew 26:52.

observation. He knows all things because they are in his mind before they are in actuality and they only remain in actuality so long as he wills them. Naturally, then, he knows the future and can tell us of it through his Spirit in his prophets. We are all dependent on God for "life and breath and all things".[54] Knowledge is one of the most important gifts included in these "all things". Independent knowledge was not part of God's created purpose for us.[55] We were to be dependent on God for the knowledge he saw it was wise for us to have through his Spirit, as well as through our own experience of events and the experience of those who went before us.

Such limitation of knowledge of the future, which is characteristic of man as created, is an essential basis for the exercise of faith in God. To live by faith means to trust God for the future. In his word God has given us innumerable promises, both general and specific, of his protection and provision for us in our future. We are to glorify him by trusting him. Faith in God, expressing itself in attitudes and actions, is the true worship of God. Without faith in him it is impossible to please him.[56] To live by faith in God is the most characteristic feature of human life as God created it. Naturally, therefore, Jesus, the perfect man, lived by faith. His faith was tested in his temptations throughout his life and his ministry. The testing reached its acme in his passion. In Hebrews chapters 11 and 12 the author lists a host of God's people who lived by faith, mentioning some of the actions which expressed that faith. The supreme example of faith that he lists is Jesus "the sole leader and completer of faith... who endured with patience the cross".[57]

We, too, are to live by faith. Our knowledge of the future is contingent on God. We know from his abundant promises what he will be for us in the future, though we depend on events to know what that future will be. But we know from God's word how we should behave when that future comes, and as we trust God to be faithful, so we glorify God, we worship him and we are united with Christ in bringing in God's rule, God's kingdom. The prayer, "Your kingdom come" implies,

54. Acts 17:25.
55. Genesis 3:22.
56. Hebrews 11:6.
57. Hebrews 12:2.

for us, our faithfulness to a faithful God. This overthrows Satan.

Our Lord's knowledge, which he received from his Father in his incarnate life, was not the sort of knowledge that excluded contingency. With God nothing is contingent; he sees the end from the beginning. Human knowledge is contingent, for we do not know all the causes, nor the wills of others (or of ourselves) which go to make up the event.

Nor did our Lord's knowledge exclude faith: knowledge which rests on the character of God. It is sure knowledge but it is different from the clear knowledge which arises from all the knowledge of all the causes, the knowledge of the wise, righteous and loving will of God, the ultimate cause, and which God alone knows. Thus our Lord's knowledge was truly human knowledge. Contingent prayer would be impossible otherwise and so, too, would faith.

Yet when our Lord prayed "Let this cup pass from me, for all things are possible for you", his knowledge of the future must have been contingent. He would not have prayed thus if he had known that it was not God's will that the cup should pass away. But this he learned from the events which immediately followed, so that he accepts the cup as "The cup which my Father gives me".

In taking our nature and becoming man Jesus accepted the limitations of human nature in its perfection. Thus he accepted the limitation of knowledge that goes with human nature.

ASSORTED NOTES

1. He did not know what was, humanly speaking, contingent on other people's will, for example, who touched him.
2. But he did know what was in man. Thus he knew how man would react. We also know this partially, and grow in knowledge of human nature with growing experience. Jesus knew human nature fully, but this is essentially human knowledge.
3. Jesus did not know what the Father had retained in his own knowledge, for example, the day of the end of the age.

His sinlessness would prevent him from saying anything that was beyond his knowledge. Therefore all his words remain utterly reliable and none will pass away.[58]

Within the Trinity, the knowledge of the Son springs from the initiative of the Father. "The Father loves the Son and shows him everything he does".[59]

In the Garden of Eden man depended on God for his knowledge. But man sought to be independent of God and to be his own source. This was forbidden, but man in a way achieved it by disobedience. He became like God, knowing good and evil. It was really a form of ignorance, for through his disobedience he had cut himself off from fellowship with God, who is the source of knowledge.

In the incarnation, God was restored as the source of man's knowledge. Jesus knew what the Father in his wisdom revealed. He revealed it sometimes supernaturally, sometimes by ordinary means, for example, by the study of the Old Testament, by instruction of others, by experience of life. Thus our Lord sometimes gave evidence of extraordinary knowledge, sometimes of ordinary knowledge and sometimes of ignorance in those matters which the Father in his wisdom kept within his own will.

Prayer—which is petition—implies lack of specific knowledge.

58. Matthew 24:35.
59. John 5:20.

Chapter 10

The work of Christ; the faith of Christ; the obedience of Christ; the curse of Christ

 HAVE BEEN WRITING A LITTLE BIT OF theology. It is wonderful how the passages of the Bible stand out clearly with deep meanings, although one has been reading them over and over again for years, and knows their general meaning.

Growing in knowledge of what the Bible says is a great encouragement in reading the Bible daily. The devil is at work to stop us and distract us, of course, as well as to distract and stop us praying. But we all must persevere, as it is the life-line to relationship with God, and to joy, peace and hope.

The verses I have been thinking of are the verses which speak of Christ's obedience being the ground of our salvation, that is:

Romans 5:19: "As through the obedience of the one person many were justified" (made righteous).

Philippians 2:8: "He was obedient to death, even the crucifixion" (the expression is being killed by being hanged on a tree, which is the sign of being under God's curse). "He became a curse for us"[2] during the three hours of darkness on Calvary. That is, he experienced hell for us on the cross.

Faith and true obedience are one. True obedience is loving obedience springing from the heart because you know the wisdom and the righteousness and the love of the One who requests your obedience, and that he has the right to request obedience.

---

1. A sermon; date and occasion unknown.
2. Galatians 3:13.

Jesus' obedience was perfect all his life; that is, his faith in his heavenly father never wavered; that is, it issued in perfect obedience. The New Testament often speaks of Jesus' faith as the basis of our salvation, just as it speaks of Jesus' obedience as the basis of our salvation.

We know what we ought to do, that is, the right thing, the fair, pure, just, kind thing in every circumstance, but the content of obedience, the thing we have to do, is indicated by the circumstances we find ourselves in.

God is in complete control of our circumstances. In some circumstances, obedience is quite simple, though in others much more difficult. This latter Christ realized in Gethsemane when he prayed so strenuously to his heavenly Father that his Father might alter the circumstances which appeared to be looming. But when the circumstances (i.e. his arrest) indicated what the cup was that his Father was giving him, he drank it in perfect faith in him, and perfect obedience.[3]

That is, he learned obedience by the things that were happening to him, in this case by what he was suffering. As Hebrews 5:8 says, "he learned obedience by what he suffered", that is, he learned by experience what was involved in obeying fully. I believe this comes out most clearly in the cry of desolation from the cross. It was a question implied by faith for it was directed to his heavenly Father (Psalm 22:1, "My God, my God, why have you forsaken me?").

There was no shaking of the fist in God's face. It sprang from his suffering, the awful depths of hell which could not be grasped[4] by the human mind until experience showed what was involved in bearing the penalty of sin. But Jesus persevered in obedience, that is, the right thing in the circumstances. He was involved in doing the right thing by remaining unshaken in faith in almighty God and in the perfection of his character. His faith remains unshaken till the end when a great shout of joy will be in [...][5] to say: 'It is finished!" and "Father, into your hand I commend my spirit".

And what a great expectation of joy he received (alluded to in Hebrews 12:2). We who are justified by Christ are of one spirit with

---

3. John 18:11; Matthew 26:53-54.
4. "be grasped' has been added. Original unclear.
5. Word missing.

him.[6] We who are saved by faith in him are saved by his faith and his obedience as he bore perfectly our penalty, and will share his joy in all its many facets.

We are called to the privilege of sharing his sufferings in faith and obedience, and so winning the victory over the world, Satan and sin, as Jesus did. Sharing his victory, that is, his trust/faith in God who controls all circumstances, who will not allow Satan to overcome us in those temptations which will be too strong for us.

But it is God's purpose that, in these temptations, we obey by seeing him who is invisible, and so remaining strong in faith in our God and Saviour, as Jesus did.

6.   1 Corinthians 6:17.

him. Whatever means of faithful love we use for us and that the obedience as he bore pain any penance and suffering his joy in all he suffered.

We are called to the privilege of sharing his suffering and obedience, and so winning the triumph of his world appeases and Jesus did restore his nature in us in us, the Lord his movement in and won us to all sanctification which will not allow Spirit to work save in those intentions which will be too strong for us.

With this one purpose then, in our accomplishment we offer by seeing that all conscience that so much greater cost in us than our God and Saviour Jesus Christ.

Chapter 11

I WAS ASKED TODAY HOW THE CRUCIFIXION of Jesus fitted into a religious view of the world. It is an important question because it is only through the crucifixion that we can escape the penalty of not doing what we know we ought to do and of doing what we know we ought not to do. When we act against our knowledge of right and wrong we will certainly be condemned; we will not escape even though for the time being we may have forgotten all about it. All our actions are always present in the mind of God and our memory will revive on the judgement day. But Jesus can save us from this lost eternity through his cross and we can begin to experience this now before the judgement day comes, as it surely will come, as surely as today followed yesterday.

Let me explain how the cross of Jesus saves us.

Jesus of Nazareth lived a perfectly good life. You might think that this would make him popular, but on the contrary, people find a good life a threat. They do not like it; it points the finger at their own short-comings; it makes them feel uncomfortable. They do not like that sort of person in their group. Jesus predicted that this would always be so. He told his friends, "if they have persecuted me they will persecute you also".[2] Christians in Cambodia and South Vietnam are experiencing this now. We ought to pray for them that they may be faithful to the end and so obtain the crown of life. We do not know how soon our turn will come: it may be sooner than you think!

Now Jesus always reacted in a right way to the persecutions he experienced. For example, a disciple betrayed him but he did not vituperate; he was gentle. His associates misunderstood him, yet he continued to serve them. When unjustly arrested and when lies were

---

1. Protestant Faith Broadcast, 4 May 1975.
2. John 15:20.

told about him in court, he did not answer rudely; he did not threaten; his reaction was always right. He kept his self control, he kept his kindly love, he was thoughtful for the needs of others. He spoke words of encouragement to the man dying next to him, and he prayed for those who were killing him. In a word, Jesus never gave way under the cruel and painful suffering, the unjust accusations and condemnation and the falsehoods with which he was surrounded. But in the midst of this piled-up wickedness of men and devils, he did what was right at every point. It was a complete victory over sin and wrong, the first such complete victory ever won on this earth. That is why it can save us, because it defeated the sin that drags us to hell.

But there is more to it still. Jesus not only did the right thing to his fellow man in the midst of the cruelty and injustice heaped on him by men led by Satan, but he also did the right thing with regard to what God asked him to bear for our sakes. Jesus underwent the spiritual penalty for our wrongdoing. Everything we do wrong has consequences that cannot be avoided, but Jesus willingly identified with us and bore the penalty. We may learn a little of the awfulness of this experience as we contemplate the agony of Jesus as he faced his coming death, wrestling in prayer in the Garden of Gethsemane on the evening before the crucifixion. On the afternoon of Calvary itself the uncanny darkness was an outward expression of the darkness of sin's separation from God which Jesus was bearing. The depth of his spiritual suffering was indicated in his words on the cross, "My God, my God, why have you forsaken me?" Throughout the bitter agony Jesus was gladly obedient, he was the divine Lord, as man bearing man's sins in himself.

Through that suffering and death perfectly borne, the penalty and power of our sins have been blotted out. That is why if we pray to Jesus the king we may face the judgement day without fear, for our *wrong* doings are hidden out of sight by Jesus' perfect *right* doing. He identified with us in our sin so that we might be identified with him in his goodness.

Jesus, the complete victor, rose again from death. This was to be expected, for death is the penalty for sin and victory over sin means victory over death. He rose to God's right hand and now rules over every enemy—over sin, death and the devil. If we pray to him as our Lord, his victory is ours, our sins are forgiven, we have him as our friend and he will raise us from death to be with him forever.

Chapter 12

SOME ASPECTS OF THE ATONEMENT[1]

I HAVE BEEN ASKED TO ADDRESS THE Tyndale Fellowship of Australia on some aspects of the Atonement, and in seeking to discharge this privilege, I wish to examine two misunderstandings of the satisfaction of Christ which are current at present, and which have consequences affecting evangelical faith and practice. The first is exemplified in the *Report of the Lambeth Conference of Anglican Bishops* in 1958. It has bearing on the theology and conduct of the service of the Lord's Supper. The second is to be found in the writings of seventeenth century Calvinists and their modern successors, and has bearing on the way the gospel is presented in evangelism.

— I —

The centrality of the doctrine of the cross in the Christian message is not open to dispute. It is underlined by St Paul's summary of the gospel he preached at Corinth: "Christ crucified".[2] This is a paradoxical phrase. "Messiah crucified" was an enigma; the words are not self-interpreting. Why should the Messiah accomplish his mission through the way of the cross? What happened in the crucifixion? What is involved in it for the crucified One? These questions can never be completely explicated. We must be content with partial knowledge.

St Paul, in summarising the gospel which he preached at Corinth, described it as preaching "Christ crucified". He used an equally succinct phrase in Acts 20 to describe the gospel that he preached at Ephesus. On that occasion he spoke of "preaching the kingdom".[3] We

1. An undated paper delivered to the Tyndale Fellowship of Australia.
2. 1 Corinthians 1:23.
3. Acts 20:25.

may equate these two phrases, for they have reference to the same subject; that is, 'Christ crucified' and 'the kingdom' are one, for they are both the content of St Paul's gospel. A synonym for 'the kingdom' might be 'the sovereignty'. We see that 'the sovereignty' was the theme of St Paul's message, and that it centred on the cross, for it was at Calvary that the kingdom was decisively vindicated and demonstrated.

Christ's victory at Calvary is celebrated in the Old Testament, *inter alia*, in Psalm 2. This psalm is applied by the early Christians to the crucifixion of the Messiah.[4] It was at the cross that the kings of the earth set themselves, and the rulers took counsel together, against the Lord and against his Christ, and it was there that the machinations of the world, and the prince of the world, were dashed in pieces like a potter's vessel.

Now, the writer of the Apocalypse uses the terminology of Psalm 2 to describe the great conflicts of the world powers with the armies of heaven, which his visions embraced.[5] In all these verses we have an echo of the psalm as understood by the early church, which saw the kings of the earth gathered together against the Lord and against his Christ. This phraseology in the Apocalypse is only to be expected. After all, no Armageddon can be as fundamental as the Armageddon of Calvary. Every subsequent 'gathering together' of the servants of Satan against Christ is a less serious challenge against the sovereignty of God, than was that gathering together against Christ at Calvary. That was the decisive Armageddon. Subsequent Armageddons (and they are constant) and the final Armageddon, whatever form it may take, will all be fought in the light of that decisive victory. Or, to use parallel imagery, Christ crushed Satan's head at Calvary. That was the bruising foretold in Genesis 3. Yet the spiritual conflict continues,[6] and Satan is yet to be bruised under the feet of the saints.[7] The promise in the Garden was pre-eminently fulfilled at Calvary, and it is progressively being amplified in the experience of Christians in the world. So, too, the message of Calvary is the message of sovereignty once for all vindicated, and yet of a sovereignty still being worked out in victories over Satan.

4. Acts 4:25-30.
5. Revelation 16:14; 19:19; 20:8.
6. Ephesians 6:12.
7. Romans 16:20.

The death of Christ was the victory;[8] the resurrection the consequential glorification. But in what way was the death the victory? In what did that death consist? In Philippians 2, St Paul stresses the obedience of Christ. It is not hard to see how obedience in the face of temptation is a victory. But here we must be careful to state the matter accurately. It is not merely the willingness to obey, nor even the obeying considered formally, but the *content* of the obedience itself (i.e. the thing obeyed in) that was the victory. But what was this? What was it that God asked of Christ? Certainly this obedience which Christ rendered included the manifestation of a God-like character amid adverse circumstances. It included, that is, the repulsing of Satan's temptations to revile when reviled, or to threaten when suffering, and such like; it included thoughtfulness for others rather than for oneself, and the committing of one's cause in perfect faith to a faithful Creator.[9] All these things God asked of Christ, as he asks them of us—obedience, that is to say, to the law of God for men.

But there is clear indication in the Scriptures that God asked of Christ not only obedience in these, but obedience in something far deeper than these. Christ, in fulfilling the will of God "bore our sins".[10] He became "a curse for us".[11] He was "made sin for us".[12] "The Lord laid on him the iniquity of us all".[13] Here is a level of obedience which far transcends anything God asks of us. It is most important to recognize that though our obedience and Christ's are alike when viewed as to what is the proper response of man to God's will; yet from another point of view, that is to say, with regard to what it was that God asked by way of obedience, there is a great chasm between the obedience of Christ and our obedience. Of us God asks perfect conformity to the moral law. Christ rendered that. But of Christ God pre-eminently asked the bearing of the sin of the world. This was the real commission that Christ received from the Father. This was the purpose of his coming into the world, and the most acute of Satan's temptations was to

8.   Colossians 2:15; Ephesians 2:16; John 12:31.
9.   1 Peter 2:21-23.
10. 1 Peter 2:24.
11. Galatians 3:13.
12. 2 Corinthians 5:21.
13. Isaiah 53:6.

shrink from this cup the Father was giving him. We glimpse the depth of the temptation, and the consequential greatness of the victory in the agony in the Garden of Gethsemane. The cross was a victory not only in that it repulsed the temptations to which sons of Adam normally succumb, but more centrally, in that it was the repulsion of the most profound temptation a man could be subjected to, namely the temptation to shrink from and refrain from rendering that profound obedience which God was asking of Christ.

However, the cross was a victory from another and more fundamental point of view. It was the acme of God's exercise of sovereignty. We tend to think of God's sovereignty as most clearly seen in his control of inert matter, his control, for example, of the wheeling planets or the spinning electrons; but this is not so. Moral evil is the most intransigent foe to the rule of God. The cross was complete victory over evil in its deepest developments, for through it God brought to nought the devil, by providing a way of forgiveness through sin-bearing. At one stroke the wiles of Satan, begun in Eden, by which men were set at enmity with their Creator, and which were to lead to their eternal perdition, were overthrown. The work of the devil was pulverised. Forgiveness was provided in place of wrath, and the sovereignty of God over evil was matchlessly vindicated. The very centre of this victory was that Christ underwent the curse which was ours. God made Christ to be sin for us. He laid on him the iniquity of us all.

THE LAMBETH REPORT

Sin-bearing and substitution are at the very centre of this victory of the Atonement. It was the willingness to be a substitute for sinners here which was the index of Christ's obedience. His obedience cannot be properly conceived of apart from a clear recognition of what it was that God asked of him, i.e. sin-bearing for others. Yet this is the very thing that many modern theologians of the atonement fail to do. To speak of Christ's obedience in a general way, without recognition of that unique thing which God asked of Christ by way of obedience, leads to a very inadequate notion of the atonement, by failing to recognise the wide difference between the obedience we render, and the obedience Christ rendered. In particular, it leads to the error of equating our obedience and Christ's obedience as though they were both of a type. This error finds illustration in the *Committee Report of the Lambeth Conference of Anglican Bishops* in 1958. In speaking of Christ's sacrifice on Calvary, the Report says:

> *This sacrifice is a sacrifice of willing obedience, "Lo I come to do Thy will O God" (Heb 10:7; Phil 2:8), and inasmuch as Christ is not only perfect and representative man, but also the eternal Son of God, "this act of will is not only the one perfect response of humanity to the will of God, but it is also the will of God going out to man in yearning love" (see C. F. D. Moule* The Sacrifice of Christ, *p. 26). "The new man, the Adam who is Christ, fulfils in the Cross the thanksgiving of man to God. In Christ the fulness of God giving himself to man meets with the fulness of man offering himself to God" (Bouyer* Life and Liturgy, *p. 131).*[14]

Only a failure to distinguish and isolate what it was that the Bible says God asked of Christ in obedience can explain this strange language of the Report, which turns the curse of Calvary into a thanksgiving of man to God. Christ's obedience consisted in unflinchingly bearing our sins. *The Lambeth Report*, following Professor Moule and others, has confounded the willingness to obey and the obeying, with the thing obeyed, as though the coming to do the will of God (in the verse they quote from Hebrews 10) was the important thing. It is not even the doing of the will, considered 'formally', but the doing of the will considered 'materially', that is the essence of the work of Christ. Thus the writer to the Hebrews goes on to say "*By which will* we are sanctified".[15] That is, our salvation is grounded on the *content* of the will of God, which Christ fulfilled. The Lambeth bishops, however, are content to describe the sacrifice of Christ as an "act of willing obedience" and as "a sacrifice of willing obedience". But it is not possible to understand 'an act of obedience' without reference to the thing in which obedience is rendered, in Christ's case, the sin-bearing. But this, in fact, is what the Lambeth Bishops have not done. Indeed, they appear to be

14. *Report of the Lambeth Conference 1958*, 2.84.
15. Hebrews 10:10.

unaware that Christ's 'act of willing obedience' had any content to it at all! The willing obedience was not the essence of Christ's sacrifice, but rather it was the necessary concomitant of any offering acceptable to God. Unless we are prepared to say that it is not possible to offer anything to God but obedience, we must distinguish between the formal obedience in offering God what he asks for, and the actual offering itself. Thus the quintessence of Christ's sacrifice is not the willingness to obey, nor obeying in itself; but is rather the thing obeyed in, namely the enduring of the just penalty of sin inflicted at the hand of God for the propitiation of the wrath of God against sinners.

The failure to analyse what it was in which the obedience consisted leads to failure to differentiate between the character of our obedience and the character of Christ's obedience, and in turn has led the Lambeth Report to an inadequate theology of the Lord's Supper. This they interpret as being an offering of ourselves in the offering of Christ, which we make on his behalf to the Father. Our obedience and Christ's obedience are thought of as of a kind, and we are said to offer both to God in the Lord's Supper. Indeed, they say that if redemption is a past act, we can only enter into it in the Lord's Supper by either 'repeating it' or 'remembering it' (as though this latter were a bare and insipid activity!). They seem unaware of the Reformed doctrine that in the Supper we enter into Christ's death by *believing* it, accepting it by faith, and so receiving the benefits which God designed should flow from it, and thus praising and glorifying God. The truth is that in the Supper we appropriate the benefits which Christ's obedience in sin-bearing brings to us, and do not 'offer' either his obedience (i.e. his sin-bearing) or ours, or both together, as the Lambeth Report puts it. Our obedience (always partial) of conformity to the law of God is an obedience of response to the love of God in Christ, and it can never be equated with the sin-bearing which God asked of Christ and in which he obeyed perfectly once for all, and on the basis of which remission of sins and all other benefits of his passion are daily offered to us.

Cranmer puts the matter thus: "Although it be one Christ that died for us, and whose death we remember, yet it is not one sacrifice that he made of himself upon the cross and that we make of him upon the altar or table. For his sacrifice was the redemption of the world, ours is not so: his was death, ours was but a remembrance thereof: his was a taking away the sins of the world; ours is a praising and a thanking for the same; and therefore his was satisfactory, ours is gratulatory."[16]

The failure to analyse in what Christ's obedience consisted leads to the notion that Christ's redemptive work was not confined to Calvary. Redemption is said to be ongoing now in Heaven. Thus Professor Moule speaks of "the stream of Christ's obedient love which flows continually to the Father".[17] To maintain this view, it is necessary to minimise the scriptural testimony of 'once-for-allness' (the *hapax* and *ephapax* of Hebrews, and the *tetelestai* of John), by limiting it to an earthly shadow of a heavenly continuous redemption, as well as to ignore such teaching as "He was made sin for us" and "He became a curse for us", for it is impossible to think of Christ in Heaven as still under the curse of God. Indeed Moule explicitly rejects the church doctrine of propitiation.[18]

The Lambeth bishops (following Moule,[19] who bases himself on, and quotes at length, Dom Gregory Dix, who is a most unsafe guide to the theology of the Reformation) believe they have solved the dialectic of the medieval and Reformed view of the Lord's Supper. They deny that "the redeeming work of Christ is limited to the cross as a past act". Consequently they believe that in the Lord's Supper we enter into and take our part in an ongoing work of redemption that is now being offered by Christ to the Father in Heaven. "Christ with us offers us in Himself to God". Our obedience and his are fused, because they are thought of as of a kind.

But the Scriptures clearly teach that the work of redemption is finished. It has been accomplished by Christ alone. Already the Redeemer has received the reward for his work, which is finished and accepted. It is not possible to square with the teaching of Scripture any doctrine of the Lord's Supper which turns that Service from a supper into a sacrifice—from a thanksgiving for God's provision and a receiving of it, into an offering to God from us or from Christ, or worse still, from

16. Thomas Cranmer, *Works of Cranmer*, Parker Soc. (Cambridge: Cambridge University Press, 1844), 2.359.
17. C. F. D. Moule, *The Sacrifice of Christ* (Philadelphia : Fortress Press, c1964) p. 49.
18. *ibid* p. 46.
19. *ibid* p. 49ff.

both on a level together. The growing desire to stress the 'people's offering' of bread and wine, and of money, in the Lord's Supper is a direct result of this erroneous correlation of Christ's obedience and our obedience in redemption. It changes the service from a remembrance of Christ with faith and thanksgiving into an activity of ourselves.

— II —

LIMITED ATONEMENT

Substitution in sin-bearing is the centre of the New Testament doctrine of the Atonement, as well as the Old Testament adumbration of it. A realisation of this makes impossible the concept that Christ's redeeming work is continuing in Heaven now, or that we can join our obedience to his as part of the act of redemption.

On the other hand, there is a way of viewing Christ's satisfaction for sin which limits it in extent, so that Christ's atonement is not co-extensive with humanity, but is limited to those elect of God only. However, that the work of Christ extends uniformly to the whole of humanity becomes clear when it is considered under the following heads:

(a) The Incarnation. When Christ took man's nature in the womb of the blessed virgin, he took the nature which all men share, and not the nature of the elect only.

(b) Christ's Perfect Righteousness. When Christ lived a life of perfect obedience to the law of God, he fulfilled the obligation which rests on all men equally, and not an obligation which the elect alone have.

(c) Christ's Victory. When our Lord overcame all the wiles of the devil and bound the strong man, he overcame the common enemy of mankind, and not the enemy of the elect only.

(d) Christ's Bearing of the Curse. When our Lord, through his death on the cross, became a curse, he bore the curse which God threatens against all breakers of his covenant, and not the curse which is particularly applicable to the elect.

From this it will be seen that the work of Christ viewed in itself, and apart from its application, is co-extensive with humanity, or, in the old phraseology, "Christ's work is sufficient for all". Thus William

Cunningham wrote: "The atonement, viewed by itself, is just vicarious suffering, of infinite worth and value, and, of course, intrinsically sufficient, to expiate the sins of all men".[20] This may be underlined by reflecting, in contrast, that traditional theology has never regarded the atonement as intrinsically sufficient to expiate the sins of any fallen angel: that is, Christ has died for all men in a way he has not died for any fallen angel, and thus we may give a straightforward exegesis to those Scriptures which assert the universal extent of the atonement.

Thus *from the point of view of the preacher,* Christ has died for all his audience. All may accept the proffered salvation which Christ has provided. The preacher is not concerned with the intended application of the atonement, which at the time of the preaching still lies hidden in the counsel of God. Thus, from the point of view of the preacher presenting the gospel (which is the same as our point of view), all have an equal interest in the death of Christ. Were it not so, and not true that Christ had died for all men, it would not be possible to extend a universal offer; for the offer, if it is to be a true offer, must rest on true and adequate grounds, which cannot be less than the death of Christ for those to whom the offer is being made. Thus if the gospel is offered genuinely to all, it can only be offered because Christ died for all, and if for all, then the preacher is at liberty, and indeed obliged, to press home the offer, and to say to each sinner individually, "Christ has died for you".

The extent of Christ's work is not limited in itself, but only in the intentions and purposes of God, and consequently in the application of its benefits to those whom God had foreknown and predestined to be conformed to the image of his Son.

In intending to reconcile the elect only, the method God has chosen has been to make all men reconcilable. Both Calvinist and Arminian are right in what they affirm, but the Arminian is wrong in what he denies. The Arminian affirms that Christ made all men savable, and denies that he saves any. The Calvinist affirms that Christ saves the elect; but some Calvinists are inclined to speak as though the atonement in no wise affects the savableness of any others. Cunningham states, "The intended destination of the atonement was to effect and secure the forgiveness and salvation of the elect only...

20. William Cunningham, *Works of William Cunningham* (Edinburgh: T. & T. Clark, 1863) vol iii, p. 364.

God did not design or purpose, by sending his Son into the world, to save any but those who are saved".[21]

This is correct. Cunningham thinks that the doctrine of limited atonement follows, but this is a non sequitur. For the method by which the elect are saved is that they and the non-elect alike are made savable by Christ's death for mankind, if they will repent and believe, which God commands all to do. But only the elect do so, for only the elect receive the necessary grace, which grace to repent and believe was merited and purchased by Christ for his sheep; so that ultimately they are the only ones for whom Christ died.

All men receive benefits from Christ's death. This is agreed. It should be further agreed that one of these benefits is savableness—which no fallen angel has received. Thus it is true to say that Christ is a ransom for all, without limiting the word 'all', nor limiting the word 'ransom' to that which is less than complete salvation. The word 'for' is capable of two levels of meaning. Just as there are two levels of meaning in "Saviour of all men, especially of those that believe",[22] so there are two levels of meaning in "He died for all", and "Christ died for his sheep", and in "He is a Saviour of all", and "He saves his people".

It is not what limited atonement states positively, but what it states negatively, that is objectionable (that is, the use of the word 'only' for the more appropriate 'specifically', or 'especially').

In the phrase "Christ died for the elect", the word 'for' is ambiguous. If it implies intention, it is true. Thus Scripture affirms that Christ came to save his people from their sins. But if it applies to the extent of his atonement, it is not true; so that, with the Church of England Catechism, we are right in affirming that "Christ redeemed me, and all mankind"; and with the Synod of Dort that he efficaciously redeemed only the elect.[23] It is regrettable that the Westminster Confession has

21. *Works III*, p. 347.
22. 1 Timothy 4:10.
23. *Dort* 2.8. The Synod of Dort was convened by the Dutch Reformed Church in 1618-19 to deal with the 'Arminian controversy' (and other issues). It issued the five articles which came to be known as 'The five points of Calvinism', the third of which is 'a limited atonement'. By 'limited atonement' the Synod meant that the Christ's death was "sufficient for all but efficient for the elect".

gone beyond this scriptural position of the Synod of Dort, to confine the redemption of Christ exclusively to the elect. "Neither are any other redeemed by Christ...but the elect only" (3.6).

To deny, as "limited atonement" does, the propriety of laying on the conscience of the unconverted their duties to repent and believe the gospel, by telling them "Christ died for you", is improperly restrictive of the scope of the atonement, as seen from the point of view of preacher and hearer.

Owen rejects the concept that the decree of redemption is antecedent to election, with the retort "cui bono?"[24] This appears to be his only argument. Palmer uses the same argument, "There would be no sense, no use, no purpose in sending Christ to die for those whom he knew would never accept Christ".[25]

But this argument is a *non sequitur*. It also smacks of anthropocentrism (i.e. Arminianism). God is glorified even in those who are perishing. Even to these the gospel is a sweet savour of Christ unto God, though a savour of death unto death.[26] This could not be so if in the mind of God those not being saved were quite outside the scope of Christ's redemption.

'Limited atonement' in its commonly accepted modern use amongst Calvinists is a textless doctrine. This is a fatal defect for any doctrine for which a place in Reformed Theology is sought. The Bible certainly affirms that Christ laid down his life for his sheep, and that he purchased his church with his own blood; but nowhere is the sentiment expressed negatively, i.e. that he died for his sheep only, or that redemption is to be spoken of the elect only; and in fact biblical phraseology is opposed to such expression, e.g. 2 Peter 2:1, where it is affirmed that apostates were amongst those whom God had purchased.[27] Salvation and redemption are terms which properly belong to the elect (see, for example, the 'new song' of the living creatures and the elders before the Throne in Revelation 5:9). But in a secondary

24. John Owen, *The Death of Death* (London: Banner of Truth Trust, 1959) p. 37. Literally, "What good is it?"
25. Edwin H. Palmer, *The Five Points of Calvinism* (Grand Rapids: Moelker Printing, [1954?]) p. 37.
26. 2 Corinthians 2:15, 16.
27. Cf. also Romans 14:15, 20; 1 Corinthians 8:11.

sense, salvation and redemption through the death of Christ are spoken of in Scripture as applying to all men. A recognition of this terminology will prevent a harsh classification of humanity into the savable and the non-savable, after the fashion of the Valentinians.[28]

To summarise:

1. No purpose or intent of God ever fails.

2. The purpose of Christ's death was the salvation of the elect. Christ's death effects this.

3. It does not follow from these two points that the atonement (i.e., the work of Christ in discharging the penalty of the sin of mankind and fulfilling the obligations of the law) has reference to the elect only.

4. As the result of the atonement, all may be saved if they will repent and believe. So all may be told "Christ has died for you; therefore accept the proffered salvation".

The doctrine of 'limited substitution', which is used to defend 'limited atonement', goes too far. Thus B. B. Warfield in criticising Amyraldists[29], says that they alter the character of the atonement, and asks: "If sin is removed by Christ's substitution, what remains as a barrier to the salvation of sinners?"[30] But this proves too much, by excluding the paradox (as Barth does on the other side of the paradox). For the elect are not saved at the moment that the substitutional atonement was made at Calvary, nor is their sin then removed from them. This takes place only on the application of the atonement to themselves in regeneration. Till then, the elect are children of wrath, as the rest.[31] If the doctrine of substitution is to be pressed to support limited atonement, then it means that God is unjust to hold the elect accountable for their sins before they have turned to him in faith. An example of this erroneous

28. The Valentinians were a 2nd century gnostic sect who divided all mankind into three distinct categories: the pneumatics (i.e. themselves) who alone had access to the secret 'gnosis' (or knowledge) of salvation and would enjoy eternal bliss; other Christians (the 'psychics') who might inhabit a lower level of heaven; and the rest of mankind (the 'hylics') who were destined for damnation.
29. Amyraldists follow the system of Reformed theology put forward by Moise Amyraut in the 17th century. They hold to the formula: "Jesus died for all men sufficiently, but only for the elect efficiently".
30. B. B. Warfield, *The Plan of Salvation* (Grand Rapids: Eerdmans, 1935) p. 95.
31. Ephesians 2:3.

use of the doctrine of substitution to establish limited atonement may be drawn from *The Five Points of Calvinism* by Edwin H. Palmer, now on the faculty of Westminster Theology Seminary. Dr Palmer writes, "Finally, a conclusive argument is to be drawn from the nature of Christ's atonement. Is the atonement a substitution or not? It must be one or the other. Do we believe in the vicarious or substitutionary death of Christ or not? If so, then those for whom he died must be free from the penalty of the law because Christ satisfied the law. If Christ was the substitute for all men, then all men would be free from God's wrath and condemnation. For the atonement is objective. Christ paid for all. And if Christ paid for all, then all men are free. But of course even the Arminian will not assert that the unrepentant is free from the penalty of the law. Therefore he should admit that Christ did not die for the unrepentant. It is either-or. Christ's death was a substitute or not. And if it was an actual substitute, then the persons for whom it was made are free. But this obviously cannot apply to all men."[32]

If Christ's substitution is conceived of in this pecuniary way, it would follow that all the saints are free from the wrath the moment the substitution is made and accepted. Otherwise God would be unjust.

The particularism which is characteristic of Calvinism ought not to be applied at the point of the making of the atonement, but at its application. If supralapsarianism[33] is to be rejected, because "particularism, in the sense of discrimination, belongs in the sphere of God's soteriological, not in that of his cosmical, creation", so that the decree, or election belongs logically after the fall, as Warfield argues,[34] then on the same argument the decree of election is logically after the decree of atonement, where also, in fact, it belongs in the working out of the application of salvation. That is to say, the atonement is general, its application particular. If the reply is made that Scripture affirms that Christ entered the world to "save his people from their sins", it should

32. *Op cit* p. 40.
33. Supralapsarianism is the doctrine held by some Calvinists that (in logical order) God decreed both election and reprobation before the fall (*supra* above, *lapsus* fall). In this system, God's first decree was to glorify himself by electing some to salvation and others to damnation; the decrees to create the world, to permit the fall, and to provide salvation for the elect through Christ logically followed.
34. *The Plan of Salvation* pp. 88, 89.

also be noted that Scripture affirms God created his people to be his glory and praise.[35] But since the infralapsarian[36] does not regard this latter as establishing the decree of election prior to that of creation, he should not regard the former as bearing on the question whether the decree of election is subsequent to that of atonement.

Finally, it should be noted that limited atonement (as distinct from effective redemption) is not affirmed in the decrees of the Council of Dort, so it cannot be regarded as an essential bulwark against Arminianism. It finds no support, but the contrary, in the writings of Calvin. On Hosea 13:14, Calvin commented: "God does not here simply promise salvation but shows that he is indeed ready to save...the obstinacy of men rejects *the grace which has been provided* and which God willingly and abundantly offers" [my italics]. Moreover, it lacks the positive Scriptural testimony which the other four points of 'tulip' (let him that readeth understand!) are so rich in, so that it ought not to be placed on an equality beside them. Indeed, it appears to run counter to some plain verses in Scripture, such as "denying the Lord who bought them".[37] It cuts away the basis of a genuine offer of the gospel to all the world, and blunts the point of evangelism in preventing the pressing home of the claims of Christ on the consciences of the hearer, by interdicting such phrases as "Christ died for you", "God so loved you...".

The object of the doctrine of limited atonement is to ensure the truth that Christ's death saves his people effectively, as against the Arminian doctrine of general redemption, which holds that by the atonement Christ redeems all men, without necessarily effecting the salvation of any. But while rightly stressing that the atonement saves those whom God intends it to save, we should not speak of the substitution of Christ on Calvary in such a way as to overthrow other Scriptural points of view. Limited atonement as commonly propounded, introduces unscriptural concepts into the doctrine of God's relation to the world, and may prove an Achilles' heel for the revival of Reformed theology.

35. Isaiah 43:7.
36. Infralapsarians (*infra* below, *lapsus* fall) argue that the logical order of God's decrees is as follows: to glorify himself through creating mankind; to permit the fall; to elect some of the fallen race to salvation, and to pass by others, consigning them to damnation; to provide salvation through Christ for the elect.
37. 2 Peter 2:1.

Chapter 13

THE BAPTISM AND THE FULLNESS OF THE SPIRIT[1]

1. The Holy Spirit
2. Anointed with the Spirit
3. Pentecostal power
4. The Holy Spirit in the Trinity

1. THE HOLY SPIRIT

THERE IS A GOOD DEAL OF TALK THESE days in all the denominations, including the Roman Catholic denomination, about being baptised with the Holy Spirit and being filled with the Holy Spirit and consequently speaking in tongues, (that is speaking unintelligent sounds), which are said to be the sign that God is present in the heart. It is worth examining this phenomenon.

The teaching and the experience of the Holy Spirit is a unique feature of Christianity. The phrase 'Holy Spirit' is a synonym for the 'Spirit of God', that is for God himself, and the gift of the Spirit means that God gives himself to his children, Spirit to spirit. Through the Holy Spirit we are in personal relationship with our God, in the same way as men are in relationship with each other through their spiritual, that is personal, fellowship.

The work of God's Spirit in the world is to perfect God's purposes. Thus in Genesis 1 the Spirit of God is at work in the creation, and in Psalm 104:30 and Job 33:4 the Spirit of God brings nature to its fulfilment. In the endowing of Bezaleel and the Mosaic elders and the judges of Israel, the Spirit of God brought the natural gifts of these persons to

---

1. An unpublished paper.

their completion in order that God's purposes through them and these gifts might be accomplished, for example, the building of the tabernacle on the one hand and the governing of his people on the other.[2] God's ultimate purpose in creating men and women is that they might be in fellowship with him, and this is brought about by God's Spirit dwelling with our spirit after we have been forgiven and made God's sons and daughters through salvation in Jesus.

The Spirit is the spirit of the knowledge of God; that is, experience and fellowship with God in the same way as we know a person. During his ministry Jesus said that he alone knew the Father.[3] This was because, up till then, he alone had received the Spirit of the knowledge of God. But in the same verse Jesus promised to give this knowledge of God, this fellowship with God, to his disciples, and this he fulfilled by giving them the same Spirit of God, so that all who believe in Jesus have this Spirit of God[4] and all have this knowledge and fellowship.[5]

This is the fulfilment of the promise of the Old Testament, that in the time of the Messiah all of God's people would receive the fullness of God's Spirit, that is, would be in permanent and full relationship with God so that all could know God.[6] This promise was couched in metaphors drawn from water; thus the Spirit is to be poured out,[7] the Spirit is to be sprinkled as water is sprinkled,[8] the Spirit flows out from God's presence like a river.[9] In particular, the gift of the Spirit of God is to be pre-eminently given to the Messiah[10] and it will result in a relationship of knowing God.

In the New Testament, the Old Testament promises are fulfilled. Jesus is the man filled with the Spirit.[11] Thus he becomes the exemplar of the Spirit-filled man. It is worth noting that he is not an enthusiast

2.   See Exodus 35:31; Numbers 11:17; Judges 3:10 etc.
3.   Matthew 11:27.
4.   John 7:39.
5.   1 John 1:3; 2:13-14, 20.
6.   Jeremiah 31:31-34.
7.   Isaiah 32:15; 44:3; Joel 2:28; Zechariah 12:10.
8.   Ezekiel 36:25-27.
9.   Ezekiel 47:1ff.
10. Isaiah 11:2.
11. Acts 10:38; Luke 4:1-18; John 1:32; 3:34.

but his character is selfless, full of joy and peace. He is devoted to his duty; that is, he obeys God exactly, sensitive to the slightest sin (compare his rebuke of Peter). He exercises signs of his messianic office through miracles, but there is no suggestion anywhere that Jesus spoke in tongues.

The gift of the Spirit to those who believe in Jesus follows from Christ's victory on the cross and his exaltation and crowning at God's right hand.[12]

Jesus himself had prophesied that this would be so, using water metaphors drawn from Ezekiel 47.[13] John the Baptist had himself predicted it, using a water metaphor drawn from his own practice of baptism. He said that the Messiah would baptise with the Holy Spirit. St Paul uses the same water metaphor of baptism to describe the experience of every Christian in receiving the Spirit[14] and he adds a second water metaphor drawn, doubtless, from the experience of the children of Israel in the wilderness, saying that all Christians have been made to drink of one Spirit. There is no doubt that the two halves of this verse are identical in meaning and refer to the experience which follows from the victory of Christ for all who believe. Every Christian has this relationship with God through his Spirit.[15] God will deepen our experience of his presence and fellowship if that is really what we want in life. Jesus promised that God would give the Holy Spirit to those who ask him:[16] "If any man thirst let him come to me and drink".[17]

The result of the Spirit's work is life; God is life and the Spirit is God. It is the Spirit of God who confers natural life[18] and it is the same Spirit who confers spiritual life. Thus in Titus 3:5-6 the beginning of spiritual life in the believer is referred to in the hendiadys of the washing and renewing of the Holy Spirit.

The Spirit's presence is the presence of Christ, and it is through Christ's Spirit that we have fellowship with Christ. He is his Spirit:

12. Acts 2:33.
13. John 7:38-39.
14. 1 Corinthians 12:13.
15. Romans 8:9.
16. Luke 11:13.
17. John 7:37.
18. Psalm 104:30.

"I will come to you", "My Father and I will make our abode with him".[19] The Spirit's presence ensures that the Spirit's character, that is God's character, that is Christ's character, is manifest in us.[20] The test of the Spirit's presence in anyone is the fruit of the Spirit manifest in the life of that person and, in particular, the character of love and righteousness, for "God is love" and "God is light and in him is no darkness at all".

As in the Old Testament so in the New, the Spirit of God endows his servants for service in the church. These gifts are, of course, based on natural gifts as in the Old Testament, for example, Bezaleel and the Elders. Thus Peter's and John's gift of leadership and boldness is the work of the Spirit in harnessing natural aptitudes. God works through his own gifts. He knows whom he has called before the foundation of the world.

The gifts Christians receive in the New Testament are for many different purposes; for example, boldness to witness, gifts of service such as hospitality, gifts in connection with the gospel (apostles, prophets, evangelists, pastor-teachers), evidential gifts (healing, tongues), gifts of administration (helps and governments) and so on.

In Ephesians 4 when St Paul lists the gifts that the ascended Christ gave to mankind he has four categories. All four are ministries of the Word. First, apostles, who are witnesses to the resurrection and so are foundation stones of God's revelation. Then come prophets, who fill out the revelation. By the nature of the case these two ministries have ceased now that the revelation of God in Christ is complete. The other two ministries in Paul's list are evangelists and pastor-teachers. These two ministries are still with us as they are the ongoing essential ministries, the preaching of the Word to those outside and the preaching of the Word to those who have responded.

In considering the phrase "filled with the spirit' or "full of the Spirit" as it occurs in the New Testament, it should be noted that this also is a water metaphor. In Ephesians 5 being filled with the Spirit is contrasted with alcoholic intoxication. Apart from this instance all the other references occur in Luke's writings. The phrase is based on the Old Testament language and is normally in two parts, with the second

19. John 14:18, 23.
20. 2 Corinthians 3:18; Galatians 5:22; 1 Corinthians 13.

part explaining what the work of the Spirit is to which reference is made. Thus a typical construction is: so-and-so was full of the Spirit and he.... It occurs in Luke's gospel pre-Pentecost, for example, "Elizabeth was filled with the Holy Spirit and she lifted up her voice";[21] "Zecharias was filled with the Holy Spirit and prophesied";[22] "Jesus, full of the Holy Spirit, was led by the Spirit into the wilderness being tempted by the devil...and Jesus answered him".[23]

After Pentecost the same phrase is used by Luke in Acts: "Stephen, full of the Holy Ghost, looked steadfastly into heaven and saw the glory of God...and said...".[24] Luke uses the verb similarly, "filled...and": "They were all filled with the Holy Ghost and began to speak with other tongues";[25] "Peter, filled with the Holy Ghost, said to the people...";[26] "They were all filled with the Holy Ghost and spoke the Word of God with boldness";[27] "Saul, filled with the Holy Ghost, fixing his eyes on him said..."[28]

It is worth noting that these actions which follow filling with the Holy Spirit are actions of speaking. The presence of the Holy Ghost gives power to speak the Word of God. There are further examples. The reference to the gift of the Spirit to John is followed immediately by a prediction of the effectiveness of his preaching;[29] similarly the statement that Paul will be filled with the Spirit[30] is followed by the statement that he preached the Word of God with boldness.

The other references to being full of the Spirit in Luke are similar but, instead of the action of preaching or speaking, some gift of character is referred to in the second part. Thus the Seven are men full of the Holy Spirit and wisdom;[31] Stephen is a man full of faith and the

---

21. Luke 1:41.
22. Luke 1:67.
23. Luke 4:1.
24. Acts 7:55.
25. Acts 2:4.
26. Acts 4:8.
27. Acts 4:31.
28. Acts 13:9.
29. Luke 1:15.
30. Acts 9:17.
31. Acts 6:3.

Holy Spirit;[32] Barnabas, of goodness;[33] the disciples were filled with joy and the Holy Spirit.[34]

This style of language which St Luke uses is drawn from the Old Testament. For example: "the Spirit of the Lord came mightily upon Samson and he rent the lion as he would a kid";[35] "the Spirit of the Lord came mightily upon Samson and he went down to Ashkelon and smote 30 men".[36] Compare Judges 3:10—"the Spirit of the Lord came upon Othniel and he judged Israel".

We may conclude that Luke's use of "full of the Spirit" or "filled with the Spirit" is linguistic, based on the Old Testament and is used by St Luke to indicate some action, normally preaching the gospel, which the indwelling Spirit of God enables his servants to accomplish, or else some abiding character of the Christian such as joy or faith or wisdom or goodness. In the former case we are reminded of what Jesus promised, that the Holy Spirit would speak through his disciples when they were called upon to witness for him;[37] and in the latter case of what St Paul says is the fruit of the indwelling of the Spirit: love, joy, peace, faith, goodness, and so on.[38]

It should be noted that the phrase "fullness of the Spirit" is not a biblical one and that "full of the Spirit" is normally an opening for a phrase to indicate in what way the Spirit is expressing itself and that, with the one exception of Ephesians 5, it is entirely a Lucan phrase.

With regard to the phrase "baptised with the Spirit", this phrase was first used by John the Baptist,[39] who baptised with water those who had been alerted by his preaching to the imminence of God's reign, that is, the imminence of God's judgement.

The only way to prepare for this coming event was repentance including, of course, the consequent life which accorded with repentance. John called his hearers to this radical repentance, to be expressed

32. Acts 6:5.
33. Acts 11:24.
34. Acts 13:52.
35. Judges 14:6.
36. Judges 14:19.
37. Matthew 10:20.
38. Galatians 5:22-23.
39. Matthew 3:11.

by baptism at his hands in the River Jordan. Baptism was the outward sign of repentance (that is, death to the old life), in view of the hope which his preaching set before them of the coming of God's kingdom. That kingdom would come when the Messiah came. John described the Messiah's ministry of judgement in terms of baptism, a metaphor drawn, naturally, from his own activity. John, however, contrasted the Messiah's baptism very sharply with the baptism of water.

The Messiah's baptism is not a baptism of water but a baptism of the Holy Spirit and fire, that is to say, it would be a baptism of judgement, for when the Messiah came he would purify his people as a refiner's fire and wash them as with fuller's soap.[40] His coming then would be a baptism or washing of fire. Isaiah 4:4 speaks of the same events as a purging of the people of God through the Spirit of judgement and the Spirit of burning. That is to say, God's Holy Spirit would judge and so purify his people by burning up the dross. This was doubtless the background of John's thoughts when he foretold that the Messiah would baptise with the Holy Spirit and fire. Jesus himself acknowledged this was the purpose of his coming, to come with the fire and the sword of judgement.[41] But the time for the judgement, "the day of vengeance of our God", was not yet.

It is important to note that the Messiah's baptism was baptism with the Spirit; John's baptism was baptism with water. The Messiah's baptism is not baptism with water and the Spirit.

It was part of the Old Testament prediction of the messianic age that the Messiah would not only be united with the Spirit but that in all God's people the Spirit would be poured out. This is what Jesus confers as a consequence of his victory and exaltation. He pours out (note the water metaphor based on the Old Testament) his Spirit on all his disciples.[42] This is the baptism with which the Messiah baptises, pouring out his Spirit as John presumably poured water on those who were his disciples. It is worth perhaps noting that the phrase "baptism of the Spirit" is always used in a group context.

At the beginning, the gift of the Spirit was accompanied by outward manifestations; there are five occasions in the New Testament when the

40. Malachi 3:2; Isaiah 66:16.
41. Cf. Luke 12:49-51 and Matthew 10:34-35 with Isaiah 66:16.
42. Acts 2:33.

Spirit is given for the first time: to Jesus at the beginning of his ministry; at Pentecost when the disciples of Jesus received the Spirit; at Samaria; at Caesarea when the Gentiles received the Spirit; and at Ephesus when John the Baptist's disciples received the Spirit. The gift of tongues is mentioned on three of these occasions but it would seem that, from the time of Pentecost onwards, tongues were absent from the Jerusalem church, for when tongues occurred at Caesarea Peter remarked that it reminded him of what they had experienced "in the beginning".[43]

God always gives his gifts in accordance with our natures, of which he himself is the Creator and giver. Consequently, speaking in tongues will be based on a psychological and physiological characteristic in human nature. The elevation of spirit, which the Holy Spirit brought to those who were hearing for the first time the wonderful truths of the gospel and who were brought into a new fellowship with God, led to the speaking of tongues. And we may ask whether this was not intended to be evidential. The Holy Spirit's presence is not now indicated by the speaking with tongues so much as by the transformed character and the power to live the Christian life and to testify to the gospel in whatever way God calls us to.

However, the psychological and physiological ability to speak with tongues will still remain in the human frame, so that if our spirit is elevated, from whatever cause, it may well lead to glossolalia, that is speaking with tongues. But, unless it is the work of the Spirit, glossolalia is of no spiritual significance, merely psychological. I am of the opinion that the modern phenomenon of glossolalia, or speaking with tongues, is psychological and not, in itself, a manifestation of the Spirit of God.

The Spirit of God is the presence of God. He has promised his presence to all who believe in Christ.[44] If we open the door of our life he will come in and he will join us in fellowship round a meal, as it were.[45] We have only to ask for God's presence, for Christ's presence, in our heart to receive him. Jesus said that God will give his Holy Spirit to those who ask.[46] This is the great privilege and experience which the Christian religion brings: to know God through his indwelling Spirit.

43. Acts 11:15.
44. John 7:39; Acts 2:38.
45. Revelation 3:20.
46. Luke 11:13.

2. ANOINTED WITH THE SPIRIT

We modern Christians customarily speak of Jesus as the 'Lord Jesus Christ' and we treat this as a single three-fold name. In doing this we lose sight of some very important truths. Jesus was known to his contemporaries as 'Jesus', the Greek form of Joshua. It was not an uncommon name and so, to distinguish him from others of the same name, he was often referred to as 'Jesus of Nazareth', from the town where he had been brought up. His followers called him the 'Lord' because they recognised that he was divine, and so they gave to him the name which the Old Testament used for God. The test of being a Christian is whether we are able to say that Jesus is Lord—Lord, not merely theoretically but personally, accepting his lordship over our own lives.

The other term of the trilogy, namely 'Christ', was used by Jesus' followers to draw attention to the unique mission that Jesus as man ful-filled. He was God's Messiah (which is the Old Testament word for 'Christ'). 'Messiah' in the Hebrew, or 'Christ' in the Greek, simply means the 'anointed one' and refers to the Holy Spirit promised by God.[47] Jesus was the man whom God anointed with his own Spirit.

The advent of a king who would rule in God's name, according to God's heart and will, had been predicted by the Old Testament prophets, and, in particular, by Isaiah in the well-known passage: "unto us a child is born, unto us a son is given, and the government shall be upon his shoulder...of the increase of his government and of peace there shall be no end...and the Spirit of the Lord shall rest upon him".[48] Kings are commissioned by anointing and the Messiah King, Christ the King, was anointed not with the symbol of oil but with the reality of the Holy Spirit. Thus Isaiah prophesied of the Christ: "the Spirit of the Lord God is upon me because he has anointed me to preach good things to the poor..."[49]

In the gospels we read how the Holy Spirit came on Jesus at the beginning of his ministry. It is this gift of God's Spirit which the term 'Christ' points to. Jesus is the Christ, the anointed One, the One who has received the Spirit of God and so, in Acts 10, Peter tells Cornelius

47. Isaiah 11:2.
48. Isaiah 9:67; 11:2.
49. Isaiah 61:1.

"how God anointed Jesus of Nazareth with the Holy Spirit and with power, how he went about doing good and healing...for God was with him".[50] John the Baptist described how "I saw the Spirit descending as a dove out of heaven and it rested upon him".[51]

To possess the Spirit of God means to be in a relationship with God. And to possess the Spirit fully, as Jesus did, means to be in full personal fellowship with God, Spirit to spirit. It was a consequence of this relationship that Jesus carried out his ministry. Through the power of the Spirit his human life and character conformed at every point to the character of God. He was the image, the reflected likeness of God. "He went about doing good"[52] and by the power of the Spirit he performed the signs and wonders of the miracles as evidence of his Messiahship.

The healing of the sick,[53] the opening of the eyes of the blind, the healing of the dumb, the restoring of the lame and the deaf,[54] the raising of the dead by the powers of the Spirit[55] and the preaching of the gospel to the poor[56] were the things which the Old Testament predicted the Messiah would bring about when God's kingdom came. And thus Jesus, the Messiah, the Christ, the One anointed by God to be king after his own heart, not only preached the gospel of the kingdom but accompanied his preaching with acts of goodness in accordance with God's character as occasion served, and so drew attention to the fact that God's King was now, after so many centuries, present.

Jesus is the exemplar, the example par excellence of the Spirit-filled man, the Spirit-led man. The fruit of the Spirit to which Paul refers—love, joy and peace—were all present in Jesus' experience and showed up in his character. He was full of faith and obedience and thankfulness. He was not (as far as we can judge from the records) temperamentally an enthusiast nor did he get excited. His object in life was what should be every Christian's desire, always to do what is right.[57]

50. Acts 10:38.
51. John 1:32.
52. Acts 10:38.
53. Isaiah 53:4; Matthew 8:17.
54. Isaiah 35:5.
55. Ezekiel 37:12-14.
56. Isaiah 61:1.
57. Hebrews 13:18 (NEB).

This keenness and readiness to do the will of God resulted from knowledge on the one hand and prayer on the other —knowledge of the truth of God, of the heavenly world, of the transientness of this life and of the conflict with the devil in which we are involved; and prayer, which is fellowship with God on the basis of the truth of his Word. Knowledge (which comes from hearing, reading and meditating on God's Word) and prayer in agreement with that knowledge, are the two means by which the Spirit of God leads us in the way of God's Will.

Not only is Jesus the exemplar of the Spirit-filled man, but he is the source of the Spirit's presence in the people of God. He had promised this gift in John 7:38-39; 16:17 and 20:22, and Peter had interpreted the Day of Pentecost as Jesus pouring out of his Spirit from his heavenly throne.[58] Like their master, all Jesus' followers are anointed with the Spirit.[59] Together with Jesus they form the Christ.[60] The gift of the Spirit to his people is consequential on Christ's exaltation. The Spirit's presence in our hearts is the presence of Christ, the presence of the Father.[61] The test of the Spirit's presence in any person's life is the fruit of the Spirit in the character and, in particular, love and righteousness. This is the only real test, the test of character, for only the Spirit of God can give this fruit. It is, however, possible to exercise powers which might appear to be spiritual without being so. For example, it is possible to prophesy in Christ's name without having the Spirit of Christ, or to speak with tongues without having the Spirit of Christ. This is plain from what Jesus says in Matthew 7:22-23 and from what St Paul says in 1 Corinthians 12:3 and 13:1.

The Spirit of God not only transforms us into the character of Christ[62] but he also gives us power. Jesus promised: "You shall receive power when the Holy Ghost is come upon you and you shall be my witnesses".[63] What is meant by this power? Primarily it means the power to live a Godlike life in contrast to the powerlessness of the people of God under the old covenant when they said with their lips "all

58. Acts 2:17-18.
59. 1 John 2:20.
60. 1 Corinthians 12:12.
61. John 14:18, 23.
62. 2 Corinthians 3:18.
63. Acts 1:8.

the Lord has spoken we will do and be obedient",[64] but immediately they turned aside and made a golden calf and worshipped it. The rest of their history was in keeping with this. They had no power to resist the devil, and they were led by him into all sorts of godlessness, immorality and idolatry.

The Christian, however, in receiving the Spirit of God, receives power to live the Christian life, that is to say, power to put the devil to flight.[65] What greater power imaginable is there than this? It is the power to trample down Satan under our feet[66] (this power includes, of course, the power to drive out devils in the name of Jesus from those who are devil-possessed—all Christians have this power); the power to enable us to keep on keeping on in the Christian life.[67]

The promise includes power to witness. This will primarily be, of course, the witness of character, for words without character to support them are empty. But it extends to a witness to Jesus with our words. Through the Holy Spirit we have power to witness according to our circumstances and calling. Thus, if we are brought before kings and governors, as were those early Christian disciples, we need have no doubt that the Holy Spirit will speak through us words of witness to Christ. Or when we are called upon in a private capacity to give "a reason for the hope within us"[68] it is the Spirit of God which will prompt us to speak in a way that will glorify him. If it is the will of God to support our witness by external signs, as it was at the beginning of the gospel, this, too, will be worked through the power of the Spirit, though there is nothing to suggest that this is the way that God supports our testimony today; much more effective for testimony is the support of a transformed life and words of witness to the power of Christ which accompany it.

How do we receive this gift of God's Spirit? What are the conditions for being baptised with the Spirit and being filled with the Spirit? The New Testament knows of only one condition, namely belief that

64. Exodus 24:3.
65. 1 Peter 5:8-9; James 4:7.
66. Romans 16:20.
67. Colossians 1:11.
68. 1 Peter 3:15.

Jesus is Lord. Thus Jesus promised the Holy Spirit to all who believe in him[69] and Peter reaffirmed the promise in Acts 2:38. Nowhere in the New Testament is there any other condition laid down to be fulfilled for the receiving of the fullness of God's presence in his Spirit than the acknowledgment of Jesus as Lord. Of course there may be inadequacies in believing because of inadequacies in comprehension or, perhaps, inadequacies of teaching about Christ, and when this inadequacy is overcome there will be a deeper experience of God. But if we believe truly in Jesus as a result of a true preaching of the gospel, then Christ has promised that he will come into our lives through his Spirit; and when Christ comes in, the fullness of the Godhead comes because in Jesus the fullness of the Godhead dwells, and if Jesus lives in us through his Spirit there is power: power to live the Christian life and power to put the devil to flight.

3. Pentecostal Power

The resurrection of Jesus was a display of power; the stone rolled back, Jesus rose from death. There is a tremendous amount of power built into the world by its Creator. Think of the power locked up in the atom which we have just learned to release. It has been there since creation! And what marvels are still to be discovered by us in God's world? God is the source of all power—physical, psychic and spiritual—and it was his Spirit who raised Jesus from the dead. It is the Spirit of God, St Paul says in Romans 1, who brought about this great vindication of Jesus, this resurrection which justified his life of righteousness, of obedience, and his victory over every aspect of sin.

Before his ascension Jesus promised his disciples that they would share in this power from God. "You will be clothed with power from on high",[70] he said and again, "You shall receive power when the Holy Spirit is come upon you".[71] God's Spirit is the Spirit of power. This power was manifested in the early days of the church when the apos-

---

69. John 7:38, 39.
70. Luke 24:49.
71. Acts 1:8.

tles first preached the gospel. We read that "with great power they bore witness to the resurrection".[72] They convicted the hearers of the truth and crowds were converted, 3000 in one day. Their preaching was accompanied by miracles as signs that God was with them.

Not only the apostles, but people like Philip and Stephen were supported in their preaching by the power to perform signs and wonders. St Paul says that his preaching was accompanied by similar expressions of the power of God. He speaks of the "signs of an apostle", which he performed.[73] This phrase is interesting as it indicates that not every Christian performed miracles but that they were testimonies which God gave to the apostles at the time of the founding of the church. With the passing of the apostles, these signs of an apostle passed away too, but the power of the Spirit of God is still very much with Christians. This power shows itself in a double way.

First, the power to speak effectively, for the words of the gospel, if spoken with the Spirit's promptings, will not be mere empty sounds but will bring to spiritual life those who hear them. People who are dead in their sins without a thought about God will be converted to a living relationship with him. We see this happening all the time and it is a miracle of power, effected through the gospel.

Then, too, the Holy Spirit will give power to speak a word of testimony as the occasion calls for it. Thus, Jesus said, we are not to be anxious if we are brought even in to the presence of governors and kings for his name's sake, as the Holy Spirit will empower us to speak truly and effectively for Christ when the time comes.[74]

But much the most frequent references to the power of the Spirit in the life of the Christian are to living an 'ordinary Christian life', as we would say, especially power joyfully to endure persecutions. Thus St Paul prays: "May God strengthen you with ample power to meet whatever comes with fortitude, patience and joy and to give thanks to God".[75] The power to be thankful and joyous, even in adverse circumstances, is the power which St Paul here associates with the Holy Spirit.

72. Acts 4:33.
73. 2 Corinthians 12:12.
74. Matthew 10:17-20.
75. Colossians 1:11.

He refers to the same power of the Spirit in 2 Timothy 1:6-8 and again in Romans 15:13. He wrote how the Romans were "abounding in hope in the power of the Holy Spirit". Living expectantly, waiting for God's promises, is the work of the Spirit; it is the power that the Spirit gives according to St Paul. He writes similarly in Galatians 5:5-6 that it is the Spirit who is the source of hope in the Christian. In Ephesians 3:16 St Paul says that the power which the Spirit brings into the Christian's life is the power to understand and to express in our life something of God's love for us.

Thus we see that, when Jesus promised his disciples power through the Holy Spirit's presence, the New Testament understands this as fulfilled in the power to lead the Christian life and to rejoice in hope in God. This is no slight power. For, putting it negatively, it can be expressed as putting the devil to flight;[76] or as trampling down Satan under our feet.[77] This is real power, power to live acceptably to God, joyfully and hopefully as we wait for the coming of Christ.

In the Old Testament the people of God promised to be obedient[78] but very quickly fell into all sorts of disobedience and idolatry. Their good resolutions were not accompanied by power. They were in word only. They had no power to transform words into deeds and character. God had not written his will in their hearts by the presence of the Holy Spirit. But now, through the death and exaltation of Christ, we have been given power, the power of God's own presence, and this expresses itself, primarily, in the power to lead the Christian life at home or at work, at school or wherever it may be.

This is the basis of all our witness and testimony to God. If our life is not consistent with our words, our testimony is useless. But on the basis of our consistent Christian life, brought into being by the power of the Spirit within us, the same Holy Spirit will enable us to witness with our words powerfully as we have opportunity. It may be simply in giving an answer to those who ask us about our Christian hope. It may be preaching the gospel more formally in the ministry of the Word in the church or as an evangelist. Or it may be testifying in times of persecution when the Holy Spirit has promised to speak through us.

76. 1 Peter 5:8-9.
77. Romans 16:20.
78. Exodus 24:3.

The Christian religion is a religion of power, not just the outward miracles, for similar miracles Jesus himself said could be done by those who had no relationship with God at all, but the power of the changed life of the faithful and testimony which God uses to convert and bring to life the spiritually dead.

On Easter Day God raised Christ from the dead and raised all of us from spiritual death through Christ and he will raise us at the last day in the general resurrection. For God is the God of power and his purposes will never fail.

4. THE HOLY SPIRIT IN THE TRINITY

When the Roman Catholic theologian, Hans Kung, was in Australia, in one of his addresses he mentioned how long a time it had been for him to reach the conclusion that the Christian message is 'Jesus, Jesus himself'. We probably all agree in theory that this is the true message, but if we reflect on the preaching we hear and the way that our own thoughts run, we will recognise that Jesus, Jesus himself, is not in fact the centre of our message as he should be, or the centre of our thinking about Christian things. Yet the biblical testimony about Jesus is so profound and exalted in concept that we must never think of ourselves or of God apart from Jesus.

In a word, Jesus is Emmanuel, God with us, the almighty Creator with us in human flesh, in human life, in human nature. Jesus is to be the object of our divine worship: "He who honours not the Son, honours not the Father".[79] Jesus is the object of our faith. "You believe in God..." he told his disciples, "...believe also in me".[80] Jesus is the One to whom we offer our prayers: "If you should ask me anything I will do it" he promised.[81] He is the One who forms his church, bringing his people into heaven where he is: "I go to prepare a place for you...I will come again and receive you unto myself that where I am you may be also".[82]

79. John 5:23.
80. John 14:1.
81. John 14:14.
82. John 14:2, 3.

The words and works of Jesus are those of God the Father.[83] He is one with the Father, and the Father with him.[84] Jesus promised his disciples that we would share in this unity with God and we share in it through Jesus' presence in our own life: "I will not leave you orphans, I will come to you".[85] Or, again, he speaks of this same experience as the Father and the Son coming and making their abode with the believer.[86]

In his prayer which concluded the discourse in the Upper Room, from which I have been quoting, Jesus prays for the unity of believers, that is unity with the Father and the Son. His words were "that they may all be one, even as thou, Father, art in me and I in thee, that they also may be in us".[87] This is no organizational unity but the closest unity of persons, Spirit with spirit. And a little later he prayed similar words, "that they may be one, even as we are one, I in them and thou in me, that they may be perfected into one".[88]

This presence of Christ in the believer which brings him into unity with God—Father and Son—is brought about by the presence of Christ in the inmost personality. As St Paul puts it: "Christ in you". Another way of speaking of this is saying that the Spirit of Christ is in the Christian. The Spirit of God, the Spirit of Christ, the Holy Spirit, are all three names for God in his relationship to us in our spirit.

It is important to recognise that the Holy Spirit is not to be thought of as a separable aspect of God, for the Spirit is the Spirit of Christ, Jesus himself. It is worth noting that, in these chapters spoken in the upper room in St John's gospel, Jesus speaks about himself as going to the Father, not to the Father and to the Spirit. Again we gather from Jesus' words that it is the Spirit who comes to the Christian when the Father and the Son come.[89] Similarly, it is the Spirit who unites us with Christ in that unity referred to in the prayer of the 17th chapter though, again, it is worth noting that the Spirit is not mentioned in this chapter.

We are not to think of the Spirit as a separate experience from the

83. John 14:10.
84. John 14:11.
85. John 14:18.
86. John 14:23.
87. John 17:21.
88. John 17:23.
89. John 14:23.

experience of Christ or of our relationship to God. It is the work of the Spirit to centre our thoughts on Christ who is God with us, incarnate God: "He shall glorify me, for he will take of mine and declare it unto you. Whatsoever the Father has is mine. Therefore I said that he takes of mine and shall declare it unto you".[90] It is the work of the Spirit to reveal the Father and the Son to the Christian.

The Spirit has not any independent work, and thus there is no prayer in the Bible directed to the Spirit. Prayers are offered to the Father and the Son but never to the Spirit. We are not to think of the Spirit apart from the Father and the Son. The Father is in the Son and the Son in the Father and the Spirit is the Spirit of the Father and the Son, the Spirit of God, God himself. Jesus speaks about the Father from whom he came and to whom he goes, and with whom he is one, and he speaks about the Spirit who will come in his name. The Spirit is Christ. This is plain when Jesus says: "A little while and you behold me no more and again a little while and you shall see me".[91] These verses refer, primarily, to the coming of Christ through his Spirit.

The work of Jesus was to do the will of the Father. In his prayer in chapter 17 he said, "I glorified thee on the earth having accomplished the work that thou hast given me to do".[92] The Christian has the same calling—to do the will of God—and it is the Spirit in the heart of the Christian which enables him to fulfil this. St Paul spoke about the fruit of the Spirit being love, joy, peace and all the other virtues that it is God's will that our lives should reflect.

The Spirit of God is the Spirit of love. But our love for God is the same as our obedience to his will. It is a mistake to think that love is an emotional tingle, as it were, an excitement of our spirit. In the upper room, when Jesus spoke at length about the Spirit, there is no suggestion that this emotion would be the result of the Spirit's presence. Obedience to God is what the Bible calls love for God. St John, in his first epistle in chapter 5 verse 2 wrote, "By this we know that we love the children of God, when we love God and obey his commandments. For this is the love of God, that we keep his commandments". Love for God, that is

90. John 16:14.
91. John 16:16.
92. John 17:4.

obedience to God, is the fruit of the Spirit's presence. Love is not an ebullient feeling but the doing of your duty. As John wrote "Love one another. And this is love, to walk after his commandments".[93]

The work of the Spirit may be summed up, first of all, as that of centring our thoughts on Christ and, secondly, as producing in our lives the character of Christ so that we do the will of God. This will, in turn, lead to the conversion of the world for, although the world cannot recognise the Spirit of Christ, it can recognise the Christian character. Jesus said that when the Spirit of God comes to the Christian he will convict the world.[94]

There is a third work of the Spirit and that is bringing the believers into unity with God—Father and Son—through the Spirit, so creating fellowship. "I in them and thou in me" is a reference to this unity and relationship which the presence of God's Spirit creates between the believer and God. The Spirit's presence is our glory as it is the glory of our Saviour. Although the Holy Spirit is not mentioned by name in the prayer of Jesus, I believe that he is referred to when Jesus speaks about the glory which he himself has received and which he has passed on to his disciples. "The glory that thou hast given me I have given unto them that they may be one, even as we are one".[95] The Holy Spirit who unites us with the Father is our glory. He is also referred to in the last verse of the prayer though, again, not mentioned specifically. For it is the Spirit of love which leads to obedience and the doing of God's will towards others. Love, that is obedience, is the result of knowledge of God, of his character and of his will. Christ is the source of knowledge and love. This is the same thing as saying that the Spirit is a Spirit of knowledge and of love. Thus our Lord concluded his prayer: "I have made known unto them thy name and will make it known, that the love wherein thou lovedst me may be in them and I in them".[96] The Holy Spirit is the "I in them", to quote our Lord's last words; "I in them" means God's Spirit in us. And Jesus equates this with the love of God when he says "that the love wherewith thou lovedst me may be in them and I in them".

93. 2 John 6.
94. John 16:8.
95. John 17:22.
96. John 17:26.

When we think of the Holy Spirit we must think of Jesus within us, uniting us to himself, to the Father and to one another, and producing in us love, not excitement or ebullience but solid love, that is, the doing of the will of God in our daily relationships and living in his presence.

If we conform to our Lord's teaching in John chapters 14-17, we will not think of the Holy Spirit as a separable experience. Whitsunday is the commemoration of the day when Jesus poured out his Spirit on all flesh, the day when the Father and the Son made their dwelling with the believer in a new way. The coming of the Spirit leads us to Jesus, who was in the Father and the Father in him. Our message is Jesus, Jesus himself, and our experience is Jesus, Jesus himself.

Chapter 14

THE UNIQUENESS OF CHRIST
AND THE CULT OF MARY[1]

*C*HRISTIANITY IS THE RELIGION OF AN event, an event so stupendous that it transcends the powers of our imagination: that God, the source of all, the creator and upholder of the whole universe, should come into a new and intimate relationship with mankind in Jesus Christ. He was manifest in the flesh. Though he was rich, yet for us he became poor. He humbled himself, leaving aside his glory, and taking the form of a servant became man.[2] God has entered into a new and permanent relationship with his creation in this man. This is the Christian message.

When you reflect on it, it is most extraordinary and breathtaking that the Son of God should enter into this intimate relationship with us and take our nature as man, though remaining God, subjecting himself to our life and experiences, being tried and tested in all things as we are, in order that by overcoming temptation and suffering and death as man and for man, he might save us from the consequence of our sins and bring us into eternal fellowship with himself. Through his death Jesus became victor over sin, bearing its penalty, repulsing its temptations, never wavering in faith. He was completely triumphant for us and so was raised from the dead, that in Jesus mankind might enter the fulfilment of God's purposes of having dominion over all creation. Christians await with eagerness the culmination of God's purposes when the Lordship of Jesus will be manifested and made complete at his coming.

"God was in Christ" said St Paul, "reconciling the world to himself"[3]

1. Protestant Faith Broadcast, 28 March 1976.
2. Philippians 2:5ff.
3. 2 Corinthians 5:19.

and Jesus told his disciples that as the Father had covenanted with him for a kingdom so he covenanted with his disciples that they should share in that kingdom.[4]

In view of the epoch-making character of Jesus' life and death and resurrection and coming again, it is not surprising that Jesus is the centre of New Testament religion. Our Lord himself clearly taught this. Thus he invited all who were weary and heavy laden to come to him and he would give them rest;[5] and he told Philip, "he that hath seen me hath seen the Father".[6] Ordinary preachers point away from themselves to God, but Jesus pointed his hearers to himself, for he was the revelation of God.

The apostles bear the same testimony to the absolute centrality of Christ in the Christian gospel and in the Christian life. St Paul told the Corinthians that he determined to know nothing among them save Jesus Christ and him crucified.[7] All the New Testament writers are full of the hope of Christ's return, which will bring God's purposes for mankind to their fulfilment.

We must be on our guard against the temptation of displacing Christ from the centre of our understanding of the world's history or of our own relationship to God. There is, for example the temptation to substitute the less personal idea of the church. Preachers are tempted to urge their hearers to come to church to join the church and so on, rather than make the personal call to recognise Jesus Christ as Lord and Saviour, and submit to his will and pray directly to him.

In the Roman Catholic denomination the cult of the Virgin Mary has had the disastrous effect of displacing God in Christ from the centre of religious devotion. Many of the attributes which the New Testament ascribes to Christ are duplicated in Roman Catholic tradition with regard to the Virgin Mary. For example, the Scriptures affirm that Jesus, who is the image of God, was sinless; that though tempted like us in everything, he did not yield at any point. It is important to remember that this victory was not for himself alone but

4. Luke 22:29.
5. Matthew 11:28.
6. John 14:9.
7. 1 Corinthians 2:2.

for all of us who put our faith in him, for we are saved by this victory over sin which reached its acme at Calvary.

The Scriptures affirm that Jesus was sinless, but at the same time state that the rest of mankind are sinners. There is none righteous, no not one, said St Paul.[8] However, Roman Catholic theology now teaches that the Virgin Mary was sinless as well. It teaches that not only did she commit no sin in her life, but she was free from the taint of original sin as well. However, the Bible is completely silent about such sinlessness; in fact the Bible suggests the contrary, for more than once her actions are found to have been mistaken. Moreover the Bible teaches that death is the result of sin: "Death passed upon all men for that all sinned".[9] Now Jesus, though sinless, died because of other people's sins. "He was made sin for us," said St Paul[10] and Isaiah prophesied, "The Lord laid upon him the iniquity of us all".[11] But what of the Virgin Mary's death if she was sinless? Roman Catholics admit that the Virgin Mary died, but if she was free from all actual and all original sin, then St Paul's statement "Death passed upon all because all *sinned*" would be untrue.[12]

The theory of Mary's sinlessness presents a difficult theological problem. The rest of us are saved because we are sinners, but on this view Mary was not a sinner, being free from original as well as actual sin. What then does Mary mean when in her song known as the Magnificat, she calls God her Saviour? On this theory it can only mean that she is saved from becoming a sinner as the angels are saved from becoming sinners, saved by God's power and enabling and not saved from the consequences of being sinners by Christ's redemption, as we are. St Paul teaches us in Romans 5:8, that Christ died for sinners, but if Mary was sinless, how can she be regarded as redeemed by Christ's death? How can she even be a member of the church, for the song of the church is given in Revelation 1:5, "Unto him that loved us and *washed us from our sins* by his blood…to him be the glory and the dominion for ever and ever".

8.   Romans 3:10.
9.   Romans 5:12.
10. 2 Corinthians 5:21.
11. Isaiah 53:6.
12. Romans 5:12.

Not only is the Bible doctrine of Christ's sinlessness duplicated by the non-biblical teaching that Mary was also sinless, but Christ's resurrection is duplicated by Mary's resurrection or assumption.

In 1950 the Pope made it an article of the Roman Catholic faith that the body of the Virgin was resurrected after death and transferred to heaven. Before this time Roman Catholics were free to disbelieve this, but now the Roman Catholic who deliberately disbelieves this teaching is regarded as being condemned to hell for disbelieving it. Needless to say, there is not the slightest trace in the New Testament of this doctrine of the assumption of the Virgin Mary. Moreover, it was unknown in the first four centuries of the Christian church. Proof of this, for example, is that it was unknown to St Ambrose, or St Epiphanius who investigated the question of the virgin's death. They are quite unaware of any idea that her body had been raised after death and taken to heaven. The idea first occurs in some of the heretical apocryphal gospels. A book teaching the assumption of the virgin was actually condemned by Pope Gelasius I. However, by the sixth century the doctrine had been accepted by the orthodox, mostly on the authority of what were thought to be statements of Jerome, Augustine and Dionysius, but which are now recognized by everyone as being spurious.

Gregory of Tours, who died in 594, gives the story in the following form: "All the apostles were assembled in the house of Mary to watch by her death bed when Jesus appeared with his angels, received her soul and gave it over to the archangel Michael. When on the following day they were about to carry her body to the grave he appeared again and took it up in a cloud to paradise, there to be reunited to the soul". The story appears in a more extended form in St John of Damascus. Not only the angels and the patriarchs stand around the death bed with the apostles, but even Adam and Eve are there calling their descendant blessed for removing the curse which through them came into the world.

This doctrine of the assumption to heaven of the body of the mother of our Lord after her death parallels Jesus' resurrection and ascension and detracts from the uniqueness of our Saviour.

Then there is the question of prayer to Mary. New Testament Christians were characterized by the fact that they prayed to Jesus. Thus St Stephen as he was being stoned to death said, "Lord Jesus, receive my spirit", and in 1 Corinthians 1:2, St Paul described Christians as those "who call upon the name of our Lord Jesus Christ", as did Ananias in Acts 9:14.

Never, throughout the Bible, whether in Old or New Testament, is prayer or intercession ever offered to any but to God. It is difficult to see how it could be otherwise. God is omniscient, knowing all that happens in the world, which he sustains. Thus he can hear prayers; but how can the saints, including the Virgin Mary, hear the myriads of prayers which Roman Catholics direct to them, for they are not omniscient as God is, nor present throughout his creation as he is, but are in heaven. Only God can read our hearts and can hear and answer prayer.

Throughout the Bible there is not the slightest hint that we should pray to the Virgin. If God had meant it otherwise would his Spirit have given us a Scripture with not even a mention of Mary throughout the Epistles, though these reflect the life of the Christian church? Yet how many myriads of miracles are attributed to her intercession these days! I am not aware of any that are attributed to Christ. This in itself is sufficient proof that these are not the result of the Spirit that inspired the Bible, for the Spirit of God will glorify *Jesus*, so our Lord foretold in John 16:14, "He shall glorify Me".

The Rosary is a most popular form of Roman Catholic Prayer. It is said in honour of Mary and consists of 150 repetitions of a prayer to Mary for salvation, together with fifteen repetitions of the Lord's Prayer.

To pray to Mary depresses our concept of the goodness of our Heavenly Father and our Lord Jesus Christ. One illustration amongst numerous examples is sufficient. Bernard of Clairvaux (*Sermon on the Nativity IV*) said "Dost thou fear the divine majesty in the Son? Wilt thou have an advocate before him? Flee to Mary."

In the New Testament, Christians looked for the coming of the Lord Jesus with a fervent and sure hope. Here again the teaching about the Virgin Mary has duplicated Jesus' prerogatives, for a favourite description of her in Roman Catholic devotion is "our hope". But it is Christ in his coming who is our hope and for whom we look.

If we examine the New Testament, apart from the birth narratives where, of course, Mary occupies a prominent and honoured place in the story, there are, in fact, very few references to the mother of our Lord; just a few in the Gospels and one only in the first chapter of Acts; after that no more at all. Throughout its pages Jesus Christ is central in the thoughts and hopes of Christians and in their prayers, and we must keep the same emphasis.

The cult of Mary distorts and obscures the true doctrine of Scripture. Yet in avoiding what is rightly regarded as excess, we must not overlook the wonderful privilege Mary was given, that of being mother of the Saviour; yet a similar privilege is given to us all, that of being closely related to the eternal God by his taking our nature to be our Saviour.

Mary sang, "My spirit has rejoiced in God my Saviour, for he has looked upon the low estate of his handmaiden".[13] This is true: and it is true for all of us. God has looked upon our lowliness and has shared it; taking our nature so that through the victory of his death he might bring us into an eternal relationship of being his sons and daughters. Never let this be obscured in your mind.

He alone is our hope, to him alone should we direct our prayers and to him alone be the glory.

13. Luke 1:47-8.

Chapter 15

GOD'S WORD[1]

*T*HE BIGGEST CHANGE IN THE CHRISTIAN religion this century compared with all previous centuries has been the change in the attitude of Christians to the Bible. In the past, the Bible has always been regarded as God's infallible word. What the Bible says, God says. But nowadays in many of the denominations this has changed, and is changing, and this change is having very widespread effects. The Christian religion cannot survive where the Bible is not regarded as God's book, even though the shell, that is the organisation, remains much the same. For Christianity is a supernatural religion, and this requires a supernatural word from God, telling us of himself, and of his purposes and will for men. Nowadays, however, Christian leaders teach not a supernatural God but a God in nature, the ground of our being, and Christian ministers and church programs are concerned with bettering this world rather than proclaiming a message about the next. The reason for this change is a simple one, namely, loss of faith in the Bible as God's Word. Without a supernatural word from God it is impossible to maintain a supernatural view of life and supernatural expectation of the coming of Christ in his kingdom. That is, unless the Bible is believed to be God's infallible word, Christianity cannot survive. The name and the church organisations will survive, but their content will be changed, for Christianity is a supernatural religion. Christianity believes in a supernatural God, One who stands over and above nature, who created us and the whole universe, by calling it into existence simply by a decision of his will. Science tells us a little of the process which God used in bringing the world to its present form, but the fact remains (on which science is unable to make any comment) that God is the originator and director of that process.

1. Probably lecture notes for a course delivered at Moore College. Subheadings did not appear in the original manuscript.

THE SOVEREIGN GOD IS THE AUTHOR OF THE BIBLE

God is a supernatural God standing above nature, not only as its Creator, but also as its controller. Not a single event takes place in the universe that he does not control, not even the movement of the smallest electron in the most distant star. The thought is, of course, too stupendous for us to apprehend. Our minds are stupefied by the concept, for we are inclined to think of God in terms of things we know, thinking of him as a general manager of a department store who has to delegate detail to his subordinates. Of course this is not so. God who created all the details knows and controls them all.

God is the controller, not only of inanimate things but also of the minds and wills of men, even of sinful men. You may find this a difficult thought, but we act on its truth every day, when we trust God to protect us.

God's control of nature is through nature. He is the author of nature. Therefore it is not surprising that he should work in accordance with the laws of his own creation rather than against it. God does not find the laws of nature something intransigent, which get in the way and thwart his will, but rather he works through nature, which he designed for this purpose. Thus when he carried out his will through men, he works in what we would say is a natural way; nevertheless it is God who is carrying out his will exactly as he wills.

The all-sovereign God is our Heavenly Father who loves and cares for his creation and who wills to enter into fellowship with us, even though we are rebels against his sovereignty and love. Thus, we believe in a supernatural God, not only as Creator and Controller, but also as revealer of himself. He has made himself known to men. Centuries ago he called Abraham and Moses and sent his prophets to the children of Israel in order to make himself known to them, to show what his character is, and to call men into fellowship with himself. God's supernatural revelation of himself reached its acme in the coming of the Lord Jesus Christ, the divine Son of God. His name is 'Immanuel', which means 'God with us'. His perfect life, the sublimity and truth of his teaching, his powerful miracles of love, and his own claims and teaching about himself all testify to the truth reflected in that name Immanuel. He was indeed God with men, his coming a most remarkable supernatural event, but entirely in keeping with our supernatural God, and, of course, our salvation through the death and resurrection of Christ is supernatural.

The inspiring of the Bible by the Spirit of God is part of this same movement of God in revealing himself to men in order to save them by restoring them to fellowship with him. It is a supernatural book.

Although written by men and faithfully reflecting the divergent characters and historical situations of the authors who wrote the sixty-six books that make up the Bible, the most important fact and the fact that gives the Bible its unity is that the Holy Spirit of God was the true author. He used the writers, not forcing their wills or their minds or their thoughts, but working through these things of which he himself was the creator, so that what they wrote was not only their own words but more importantly God's words; words infallible for the purpose for which God inspired them, namely, to teach us about himself and about his relations with men.

I do not think we need spend time considering whether God could give us a book which, though written in a perfectly natural way, by men—sinners and ignorant of many things though they were—yet would in every point exactly reflect the perfect mind of God for us. God's sovereignty over his own creation sufficiently answers this. The question remains whether he has done so, and to what extent, and for what purpose. St Paul in 2 Timothy 3:16-17 sums up the traditional Christian answer: "Every Scripture is inspired of God and profitable for teaching, for reproof for correction, for instruction which is in righteousness, that the man of God may be complete, furnished completely unto every good work".

REASONS TO BELIEVE THE BIBLE IS THE WORD OF GOD

There are many reasons why Christians traditionally have believed the Bible to be a supernatural book and the true word of God. Of course, the final reason is that they hear God's word in it, for when God speaks to the conscience which he has created, it would indeed be strange if his voice was not recognised by his children, to whom he has given his Spirit. As Jesus said, "My sheep hear my voice and they follow me".[2]

2. John 10:27.

But before we reach that final reason there are some preliminary considerations worth noting.

To start with, the Bible itself claims in many places to be the word of God. How frequently this introductory phrase occurs: "Thus saith the Lord". Then, too, the Lord Jesus Christ's testimony to the divine inspiration of the Bible is very clear, and for Christians who believe that Jesus Christ is the divine Son of God, that in itself should be quite sufficient. Jesus knew his Bible thoroughly. He had plainly read it regularly and carefully. He based his teaching on it and regarded it as of final authority. Thus, when he was tempted by the devil, to each temptation he simply quoted a phrase from Scripture saying, "it is written", or as we might put it today, "The Bible says". For him this was final. Jesus testified to the infallibility of Scripture by saying in John 10:35, "The Scriptures cannot be broken". After his resurrection he reproved the disciples for their slowness to believe all that the Scriptures said and he spent the last hours of his fellowship with them expounding the Scriptures.[3]

A very interesting illustration of Jesus' view that whatever the Bible says, God says, is found in Matthew 19:5 where Jesus quotes a verse from Genesis 2, reminding his hearers what God the Creator had said in the beginning, with regard to husbands and wives, "For this cause shall a man leave his father and his mother and shall cleave unto his wife and the two shall become one flesh". In Genesis this verse is actually the comment of the writer, but Jesus said unequivocally that God was the author of the sentence. We see that for Jesus the words of the Bible, no matter who was the human writer, are the words of God.

Another interesting verse is Matthew 22:31. Jesus was replying to the Sadducees who denied the resurrection and he was establishing the truth of the resurrection by a verse from Genesis. He prefaced the quotation of the Old Testament with the question "Have you never read what was spoken unto you by God?" By this sentence Jesus showed that he regarded the Bible as the Word of God, "spoken by God". And it is the written words of Scripture, not merely the thoughts or events behind them, which Jesus called the Word of God, for he asked "Have you not read what was spoken to you by God?" It is the written word, the sentences and propositions of Scripture, which Jesus designated as

3.   Luke 24:25-27, 36-49.

the word spoken by God. And thirdly, note that the written Scripture is revelational. It is not merely the record of a revelation from God to their leader. Jesus asked, "Have you not read what was spoken to you by God?" God speaks to us as we read his word. For the word of God is a living word, never merely a thing of the past.

The same attitude to Scripture is reflected in the rest of the New Testament. For example in Hebrew 3:7 a verse from the Old Testament is introduced by the words, "Even as the Holy Ghost saith", making clear that the New Testament writer realised that though the verse was written by the psalmist, the ultimate author was God. Similarly in Acts 1:16 a quotation from the Bible is introduced by the phrase, "The Scripture which the Holy Ghost spoke by the mouth of David". This is an interesting illustration of the two-sided truth. David wrote the words naturally and freely, drawing on his experience, yet the true author was the Holy Spirit who was infallibly directing those faculties, which he himself had given to David. (Compare this with Acts 4:24, 25 where there is a very similar introductory formula.)

There is an important verse in 2 Timothy 3:16 where St Paul commends Timothy because he had known the Bible from his earliest years. The Apostle affirmed that the Bible is able to make the reader wise unto salvation through faith in Christ Jesus, adding, "Every Scripture is inspired of God and is profitable for teaching, for reproof, for correction, for instruction which is in righteousness, that the man of God may be complete, furnished completely unto every good work".

The Greek word here translated "inspired of God" is *theopneustos*, that is, *breathed out* by God. It is the final written word, the end-product, which is under consideration and which is said to be God-breathed. We sometimes think of God's inspiration as being confined to inspiring thoughts or controlling events of history. But the apostles speak of God's inspiration always as the finished product, the spoken or written Word. Of course, such inspiration includes inspiring the thoughts or directing the actions, but it does not stop there. It is the Scripture, the final written Word that is breathed out by God, according to the apostles.

Thus, St Paul speaks of the Bible as "the oracles of God",[4] that is, infallible utterances, infallible sentences, for this is the meaning of the

4.   Romans 3:2.

word 'oracle'. Similarly in 2 Peter 1:19 we read of Scripture that "men spake from God, being moved by the Holy Ghost". Essentially, the Bible is from above. God the Holy Spirit is the prime author. God is able to control his creation so as to fulfil his purposes without destroying his creation, therefore the words of Scripture can be divine words without ceasing to be human words. The church, the Christian community, witnesses to the Bible that here is indeed the Word of God.

THE CHURCH AND AUTHORITY

Sometimes it is contended that the church has given us the Bible and so the church is superior or at least equal to the Bible in authority. This is the position of the Second Vatican Council and the Council of Trent which said that Church tradition was to be received with veneration equal to the holy Scriptures. But although the church witnesses to the Bible as the Word of God and hands it on to us, it does not give us the Bible in the sense of originating it, but itself receives it as a gift from God. The books of the Bible were written *to* the church, not *from* the church. For example, the prophets were sent by God to his church. Sometimes the words of Scripture were received in a very hostile manner by the church. For example, Jeremiah's prophecy was rejected by the Old Testament church to which it was sent. So, too, the New Testament was written to the church by the Apostles. Then again, we need to remember that when the Christian gospel was first preached, the preachers brought the Bible with them in that they handed over to the new converts the Old Testament which comprises the greater bulk of our Bible and which the preachers had themselves received as God's infallible Word, and by which they asked their hearers to check the gospel they were now preaching. In the same way today, the church, often in the person of parent or Sunday School teacher, hands on to us the Bible which it has itself received, adding its word of testimony that in the Bible the voice of God is to be heard. Again it is sometimes argued that the Bible is incomplete, and that it needs to be supplemented by church tradition as a source of revelation. But the Scripture itself contradicts this. In 2 Timothy 3:16 St. Paul three times over affirms the sufficiency of the Bible "that the man of God (i.e., the Christian) may be complete, completely furnished to every good work". Thus, Scripture establishes that when God gave the Bible as a source of revelation he gave what was complete and sufficient and which does not need to be supplemented. St John says the same in John 20:30, 31. He comments that there are many other things that he could have included in his gospel but what he had included was sufficient. His words are: "Many other signs therefore did Jesus in the presence of his disciples which are not written in this book but these are written that ye may believe that Jesus is the Christ, the Son of God, and believing you might have life in his name".

Sometimes it is said, in support of the notion that the teaching of the church is as infallible as is the teaching of Scripture, that God has promised the guidance of his Spirit to the church (which is, of course, true) and that as a consequence the church's teaching must be infallible. But this does not follow, because the guidance of the Spirit is not given for the purpose of leading us to infallibility. The Holy Spirit's guidance is promised to the individual Christian as much as to the church as a group. For example, Romans 8 tells us that whoever is not led by the Spirit of God is not a child of God, so that all God's children are led by his Spirit. But it is quite plain that we are not led infallibly in the sense that we can rely on our conclusions without needing to examine them. The same is true of the Holy Spirit's guidance of the group or the church. The result of this guidance (i.e., church tradition) is not in itself infallible but needs to be examined, and, of course, the rule by which we examine our own conclusions or church tradition is the written Word of God. Primitive Christianity and church tradition are helpful in understanding the Bible, but we should not have recourse to them to supplement what God has given us in Scripture.

It is sometimes said that the teaching of the Bible is obscure, so that the ordinary reader cannot understand it but needs to rely on the official interpretation of the church. But the fact is that the teaching of the Bible is perspicuous. It is not hard to understand. In the passage in 2 Timothy 3, St Paul congratulates Timothy on having known the Bible from when he was a child. He had been taught the Scriptures by his mother and grandmother. Anyone who reads the Bible in a modern translation can test the matter for himself, and he will find that like any other book, the Bible was written to be understood by the reader. It is true, of course, that self-willed people will twist the Bible to support their own views, to which Peter refers in 2 Peter 3:16, but in actual fact there is a very wide agreement amongst Christians about the essential teachings of the Bible. You will find that most of the differences amongst Christians are on matters about which the Bible has very little to say. It is we who are at fault in this. We ought not to erect grounds of separation, and break the bond of love and duty of fellowship, over matters not important enough to be included by God in his revelation in Scripture.

A CIRCULAR ARGUMENT?

You will have noticed that I have quoted the Bible to establish the authority of the Bible. This may be thought to be arguing in a circle; but in fact this is not so, for, firstly, Scripture may be treated simply as an historical account of what Jesus taught and what his Apostles taught. For Christians, the teaching of Jesus and the Apostles about God is of final authority and what this was may be discovered from the New Testament simply treated as an historical record; and so to quote the Bible to show what this teaching was, although in fact it establishes the authority of the Bible, is not arguing in a circle. Secondly, it must be remembered that God's Word is self-authenticating. It would be strange if this were not so, and if God needed witnesses from outside himself to testify to his authority.

Consequently, Christians, in recognising the Bible as God's word, use it as the source for Christian doctrine. In fact, all Christian doctrines must be drawn from Holy Scripture. There is therefore no reason why we should not use Scripture as a source not only for such doctrines as the Second Coming, but also for the doctrine of revelation. It is inconsistent to take the Bible's teaching about sin and judgement and incarnation and salvation, but yet refuse to accept its testimony as to what is the nature of God's revelation through its written pages.

It is contradictory to acknowledge Christ's authority as a teacher on divine matters and reject his teaching about God's relationship to part of his creation, namely his relationship to the words of Scripture. For Christ clearly taught that the Bible is God's Word and cannot be broken.

Again, it is contradictory to accept the Bible as a source of doctrine, believing for example such amazing things as the incarnation, the resurrection and the second coming solely on the ground of the testimony of Scripture to them, and yet reject the doctrine of the Bible in its testimony about the character of Scripture, especially when there is such an immense weight of evidence as to what the apostolic view of Scripture was. We know nothing (and can know nothing) about the future, about such doctrines as heaven and hell, Christ's coming and future judgement, apart from the teaching of the Bible. If we accept these basic Christian doctrines on the authority of the Bible, we are hopelessly inconsistent if we reject the teaching of the Bible on the doctrine of inspiration.

CONCLUSION

We may conclude then that the Bible, being God's book, is utterly reliable in all matters in which he intended it should be our teacher. If you reflect, you will see why God should have given us a book of this supernatural character. For had he not done so it would not have been possible for us to have the same religion as the disciples or as Abraham or as those who heard the Old Testament prophets. The disciples and the Israelites were in a position to hear God's Word directly and with certainty, either from the mouth of Jesus Christ himself or from a prophet filled with the Spirit of God. But what of us? If we are to have the same religion of trust and obedience we must be in a position to hear the same sure direct Word of God. But how can this be, now that Christ has returned to heaven and prophecy has ceased? God has provided for it by inspiring in a supernatural way the Holy Scriptures, which are his direct and infallible word to those who will read them prayerfully.

There is a further consideration. The Christian religion is essentially one of faith and trust in God, but it is not possible to have true, utter trust and calm, confident faith unless we have been given a reliable word or promise in which to trust. If we sense any element of unreliability in that in which we are trusting, then to that extent trust becomes impossible and we are forced back on our own resources; prudence takes the place of trust. But the Christian religion calls upon us to have utter trust in God, which implies that we must have an utterly reliable word. And this God has given to us in the Scripture, which is utterly reliable because he has inspired it through his Spirit in a supernatural way so that its words are his words, without ceasing to be the words of the writer.

Again, Christianity is an acknowledgment of the Lordship of Christ. To take Jesus as Lord is the test of a Christian; but now that Christ has returned to heaven, how does he exercise his lordship over our hearts, or over the church, except through his clear and true word? If he had not left us his word, we could not obey him, or if that word were doubtful or unreliable, our obedience would to that extent be less than full and we would have to have reservations in our obedience. But Christ calls for complete obedience that in turn necessitates a completely reliable Word from him. This has been given to us in the Bible.

Again the Christian life is a life lived waiting for the completion of God's purposes.[5] The future is unknowable unless God tells us about it. Man cannot predict even the weather of the next few days with any certainty. Yet the Christian life as laid down in the New Testament is a life lived in the light of the certainty of the world's future according to God's purposes. This is impossible unless the Bible is the infallible word of God. If we are to live the life of hope and not be found fools, God must give us his reliable Word about his purposes. This he has done in the revelation of Jesus Christ and the apostles, preserved for us reliably in Holy Scripture through the work of God's Spirit in the writers. Any view of the Bible which mingles it with unreliable elements strikes at the very basis of the Christian religion. We may be thankful that God has given us in the Bible his inerrant Word, the instrument through which he calls us to faith and obedience, and through which he moulds in us the character of Christ. It is our duty to believe that word and to read it regularly and prayerfully and through it to trust God completely and to obey him gladly and thus grow into Christ-likeness, as we wait in confidence for the promise of our Lord's return and the coming of his kingdom.

5.   Titus 2:12, 13; 1 Thessalonians 1:9, 10; Philippians 3:20; 1 Corinthians 1:7; Romans 8:24, 25; etc.

QUESTIONS ASKED AND ANSWERED

If the Bible is the true revelation of God, why is there a difference between God in the Old and in the New Testament? The Old Testament God is a harsh judge punishing sin, lobbying for the Jews alone. The New Testament God, as revealed by Christ, is a forgiving Father, forgiving repented sin, and who is for all people.

The question reflects an erroneous hearsay view of the Old Testament. We must remember that the God of the Old Testament is the God of our Lord Jesus Christ and of the apostles. The apostles did not change their religion when they accepted Jesus as the Messiah. On reading the Old Testament it will be seen that God is there revealed as, essentially, a God of love. For example, in the very beginning in Exodus 34 he reveals his name, that is his character, as "A God of compassion and gracious, slow to anger and plenteous in mercy and truth; keeping mercy for thousands, forgiving iniquity and transgression and sin".

The ethical injunctions of the Old Testament are fully in keeping with Jesus' teaching, for example, Exodus 23:4—"If you meet your enemy's ox or his ass going astray, you shall bring it back to him"—and Jesus' summary of our duty—that is, "You shall love your neighbour as yourself"—are simply two quotations from the Old Testament. To give only one further instance, the Psalms are full of praise for God's steadfast love and mercy. Yet, at the same time, both in the Old and New Testaments, God has revealed that he is also a God of judgement. He does not ignore unrepented sin and rebellion.

Did God stop writing when he finished the Bible? Are the writings of saints who have lived since then in any way inspired? And can they further reveal God's purposes?

In Christ God has fully revealed himself for "in him the fullness of the Godhead dwelt bodily".[6] It is, therefore, inconceivable that there should be anything more that God wants to reveal to us about himself than what he revealed when he himself was present. The lives of the saints illustrate God's work in men's lives, that is they illustrate (but do not add new revelation to) what God tells us in Scripture of himself, and of his relations with us. For this reason good Christian biography is most valuable reading.

6. Colossians 2:9.

If God controls every atom and electron in the universe, and if we are made up of electrons and atoms, why do we have free will?

It is true that we have free will (which is, of course, synonymous with 'will'—the adjective 'free' adding nothing to the concept; for a will that is not free, in some sense is not a will). But our wills do not have the sort of freedom that some people think we have; for example, sinners are slaves to their sin because they are blinded by the devil and cannot choose but to sin. Though they always retain a 'formal' alternative, they have no 'material' alternative. Those who have been redeemed by Christ are set free from the external tyranny of sin so that they are now free to follow their own natures, of which God is the author; and so the regenerate person, in so far as he is free from sin, naturally loves to do God's will; but all of us, whether regenerate or unregenerate, exercise our freedom within the sovereignty of God. This relation of a sovereign will to a true secondary will is unique. There is nothing to which we can compare it, but we can see it illustrated in our experience of prayer for guidance, and in our trust for protection. For we never imagine God saying to us, in reply to our prayer, "So sorry, I can't help you, for the man you fear has free will". The Holy Bible teaches clearly that God is sovereign, working all things after the counsel of his own will; and a clear appreciation of this doctrine sets us free for energetic Christian service. The inspiration of Holy Scripture is an example of God's sovereignty which, though controlling the event, does not destroy the free working of the natures he has made.

Must you be certain of something before you have faith?

Faith is exercised towards that which is not seen but not towards that which is not known. Faith is not an uncertain venture 'on spec', but St Luke says, in Acts 1:3, it has its own infallible proofs.

Is no direct revelation possible at any stage of Christian growth between God and his creature?

The Holy Spirit is in direct fellowship with the believer but he mediates this fellowship through God's word, that is the Bible. The Bible also serves as a test of experience, in order that we may detect spurious experience which does not come from God but, perhaps, from our own psychic nature, from experience which comes from the indwelling of the Holy Spirit. If what we experience does not conform to the word of God, it does not come from God.[7]

Is it not true that the New Testament is the product of the church?
No part of the Bible is a product of the church. For example, St Paul
says in 1 Corinthians 2:13, "We speak not in words which man's
wisdom teacheth but which the Spirit teacheth", and in 2 Peter 1:21,
"The Scriptures were written by men borne by the Holy Spirit". The
Bible was written by members of the Christian community but written
to it, not from it. The community sometimes was most hostile.
Jeremiah's prophecies are an illustration, where the head of the
community burned the words that the prophets wrote.

*If the Bible is infallible and inspired from beginning to end, what answer
is to be given to geologists and the like who have disproved the story in
Genesis concerning the time of the formation of the world?*
God has given us the Bible for certain purposes and has used the natural
faculties and gifts of learning of men in doing this. Since God is its
ultimate author, it is infallible and perfect for his purposes. He has
over-ruled so as to exclude any mistakes that would mar it. This does
not imply that God, of necessity, must inspire it in such a way as to
exclude what we would regard as imperfections if the Bible is used for
other purposes, for example, as a source book for learning Greek
grammar. In inspiring Genesis to teach us about God as Creator and
man as sinner, God has obviously used a writer who thought in ways
not unlike his contemporary cosmologists. I do not think that we can
require, of necessity, the Holy Spirit to have inspired Genesis so that it
conforms to today's science, but to final science, whatever that might
be. What we may say is that in Genesis 1-3 all errors with regard to God
and his relation to the world and to man have been excluded, for it was
to give a knowledge of these things that God caused the Bible to be
written. All truth which the Bible was written to give a knowledge of,
that is all truth which the Bible teaches, it teaches infallibly. Thus, if we
read it in a straightforward way we will form a true concept of God's
relation to the world and of our relationship to him and to one another.

7.   Deuteronomy 13:1-3.

Chapter 16

PROPOSITIONAL REVELATION, THE ONLY REVELATION[1]

*T*HE OBJECT OF THIS ARTICLE IS TO counter the current notion that there is no such thing as "propositional revelation", and, on the contrary, to establish the fact that all revelation, insofar as it reveals God to us, is propositional.

PROPOSITIONAL REVELATION UNDER ASSAULT

For some time now it has been fashionable to deny what is called propositional revelation . The term has been coined by those who are opposed to the concept, and by it they appear to mean that revelation is not given to us by God in the form of truths couched in words, or propositions, but that all the revelation that God has give has come to us primarily as acts and events. Thus, Dr Leonard Hodgson, former Regius Professor of Divinity in the University of Oxford and Canon of Christ Church, writes: "The 'Word of God' is not a proposition or a series of propositions prescribing what we are to believe or think. It is a series of divine acts, when they are reflected on by the mind as it seeks to grasp their significance. The revelation of God is given in deeds: the doctrines of the faith are formulated by reflection on the significance of those deeds". Hodgson denies that there exists for us "revealed doctrine, presented by God, ready-made in propositional form". He goes on to argue for the "substitution of revelation in act for revelation in propositions" a concept which solves some of the antimonies between philosophy and theology.[2] Dr John Burnaby, former Regius Professor

---

1. First published in *Reformed Theological Review,* vol xix, 1, February 1960.
2. L. Hodgson, *The Doctrine of the Trinity,* (London: Nisbet, 1944), pp. 22ff.

of Divinity in the University of Cambridge, in his lectures on "Christian Words and Christian Meanings" writes in the same strain.[3]

The Right Reverend J. C. Vockler, formerly of Adelaide, has traced the concept that revelation is in deeds and not in words to F. D. Maurice and Bishop Charles Gord, implicit in whose writings was the notion that "the Bible is not the revelation of God so much as the record of that revelation and more importantly, that God's revelation is a self-disclosure in action. Revelation is through *events*, not in propositions". Archbishop William Temple argued in a similar manner, and Vockler goes on to say that through Temple's writings "we are clearly rescued from the notion of propositional revelation and our attention is focussed on the activity of God in history, both generally and specifically, as the mode of divine self-disclosure".[4] Temple indeed makes a great deal of this denial of propositional revelation. In *Nature, Man and God* he asserted, "There is no such thing as revealed truth. There are truths of revelation, that is to say, propositions which express the result of correct thinking concerning revelation; but they are not themselves directly revealed."[5] The explicit denial of "propositional revelation" may be traced back as far as George Tyrrell, the Roman Catholic modernist, who wrote: "revelation is not a statement, but a showing...God speaks by deeds, not by words".[6]

PROPOSITIONAL REVELATION IS TAUGHT IN SCRIPTURE

The denial of "propositional revelation" is the denial that God reveals himself to men through the medium of words, that is to say, through meaningful statements and concepts expressed in words, for such is the only sense that can be given to the word "propositional" in this phrase. The denial that revelation is propositional in form, though widespread and repeated nowadays from writer to writer, runs counter to the

3.   J. Burnaby, *Christian Words and Christian Meanings*, (London: Hodder & Stoughton, 1955).
4.   J. C. Vockler, *Communitas*, 1959, pp. 42ff.
5.   W. Temple, *Nature, Man and God*, (London: Macmillan, 1935), p. 317.
6.   G. Tyrrell, *Through Scylla and Charybdis*, (London: Longmans, 1907), p. 287.

biblical view of revelation. The view of the Bible is that revelation is essentially propositional. This may be established in two ways. First, by considering how the Bible describes revelation, and secondly by examining biblical revelation to see what in fact its nature is.

On the first point, it should be noted that the Bible regards words spoken and, in particular, written, as being the bearer of revelation. For example, St Paul describes the Old Testament as "the oracles of God".[7] It is the words of the Old Testament which are referred to as "oracles" (or logic). The same term is employed by Stephen in Acts 7:38, where the law at Sinai is described as "living oracles" and the phrase "oracles of God" is used in Hebrews 5:12 and 1 Peter 4:11. An oracle is a revelational utterance, or, in other words, a revealed truth. Its revelational character lies entirely in the words. The words may be descriptive of an event, or of a concept; but in both cases the words form propositions and it is the proposition that is revelational, because it is a proposition uttered by God. This is the meaning of the phrase, "oracles of God". The apostolic writers regarded the Old Testament as a series of oracles, of which God is the author, though different prophets and lawgivers were the penmen. The concept would be common place to the Greek readers of the New Testament. (We need not, of course, follow the pagan Greeks in their unduly mechanistic concept of the methods of inspiration.) Nevertheless, the phrase "oracles of God" can imply nothing else than that the end-product, viz., the words uttered and written down, are God's words, and if God's words, then revelational of his mind and purpose and so entirely properly called "his oracles". The biblical doctrine of revelation is concerned with the end product—the words written down. Words written meaningfully are, of course, propositions. Yet it is such written words which the Bible avers to be "God-breathed".[8] It is the written word, the Scriptures, which Christ declared cannot be broken.[9] The gospel, which St Paul says is God's power to save, is adumbrated in "holy Scriptures".[10] Jesus asked the Sadducees "Have you never *read* what was spoken to you by God?",[11]

7.   Romans 3:2.
8.   2 Timothy 3:16.
9.   John 10:35.
10.   2 Timothy 3:15.
11.   Matthew 22:31.

that is, the written word is God's word to the reader.

An examination of the nature of revelation in Scripture confirms that this revelation very frequently is plainly in the form of propositions. For example, the opening verse of the Bible, "In the beginning God created the heaven and the earth", reveals one of the most fundamental facts in our knowledge of God and ourselves; and this verse is revelational (and is it profoundly so), it is because it is in the form of a proposition. No one was present when the act of creation took place, to perceive it. The act in itself revealed nothing to us. Our knowledge that God is creator is a revealed truth, and this revelation is exclusively propositional. The writer to the Hebrews affirms as much.[12] The same is true of all that has been revealed, for example, with regard to the Second Coming, or about Heaven and Hell. By the nature of things, such revelation must be propositional, for the action of the Second Coming has not yet taken place, while men cannot yet experience heavenly things. Consequently, our knowledge of future events, or of heavenly super-sensible realities, must be revealed to us propositionally, that is to say through meaningful words, if we are to have any knowledge of them whatsoever. The revelation which God has given us of the Second Coming, of the judgement day and of Heaven and Hell, form a very large and important part of biblical revelation, and are all exclusively propositional. We are enjoined in Scripture to orient our lives by these propositions about God's actions in the future. If they are not reliable and inerrant, this would be an improper injunction. Similarly, the knowledge of God's providence comes to us through propositions. For example, our Lord's statement that God is "Lord of heaven and earth"[13] is a proposition. Yet by this title a profoundly important truth has been revealed to us. God's providence is not deducible by observation of events; though having been given to us through propositional revelation we can see this doctrine reflected in events. In the Bible God is constantly represented as revealing facts about himself in propositional form, e.g., "I am the God of Abraham, Isaac and Jacob". All the great "I am" sayings of Christ, too, are propositions. Nor would these truths about Christ have been apprehended by the weak minds of men

12. Hebrews 11:3.
13. Matthew 11:25.

had they not been given as propositions. A great deal of the Old Testament revelation was given to the prophets in the form of vision. So characteristic is the vision of prophecy that the whole book of Isaiah is described as "the vision of Isaiah".[14] In revelation through vision, the event (i.e. the vision itself) is not revelational, but it is the content of the vision (i.e. the concepts which God makes known through the vision) which is the bearer of revelation. These concepts are all apprehended by the seer and passed on to the hearer propositionally, that is to say, through meaningful words forming the concepts that God put into the mind of his servant. One of the most important revelations through vision is Daniel's vision of the Son of Man in Daniel 7. Both the vision itself, and the vital interpretation of it, cannot be described otherwise than as "propositional revelation".

DEEDS ARE NOT REVELATORY

Hodgson's statement that the revelation of God is not given in words but in deeds, minimises the fact that, if the deed is to be meaningful, it must be interpreted correctly; and that it is the interpretation which brings about the revelation. Hodgson's position, by confining revelation to deeds and making the Bible merely a witness to the deeds and not itself part of the revelation, leads to foolish conclusions, self-evidently wrong. In his view, "the Word of God is a series of divine acts, to which the Bible bears witness... the revelation of God is given in deeds; the doctrines of faith are formulated by reflection on the significance of those deeds". Such a view means that the New Testament epistles are excluded from being revelation. They would be, according to Hodgson, the propositions formulated by the mind, as it reflects on the deeds of God and seeks to grasp their significance. A similar consideration applies to such statements of Christ as "God is a Spirit; and they that worship him must worship him in spirit and in truth; for the Father seeketh such to worship him".[15] This is a statement about God and his worshippers. To deny that this proposition is revelational is foolish.

A further unfortunate consequence follows from the denial of

14. Isaiah 1:1, 2 Chronicles 32:32.
15. John 4:23, 24.

propositional revelation. If the words of the Bible are made merely witnesses to the revelation of God, the unique position of the authority of the Bible is undermined and it becomes merely one witness of no greater authority and of no more infallible a character than the other two witnesses which may be brought in at this point, namely the witness of the Church and the witness of the human spirit and reason to the acts of God in experience. The dichotomy between event and the interpretation of the event, with the singling out of the former as the important element, or indeed as the sole element making up the revelation leads, as might be expected, to the ignoring of the interpretation which commends itself to the reader. Thus Brother George Every, S.S.M., writes of Father Herbert Kelly, the founder of his Community (and who "learnt almost everything first from Maurice"): "In his own reflections on the Old Testament Father Kelly had a way of going directly to the event without even noticing the interpretation given by the prophet or the prophetic historian".[16] It will be seen that if revelation is in the event rather than in the interpretation, revelation becomes like a nose of wax to be reshaped according to every man's whim. In fact, if revelation is only in event, then there is no revelation in the sense of God-given knowledge of God.

In the last resort, the concept that God's revelation is in deeds can only be maintained by a forgetfulness that God is all-sovereign over the world. The fact is that there is no event that God controls more than any other and, therefore, every event is equally revelational of some aspect of his character. Yet to say this is to say that no event is revelational in itself. For example, God controlled the migrations of the Syrians from Kir and the Philistines from Caphtor as completely as he brought up the Israelites out of Egypt.[17] What is it then that makes the tribal migrations of the Israelites pregnant with revelation throughout the Old and New Testaments, while those of their related tribe, the Syrians, reveal only the one fact of God's general providence to which Amos alludes? Similarly, why are the invasions of neighbouring countries by the Assyrians, and the fate that overtook the Assyrians, revelational of God's character,[18] while the intertribal warfare of, say, the

16. H. Kelly, *The Gospel of God*, 1959, p. 34.
17. Amos 9:7.
18. Isaiah 10.

Maoris, is not? It is not as though God's sovereign control is exercised any the more over the one or any the less over the other of these different events, but simply that to the one have been added interpretive propositions and statements, but not to the other. It is the proposition which is the revelation, giving meaning to the event, to our minds. The event by itself means nothing. The conclusion is that revelation is essentially propositional.

Modern theology largely ignores the doctrine of the sovereignty of God, and the important consequences of this are seen in modern theories of revelation. Temple saw the danger and sought to guard against it. His modern followers fell headlong into the pit. Dr Alan Richardson has summed up Temple's view of revelation thus:

> *Revelation is due to the twofold form of the activity of God: God controls the historical events which constitute the media of revelation, and also inspires the minds of the prophets and thus enables them to interpret the events aright. He guides the process; he guides the minds of men; the interaction of the process and the minds that are alike guided by him is the essence of revelation.*[19]

But God guides every event, every process. The new element is the infallible guidance of the prophet's mind so that he interprets the event aright. Thus it is the interpretation which is the revelation, and this interpretation is in the form of inerrant propositions. The biblical doctrine is that it is the work of the Holy Spirit not only to formulate these propositions in the mind of the inspired prophet, but to secure their embodiment in the written Scripture. The activity of God in controlling events is continuous and unchanging (though the purposes of his control will vary); but the gift of interpreting the event aright is sporadic.

GOD INTERPRETS EVENTS

For an event to be revelational it must be interpreted by God himself. This and not merely some human reflection on the occurrence is the real differentiating factor. God interprets through his Word, given in the form of propositions and statements about the event. Thus, for the

19. A. Richardson, *Christian Apologetics* (London: SCM, 1948), p. 146.

prophets, the word of the Lord was not the event but the interpretation of the event which had been given them by the Spirit. The same is true of that supreme event, the life, death and resurrection of Jesus Christ. There would have been no revelation in Christ's ministry were it not for the interpretative statements of our Lord and his apostles. It is the proposition then that is the revelation, not the act itself.

Temple states, on the contrary: "the faith in which his early followers believed that they had found salvation did not consist in the acceptance of propositions concerning him, nor even in acceptance of what he taught in words concerning God and man, though this was certainly included; but in personal trust in his personal presence love and power".[20] This statement contains an inner contradiction. Faith cannot be exercised except towards propositions. Certainly, Christian faith (and in particular the disciples' faith) was not exercised towards propositions about material things, but towards propositions about a Person: his power, and his promises. Nevertheless, the disciples' trust in Christ's presence, love and power was ultimately based on the acceptance of propositions about these things which had been formulated in their minds. The case is no different, though more obvious with regard to those who "not having seen, yet have believed", for their knowledge of Christ's presence, love and power (from which their personal trust in him sprang) was conveyed to their minds exclusively by propositions. Trust in Christ is a religious experience which is a consequence of a revelation given and received ("He who comes to God must believe that he is").[21] This trust and religious experience is to be distinguished from revelation. Such experience of God is, of course, more than propositional; but the revelation on which it is based and by which it must be judged is essentially propositional. A confusion arises, unless the meanings of the word 'knowledge' are clearly distinguished. Knowledge of God in the sense of revelation of him is entirely intellectual; it is apprehended by the mind alone. It is, therefore propositional. But knowledge of God in the sense of 'fellowship with him' goes beyond intellectual apprehension and is experienced through all the avenues of our being. In this latter sense, knowledge of God is not exclusively, perhaps not even essentially, propo-

20. Temple, p. 311.
21. Hebrews 11:6.

sitional, that is, not articulated consciously into propositions; but this knowledge of God is not in itself revelational, though it illuminates revelation and suffuses revelation. Yet such religious experience must be based on revelation, and be judged by revelation if it is to be regarded as true and not spurious knowledge of God. Revelation is the test and criterion of such religious experience as to whether it is knowledge of God, and the revelation that forms this test is the words of the Scripture and the propositions that these words form.

Denial of "propositional revelation" makes Christian faith impossible in its fullest and deepest expression of trust, for it is impossible to trust absolutely unless we have a sure word of God. Such denial restricts Christianity to a religion of works, that is, to following and obeying Jesus Christ as best we can. Moreover, denial of propositional revelation makes the lordship of Christ impossible, for it is only by the sceptre of his word that he can exercise that absolute lordship over men's consciences and wills which is his by right. For it is wrong to give absolute obedience to an uncertain command or to place absolute trust on an uncertain promise.

INERRANCY AND PROPOSITIONAL REVELATION

Denial of propositional revelation goes hand in hand with a denial of inerrant revelation. An illustration of this may be taken from *The Christian in Philosophy* by Professor J. V. Langmead Casserley who writes:

> For the most part, the biblical conception of revelation is not propositional but historical. The God of the Bible is made known, or rather makes Himself known, not in words but in events. The Bible is not a series of saving propositions... but a propositional record of saving events. Its actual language, as is inevitable when human speech grapples with the problem of describing the singular, is partly adequate and partly inadequate.[22]

It is commonplace nowadays to assume, as Casserley does, that the words of the Bible, being human words, must inevitably (either

22. J. V. Langmead Casserley, *The Christian in Philosophy*, (London: Faber & Faber, 1951), p. 190.

through natural human inadequacy or the presence of sin) distort God's revelation. But the assumption ignores the power of God expressed in the divine rebuke, "Who made man's mouth?".[23] To assert that its Creator (who saw all from the beginning) cannot fulfil his purposes which he determined on from eternity, namely to reveal himself infallibly through human speech, betrays great impiety.

It is sometimes further asserted that, from the nature of truth, it is impossible that there should be such a thing as inerrant revelation. A simple illustration will show the falsity of this. If when the clock strikes four, I state "The clock has struck four", I have made a propositional statement which is true if words mean anything and this truth remains characteristic of the proposition, even if (a) my hearer misheard me through deafness, (b) failed to apprehend my meaning through faulty knowledge of English, or (c) there was no-one present to hear me. If it is possible for an ordinary human to make a completely true proposition which is a revelational fact for those who have ears to hear, it is again the height of impiety to say that God cannot ensure that his servants do so, if he will; and not make one such true proposition only, but to make a whole series of them within the pages of the Bible, and to exclude from among them any erroneous propositions, if he will— words not only true, but to the point, that is, they are words which God has spoken to us who read them. That God has in fact done so must be believed by all who give credence to the teaching and attitude of Christ and of his apostles (and, indeed, to the whole of Scripture itself) with reference to the character of holy Scripture. The apostles explicitly affirmed that their words were the words of God, and that the propositions that they penned were verbally inspired by the Holy Spirit, e.g., "We teach not in words which man's wisdom teacheth, but which the Holy Spirit teacheth",[24] and "When ye received from us the word of the message, even the word of God, ye accepted it not as the word of men, but, as it is in truth, the word of God".[25]

It is highly inconsistent, and springs from no discernible principle, that modern-day theologians should accept the authority of Christ and

23. Exodus 4:11.
24. 1 Corinthians 2:13.
25. 1 Thessalonians 2:13.

the apostles (and of Scripture in general) with regard to God and his relation to his creation, while rejecting that authority with regard to God's relation to the words of Scripture, themselves a part of that creation.

Chapter 17

THE CANON
AND BIBLICAL THEOLOGY[1]

1. The formation of the canon
2. The canon and inspiration
3. Prophecy and canon
4. The end of "biblical theology"

1. THE FORMATION OF THE CANON

*T*he word 'canon' means 'a measuring rod', and thus it has a double application with regard to the Bible. The original and fundamental meaning is that the books which compose the canon are the measuring rod or rule by which the church measures doctrine. Thus the canon, that is, the books which comprise it, is the standard by which Christian truth is to be tested.[2] But secondly, the word 'canon' refers to the list of books which make up the canon or rule. It is this latter use of the word which is the subject of this article.

Primarily, the word canon refers to the character of the books. They are the rule by which our religious ideas are to be measured. They are this because of their character, which is the result of God being their Author. They are inspired by him for the purpose of being a revelation of himself. Being the words of God, they are of supreme authority. If a writing is not canonical in this sense of being inspired by God as a revelation, that is, if it is not God-breathed, no decision of church or council can ever confer this character of canonicity on it.

---

1. This chapter is a combination of four addresses (compiled by Dr Knox). The source of the original manuscript is footnoted at the beginning of the relevant section. The occasion of this first section is uncertain.
2. Acts 17:11.

On the other hand, if it is inspired by God, no adverse decision of the church can ever detract from its character and God-given canonicity. That there was such a body of documents having this character in existence at the time of our Lord and his apostles, is evident from the attitude and words of our Lord and his apostles, and it is not difficult to establish by historical research, that these documents were what we know as our Old Testament.

Thus, when the Christian church was brought into being by the preaching of the gospel of Jesus Christ by the apostles, it had from the beginning a canon of Scripture. It was never without a Bible, that is to say, without books which were regarded as of absolute authority in matters of faith and conduct. When, at the beginning of the gospel, Jews were converted to put their faith in Jesus as their Messiah, they did not abandon their Old Testament, nor modify their views with regard to it, except to see Jesus Christ as fulfilling it. Similarly, when Gentiles were converted, they were converted into a church where the Old Testament was already prized as the very word of God. Thus the Christian church was not required to form for itself the idea of a canon (or, as we would say, a Bible), that is, a collection of books given by God to be the authoritative rule of faith and practice. It had a canon from the beginning.

But the question arises, how was it that the early Christians who so highly prized the Old Testament Scriptures, added to these Scriptures fresh writings which they placed on a level with the Old, as fully inspired by God himself? The explanation is to be found in the presence within early Christianity of apostles and prophets,[3] who were recognised as being the instruments of the Holy Spirit to bring to completion the revelation of God in Jesus Christ, the incarnate Son of God.[4] The apostles and prophets were the recipients of revelation.[5] The church of the apostles' time recognised the activity of the Holy Spirit in revelation, as we see from 1 Timothy 4:1 and 1 Corinthians 2:9-16. The apostles were conscious that their words were authoritative.[6] St Paul was conscious that his writing was revelational. Just as Moses was a minister

3.   1 Corinthians 12:28; Ephesians 2:20; 4:11.
4.   Ephesians 3:5; Romans 16:26; Colossians 1:26; Titus 1:3.
5.   Ephesians 3:5.
6.   1 Thessalonians 2:13; 4:2; 2 Corinthians 10:8; 13:10.

of the Old Covenant, and was read regularly, so the apostles were ministers of the New Covenant which Christ had instituted in his death.[7] They were conscious that their writings had divine authority, and were to be read along with the Old Testament Scriptures.[8] Their writings were to be included in the standard of faith and conduct, so that obedience to them was to be the condition of Christian fellowship.[9]

It is interesting to note that neither our Lord, nor the New Testament writers, although they held clear and strong views of the authority of Scripture, defined the limits of canonicity. In this, doubtless, the providence of God may be seen, for the infant Christian church did not have a closed canon, but one that was augmented from time to time, as the apostles either wrote or authenticated those books which we now know as the New Testament. We should not regard it as accidental, but rather providential, that the limits of canonicity were not settled among the Jews themselves until after the separation of the unbelieving Jewish community from the Christian church. Had the limits of the Scripture been a firm and closed question in the time of our Lord and his apostles, so as to be reflected in their teaching, the addition of the New Testament books to the canon would have presented a difficulty for the Christian community. As it was, we can see from the pages of the New Testament that the apostolic writings were placed by the apostles themselves alongside the Old Testament as Scripture.[10]

There are three distinct things to keep in mind when considering the canon. (1) How the books came to have their character as canonical; (2) how the books came to be accepted as canonical, that is, how the canon came to be formed in the second sense of the word; (3) how the books composing the canon may be verified and tested as canonical in the first sense of the word, that is to say, as God-inspired and, therefore, the standard by which faith and practice is to be shaped.

With regard to the first question, Holy Scripture was written by the inspiration of the Holy Spirit, and, therefore, such books have the character of canonicity, that is, they have the authority of God from the moment of their composition. The Christian church cannot by any

---

7.   Ephesians 3:4-4:1.
8.   E.g., 1 Thessalonians 5:27; Colossians 4:16; Revelation 1:3.
9.   2 Thessalonians 3:14; 1 Corinthians 14:37.
10. 1 Timothy 5:18; 2 Peter 3:15, 16.

of its decisions either add to, or detract from the character of such a book. If it is inspired by the Holy Spirit, it has the character of canonicity from the time of its composition. The second question is which books should be regarded as having this character.

With regard to the Old Testament, this second question is shrouded in the mist of history. All that we may say is that the Old Testament canon was accepted by the Jewish church and by our Lord and his apostles, at the time of the beginning of the gospel. With regard to the New Testament books, the history of their formation into a list of recognised books is not altogether clear, as the evidence has not fully survived, but it was probably as follows. A book would be authoritative from the time that the prophet or the apostle wrote it and imposed it on the church to which it was addressed, as an authoritative word, and it would be recognised as authoritative by all that section of the Christian church which knew of its apostolic authorship, and of its imposition by apostolic authority on the Christian church. However, New Testament books were written to local Christian communities, and there would, therefore, be a passage of time between the writing of any book (with its acceptance by the local church to which it was written), and the acceptance of it throughout the whole Christian fellowship. Time would have to elapse before the book was known throughout the worldwide Christian church. We know that the early Christian church was conservative in its willingness to recognise books as canonical, and this, of course, was right, and is our safeguard. It was no light thing to place fresh books alongside the Old Testament Bible, as being equally God-inspired. In fact, it was not till the end of the fourth century that the Christian church came to one mind about all the New Testament books which it included in the list of the canon.

The third question then is how may we know that any particular book is rightly included in that list? Some theologians affirm that it is the decision of the church, which confers canonicity on a book. But this is not so. All the church can do is to recognise the character of the book, and for the great bulk of our New Testament books, this character was recognised without dispute by Christians from the time of the composition of these books, for they were received at the hands of the apostles.

Most of our New Testament was received everywhere in the church from the beginning. No New Testament book was rejected everywhere and then accepted. But some books were known only locally at first, and the passage of time was needed for them to be accepted universally. (The history of this growing unanimity on the part of the church with regard to what should be included in the canon is traced in the textbooks).

A test that may be applied to a book claiming canonicity is the conformity of its doctrine with the rest of Scripture. For if a book is in reality canonical, the Holy Spirit will have been its author, and this implies that its teaching about God will be in conformity with the teaching of all those other books of which the Holy Spirit is also the author. In this way, the remarkable agreement in doctrine and ethics throughout the pages of the Bible is a striking vindication of the truth of the inspiration of Scripture and the correctness of the canon.

The canonicity of a book is sealed for us by the fact that the Christian church has heard God's voice in it through the centuries. The word of God is active. Christ's sheep, our Lord affirmed, hear his voice. Each generation in the church receives the Bible as the word of God and hands it on, adding its own testimony to the uniform testimony of God's people who have gone before, that in these pages, Christ's voice is indeed to be heard. The church may recognise the canon as something already existing. It cannot, by its decision, confer canonicity; for no church or council can confer authority on a Word which is already the source of authority because breathed forth by God and because it attests itself in the heart of the believer by the testimony of the Spirit as God's Word.

2. THE CANON AND INSPIRATION[11]

The New Testament provides clear evidence that the first Christians accepted without question a body of literature which they designated the Scripture, which was of a special sacred and divine character. Jesus and the apostles quoted this literature with the introductory phrase "It is written", and this indicated final and absolute authority of the quotation.[12] It was their opinion that what was written in Scripture, God

---

11. A paper read to the Fellowship of Biblical Studies Symposium, 24 March 1976.
12. Matthew 4:4, 7, 10; Romans 1:17; Galatians 3:10, 13; etc. cf. Matthew 21:42; Luke 24:27; John 7:42; 10:35; 20:9; Romans 11:2.

spoke both originally and to the present readers,[13] and he continued to speak the written Scripture.[14] It is therefore an obvious but important truth that the Church did not require to form for itself the idea of a collection of books given by God to be an authoritative rule of faith and practice. That is, it did not form for itself the idea of a Bible or a canon. The church did not grow spontaneously but was founded; and the apostles, the authorative teachers sent by Christ, carried with them a body of divine Scriptures which they imposed on the churches which they founded, to be received with the same absolute authority as Jesus and the apostles had received these books. That is to say, these written words were to be received as the very words or oracles of God.[15]

We do not know the way the books of the Old Testament came to be recognized as the very words of God, though it is plain that they were recognized in this way by the Jews of our Lord's time, a recognition which our Lord and the apostles shared and commended. Josephus and the author of 2 Peter were of the opinion that the books were written through the work of the Holy Spirit of prophecy. Because Josephus believed that prophecy ceased after Ezra, he was convinced that there could be no sacred Scripture written from that time onward.[16]

With regard to the New Testament, the extraordinary fact that has to be explained is how the first Christians who held the highest possible views of the character and authority of Scripture came to add to the canon books written in their own time. The explanation is their conviction about the presence of the Holy Spirit of prophecy and the presence of the apostles commissioned by Christ and endorsed by him with the signs of apostleship. The early Christians were convinced that the Spirit had been poured out upon them and that all Christians had received the anointing of the Holy One. Christians experienced the Spirit as the spirit of revelation.[17] It was the consciousness of the Spirit's presence and activity which made it possible for the first Christians to accept the possibility (in contrast to Josephus) of new

13. Matthew 19:5; 22:31; Acts 2:16 and Romans 9:25; 2 Timothy 3:16.
14. Hebrews 3:7; 10:15.
15. Matthew 19:5; Romans 3:2; Hebrews 3:7.
16. Josephus, *Against Apion* 1:8.
17. 1 Timothy 4:1.

Scriptures, and within the New Testament there is a recognition of the phenomenon of New Testament Scriptures.[18]

Though the consciousness of the Holy Spirit's presence made the concept of additional Scripture acceptable, it did not follow that everything that a Christian said or wrote with the help of the Spirit should be treated as Holy Scripture and added to the corpus. What was required was the authentication by apostolic authority. There is clear evidence of this in 1 Corinthians 14:37 where St Paul makes a distinction between the words of an apostle and of a prophet or spiritual man. It was the mark of a prophet or a spiritual man that he would recognize that the apostolic writings are the commands of the Lord. St Paul gives no indication that all prophecy within the Christian church had the character of being the command of the Lord; indeed he himself felt free to set aside prophetic warnings.[19] But the apostolic word was of a different character. It was the norm for behaviour, and it bound the conscience.[20] Apostolic letters were to be read in the church assemblies in the same way as the Old Testament was read each Sabbath day in the synagogues[21] and doubtless also read by Christians at their assemblies. Thus by apostolic authority the apostolic letters were read along with the other Scriptures[22] and were to be regarded as the commandments bf the Lord. It is not surprising therefore that they were included in the term 'Scriptures', as for example all Paul's letters are in 2 Peter 3:16 and Luke's Gospel is in 1 Timothy 5:18. (There is no reason for excluding the New Testament Scriptures from 2 Timothy 3:16). The same identification is observable in the Apostolic Fathers. Polycarp united the Psalms and Ephesians "in the sacred books...as it is said in these Scriptures 'be ye angry and sin not' and 'let not the sun go down upon your wrath'".[23] Similarly *2 Clement 2:4*, after quoting a passage from Isaiah, adds "again, another Scripture 'I came not to call the righteous but sinners'". Ignatius was conscious of a canon of New Testament

---

18. Romans 16:25; Ephesians 3:3; 2 Peter 3:16; 1 Timothy 5:18.
19. Acts 21:10, 11.
20. 1 Thessalonians 4:2; 2 Thessalonians 2:15; 3:14; 1 Corinthians 14:37; Philemon 8; 1 Timothy 5:15, 4:11; cf 1 Peter 1:12; 1 Corinthians 2:13; 1 Thessalonians 2:15.
21. Acts 15:21.
22. 1 Thessalonians 5:27; Colossian 4:16; Revelation 1:3.
23. *Polycarp to the Philippians XII.*

Scriptures that he placed alongside the Old Testament.[24] He called these Scriptures "the gospel and the apostles". Just as in the New Testament the title 'the law' is used for the whole of the Old Testament so 'the gospel' is used by Ignatius of the whole of the New: "Give heed to the prophets and especially to the Gospel".[25] In *The Testaments of the 12 Patriarchs* the Acts and Pauline epistles are included in the concept of Holy Scripture.[26]

> *What needs emphasis at present about these facts is that they obviously are not evidences of a gradually-heightening estimate of the New Testament books, originally received on a lower level and just beginning to be tentatively accounted Scripture; they are conclusive evidences rather of the estimation of the New Testament books from the very beginning as Scripture, and of their attachment as Scripture to the other Scriptures already in hand. The early Christians did not, then, first form a rival 'canon' of 'new books' which came only gradually to be accounted as of equal divinity and authority with the 'old books'; they received new book after new book from the apostolical circle, as equally 'Scripture' with the old books, and added them one by one to the collection of old books as additional Scriptures, until at length the new books thus added were numerous enough to be looked upon as another section of the Scriptures.*
>
> B. B. Warfield[27]

The apostles were instructed and commissioned by Jesus to be the founders of the gospel. In the forty days after the resurrection he instructed them in the things concerning the kingdom of God,[28] and in the prophecies of Scripture with reference to himself.[29] The sermons in Acts and the instructions and injunctions in the apostolic letters will reflect this teaching of Jesus.

Before his death he promised that the Holy Spirit would reveal truth which the apostles were not then in a position to receive from him. The

---

24. *Ignatius to the Philadelphians V.*
25. *Ignatius to the Smyrnians VII.*
26. *T. Ben 11.*
27. B. B. Warfield *The Inspiration and Authority of the Bible*, (London: M.M.S., 1951), p. 412.
28. Acts 1:3.
29. Luke 24:44-47.

Spirit would lead them into all truth since the Spirit would reveal his mind.[30] The apostles were commissioned by Christ to be his mouth-piece.[31] They spoke, they were God's messengers[32] and wrote with authority[33] and Christ gave them signs confirming their authority.

It was through the apostolic and prophetic ministry that the New Testament revelation was given[34] and received.

The limit of the canon

It is inconceivable that Jesus and his hearers did not know what he was referring to when he said "the Scripture cannot be broken".[35] It is equally inconceivable that St Paul did not know what books were con-tained in the Scriptures which he commended the Jews of his time for preserving or that the apostles did not know what Old Testament books they were imposing on the Gentile churches. What were these books?

▸ The nearest contemporary evidence of what these books might be is Josephus when he confined the Scriptures to 22 books.[36] Josephus' views were forcefully reiterated by Cyril of Jerusalem in his catechistical lectures[37] and endorsed by Jerome.

▸ It is worth noting that Philo in his voluminous writings never quoted from the Apocryphal Old Testament. It is not intrinsically likely that Josephus or the so-called Council of Jamnia should have innovated by excluding these Apocryphal books if they were already received as Scripture.[38]

---

30. John 16:12-15.
31. Luke 10:16; Galatians 4:14.
32. Galatians 4:14; 1 Thessalonians 2:13.
33. 1 Corinthians 14:37 etc.
34. Ephesians 3:5.
35. John 10:35.
36. *Against Apion* 1:8.
37. 4.35.
38. The Council of Jamnia, said to have taken place in around AD 90, is sug-gested as the point at which the Hebrew canon was authoritatively closed by a group of 72 elders. Evidence regarding the nature, and even existence, of the Council of Jamnia is sparse.

➤ Moreover, the Old Testament canon that Jesus knew had the same order of the Old Testament books as the 'Palestinian' canon of Josephus. It is very difficult to see how the Deuterocanonical books could be included in this order.

Because of this evidence, the Apocryphal or 'Deuterocanonical' books of the Old Testament can only be regarded as having very doubtful claims to have been spoken to us by God. The Council of Trent, however, regarded them as of inspiration equal to the rest of the Old Testament. But just as it is a principle of Roman Catholic moral theology that doubtful orders ought never to be exercised and that doubtful laws do not bind the conscience, so deuterocanonical books ought not to be put alongside undoubted Scripture. Normative authority over the conscience must be absolute, or it is non-existent. God's word binds the conscience and, being God's word, does not admit of degrees.

Similarly, with regard to the New Testament canon, a writing is either God's word (as understood by Jesus and the apostles) or it is not. The activity of the Holy Spirit and Christ's commission of the apostles are the two factors which provide the possibility of New Testament Scripture. Scripture inspired by the Spirit is authoritative from the moment it is written. It is recognized as authoritative when known to have apostolic authorisation. The first recipients of these writings would know of this authorisation from the beginning. Other Christian churches would learn of the existence and authorisation of these Scriptures through the lapse of time. In this way the canon of each church would grow in volume though not in authority. If it were to be established that a writing was not accepted as Scripture by its recipients when it first appeared, this would be *prima facie* evidence that it was not Scripture (e.g., the *Shepherd of Hermas*). However, the re-examination and the weighing of the evidence for the inspiration of a book already received is not evidence of this, but only of the scrupulous care that Christians took in the formation of their canon, which should reassure us in using this canon in as much as we no longer have access to the evidence through which it was formed.

3. PROPHECY AND THE CANON[39]

Prophecy may be defined as men speaking from God, being moved by God's Spirit.[40] Prophecy is God's words spoken through the agency of men, e.g. "God spoke by the mouth of David".[41] Put another way, prophecy is human words spoken by men which are God's words because he has spoken them through his influence and control of the speaker. Thus Balaam told Balak that he was unable to say just anything that Balak wanted, but could only speak the words which God gave him.[42]

Before we look more closely at the phenomenon of prophecy, we must examine whether human language is able to be a vehicle for the expression of accurate and infallible divine communication. We note first that God created mankind in his own image. This includes the concept that human personality has an affinity with the divine and that human relationships are reflective of the divine nature and character so that language drawn from human experience is a reliable medium to describe in a true way divine thought and character and actions. Consequently it is possible for God to use human language directly and not merely analogically to describe his relationship with us.

The Bible tells how God has used human language to speak to men directly; for example, at the burning bush God addressed Moses directly,[43] and at Sinai God spoke directly to the children of Israel the Ten Words.[44] During his incarnate life our Lord Jesus Christ taught his contemporaries the things of God using direct human language. Thus Scripture testifies that God has used human words for direct communication between himself and men. There is no suggestion in the context that he was using the language analogically, but on the contrary simply, directly and normally, as we would use it in communicating one with another.

39. Paper read at a Symposium at St Barnabas Anglican Church, Broadway, Sydney, 27 October 1975.
40. 2 Peter 1:21.
41. Acts 4:25.
42. Numbers 22:38; 23:5.
43. Exodus 3:4ff.
44. Exodus 20:1-17.

Besides these words directly addressed by God to men, there is another phenomenon, namely, God addressing us through prophets. For example, we frequently read in the Old Testament "Thus says the Lord" followed by words in direct speech addressed to us by God. These words of God through the prophet are not men's words about God but are God's words addressed to us. This is how the prophet designated them and this is how they were received. Consequently these words will have the character of infallibility, that is to say, of utter reliability and truthfulness; and they will be perspicuous, able to be understood by the hearer, for this was God's purpose in speaking them; and they will be authoritative over our words and conscience, being the words of God.

Holy Scripture brings before us a third phenomenon. Not only are there direct words of God spoken at Sinai or in Galilee, and also words spoken by prophets, but thirdly there is the phenomenon of written prophecy. God not only used the mouth of his servants but also the pen of his servants, and so we have the fact of Holy *Scripture*, that is to say prophetic *writings*. The New Testament testifies to this third phenomenon (in, for example, Matthew 19:5). Here Jesus makes reference to words that he ascribed to God, which were never spoken but were written from the beginning. In fact, the whole of the Old Testament has this character of being written prophecy and has received the imprimatur of Jesus when he said "the Scripture cannot be broken", for only God's word has this infallible, unbreakable characteristic. Notice that it is the Scripture—the written word, the word which we have—to which Jesus testified that it was God's word.

Jesus taught that what the Scripture says, God says. Consequently, Jesus appealed to the Scripture as final authority. He repelled the temptations of Satan with the phrase, "It is written". That is to say, this written word has final authority, because it is God's word. He confidently expected all the Old Testament prophecies to be inevitably fulfilled. What is written must be fulfilled.[45]

The same attitude to Holy Scripture is reflected in the rest of the New Testament. In Acts 1:16 and 4:25, the apostles speak of God as the author of the words of the Old Testament. So too in Hebrews 3:7, the writer, quoting Psalm 95, bypasses the human author with the

45. Luke 22:37.

phrase, "The Holy Ghost says". St Paul puts the matter in a nutshell in 2 Timothy 3:16 in which he states that Scripture is "God-breathed". The words are God's words. Just as the words I breathe are my words, and reflect what I want to convey, to the best of my ability, so the God-breathed Scriptures are God's words and reflect God's intentions perfectly and completely. Therefore, Holy Scripture, since it is the word of God, is true in respect to all the things that God is saying through it. It will be infallible, that is to say, utterly reliable; it cannot be broken or proved wrong; it must be fulfilled. It will also be able to be understood, because this is God's purpose in giving it, and it will be sufficient because this again is God's purpose that the men of God might be completely furnished for every good work.[46]

It is necessary to distinguish what God is saying from the form of the language through which this word comes. This is true in all human writing and is also true of Holy Scripture. For example, if we use a metaphor we distinguish between what is intended to be said and the form in which it comes. If I were to say "you are a donkey", you would be mistaken if you tried to prove this wrong by showing that you did not have four legs or unduly long ears; indeed that endeavour would only prove the truth of my statement! We see then that in all language we must distinguish between what is intended to be said and the form in which it comes. What God intends to say will be true, or else it was not God who said it. Similarly, it will not be stated ambiguously nor will the form of the language be misleading. Thus, if God intends to teach us about history or about science as a means by which we are to learn about him, then those statements about history and science will be true, for if they are not, God never said them. For the most part it is not hard to find out what a passage is intending to teach, nor to distinguish the teaching from the form in which it is expressed. This is the sense in which the written Scripture is infallible and true.

Of course it has always been possible to reject the notion that God has spoken and to attribute the words which say "Thus saith the Lord" to the religious imagination of the writer and to explain Scripture as merely human reflections about divine truth. It is possible to reject the authority of Paul or the other writers of the New Testament as though

46. 1 Timothy 3:17.

God's Spirit was not speaking through their penmanship. But prophecy was a recognized phenomenon in biblical times. Jeremiah, for example, distinguished clearly between true prophecy and imitative prophecy,[47] and we must face the question where there is such a category as true prophecy, because if it is a fact then it becomes central to all our discussions of our knowledge of God. Yet in present day writings on the character and authority of Scripture the concept of prophecy is often overlooked. If we agree that there is such a thing as prophecy it means that prophecy is distinct from all other human literature. Prophecy is from heaven, the word of God: infallible, true, utterly reliable, meeting our needs, never can be broken and will always be fulfilled. All other human literature, however inspiring, however true, however helpful, is from men.

The concept of prophecy involves the concept of the Canon, that is, the list of writings recognized as prophetic and therefore authoritative. It is conceivable that we may make a mistake in our list of writings; we may include in the canon literature that God has not spoken in this prophetic way, or we may thrust out of the canon that which God has spoken. But, if we believe there is prophecy, then we must have a canon, that is to say, a list of what is prophetic and thus different from all other human literature.

The Christian church has always had a canon. In the time of Jesus and the New Testament the concept of Scripture as the word of God was already firmly established and Jesus and the Apostles testified to it. Paul commended the Jews of his time as having preserved the oracles of God; that is to say he confirmed the canon of his time. The concept of deuterocanonical books, if this is taken to mean a second level of authority, is of course a fantasy. Books are either God's prophetic word or not, and if not, they are to be classified with human literature and excluded from the canon of Scripture, however helpful or true they may be.

It is not hard to see how the New Testament canon must have been formed. For example, when St Paul wrote a letter to a Christian church he was writing to a community who already had the concept of holy Scripture as distinct from other literature—yet we find that the recipients added his letter to Scripture. It must be because they were as

47. Jeremiah 26:15; 27:15.

firmly convinced that his writings were prophetic, as the hearers of Isaiah were that he was a prophet, and St Paul endorsed this conviction. His message, he said, was not the word of man but of God. You may, of course, think Paul was wrong, but the early Christians did not think this was so. They put his book into the canon because they believed the Spirit of God was speaking through the apostle. So it must have been with all New Testament books. That is to say, the first recipients must have received these books as prophetic, because the character of prophecy cannot grow in a writing. It is either there as the ink is drying on the paper, or it is never there. Thus, a book would need to have been accepted as prophetic by the first recipients for anyone else to accept it as prophetic. The canon grew in the sense that it grew as more prophetic books were written, and in the further sense that different Christian churches enlarged their canon by receiving copies of New Testament prophecy from churches who had received them in the first place. But it did not grow in the sense that a book, not at first received anywhere, was later put in. That is an impossible concept in view of the very high authority given to the canonical Scriptures by the early Christians. It is only because they were persuaded that the holy Spirit was speaking also through the writings of the apostles that they could have put these writings alongside the Scripture of which Jesus said that God had spoken it.

The concept of canon is a simple one; it is simply putting certain writings into the pigeonhole of prophecy, while all other literature goes into the other pigeonhole. There is no mystique about the canon. There may be a mistake in the list, though there is little likelihood of this. Christians today receive the canon through those that first received the documents and accepted them as prophetic. The only test nowadays is the test of consistency. Plainly, if a writing is inconsistent with the rest of the canon God could not have written it.

Everything that is rightly in the canon is the word of God, so that whatever the document is plainly teaching, God is teaching. We will need of course to use the reflective gifts given by God to us and to others, to find out what God is teaching us through these historic documents. For the most part this is plain, but sometimes it needs some degree of exegetical skill to elucidate the meaning. For example, we need to elucidate the principle that is being expressed from the cultural form through which the principle is expressed. For if the culture changes, the form of expression may no longer be appropriate, but the principle taught us through this expression will be abiding and part of God's revelation to us. We are not however at liberty to set aside what Scripture teaches once this is established, for Scripture is authoritative. It is God's word to us and his word is infallible, reliable, and will not trip us up. From this it follows that God will not speak one sentence of a writer and not the next; just as when Isaiah said, "Thus saith the Lord", the whole of what he said under this heading was the word of God. Of course the prophet may be a false prophet, or the apostle, a false apostle. But this was not the view of the early Christians with regard to our Scriptures. Though we are at liberty to believe that the early church made a mistake in its inclusion of any particular book (or part of that book), and so may reject this from the canon, we are not at liberty to pick and to choose from among the statements of a writer that we accept as prophetic as to what we would like to believe or to obey.

4. THE END OF 'BIBLICAL THEOLOGY'[48]

This is an important article.[49] It sings the swan-song of biblical theology as this term is applied to a phenomenon of the immediate post-war world of biblical studies. It is a short article of only seventeen pages. Barr acknowledges that biblical theology is a broad term but for the purpose of the article he distinguishes three senses. Firstly, the term describes a movement in modern theological studies which reasserted the authority of the Bible though in a changed form, and secondly, as a sub-section of this movement, he uses the term to describe the writing of books which are theologies of the Old or New Testament. Thirdly, he uses it in a further sub-division for monographs which take

---

48. A review of the article entitled, "Trends and Perspectives in Biblical Theology" by Rev. Prof. James Barr, read at the Fifth International Congress in Biblical Studies, Oxford, 3 September, 1973, and published in the *Journal of Theological Studies*, October, 1974. Also read to the Fellowship of Biblical Studies, Sydney, 24 July, 1975.
49. That is, Barr's article.

a more limited area, for example, the theology of the Deuteronomist, or Luke's view of history, or the meaning of the covenant, and so on.

Barr regards G. Ernest Wright's *The Old Testament against its Environment* (1950)[50] and *The God who Acts* (1956)[51] as good examples of the movement in its hey-day. The books of the movement are characterised by two assumptions: (1) that there is a unity to be discovered in the Bible and (2) that if the Bible's teaching can be truly distilled, the distillate would have, without further argument, a normative status.

Thus the writers of the movement assumed that biblical theology was quite distinct from study of religions. Barr, however, reaches the conclusion that all this is now in the past. The history and study of religion is flourishing as never before while biblical theology has ceased. It has been absorbed by the history of religions. This should not have been the case if the presuppositions of biblical theology were right. Indeed as Barr points out, biblical theology was intended to keep at bay the history of religions and philosophical theology. But these grow stronger as it withers. It had hoped to re-state the authority of the Bible, but that authority is being questioned now more than ever before. A good example of the change of perspective is Barr's accusation that the biblical theology movement in its handling of the Old Testament failed to do justice to Judaism as a religion that stands in valid continuity with the Old Testament. In other words, Barr assumes the very thing that biblical theology denied, namely the continuum of religious experience in the Old Testament with other forms of religion and in particular with Judaism. If Barr's assumption is correct, and it is a near universal assumption nowadays, then in my judgement there can no longer be any such thing as Christian theology as a discipline in its own right. It now becomes merely a subdivision of the study of human religiosity and religious ideas. Barr affirms that instead of the unity, the theological diversity of the Bible is now accepted, and that its authority *qua* Bible, can no longer be assumed. Just as Professor Wiles regards systematic theologians like Barth as poets rather than scientists,[52] so Professor Barr likens the biblical theologian to a landscape painter imposing his own interpretative unity on the survey.

50. London: SCM, 1950.
51. London: SCM, 1956.
52. M. Wiles, *The Remaking of Christian Theology*, (London: SCM, 1974), p. 107.

It will be seen then that Barr's article is important as indicating a watershed which was crossed some time ago and from which Barr is well down the other side. Indeed the watershed was crossed by the supporters of biblical theology themselves. They are on the same side of the watershed as is Barr, though at the time they strenuously denied that they were in this position, and sought to maintain a pre-watershed stance by affirming the uniqueness of biblical religious experience. For example, Wright wrote in the foreword to *The Old Testament Against its Environment* that the purpose of his book was to "lay emphasis upon those central elements of Biblical faith which are so unique and *sui generis* that they cannot have developed by any natural evolutionary process from the pagan world in which they appeared."[53] But Barr has proved that this position was an impossible one by showing that there are now no scholars, not even Wright himself, who occupy the position dug out and fortified with such gusto in the early fifties. As Barr points out, the distinctive feature of the problem is the authority of the Scriptures, and the distinctive feature of the biblical theology school was to place the authoritative revelation of God in the acts narrated in the Old and New Testament, and not in the verbal propositions of the narrative, e.g., "The Bible is not primarily the word of God, but the record of the acts of God, together with the human response thereto.[54] As I pointed out in an article in February 1960 in the *Reformed Theological Review*, revelation through uninterpreted acts is a chimera and the tenor of Barr's article confirms that this is so.[55] The problem that Christian theologians must grapple with is whether there is a revelation from God unique to the Old and New Testaments. Biblical theology said that there was, but accepted the presupposition of modern scholarship as to the fallible character of the biblical writings, so that these theologies were forced to say that the supernatural revelation which they affirmed lay in the acts and not in the interpretive narrative of the acts. But while maintaining this position that revelation was in acts and not in propositions, they ignored one of the most fundamental of the acts of God as

53. Wright, *The Old Testament*, p. 7.
54. Wright, *The God who Acts*, p. 107.
55. D. B. Knox, "Propositional revelation the only revelation", *RTR*, vol xix, 1, Feb 1960. Reproduced in the current volume, pp. 307-317.

narrated in the Old and New Testaments, namely, the act of prophecy. Prophecy is verbal action, and in the Old and New Testaments this verbal action of God is sometimes auditory, at other times inscripturated. Indeed all our knowledge of the auditory and other acts of God comes through inscripturated prophecy, for it is this character that the Scriptures claim for themselves. Prophecy is the phenomenon that must be tackled by modern biblical and theological studies. "The God Who Acts" remains a silent God. Wright and Barr are agreed on this. Thus they are both on the same side of the watershed. They have both abandoned the God of Christianity. For it is the God who spoke that the Christian Creed affirms, "who spoke by the prophets". Thus the biblical theology school of the fifties is hoist by its own petard of ignoring the most characteristic acts of the God who acts!

If biblical prophecy is what it claims to be, and if biblical writings are prophecy as they claim and as Christ and the apostles have testified to them, then there is an authority within our reach that is unique. It follows that only religious experience which conforms to that inscripturated revelation is authentic in contrast to all other religious experience which is not based on the word of the God who spoke, not merely in acts which have perished, but in revelation contained in inscripturated prophecy, that is in words infallibly given through the action of God by his Spirit. These words remain with us today for us to read and understand and to bring us into relationship with the true God.

The fatal internal contradiction of the Biblical theology movement was that while seeking to maintain belief in the transcendent God, it exhausted any supernaturalness from the acts on which it based its knowledge of him. The phenomenon of inscripturated prophecy is the watershed. It is a thoroughly supernatural phenomenon as is the incarnation and God's speaking the Ten Words out of the fire at Sinai. If the phenomenon is accepted as actual, then the canon and tradition is merely a commentary, accurate or otherwise, on the revelation, so that both canon and tradition become subordinate and ancillary. But from Barr's standpoint they rightly become central (as he emphasises in his article), for they are then a most important aspect of the history of religion which in the face of denial of the phenomenon of prophecy and in particular, inscripturated prophecy, becomes the only source of our knowledge of religious truth. The crux then, is whether prophecy exists, for if it does it must supersede experience as the subject matter of theology.

Chapter 18

AUTHORITY AND THE WORD OF GOD[1]

$\mathcal{A}$UTHORITY IN HUMAN EXPERIENCE has its ground in the incompleteness of our human nature. It has a twofold aspect and both these facets spring from the fact that the individual life is not self-sufficient. The first aspect does not belong exclusively, nor primarily, to the religious sphere of a man's life. In the realm of everyday life most of our knowledge comes to us on the basis of authority. This is inevitable. Life is short; men have not the opportunity of learning first-hand all the facts which are needed for human existence. Viewed abstractly, it might appear that we should always be guided by reason. Yet reliance on authority is not undesirable. The reasoning power of the average man is limited, and if relied on exclusively would lead to many errors. Nor is being guided by authority antagonistic to being guided by reason. It is a reasonable thing to be guided by authority. Authority in common life represents the consensus of the experience of centuries. In addition, the expert who has devoted himself to a specialised field of study speaks with an authority on his subject. To respect and value these two forms of experience is eminently reasonable. In the aspect of authority which we have been considering, the individual human fills out the shortness of his own span of life with its scanty experience and its incomplete powers of reasoning, with the common experience of the whole race through the centuries or with the dicta of an expert. This experience whether of the race or of the specialist comes to him in the form of authority, to which he gladly defers.

But in the realm of religion authority takes on another aspect. Here we are dealing with deficiency in experience, not of the individual but

---

1. Paper delivered before the Faith and Order Commission of The Australian Section of the World Council of Churches on 16 February, 1950. First published in *Reformed Theological Review*, vol ix, 2, Winter 1950.

of the race itself. The subjects with which the Christian religion deals are transcendental in character. The events are unique. There is little place for that authority on which we rely in common life, that consensus of experience which is passed down to us by our forebears; (as for the expert, we have not, as we have in the world of science, any simple test to apply to the would-be religious expert, to know whether or not he is a guide to lead us safely to truth about God, or a mountebank[2] to follow whom leads to Hell). Yet although that common place authority on which we rely in our daily life for the most part deserts us in questions of religion, there is no sphere in which men crave authority more avidly than in the sphere of religion. It is here that we realise most vividly the deficiency of our own powers. We long for some help outside ourselves. To this wide-felt need Christianity answers plainly that the need has been satisfied. The primary category of the science of Christian theology is revelation. God has spoken. This fact is the basis of Christian Theology. God is *actus purus*,[3] and his activity towards mankind is revealing and redeeming. A moment's reflection will show that this word of God to man is of absolute authority. Through the Christian faith we learn that man is God's creature; his nature is of God's fashioning; his life is daily dependent on God's providence. Moreover, man, apart from God's illumination, is ignorant and blind. To such men, when the Word of God comes, it comes with an authority which must be absolute and final. So the question contained in the title which has been allotted to me in this paper: "Authority and the Word of God" is very easily answered. The word of God is of ultimate, binding, authority. This is axiomatic, and only requires to be stated to be convincing.

But there is a further question. The Christian faith states categorically that God has spoken, that he has revealed himself, that there is a word of God which men may hear. What is this word of God? Where is it to be found? It is a word of grace. We have not deserved that God should be our God, nor that we should be the recipients of his word. We have no power of disposal and no rights over him, but with unto-

2.   A fraud, a charlatan.
3.   A scholastic term meaning 'pure actuality', referring to the idea that God is unchanging.

ward kindness, in the freedom of his majesty, he resolved to his own self to be man's God; our God. He *tells* us that this is so. To quote Barth:

> *God's telling us: 'I am gracious to you' is the word of God, the central concept of all Christian thinking. The word of God is the word of his grace. And if you ask me where we hear this word of God, I can only point to himself, who enables us to hear it, and reply with the mighty centre of the Confession, with the second article, that the word of God's grace in which he meets us is called Jesus Christ, the son of God and the Son of Man, true God and true Man, Immanuel, God with us in this One. Christian faith is the meeting with this 'Immanuel', the meeting with Jesus Christ and in him with the living word of God. In calling Holy Scripture the word of God (and we so call it, because it is so) we mean by it Holy Scripture as the witness of the prophets and the apostles to this one Word of God, to Jesus, the man out of Israel, who is God's Christ, our Lord and King in eternity. And in confessing this, venturing to call the Church's proclamation God's word, we must be understood to mean the proclamation of Jesus Christ, of him who is true God and true Man for our good. In him God meets us. And when we say, I believe in God, the concrete meaning is that I believe in the Lord Jesus Christ.*[4]

Christ is the word of God and his teaching and his example must be of final authority to men. Yet in the days of our Lord's flesh, the word of God in Christ was not imposed directly on the souls of his disciples but was mediated to them through their perception and through their understanding. So with us, Christ is not known directly but mediately. Where is this mediate revelation to be found?

The Holy Bible is the sole primary source of our knowledge of Christ. Bishop Headlam is right when he says: "There is no trace in the early Church of any knowledge of real importance about our Lord and the apostles additional to that given in Scripture."[5] A perusal of Eusebius or of the apocryphal books of the New Testament confirms us in this opinion. Such scraps of information as survive in these pages light up by their absurdity the clear simple facts narrated by the Gospels.

---

4. K. Barth, *Dogmatics in Outline*, (London: SCM, 1949), pp. 16-17.
5. A. C. Headlam, *Christian Theology*, (Oxford: Clarendon, 1934), p. 69.

This supremacy of Scripture as the source of the word of God is not always conceded. Some theologians find God's revelation in our God-given nature, in the workings of conscience and in our intellectual and psychical functions. Thus Canon Richardson can write: "The pressure of truth or meaning upon our minds is nothing other than the impact of God upon us".[6] But unless we are to be pantheists we must distinguish between the natural working of our nature, which is the result of God's sustaining providence, and the special breaking through of God in revelation of himself in Christ; that was a unique and undoubtedly miraculous event, distinct from all other events of history.

Other theologians find in the voice of the Church that word of God to which we must give absolute obedience. For this position some plausible arguments can be made out. The Church speaks from a wealth of experience; further, her life is animated and guided by the Spirit of God. Yet there are two considerations which preclude our clothing the word of the Church with that *final* authority which belongs to the word of God.

1. The Church's knowledge of Christ is derivative. The sole source is the Scriptures. We must reject the theory of the Council of Trent that there is a double source, for our knowledge of the life and teaching of Christ and his apostles, namely Holy Scripture and the unwritten traditions preserved in the Church. We reject the theory, not because of *a priori* considerations so much as because an examination of the literature and practice of the early Church shows that it is untrue. The Church has preserved no reliable tradition of Christ and his apostles which are outside the pages of Scripture.

2. The Church's voice is not infallible. Though we believe that the Spirit of God guides the Church, this guidance is not given in an infallible way. The statement in the 21st article of the Church of England puts the matter succinctly: "Forasmuch as general councils be assemblies of men, whereof all be not governed with the Spirit and word of God, they may err, and sometimes have erred, even in things pertaining unto God".

Yet though we cannot give to the voice of the Church that final authority which belongs to the word of God, we must not lose sight of the fact that the Church has great authority. Its authority is of that type

6.   A. Richardson, *Christian Apologetics*, (London: SCM, 1948), p. 121.

of authority which we discussed in the beginning of this paper. It is the authority which properly attaches to the experience of God's working through the centuries. As we rightly submit most of our daily actions to the authority of society, so it is proper to give due weight to the authority of the Church. We do not, however, give it a binding and final authority. This belongs to the word of God alone.

The question remains: To what extent are we to identify holy Scripture with the word of God? Many modern theologians confine the function of Scripture to that of a record to God's revelational activity in history. For those thinkers, revelation consists not in communicated information, as it does for example for St Thomas Aquinas, but in personal communion. Thus William Temple wrote: "What is offered to man's apprehension in any specific revelation is not truth concerning God, but the living God himself".[7] On this view, the value of the Scriptures is that they are a record, more or less reliable, of God's acts of revelation to nations and individuals in the past. Guided by them, we may ourselves receive God's self-communication.

On this view, Scripture records God's revelation but is not itself that revelation. Indeed it may obscure the revelation. Accordingly, the labours of literary critics are directed to removing the hard husk with which fallible men have surrounded the pristine revelation. Thus such a learned and spiritually minded man as C. H. Dodd has been at great pains to examine the Gospel parables. In his book *The Parables of the Kingdom*, he reconstructs the setting of the parables. With great ingenuity and learning he shows that their setting as we have them in the Gospels was given them by the Church. As uttered by our Lord, each parable had another setting and indeed quite a different meaning. Thus the saying: "You are the salt of earth" was applied by our Lord to the Pharisees. Consequently the meaning that Jesus intended was quite different from the meaning that we obtain on reading it in a Gospel. Dodd applies the same method to all the parables.

What is the value of this sort of literary criticism? To my mind, nil. It is so utterly subjective. If we are to probe beyond the plain narrative as we have it, then there is little reason why a hundred scholars should not find a hundred mutually exclusive meanings for the same passage. The result would be that the value of the written word as a pointer to God's revelation

---

7.   W. Temple, *Nature, Man and God*, (London: Macmillan, 1935), p. 322.

would be gone. For no one would know to what truth it was pointing.

The conclusion we reach is that the fundamentalist position is the only tenable one if we are to retain that elemental Christian belief that God has spoken in a way that we can hear. The Westminster Confession puts this view succinctly in its first paragraph.[8]

Just as we believe that God has revealed himself in the course of human history through his divine activity, and that the Bible records these events, so we should believe that the giving and preserving of the Bible is itself one of these revelational acts of God. Here we must walk by faith, yet our faith is not contrary to reason.

Yet we must be careful not to believe too much. The Scriptures are authoritative for the purpose for which God designed and gave them: they are not authoritative for every purpose. Thus they are an infallible guide to the words of God in faith and morals, "to teach, to reprove, to correct, to instruct in righteousness" but if we use them for fortuitous guidance as some use a promise box, we must not expect to avoid grave mistakes. Nor were the Scriptures given for the purpose of teaching history, geography or science. They are not a primary or infallible source in these matters.

But in the realm of faith and morals, Scripture has a supreme authority, for it was, I believe, given by God for the purpose of revealing his mind in these matters. We accept the Scriptures by faith as a God-given revelation to be our guide in the sphere of faith and morals. It follows that the Scriptures must be sufficient and perspicuous if used in the way which their Author intended. That is to say, if they are read, humbly with the guidance and lumination of the Holy Spirit.

Fundamentally then, we accept the Scriptures by faith, believing that God has inspired them, and in his providence preserved them. (His providence extends, of course, to the selection of the Canon.) This act of faith, like all acts of faith, may be and should be supported by reason, and it is verified by our experience.

8.   "…The authority of the Holy Scripture…dependeth not on the testimony of any man or Church; but wholly upon God (who is truth itself) the author thereof…"

Chapter 19
REVELATION, PROPHECY AND CULTURE[1]

"Run, speak to this young man, saying, Jerusalem shall be inhabited as villages without walls, by reason of the multitude of men and cattle therein... Sing and rejoice, O daughter of Zion: for, lo, I come, and I will dwell in the midst of thee, saith the Lord. And many nations shall join themselves to the Lord in that day and shall be my people: and I will dwell in the midst of them and ye shall know the Lord of Hosts hath sent me unto you. The Lord will inherit Judah as his portion in the Holy Land and shall yet choose Jerusalem." (Zechariah 2:4,10-12)

THE WHOLE OF THE PASSAGE FROM which these verses come foretells the glory of the expansion of the people of God through the preaching of the gospel following the coming of Christ—"Sing and rejoice O daughter of Zion for lo, I am come, and I will dwell in the midst of thee, saith the Lord." In chapter nine the prophet speaks explicitly of Christ when he discloses how the King comes, "lowly, riding on a donkey". This earlier passage speaks of God dwelling among his people and of many nations joining themselves to the Lord in that day. So great will be the expanse of God's people that it was no use measuring Jerusalem with a measuring rod, as the young man was doing, because Jerusalem will have so many people it will overflow its walls. People will live in it as in villages without walls by reason of the multitude of men and cattle in it.

The passage is speaking of the Christian church, "Many nations shall

1.   Address delivered in Moore College Chapel, 1977.

join themselves to the Lord in that day and shall be my people" and of the Spirit of Jesus "Lo, I come, and I will dwell in the midst of thee, saith the Lord". In interpreting prophecy, it must be remembered that a prophet can only foretell the future in terms drawn from his experience of the present or the past. Consequently, prophecy of the great increase in the number of God's people that follows the preaching of the gospel, and of God indwelling his people through the Holy Spirit which followed the ascension and glorification of Christ, must take the form of predicting blessings on Jerusalem which was the City of God in the prophet's day. In conveying the mind and purpose of God for the future the prophet had no alternative to using the terminology of his own time. Thus, the great blessing of the Christian church is predicted as the desert blossoming as the rose, or as the waters flowing out of the Temple and bringing fruitful fertility wherever it goes.

It is a great mistake to take the terminology of prophecy literalistically. The New Testament itself gives the key that such terminology is not to be interpreted literalistically. For example, John the Baptist was not Elijah reincarnate. Nevertheless he was the fulfilment of the prophecy that God would send Elijah before the face of the Messiah to prepare his way before him. Malachi, in predicting the future, only had his own experience to draw upon, in this case, from the past. If this principle of interpreting prophecies is not understood, the interpreter is forced to literalism, and the only conclusion then left is that all prophecy not already interpreted in the New Testament is still in the future and this means that huge sections of the Scripture then are locked up for some future time and have no relevance for ourselves or our instruction, and we are impoverished and deprived of the nourishment from the Word of God that was intended for us. But common sense indicates and the New Testament illustrates for us, that we are not to interpret prophecy literalistically. It will be literally fulfilled but not literalistically. We are to give thought to what its spiritual fulfilment is.

When we are seeking to find the mind of God given to us in Scripture, we should recognise that God will give us his mind in terms of the life structure of the writer because there is no other alternative. This is true not only of the mind of God given by way of prophecy, but also with regard to ethical behaviour. God's word will always be directed to specific ethical situations and will take the form of injunctions suited to the situation of those addressed and clothed in the culture of the time. If we live in a different culture those specific injunctions will not be directly applicable to us, yet through these Scriptures God has given us his mind so that his children in every nation might be completely equipped for every good work. There are some relationships which never change from culture to culture, so that injunctions governing such relationships must apply universally without interpretation and reapplication, such as "Do not commit murder nor adultery". Such injunctions apply so long as men and women live in human society. But there are other cultural injunctions such as the requirement for Christian women to wear veils in church, which is no longer suitable literally in our culture, because we do not wear veils either in or out of church. Nevertheless, the injunction expresses the unchanging mind of God as this was expressed in that culture; it was God's commandment for those people and it has been written for our learning. God's mind is revealed in that command. It is silly to say Paul was speaking culturally and so dismiss his words. Of course he was speaking culturally, but he was also speaking infallibly, because the spirit of God was speaking through him, giving a command of God which applied strictly to the people who were receiving it, and it would apply equally strictly to us if we were in the same cultural situation. Nevertheless, the mind of God expressed in a command suitable to the Corinthian culture applies to us in our situation and it is our task to find out that mind, and to apply it in our culture.

The principle applies to all scriptural interpretation, for it is common sense. God in revealing his mind has revealed it not by giving a general textbook on theology, where everything is, as it were, generalised, but has revealed it for the particular situation of his people. A prophet who speaks about the future speaks in the situation and terminology of the people who are hearing him, and an inspired legislator gives ethical commands suitable to guide the behaviour of those people in their cultural situation. But prophecy and ethical instructions given in Scripture reveal the mind of God for us. We may discern it from what God said to people about how they ought to walk in their situation, but the mind of God about human relationships will always be the same and the essence of human relationships does not change. The way those relationships are expressed may change culturally. In this case the injunctions will not have a totally literal application for us, but the principle behind the injunction, that is, the mind of God, is binding on us. Thus, it is foolish, for example, to thrust aside St Paul because he was a man of his time, speaking in terms applicable to his time and culture.[2] We are to find out what God is saying to us through what he said through Paul to people in that foreign culture.

I will return to my passage. The message is "Run, speak to this young man, Jerusalem shall be inhabited as villages without walls". This is a word of encouragement that God will come and dwell among us. This has been fulfilled with the coming of Christ and his Spirit. "And many nations shall join themselves to the Lord in that day." This is a prophecy of the ingathering of Christ's people through the preaching of the gospel. There are many other passages in the Old Testament on the same theme. Take, for example, Isaiah 27:13: "And it shall come to pass in that day, that a great trumpet shall be blown; and they shall come which were ready to perish in the land of Assyria, and they that were outcasts in the land of Egypt and they shall worship the Lord in the holy mountain at Jerusalem".

The trumpet was the one instrument then available for gathering people. "A great trumpet shall be blown", means that God will gather his people. The prophecy makes reference to the only two great nations of the world in those days, Assyria and Egypt. "People ready to perish" is a reference to humanity dead in their trespasses and sins. "And they shall worship the Lord in the holy mountain at Jerusalem", Jerusalem was the only place they could worship him in those days. For if they were going to worship God, that is where they had to come to worship. This was, therefore, the terminology the prophet used in predicting the truth that the time would come when Christ would gather his elect from the four corners of the earth that they might worship him in spirit and in truth. A further example is seen in Isaiah 66:19-20:

> *"I will set a sign among them, and I will send such as escape of them unto the nations, to Tarshish, Put and Lud, that draw the bow to Tubal and Javan, to the isles afar off, that have never heard my fame, neither have seen my glory; and they shall declare My glory among the nations. And they shall bring all your brethren out of all*

---

2.   Original sentence incomplete. The words "was a man...time and culture" have been added.

the nations for an offering unto the Lord, upon horses and chariots, and litters, and mules, and upon swift beasts, to my holy mountain, Jerusalem, saith the Lord."

There again, the language, the images are drawn entirely from the daily life and culture of those days. The nations mentioned—Tarsus, Put, Lud, Javan, "the isles afar off"—was the whole known world. By the assertion that God led people out of all the nations for an offering to the Lord "upon horses and chariots, and litters and on mules, and upon swift beasts", the prophet was saying that every possible form of transportation then known would bring these people to God (that is, to Jerusalem of course): "and I will take them for Priests and for Levites, saith the Lord". Now this is not going to be taken literally as though they could be incorporated into the Levitical priesthood. It is a reference to the status Christians enjoy of serving in God's presence, for all Christians now have access into God's presence through the blood of Christ just as in those days the Levites and priests had access to the Temple and to the holy of holies. Thus this prophecy has been fulfilled with the preaching of the gospel.

I turn to one passage in the New Testament, which uses some of this imagery. Matthew 24:29 says, "But immediately after the tribulation of those days [i.e. after the destruction of Jerusalem in AD70, see Luke 21:20] the sun shall be darkened, and the moon shall not give her light and the stars shall fall from heaven, and the powers of the heaven shall be shaken." (This is Old Testament language to describe the disturbance of the *status quo*, the 'turning of the world upside down', through the preaching of the gospel.) "Then shall appear the sign of the Son of Man in heaven." This last phrase takes up the concept of a sign which occurs in Isaiah. God will give a sign, that is, a standard to rally round. What is that sign? The sign of the Son of Man in heaven, that is, that Christ has ascended to the right hand of God and that he is now ruling. He has come in the clouds of heaven to his throne[3] and is now asking of God and receiving from him the utmost parts of the earth for his inheritance, as he is seated on God's right hand according to the promise "Sit at my right hand till I make all thy enemies thy

---

3. Daniel 7:13, 14.

footstool. Ask of me, and I will give thee the utmost part of the earth for thy possession."[4] That is the sign for the harvesting of the world, of its being brought to the condition of righteousness because Christ has gone to the Father.

That is why the world believes Christ is in heaven, crowned the righteous One. He is the sign around which the Gospel preachers rally—the sign of the Son of Man in heaven.

Our Lord's prediction continues with a quotation of Zechariah's prophecy of the conversion of the world, "all the tribes of the earth will mourn".[5] There will be a world wide repentance when they see the Son of Man coming in the clouds of heaven with power and great glory, that is to say, when they see the Son of Man seated on his throne in heaven. This mourning is the mourning of repentance. This is clear from the context of Zechariah 12. Then follows in Matthew 24:31, "He shall send his angels with the great sound of the trumpet". The sound of the trumpet is accompanying imagery of the gathering of his elect. Now, in the Septuagint translation of Zechariah 2, verse 6, you will find this very same word *sunago*, "I will gather". Now of course the word 'church' means 'gathering'; Christ gathers his elect, he brings his church. And how does he do it? The sound of the trumpet of course is merely prophetic imagery. Jesus foretold that he would gather them from the four winds of heaven. That is a quotation from Zechariah 2. Zechariah foretold the gathering of the nations. Jesus declared it would be fulfilled in the lifetime of his hearers.[6] He will send his angels and gather them in. In the Greek the word is *angelos*, the ordinary word for 'messenger'.[7] We have been taught to pray "that he will send forth his labourers". He sends his messengers. Jesus chose the 12 apostles as his friends and so that he might send them out as messengers. For example, John the Baptist was said to be "the messenger of the Lord" ("angel" in the Gospel), and John the Baptist's friends are said to be the "angels" of John the Baptist, translated of course "messenger"—

---

4.   Psalm 2:8.

5.   Zechariah 12:10, cf. Revelation 1:7.

6.   Matthew 24:34 , "I tell you the truth, this generation will certainly not pass away until all these things have happened".

7.   See further below, "Translating 'angel' in the New Testament", pp. 363-372.

messengers of John. I think that there are other passages where angels ought to be translated "messenger". For example Paul told the Galatians "You received me as an angel of God";[8] "You received me as a messenger of God" is probably better. God's ministers are his messengers whom he has sent. They have been sent as labourers into the harvest as Christ was sent by the Father. "As the Father has sent me so send I you".[9] We are sent. It is better to speak of "being sent" than of "being called" when speaking of the Christian ministry. "Calling" is a status concept, and in the New Testament refers to being called to be a Christian, called into God's presence. Then God sends us out, he sends us as labourers into his harvest, he sends us as messengers to gather in his elect, "I will set up a sign among them and I will send survivors to the nations…and they shall bring all your brethren from all the nations".[10] God sends out his messengers and brings in his people into his gathering, his church. "He shall set up a sign for the nations and shall gather the outcasts of Israel and gather together the dispersed of Judah from the four corners of the earth".[11] We have been sent with the gospel to gather in God's elect. It is a glorious ministry because as the prophets foretold, it is a successful ministry. It is not a ministry of death as Moses' ministry was; it is a ministry of glory. For God has great purposes to bring in the multitude of the nations. So multitudinous will be the ingathering that "Jerusalem will be inhabited as villages without walls, because of the multitude of the men and the cattle therein". It is a glorious ministry, for which we have been sent, because it is going to be a successful ministry. God is going to be glorified by persons calling upon his name, persons ready to perish being converted in the lands of Assyria, in the land of Egypt, or wherever they might be. It is to this ministry that you have been sent by Christ to be his representative and messenger, his angel.

You must not centre yourself in your ministry in any way at all, although there is always a temptation in that direction. But Christ the Sender and the ones to whom you are sent must be the centre of your life and ministry. Christ builds his church through your ministry.

8. Galatians 4:14.
9. John 20:21.
10. Isaiah 66:19, 20.
11. Isaiah 11:12.

He will gather his people round himself. It is a joyful but arduous occupation to be a harvester.

Chapter 20

INTERPRETING THE BIBLE[1]

*T*HE BIBLE HAS BEEN GIVEN TO US SO that we may have faith and hope in God, and know how to live to please and glorify him. "Everything that was written in the past was written to teach us, so that through endurance and the encouragement of the Scriptures we might have hope".[2] Scripture is spoken by God to instruct us in righteousness.[3] God has spoken the Scriptures to each of us who reads them. For God who knows everything from the beginning purposed to speak to the present reader when the words were spoken by him in former times. What we now read was spoken to us by God; this, Jesus clearly affirms.[4] Thus the Scriptures fit every age and every nationality. They are not exclusive to one people, for the Scriptures being God's word reflect God's character and his purpose to be "the saviour of the world".[5] Like any book, the Scriptures are intended to be understood by the reader whom the author had in mind; even the youngest reader is able to assimilate the truth they contain. "From infancy you have known the holy Scriptures which are able to make you wise for salvation".[6]

The subject matter of Scripture is Jesus Christ.[7] Like any book, Scripture must be interpreted in accordance with its subject, and since the whole Bible has one author it follows that every passage of Scripture must be interpreted in the context of the whole of Scripture, not setting passage *against* passage, but rather comparing passage with

1. Unpublished notes.
2. Romans 15:4.
3. 2 Timothy 3:16.
4. Matthew 22:31.
5. John 4:42.
6. 2 Timothy 3:15.
7. John 5:39; Luke 24:27, 44.

passage in order to obtain fuller light on the meaning of each. Through these simple common-sense rules the Christian reader is able to come to a clear understanding of what God is teaching him. This is especially so if he reads and studies Scripture in fellowship with other Christians to whom God may have given greater gifts of wisdom or experience in knowing his mind as revealed in Scripture.

There is in fact no real problem in interpreting Scripture. It is interpreted in the same way as any book is interpreted. The authors of books endeavour to write so that their books can be understood by the reader whom the author has in mind. God had each reader in mind.[8] Human authors may fail in their objective, but the divine author's purpose never fails. God wrote the Bible through his servants for the present day reader. His power, wisdom and omniscience ensured that we, when we read it in a straightforward way, could understand it and know what it is that God is teaching us in it. He had each of us in mind when the Spirit spoke in the first place; and, like any author, it was his intention that we should understand it as we read it.

The Bible, however, has this remarkable characteristic which human authors cannot achieve. It directs its word to peoples of cultures other than our own and yet God speaks to us through these culturally conditioned words. Since God's mind never changes, if we strip off the cultural situation that is exposed, we are able to apply the word of God to our own situation. This requires no particular expertise but is a common sense activity. The simplest reader can recognise the difference between cultures, although there may be more than one level of reality which the truth of Scripture comprehends. While the plain and literal sense is the true and only sense of Scripture, literalism, which slavishly copies the cultural setting of the word of God (for it must come in the cultural setting of those to whom it was originally addressed) is easily seen to be a false way of arriving at God's mind to us in our cultural situation.

God speaks to us in our situation through his written word spoken originally to other situations. That was his intention when that word was first written. It will, therefore, be understandable to us by ordinary gifts that he has given to us as we read it—gifts of intelligence, knowledge and

8.   Matthew 22:31; Romans 15:4; 1 Corinthians 9:9, 10.

Christian fellowship—so long as one interprets it in the context of all that God has spoken to us, that is, every passage of the Bible should be interpreted in accordance with the whole. This is common sense. The one author does not contradict himself nor include irrelevancies, which have no place in the whole. The interpreting of Scripture is not beyond the scope of the simplest of Christians if he is prayerful, has a teachable mind and is willing to accept the help of his fellows.

Hermeneutics is mostly a bogey word. We don't need it for ordinary books and we don't need it for the Bible.

God is the author of Scripture, therefore interpret Scripture in accordance with Scripture. Christ is the subject matter. A book must be interpreted in accordance with its subject matter. Scripture was written by God with the present day in mind; therefore the present day reader will be able to understand it.

It was spoken to the cultural situation of the first readers. We must perceive Christ and apply it to our situation.

Chapter 21

INCOMPREHENSIBILITY[1]

*I*F I WERE TO WRITE YOU A LETTER WITH care and clarity setting out in detail why I wanted you to do each thing, nothing would be incomprehensible to you. If I included a blank sheet with nothing written on it, this sheet would be incomprehensible.

God has told us of his character and what our actions should be as a result of this knowledge. There is nothing incomprehensible in what he has told us.

For example, he has told us that he is sovereign in election, and that we are responsible for our actions. There is nothing incomprehensible in these two statements. On the contrary, their truth is confirmed in our judgement and our experience. He has not told us how these two facts are related. But this does not make them or him incomprehensible.

Ignorance is not incomprehensibility.

1. Note, dated August 1989.

Chapter 22
UNIVOCAL LANGUAGE[1]

*T*HE WORD 'FATHER' AS APPLIED TO God means exactly the same as when applied to men. It indicates a relationship. But because of the human condition, and because of sin, not every aspect of a father, as experienced in human life, is applicable to God. Despite that, the essential aspects of the word 'father', are exactly applicable to God.

The non-essential, and the aberrations, which do not apply, are made clear by the context of the use of the word, as is the case in ordinary language.

The context of every application of the word 'father' to God is the whole Bible. Thus the Bible makes clear what the features of the word are as applied to God. They are all descriptions of the relationship between God and ourselves.

Thus, from God we have our origin. This is an essential element of the word.

God cares for us as a father does. This is an equally essential aspect of the true meaning of the word 'Father'.

"The Lord your God carried you as a father carries his son."[2]

"As a father pities his children so the Lord pities those who fear him."[3]

"God trains his children like a good father does."[4]

1. Note, dated 1987.
2. Deuteronomy 1:31.
3. Psalm 103:13 .
4. Hebrews 12:5-10.

Chapter 23
COVENANT THEOLOGY[1]

"IT TOOK THE THEOLOGIANS OF THE post-Reformation period to explain the transmission of sin in terms of the federal or covenant relationship in which Adam stood to God on behalf of the race, so that when the head of the covenant fell, he dragged the race with him. This idea is central to Covenant Theology as a whole, since its basic principle is that since man was ruined through a representative, man can be restored through a representative."[2]

There is nothing in the Scriptures to suggest this covenant concept.

Man's relationship to Adam is much more realistic than his being a nominated representative. Similarly, the Christian (who is in Christ) has a relationship to Christ that is as real as can be. He was "in Christ", crucified with him, raised with him. In Covenant Theology, it is plain that Christ can only represent the elect. Hence limited atonement, presumably.

1. Note, dated April 1979.
2. R. A. Findlayson, *The Story of Theology*, (London: Tyndale Press, 1963), p. 30.

Chapter 24

TRANSLATING 'ANGEL' IN THE NEW TESTAMENT[1]

$\mathcal{T}$HE ENGLISH WORD 'ANGEL' IS A transliteration of a Greek word which is of frequent occurrence in Classical and Hellenistic Greek and which uniformly means 'messenger', 'the bearer or proclaimer of tidings'. It is ordinarily used of human messengers but it could be applied to anyone who bears a message, for example, the birds in augury or the god Hermes who was the messenger of his fellow deities. In Hebrew the corresponding word for messenger is *mal'ak*. It occurs 200 times in the Old Testament and it is translated in the English version exactly equally of human agents who bear messages and of angels. When we turn to the New Testament the word is still used in its ordinary sense, both of human messengers sent by God and those sent by man. For example John the Baptist is called the Lord's messenger (Greek *angelos*) in Mark 1:2, Matthew 11:10, Luke 12:24, while the friends of John the Baptist whom he sent to enquire of Jesus whether he was the Christ, are called the messengers (Greek *angelous*) of John in Luke 7:27. And when Jesus was preparing to make his final journey to Jerusalem He sent messengers into the villages in front of him to make ready for his coming. Here again the Greek is *angelous*. In St. Paul's second letter to the Corinthians (12:7) he describes the thorn in the flesh from which he was suffering as something sent from Satan. It is, he says, a messenger of Satan (Greek *angelos*), while James (2:25) described the two spies who entered Jericho and lodged with Rahab as messengers (Greek *angelous*).

These occurrences of the word *angelos* in the New Testament reflect the normal Greek usage. *Angelos* was the ordinary word for messenger. But although the word occurs 188 times in the New Testament it is only given its ordinary meaning on 7 occurrences in the English versions and is translated as 'angel' in the other 181 places. The question arises whether this overwhelming preference for the translation 'angel', meaning a super-

1. Unpublished paper.

human spiritual being, has not falsified the meaning of some passages of the New Testament where the Greek *angelos* occurs. Although, for example, Kittel's word book is emphatic that the word 'angel' only refers to human messengers on 4 occasions in the New Testament, this may well be wrong. It is not unlikely that the universal meaning in Greek literature, and which also is used in the New Testament, may not be the meaning in passages which are at present mistranslated by being referred to angelic beings instead of human messengers.

Some passages which deserve our examination are as follows:

Acts 7:53: "you who received the law as it was ordained by angels and kept it not". It is difficult to give much meaning to the phrase "as it was ordained by angels". Its meaning becomes clearer if it is recognised that Stephen, by the word 'law', is referring to the whole mind and will of God as revealed in the Old Testament Scriptures. This law came to the people of God by the hand of prophets. Jeremiah, especially, emphasised that God from the beginning of the history of Israel had persevered in sending his prophets to make clear his will, though the children of Israel refused to listen. Thus the Old Testament passage which may be the basis of Stephen's words is Jeremiah 26:4,5 where the prophetic message is said to be the law of God which the children of Israel refused to keep: "If you will not hearken to me, to walk in my law which I set before you, to hearken to the words of my servants the prophets in rising up early and sending them, but you have not hearkened, then will I make this place like Shiloh". The prophets revealed, but more particularly laid on the conscience of their hearers, the law of God. It was notorious in the Old Testament that the people refused to listen to the prophets enunciating God's law.

The concept of God endorsing his law through a succession of prophets in Israel occurs frequently in Jeremiah and receives its classical statement in the last chapter of Chronicles (36:15,16). This passage is important because the prophets are here said to be messengers (Hebrew *mal'akim*) of God. The word occurs twice in the passage and it is plainly synonymous to the prophets whom Jeremiah says God continually sent. The passage is as follows "The Lord, the God of their fathers sent to them by his messengers, rising up early and sending; because he had compassion on his people and on his dwelling place: but they mocked the messengers of God and despised his words and scoffed at his prophets". From this passage it is plain that the prophets were God's messengers and are given the title of messenger, the Hebrew being *mal'akim*, and the Greek Septuagint *angelous*. These words would also be in Stephen's mind as he spoke before the Sanhedrin, for they were the final words of their (Hebrew) Bible and exactly fitted the situation he was in. His speech had traversed the history of Israel and he summed it up in conclusion by the Sinai words of the Bible and applied it to his hearers. This confirms the likelihood that he used the word *angelos* in the same sense that it was used in this passage, as a synonym for 'prophet'.

Consequently in expounding Acts 7:53 we need not search for or invent some unknown Jewish fable about angels being the agents of God in the giving of the law, or read into Deuteronomy 33:2 more than it plainly says, but rather exegete Stephen's speech in conformity with the repeated statements of the Old Testament that God sent his messengers to his people throughout their history revealing and endorsing his law (Greek *diatageis*) and laying it on their consciences. But the people and their leaders refused to receive it at God's hands through his messengers the prophets.

Similar considerations lead to a reinterpretation of Galatians 3:19 "the law was ordained through angels by the hand of a mediator. Now a mediator is not of one, but God is one". It has been said that this verse has received almost 300 different interpretations. It is plainly a difficult verse to exegete. But it makes good sense if it is translated as follows. 'The law was given and endorsed through the prophets by way of mediation. Now there was not one mediator only (i.e. there was a succession of prophets throughout Israel's history) but God is the one and same God'. Moses was the first of these mediators, being the first of God's prophets to the people of Israel. But though there was a succession of prophetic mediators, the unity of the law with the promise is preserved by the unity of the one God. And so it follows that the law will not be against the promises of God given directly by God to Abraham—given before the law was given by God through messenger mediators. Thus in this passage also the word 'angel' should be given its ordinary Greek meaning of 'messengers'. Here again the basic thought would be in conformity with the classical expression of God's prophets as God's messengers in 2 Chronicles 36:15,16.

Included in this same group of mistranslations, where the word 'angel' in the English versions of the New Testament refers to the Old Testament prophets who were God's messengers to his people, is

Hebrews 2:2. The writer is contrasting the old covenant with its warnings to the new covenant. The old covenant came through prophets and yet its warnings proved true. How much less are Christians likely to escape if they neglect the words of the new covenant spoken not through prophets but through the Lord. The verse should be translated "if the word spoken through messengers proved steadfast... spoken through the Lord". It is true that the writer of the Hebrews normally used the Greek word *angelos* to refer to angelic beings. However, since it was also the normal Greek word of his time for messenger and since we have seen that in the Old Testament God's prophets were his messengers, we ought not to exclude the likelihood that when the author wished to use the word messenger he would use *angelos* even though he constantly used the same word for 'angel' elsewhere. Certainly other New Testament writers did this, using the Greek word *angelos*, not only of angelic messengers, but of ordinary human beings; e.g., James 2:25, Luke 7:24, Luke 9:52.

The author of Hebrews begins his letter with a contrast between the word spoken by God in time past to the fathers through the prophets, and the word spoken by God in these final days to us through his Son. After commending Christ and his work, the author launches into a comparison between Christ and angels, suggested perhaps by the opening contrast between Christ and the prophets, for the word prophet would immediately suggest 'angel' as in 2 Chronicles 36 and as is confirmed by Rabbi Yohanan "the prophets were called *mal'akim* (*angeloi*)" (*Midrash*, Wayyiqra Rabba, Ed. Mordecai Margolies p. 3).

At all events, in the opening verses of chapter 2, the author begins his first warning and returns to the contrast of the message of the Old Testament and the New, in words similar to what he had used in the first verse of the epistle; that verse relates how God spoke by (*en*) prophets and by (*en*) a son; in 2:2,3 God spoke through (*dia*) messengers (*angelōn*) and through (*dia*) the Lord. The thought is identical, namely, the inferiority of the Old, spoken by prophets in comparison to the New, spoken by the Son of God.

It should he noted that in the three references to angels and the law[2] the Greek preposition is *dia*; so the concept of agency is prominent. The emphasis is on God who is speaking through the mouth of his servants. This does not fit the concept of angelic mediation, who

2.   Acts 7:53, Galatians 3:19, Hebrews 2:2.

were not the mouth of God so much as the prophets.[3]

The commentators confidently affirm that it was a Jewish tradition at the time of the composition of the New Testament that the law was mediated by angels, and they quote these three New Testament references as the main evidence. But there is no evidence for this tradition at this time. Josephus is often cited as additional evidence, but it is plain that Josephus knew nothing about angels in the giving of the Law and that in the cited passage, *di'angelōn* should be translated not 'by angels' but 'through messengers' i.e. prophets.[4] Indeed Whiston offers the alternative "angels or ambassador"[5] and Marcus in the Loeb Classical Library edition translates the passage "we have learned…the holiest of our laws from the messengers sent by God" and adds this note "most scholars take *angeloi* here to mean 'angels', but it seems to me that the prophets or the priests are meant". The other reference to angels at the giving of the law confidently cited by the commentators is *Jubilees* 1.29. But this is a reference not to angels but to the Angel of the Presence, the Angel of the Lord of the Old Testament, who is also referred to by Stephen in Acts 7:38. Philo[6] is cited by Lightfoot on Galatians 3:19 and also by Bruce on Acts 7:53. But Philo, like Josephus, has a detailed description of the giving of the law, but without any reference to angels. In the passage cited from *On Dreams* the reference is to Moses as God's messenger and mediator. Bruce also cites the *Testament of Dan 6.2*, but this passage, although referring to the Angel of the Presence as mediator in prayer for Israel, contains no allusion to the giving of the law. It may be concluded that the existence of a Jewish tradition in the first century that angels mediated the giving of the law at Sinai has no substance, and consequently the three New Testament passages which in the English versions connect the law and angels are references to the succession of prophets, beginning with Moses, whom the Lord sent to reveal his law and enjoin it on the consciences of Israel.

Not only are prophets described as messengers of the Lord in the Old Testament (probably *mal'ak* is mistranslated 'angel' in Judges 2:1) but also priests are so described in Malachi 2:7 "the priests' lips should keep knowledge and they should seek the law at his mouth, for he is the messenger (LXX *angelos*) of the Lord of hosts." There is an interesting exact parallel in Greek literature contemporary with Malachi. Hecataeus of Abdera is quoted by Diodorus: "the Jews think the High Priest is the messenger (*angelon*) to them of God's commands (Greek *prostagmaton*)".[7]

In the Old Testament God sent the prophets as his messengers to his people. In the New Testament Jesus—Emmanuel—sends his messengers: apostles, prophets, evangelists, pastors and teachers.[8] There are three passages in the English New Testament where the word angel has been used to translate the word *angelos* when it refers more probably to these human emissaries of the Lord Jesus, his messengers to his people. A conspicuous example is Matthew 24:31—"He shall send forth his angels with a great sound of the trumpet and they shall gather together his elect from the four corners of the earth". This is a prophecy of the preaching of the gospel throughout the world which began to be fulfilled when Jesus said to his disciples, "Go into all the world".[9] Jesus' gathering of his elect is exemplified by the Lord's words to Paul at Corinth: "Speak, hold not your peace for I have much people in this city".[10] Paul was the messenger of the Lord to Corinth to gather to Christ and his heavenly assembly his children; or, put another way, to give eternal life to all in Corinth whom the Father had given the Son.[11] This passage in Matthew 24 is normally referred to the end of the world, but the reason that it is better understood as applying to the preaching of the gospel will be seen from the fact that it is accompanied by the repentance of the nations. The quotation from Zechariah which immediately proceeds these verses is a reference in Zechariah to genuine repentance and not to the anguish of judgement. Moreover Jesus sending out his angels is to take place "immediately after the tribulation of those days", that is to say, it is to follow hard on the siege of Jerusalem (Luke makes clear that "the abomination of desolation" is the Roman Army). The destruction of the Holy City brought to an end the old dispensation which had begun at Sinai.

7. *Harvard Theol Review* 48, p. 255.
8. Ephesians 4:11.
9. Matthew 28:19.
10. Acts 18:9, 10.
11. John 17:12.

From now on the Son of Man would be seen to be seated at the right hand of God[12] having come in the clouds to that throne, as foretold in Daniel 7, and a consequence of this victorious exaltation of the Lord from Calvary, the scene of his triumph, to God's right hand, the place of God's rule, would be the preaching of the gospel of remission of sins throughout the world through his messengers and the gathering in from the nations of his elect as they rallied around the sign of the Son of Man planted on the heavenly Mt Zion, lifted up above the mountains as Isaiah had prophesied.[13] Moreover, Jesus foretold with the most solemn emphasis that all this would happen during the lifetime of his hearers.[14] The whole passage is susceptible of a coherent interpretation if the word *angelos* is given its ordinary meaning of messenger and taken as a prophecy of the Christian mission to the world.

One of the places in the New Testament where the word 'angel' provides very difficult problems of exegesis is its sevenfold occurrence in the letters to the churches of Asia Minor in Revelation 2 and 3. In this passage the Spirit sends a written message through John to the angel of each church. Presumably it will be delivered to him by hand in due course. When it is recognized that 'angel' translates the ordinary Greek word for messenger, and that messenger was a regular term to describe those whom God sent to disclose his mind to his people, the exegetical problem vanishes. What the English translation calls 'angels' were the ministers of the congregation. We know from early church history that the congregations of Asia Minor were among the first to have a single presbyter/bishop as minister in contrast to the group of presbyter/bishops customary in the New Testament churches formed by Paul. The change to a single minister was natural, almost inevitable, when the minister came to be fully supported financially by the congregation. At the end of the second century it was universal. The minister of the congregation would be the natural person to receive the letter from John, just as a few years later Polycarp, the minister of Smyrna, one of the churches to which John wrote, was the recipient of the letter which Ignatius wrote the church of Smyrna.

The messenger of God is a very suitable term for the Christian

12. Psalm 110 cf. 1 Corinthians 15.
13. Isaiah 11:12, 49:22.
14. Matthew 24:30, 34.

minister. Like the prophets of the Old Testament, he is sent by God to make clear his mind to his people and to lay the law of God on their hearts. The term messenger also makes clear the unique character of the Christian ministry, diverse from the other ministers of the congregation. All Christians have gifts which they are to minister to one another. But not all are sent by God as his messengers to proclaim his word and to enjoin it, e.g. laying it on the consciences of his people. All may be said to be called (if you like) by God to minister their gifts (though the word 'called' in the New Testament is restricted to God's calling us to be his) but not all are sent. The 'sent' ministry is confined to God's messengers. This is the pastoral ministry, to be the messenger of God, to preach and forewarn, to feed and provide for the Lord's family, to seek for Christ's sheep dispersed abroad in the world, that they may be saved through Christ for ever.

In Revelation 1, Jesus is depicted in the midst of his congregations, and he is said to hold in his hand the stars which are interpreted as angels (or messengers) of the churches.[15] It is a source of strength for ministers to know, not only that Jesus is present in the congregations where they have been placed as Christ's mouthpiece, but also that he is specially related to them in their ministry, holding them in his hands.

There are two other passages where the word 'angel' ought to be translated messenger, meaning the messenger of the gospel. In 1 Timothy 3:16 there is what is apparently an ancient hymn in honour of the incarnate Christ: "Great, as is confessed unanimously, is the revealed secret of our religion. He who was manifested in the flesh, justified in the Spirit, seen of angels, preached among the nations, believed on in the world, received up in glory". The hymn begins with an oblique reference to the pre-existence of Jesus, "he who was manifest...", and it concludes with a reference to his return (*anelēmphthē*) to glory. The intermediate clauses refer to the life of Jesus, his incarnation, his victory on the cross and the progress of the gospel. "Seen of angels" is an intrusion into the order of events, and it corresponds to nothing in our knowledge of the history of the gospel. It is awkward to interpret it as referring to the ascension to the right hand of God, because this is the subject of the climactic clause "received back in glory". However when it is remembered that 'angels' translates the ordinary Greek word for messengers and when it is further remembered that messengers are those whom God sent to his people when he sent them prophets proclaiming his mind and intentions, the substitution of 'messenger' in this phrase is not only justified but it is also pregnant with meaningfulness. One of the basic strands of the gospel testimony was that the risen Christ was seen by those who went out with the gospel.[16] It was apparently a requirement for the apostles that they had seen the Lord,[17] and certainly Paul based his gospel (and that of all the other apostles as well)[18] on the fact that the risen Christ had been seen by those who proclaimed the gospel of the resurrection. Thus the phrase in 1 Timothy should read, "he who was manifested in the flesh, justified in the spirit, seen by his messengers, preached among the nations, believed on in the world, taken back in glory".

In Galatians 4:14, St Paul commended the Galatians because they had received him "as an angel of God even as Christ Jesus". It makes better sense and fits the context well if this is translated "messenger of God" because that is what St Paul was, and that is how he was received by those who believed[19] and it was for that he commended them. The Galatians also had received the gospel from him as the word of God, but now he had become their enemy because he was telling them the truth.

There are two other puzzling usages of the word 'angel' in the New Testament. In Acts 12, Peter, unexpectedly escaping from prison in the night, came to the home of Mary, the mother of John Mark, and knocked at the door. Rhoda, recognising his voice, was so excited that she left him at the door and rushed to tell all those who were gathered inside. They replied that it could not be Peter, but on her insistence they concluded it must be his angel. Rhoda had recognised Peter from his voice and insisted that it was no-one else's voice. Probably Peter had made some remarks that convinced Rhoda that she could not be mistaken. On the basis of this evidence the assembled company concluded that it was his angel. "His angel" cannot be "his guardian angel" or any other non-biblical notion of this sort, for there is no reason for thinking that such an angel would imitate his voice. The person whom Rhoda heard was Peter but his friends

16. 1 Corinthians 15:1-8.
17. 1 Corinthians 9:1.
18. 1 Corinthians 15:11.
19. 1 Thessalonians 2:13.

could not believe he was present in body. They were convinced that he was still in prison guarded by his four soldiers, for it was Herod's intention to bring him out the next day for execution. What Rhoda heard, they concluded, was his angel. His angel was Peter, speaking with his voice, but not Peter in the body. Peter was still in prison but he had sent his spirit, as it were, a messenger from himself. Thus the Christians' conclusion—"It is his angel"—ought to be translated "it is his messenger" and paraphrased "it is his spirit", not in the sense of his ghost, a pale phantom of his dead body, but "it is him in his spirit".

What appears to be a similar use of the word 'angelos' occurs in Matthew 18:10. In this passage "one of the little ones who believe on Jesus" is a reminiscence of Zechariah 13:7 and is a term for a member of the flock of God of which the Messiah is the shepherd. So when Jesus warns "see that you despise not one of these little ones", he is telling his disciples not to despise any of their fellow believers, because they are of inestimable value in the sight of God: "for in heaven their angels always behold the face of my father which is in heaven". It is a New Testament commonplace that Christians in their spirit are always in the presence of God. We have been brought into his presence by Christ and we stand in God's presence, or to use another metaphor, we are seated with Christ at God's right hand;[20] or again, we stand on Mt Zion, the heavenly Jerusalem, in the presence of God, the judge of all, and of Jesus the mediator;[21] we stand there in God's true assembly, the heavenly gathering or church of God's first-born children, along with all other fellow Christians who, like us, are awaiting the redemption of the body, but are already justified and are made perfect in spirit, and stand in God's presence.

It is in line with this truth, namely, that Christians always remain in their spirit in God's presence in heaven, that Matthew 18:10 is best exegeted. It is our Lord's way of expressing the same truth. As in Acts 12, 'angel' is used of our spirit—our messenger—representing us before God, that is, ourselves, conceived of as received by him into his very presence and standing there continually. This is the privilege of every Christian, and that is why Christians, the little ones who believe in Christ, are of inestimable value and importance and are never to be despised, because they are always beholding the face of God.

20. Ephesians 2:6.
21. Hebrews 12:22-24.

*M*Y TEXT IS TAKEN FROM ST PAUL'S first letter to Timothy chapter 3 verses 14–16, particularly verse 16. "He was manifest in the flesh, vindicated in the Spirit, seen by angels, preached among the nations, believed on in the world, taken up in glory."

In this passage, St Paul is telling Timothy his reason for writing the instructions about the ministry which take up the first part of the chapter. His purpose is that Timothy will know how he should conduct himself in the church, God's household; how the church should be organised, and how Christian character should be manifest in its ministers. He says that the church has the truth; it is in fact the pillar and bulwark of truth. By this he means that the worldview of Christians in the group that worships together is true, because they worship God as creator, as saviour and as judge and Christ as the revealed Son of God. This is the bulwark and pillar of the truth.

Outside the church there is only darkness and ignorance and that is as true today as ever it was, except perhaps that the darkness and ignorance has crept into the church through the lethargy of those who should be watching the ministers, through their failure to study, and through their failure to give themselves to their ministry. But that wasn't what St Paul was thinking of in his day. The church, that is, Christian people, is a shining light in the world, because it has the truth. And the apostle is carried away by the magnificence of this concept. Great indeed is the mystery of our religion, the *mysterion*, that knowledge revealed to those who are in the know. To Christians, God has made clear the truth about life, about the world, about time and eternity, and it is a wonderful truth. "Great is the mystery of our

---

1.   A sermon preached in the Moore College Chapel, June 15, 1979. It is included here as an example of Dr Knox's characteristic determination in tackling difficult texts, and his incisive ability to do so.

religion" or "great is the revealed secret made known to us"; unknown to those outside but known to us: the secret about the one whom we worship. Paul is carried away by its magnificence, and we need to lift our small mindedness up to compare it to the truth of the revealed religion of Scripture in the face of Jesus Christ.

At this point the apostle pens what appears to be a poem in six stanzas or rather three couplets. It is thought to be an ancient poem; it is certainly very succinct; there is not a single word in it that is not necessary and some of the normal words that you would write in fuller prose are left out. Actually, it doesn't appear to be constructed with the rest of the sentence so we don't really know what the opening section of the poem is. It begins immediately with a relative pronoun which is very hard to relate to any part of the preceding sentence, because the relative is in the nominative. The only person referred to is God, "the church of the living *God*". And then it goes on "who". Your English Bibles mistranslate the word 'who' as 'he' or 'he who', in trying to make it into English. As you will see from the Greek, it simply begins with "who", 'the one who was manifest in the flesh'. It is of course Jesus of whom they are speaking; he is the revealed truth or mystery of our religion; he is our message; he is the one on whom our whole worldview is focused.

"Manifested in the flesh"—now that of course is a phrase that is also found in St John's prologue and it reminds us of the divine person of Jesus. You wouldn't say of yourself that you are manifested in the flesh, because you were born in the ordinary way, but Christ was manifested—he appeared; he was seen in the flesh. It indicates what the rest of the New Testament makes clear, namely that Christ was pre-existent. Pre-existent in what form? The New Testament knows nothing of Arianism, so it is foreign to its spirit that he was pre-existent in the form of a created being, an angel created by God. He was pre-existent as God himself, as the Scriptures affirm.

Now you know that a great majority of our manuscripts begin the text with the Greek word *theos*: "*God* was manifested in the flesh". None of our modern editors will accept that and probably with good reason. But the meaning doesn't make any difference; that is the point I want to draw to your attention. It is God who is being spoken about because it is only God who is able to manifest himself in the flesh, pre-existently coming into being with us. As you know, the problem about the text is that *hos* which is *who* in the Greek testament only needs a little dot in the middle of the O and a small stroke on the top to turn it into *God* (*theos*) and as far as I know all the manuscripts have got that.[2] But the editors are of the opinion that it was added to some of the manuscripts at a later date. We have no real reason for not accepting that judgement of the experts, but it really doesn't make any difference to the meaning. It would certainly make the grammar better, but the meaning is the same. God was manifested in the flesh, and it reminds us that God has taken our nature, and has set before us how human life should be lived. The creator himself has lived among us and we ought to be earnest in studying with exactitude our Lord's life, his attitudes, his values, the way he related to others, because that is the pattern for life, and we need to press that upon our fellow Christians because we have diverged far from that pattern.

I need only think about our relationship to money, to give one example. Christ warned us not to try to serve two masters, yet that is what we are endeavouring to do! Even if we serve God, how many of us are consciously thinking along those lines? Christ said how foolish it is not to be rich towards God but to be rich in this earth's possessions. That is one aspect of his example: one of his values was to relate himself to other people in service. "I am among you as he who serves".[3] The opportunities of serving other people and forgetting yourself are innumerable every day, and yet we may preen ourselves if we take them once or twice in a week. But God has set us the example; he was manifest in the flesh. You can think of many other areas where you can imitate the example of Christ. For example, though he heavenly-mindedly served God, yet he served his fellow men at the same time, gave himself to prayer, trusted his Father in all things, and so on.

"Manifest in the flesh, vindicated in the Spirit"—now here is a couplet! You see, *flesh* and *Spirit*, "justified in the Spirit". Now what is that a reference to? Well I notice my English version in front of me has a capital 'S'. I think that is absolutely wrong; it is vindicated in his *own* spirit, justified in his *own* spirit. Now what does the text mean? The word 'vindicated' here is simply *edikaiothe*—'vindicated', the same word as 'righteous'. It is a term that is associated with Christ from the very earliest Christian tradition. He is "the righteous one". St Peter said very early in the Jerusalem ministry that the Jews had crucified "the

2. There is in fact a small number of manuscripts that do contain *hos*.
3. Luke 22:27.

holy and righteous one".[4] Stephen accused his hearers of rejecting those who prophesied about the coming of the righteous one, the term given to Jesus.[5] He is the righteous one. Ananias, in a very early section of the tradition, when speaking to Paul said, "to you has been given the privilege of seeing the righteous one".[6] Now Jesus therefore was described in the very earliest days of the Christian mission as "the righteous one". Why so? Because he was righteous in the final testing—even in hell, when deserted by God on the cross for those three hours, when he was bearing our sins and their penalty, he was shown to be righteous. He did not compromise his perfect relationship to God; the creature was perfectly related to the creator in faith and love and obedience, and therefore he was righteous, tested to the full. To be described as the righteous one after the crucifixion is a most suitable term for Jesus and of course it is his righteousness which is ours—we are righteous in him. Now it was in his spirit, that is to say, in his inner being that he was righteous; not in the outward action but in his relationship to God, in his obedience. Now we know from the rest of Scripture that it is Christ's obedience that saves us: "by the obedience of one man are many made righteous"[7] and Christ therefore was righteous and declared to be righteous because that is what the word vindicated here means. He was justified, declared to be righteous because he was righteous in his spirit. And we also now are righteous. We are told in Hebrews 12 that we have come into that heavenly assembly of righteous people, "the spirits of righteous people made perfect".[8] If you aren't righteous you can't possibly approach God's throne in prayer or in any other way. You can't be said to be standing in God's presence, as St Paul puts it, unless you are righteous and you are there in spirit. It is in your spirit that you have been made righteous. We are still waiting for the redemption of our body but we have been justified in our spirits, in our real being. In God's presence we are the righteous ones made perfect in Christ and we are there in that heavenly group of which we are all members and we are in each others' fellowship.

4.   Acts 3:14.
5.   Acts 7:52.
6.   Acts 22:14.
7.   Romans 5:19.
8.   Hebrews 12:23.

So here in this passage, Christ is termed "the righteous one", declared to be righteous through his obedience. So in him you have the perfect example of human life manifest in the flesh, God humbling himself and taking our nature, being born of the virgin, humbling himself to the cross. Humility is the hallmark of his character; service is the activity which flows from it. He is vindicated, proved to be righteous in his essential being on the cross. Looking at the body nailed to the cross you can't see what is going on, but what was going on was perfect obedience to God, perfect faith, and perfect love.

That is the first couplet. Now the second couplet is **"seen by angels, preached among the nations"**. Once again we have the problem of the translator not knowing what the apostle means. 'Seen' is a technical term used of the resurrection. For example in 1 Corinthians 15 you find this term constantly: "seen of James", "seen of Peter", "seen of all the apostles". The same word is used.

Now that was, as St Paul tells us, a very ancient form of words. He writes, "What I have received I have handed on to you" and then he finishes his remarks by writing "whether it is I or they" (that is, the apostles of Jerusalem or himself), "so we preach".[9] A very important part of what was preached was that he was seen, not by the whole people as St Peter says on another occasion,[10] but by those whom he had chosen. Seen, not by everybody, but seen by those whom he was sending as his witnesses, seen by his messengers. Now of course you know the word 'angel' is the ordinary Greek word for 'messenger'.[11] There is no other word for messenger in the Greek, and it is used with that meaning in the New Testament as the corresponding Hebrew word is used for 'messenger' in the Old Testament. In the Old Testament, it is more frequently used for human messengers than for messengers from God or angels. In the New Testament, perhaps the priority is reversed but certainly it is used with human messengers quite naturally. Now, as we also know, prophets are said to be God's messengers. We see that in the last chapter of 2 Chronicles where the prophets are described as God's messengers, and God rises up early and sends messengers. Now Christ sent out his apostles into the world: "the Father sent me:

9.   1 Corinthians 15:9.
10. Acts 10:41.
11. See chapter 24, "Translating 'angel' in the New Testament".

so send I you",[12] and these messengers were witnesses of the resurrection, for they had seen the Lord. As St Paul himself said, "have I not seen the Lord?"[13], and this word 'see' as I have said is very ancient in the Christian tradition referring to the resurrection.

So he was seen by those whom Christ had chosen. Of course the expression is a bit truncated in the Greek I have just been pointing out to you, and a better way of putting it would be "seen by *his* messengers". Those two little additional words bring out the meaning, but the meaning is there without them, in quite good Greek.

Thus in this poem we have the incarnation, the cross, the resurrection and then follows preaching among the nations, turning the world upside down, stars falling from heaven. That was the experience of the early church. "Preached among the nations": Christ was sending out his messengers and gathering his elect from the four corners of the earth, and it is witnessed to here because it was a marvellous phenomenon, the world turning to Christ. Something certainly to sing about as in this poem that is a hymn. So that is the second couplet. Resurrected and witnessed to by the messengers that Christ had chosen, and actually preached among the nations: the church universal now. All the nations, tribes, tongues, languages, turning to the Lord, as a result of preaching among the nations.

Now we come to the third couplet, **"believed on in the world, taken up to glory"**. It was a ministry of glory in the sense that people were believing. It wasn't a ministry of death such as Moses, Jeremiah and the Old Testament prophets were called to discharge, but it was a ministry of glory because God was gathering his elect. Paul was told that in Corinth, that very pagan city, God had many people and Paul was told to stay there until he had gathered them.[14]

"Believed on in the world"—it is rather nice for us to know that if God is sending us with his word, it will be in accordance with his purposes that that word should be believed. Again the couplet is in contrast. The early church was never forgetful of that great crowning truth that Jesus had ascended; that he has come in the clouds to the Father's throne and has received the kingdom which will be without end. He is

12. John 20:21.
13. 1 Corinthians 9:1.
14. Acts 18:10.

reigning now; he is crowned with glory and honour because of his vindication on the cross, because of his righteousness there, his victory there. He is crowned with glory and honour, and he is reigning. Says St Paul: "Christ must reign till everything is put under his feet",[15] and as we look out on the world we see it as a place where God was manifest and where God won the victory, where God sends out his messengers and where people are believing throughout the whole world.

But above all you must see the world as a place over which Christ is ruling in every detail, and that he is king. That kingdom of course will be completed. It is not yet completed, for he must reign until every enemy is put under his feet, and one day that time will come. But the early church was very vividly conscious that they were waiting for the Lord from heaven; they were worshipping one who had received all power and they were waiting for his manifestation.

Now again it appears to me that although we modern Christians give lip service to this—we believe that Christ will come to judge the quick and the dead—it doesn't play very much a part in our thinking, let alone in our imagination. We don't believe that the king will judge, that he will gather all nations before him and separate them. It doesn't play a very big part in our gospel message, although it is a very important truth that people should be aware of if they are to live in accordance with what the facts are. So we need to meditate on the fact that Christ is reigning, he has won the victory, he is taken up in glory. Then indeed we may confess with the apostle, "great is the revealed secret that God has given to us"— not to others, but to us of our religion, and that secret centres on Christ, his incarnation, his death, his resurrection, his present reign and the message that we have and the work that he is doing through that message of bringing the whole world to obedience. That is what the church should be living by; that is what the household of God should be putting their thoughts to all the time, this great truth to which we have been made privy, which has been entrusted to us. As a Christian group we are to be the pillar and bulwark of that truth, and if God sends us to proclaim it, everyone of us will have an opportunity of speaking to those who ask us. Now, he actually does send us; I trust he is sending all of us, as his messengers, to proclaim Jesus Christ as the writer describes in this very ancient Christian hymn.

15. 1 Corinthians 15:25.

BIBLE PASSAGES INDEX

*T*HE FOLLOWING IS NOT A LIST OF ALL Bible passages referred to, but an index of those Scriptural passages which are expounded, or about which some illuminating comment is made.

KNOX GEMS

$\mathcal{B}$ROUGHTON KNOX'S CREATIVE, Scripture-soaked mind was always arriving at challenging insights into the Bible and its theology.

To make the discovery and enjoyment of these gems of understanding a little easier, we have compiled the following list (arranged in page number order) as an alternative way into the contents of this volume. If your curiosity is aroused on any of these subjects, further references can be found in the general index.

ABOUT MATTHIAS MEDIA

Matthias Media is an independent, evangelical, non-denominational company aiming to produce books and other resources of a uniformly high quality—both in their biblical faithfulness and in the quality of the writing and production.

For more information about our extensive range of Bible studies, books, evangelistic tools, training courses, periodicals and audio-cassettes, visit us at **www.matthiasmedia.com.au** or contact us in any of the following ways:

Mail: Matthias Media
             PO Box 225
             Kingsford NSW 2032
             Australia

Phone: 1800 814 360 *(tollfree in Australia)*
             9663 1478 *(in Sydney)*
             int + 61-2-9663 1478 *(international)*

Fax: (02) 9662 4289

Email: info@matthiasmedia.com.au

❧ MATTHIAS MEDIA